T0270565

THE OSWALD PUZZLE

THE OSWALD PUZZLE

RECONSIDERING LEE HARVEY OSWALD

LARRY HANCOCK AND
DAVID BOYLAN

Skyhorse Publishing

Skyhorse Publishing books may be purchased in bulk at special discounts for sales promotion, corporate gifts, fund-raising, or educational purposes. Special editions can also be created to specifications. For details, contact the Special Sales Department, Skyhorse Publishing, 307 West 36th Street, 11th Floor, New York, NY 10018 or info@skyhorsepublishing.com.

Visit our website at www.skyhorsepublishing.com.

Please follow our publisher Tony Lyons on Instagram @tonylyonsisuncertain.

10 9 8 7 6 5 4 3 2 1

Library of Congress Cataloging-in-Publication Data is available on file.

Print ISBN: 978-1-5107-8340-9
eBook ISBN: 978-1-5107-8341-6

Cover design by Mei Bradford
Cover images sourced from Getty Images, the National Archives, Sixth Floor Museum, and Dallas Municipal Archives.

Printed in the United States of America

Lee Harvey Oswald with wife Marina and baby daughter June, at Thanksgiving 1962, on the way to see Lee's brother Robert. (Getty Images)

Contents

Foreword by Rex Bradford

If the Kennedy assassination is a mystery wrapped in a riddle inside an enigma, to quote a famous line from the film *JFK*, then Lee Harvey Oswald is the puzzle at the heart of the mystery. Despite the rifle found in the Texas School Book Depository being traced to him, and a whole bullet and two fragments traced to that rifle, the evidence against Oswald has always been thinner than it seems at first glance. Dallas police chief Jesse Curry summed it up a few years later: "No one has been able to put him in that building with a gun in his hand."

Was Oswald framed then, the "patsy" he declared himself to be on national television before Jack Ruby silenced him? Those at the height of government pondered this question. Assistant Attorney General Katzenbach wrote the White House on the day following Oswald's murder, opening with the statement that "the public must be satisfied that Oswald was the assassin; that he did not have confederates who are still at large…" but followed with, "Unfortunately the facts on Oswald seem about too pat—too obvious (Marxist, Cuba, Russian wife, etc.)."

What was "too obvious" was the in-your-face implication that Oswald killed Kennedy at the behest of Fidel Castro or Nikita Khrushchev, and the fear of this "solution" to the crime rocked the government. We now know that the new president Lyndon Johnson assembled the Warren Commission by invoking fear of nuclear war.

"We've got to take this out of the arena where they're testifying that Khrushchev and Castro did this and did that and kicking us into a war that can kill 40 million Americans in an hour," LBJ told his old Senate mentor Richard Russell, dragging him onto the Commission against Russell's wishes.

The Warren Commission went on to "solve" the case, declaring Oswald to be the lone assassin of President Kennedy, whistling in the dark past evidence which contradicted its pre-ordained conclusion. This verdict has been hotly contested ever since. Thousands of books have been written on the subject[1], and formerly-secret files of the Commission, subsequent investigations, the FBI, the CIA, and other agencies have created a mountainous saga of information—some 5 million pages in the National Archives—without resolution.

Some of the many books on the assassination defend the Warren Commission's view of Oswald as an unbalanced and dangerous man whose frustrations caused him to murder President Kennedy. Often they go further in this portrayal than the Commission itself, which admitted that it could find not a single instance in which Oswald expressed an unfavorable opinion of Kennedy. The Commission in the end declared that it "does not believe that it can ascribe to him any one motive or group of motives."

Other books, most of them, challenge the Warren Commission's findings. Some take on the medical, ballistics, and film evidence regarding whether any one person could have fired all the shots in Dealey Plaza. The infamous "single bullet theory," whereby one "magic" bullet caused seven wounds in two men (Kennedy and Governor Connally), is so contested, and rightly so, that several books are devoted to it alone. That undamaged and clean bullet, found mysteriously on a stretcher in Parkland Hospital and forensically tied to Oswald's rifle, has its own 60-year saga—recently added to by Secret Service agent Paul Landis' 2023 account that no, the bullet wasn't found on Connally's stretcher, but rather Kennedy's, where Landis himself placed it and then didn't tell anyone. No wonder the American public remains confused.

Many other books on the assassination go straight to the whodunit—the Mafia did it, or the CIA, or Fidel Castro, or the military, or the right wing. The problem here is that to start with motive, when discussing the assassination of the U.S. president at the height of the Cold War, leads nowhere. Got a group with a motive to kill Kennedy? Get in line.

To the extent Oswald appears in these books at all—and sometimes he is ignored entirely—he is usually a one-dimensional creature. Whether a psychopathic loner, or instead a deep-cover intelligence agent always on assignment, Oswald is too often treated as a cardboard cut-out, moved about in service of a larger narrative. Until this book.

I first met Larry Hancock in Dallas more than twenty years ago, while speaking at research conferences that he ran with Debra Conway. Larry gave talks there too, and I was always impressed by his no-nonsense approach and intellectual rigor. I learned from him the invaluable skill of separating the stories of cover-up—for which there are many possible motives, right up to "for the good of the country," I discovered—from the actual crime and conspiracy.

The Mary Ferrell Foundation, which I run, recently published Larry's *Tipping Point*; that work is in some ways the precursor to the book you hold in your hand. He and his research partner David Boylan are experts on the Kennedy-era "secret war on Cuba" and the many operatives inside and outside the CIA who populate that history. Due to the JFK Records Act, large swaths of files on that subject are now public, available due to the efforts of the Assassination Archives and Research Center which obtained them and the Mary Ferrell Foundation that put them online. In essays and other work over recent years, Larry and David have mined these records to great effect.

But this book is also and primarily about Lee Harvey Oswald, about whom the Warren Commission itself collected and published a great deal of information six decades ago. What new is there to say about him? Plenty, as it turns out. The Commission didn't have the full story, for one—this book's contributions to illuminating the formerly secret and tangled record of Oswald's trip to Mexico City, from where so many of the allegations of Communist conspiracy emanated, are clarifying and insightful. And recent years have also seen the publication of the important reflections of Oswald's best friend during his time in Minsk, Ernst Titovets.

The Oswald Puzzle is unique, though, in taking head-on the conundrum that has faced so many who have taken the time to understand the details of the Kennedy assassination. If the physical evidence shows that no single person killed Kennedy, then how could someone the Warren Commission went out of its way to portray as a "loner" be responsible at all? And yet Oswald was clearly not just some random person picked up by authorities after the fact. What then, was his role in this affair?

The authors hold no truck with sacred cows. They take the Warren Commission's own biography of Oswald and strip it of the Commission's bias, presenting a more nuanced and clear-eyed picture of this unusual young man. But they also take head-on the Walker shooting and the so-called "backyard" photographs of Oswald holding a rifle and pistol, and other stories some pro-conspiracy advocates would prefer to avoid. The result is a fascinating portrait of an unusually fearless and yes, idealistic, individual.

Those unfamiliar with the Oswald biography will encounter a very odd tale; those who think they know the story may be surprised by what they find here. And then, after laying bare the stranger-than-fiction life journey of Lee Harvey Oswald, the authors describe how his pro-Castro activities in New Orleans in the summer of 1963 landed him squarely in the sights of the anti-Castro (and by 1963, anti-Kennedy) exile movement. Hancock and Boylan tell a compelling story of what happened next.

The missing element in our understanding of the Kennedy assassination has always been the lack of a believable counter-narrative to the Warren Report, one which explains who Lee Harvey Oswald really was. Hancock and Boylan have made a profound contribution in this regard. Have they solved the puzzle of Lee Harvey Oswald, and with it some core questions about the conspiracy that took President Kennedy's life? Read this book and see for yourself.

And if you believe the story told here, then add the tragedy of this young man's life and his fate to the tragedies of November 22, 1963.

Introduction

Over the decades, history books and the media have described and defined Lee Harvey Oswald as "the assassin of President Kennedy." More recently, with a deeper view of history, and a flood of document releases and research, there has been some movement towards qualifying that description to read "the alleged assassin" or "the accused assassin."

Readers will find good cause for such a shift in terminology in *The Oswald Puzzle*. Equally importantly, they will find that the book explores the much deeper issues of who Lee Harvey Oswald really was, and what motivated him.

The historical view of Oswald originated in leaks to the media and then was solidified in the report of the President's Commission on the Assassination of President Kennedy, popularly known as the Warren Commission. But the portrait painted by the Commission is both fractured and flawed. Fractured, because the Commission itself presented conflicting views of Oswald. Flawed, because it simply ignored aspects of Oswald's life inconvenient to its conclusions.

Oswald was never tried and legally convicted of any crime, and over the following decades subsequent governmental inquiries raised doubts that the actual nature of the assassination was as simple as officially described in the Warren Commission Report. During the 1970s, first the United States Senate Select Committee to Study Governmental Operations with Respect to Intelligence Activities (known as the

Church Committee for its chair, Senator Frank Church), and later the House Select Committee on Assassinations raised key questions regarding the Kennedy assassination. Ultimately the House Select Committee report officially concluded that a conspiracy was involved in the murder of the president, and that there were multiple shooters in Dealey Plaza on November 22, 1963.

Despite those reassessments of the Kennedy assassination, history has largely been left with the characterization of Oswald originally presented in the Warren Commission Report. The Warren Report defined Oswald's character, his personality, his worldview, and his temperament—all in relation to his being presented as the murderer of the president. Even prior to the issuance of the report in the fall of 1964, during the first days and weeks immediately following the assassination, material related to Oswald was leaked from official sources to the press—first from the Dallas Police, then from the FBI (as its own report was being written over some three weeks), and as the months passed, from sources inside the Warren Commission itself. All those leaks, and all the media coverage which they generated, created a public image of Oswald which supported and solidified the charges initially placed against him. Yet at no point were those charges subject to rebuttal or challenge, simply because Oswald himself had been murdered within two days of his arrest. He had never obtained legal counsel, much less been brought to trial and legally convicted of any crime.

Over the decades, literally thousands of books and papers have been published on the Kennedy assassination. A few followed the scenario and characterization of Oswald as presented in the original Warren Report, but the vast majority revisited the attack in Dallas—and the events which followed—from a perspective of skepticism. In most instances those works either deconstructed the official story of the assassination, presented an alternative conspiratorial view of events, or perhaps most commonly, attempted both. One of this work's authors, Hancock, has previously published two such works; *Someone Would Have Talked* in 2010 and *Tipping Point* in 2021. In general, the so-called conspiracy works have treated Oswald himself from a relatively one-dimensional viewpoint, either as a tool of some conspiracy or as an unwitting actor, taken advantage of by that same conspiracy. The major difference between the works lies in either their view of Oswald and/or the size and nature of the conspiracy they discuss.

The net result of the Warren Commission's report, the subsequent congressional inquiries, and decades of books on the Kennedy assassination has left Lee Harvey Oswald as something of an enigma. What is in the history books is either misleading, or at best incomplete, in terms of what has been learned over the decades following the assassination. The minimal descriptions of Oswald given in those accounts virtually never goes beyond the original characterization of him developed in the Warren Report, which assumed him to have murdered the president, acting strictly on his own and for no specifically stated motive.

Readers who have turned to one or more of the assassination-related books will either find the characterizations of Oswald which support the view of Oswald as the sole assassin, or a broad variety of very different images of him. The majority of these portray him as either a witting or unwitting tool, instrument, asset, foil or outright dupe of some type of conspiracy—and focus on the conspiracy rather than Oswald as an individual.

This book takes a very different approach to Oswald, focusing entirely on him as an individual with his own deeply personal history and development, with a consistency in his character and worldview—all of which were in many instances the antithesis of that presented in the Warren Commission Report, and in many respects arguably different than that which has been presented in a great many books on the Kennedy assassination.

The Oswald Puzzle is first and foremost a book about Lee Harvey Oswald. It is also a book about the Kennedy assassination, but only to the extent that assassination "touched" Oswald during the last 72 hours of his life. It is a book about conspiracy, but only to the extent to which a conspiracy "used" Oswald. And it is a book about the American intelligence community—about individuals within and connected to that community—but again only to the extent that Oswald was "on the radar" and of potential usefulness to certain persons within that community.

The Oswald Puzzle is not a book about the details of the attack on President Kennedy in Dealey Plaza on November 22, 1963. It is a book about Lee Oswald as an individual, about his character and personality, and about the unique series of experiences he accumulated during the short 24 years of his life. But while it is not primarily focused on the details of the assassination, it is a book about conspiracy. To that end, the authors specifically address and explore the likelihood that Oswald was taken advantage of by individuals who used his personal goals to their own ends—resulting in the historical characterization of Oswald as something he was not, an assassin.

The Oswald Puzzle presents a variety of views of Lee Harvey Oswald, offering references to resources that allow the reader the opportunity for further exploration of the many, often conflicting views of his life. But most importantly, it is an effort to explore Oswald as an individual, with his own character, his own world view, and in particular his personal and increasingly activist agenda that drove his own activities up to the time of his arrest in Dallas, on the afternoon of November 22, 1963.

Chapter I

Viewpoints

". . . the Commission does not believe that it can ascribe to him [Oswald] any one motive or group of motives."
—Warren Commission Report, p. 423

Over the decades, two fundamentally different views of Lee Harvey Oswald have emerged. Those views have come to be so diametrically opposed it seems almost as if Oswald was a character living in different dimensions. The established, historical view is that of a radicalized "lone nut" assassin, an image presented to the public by major media in the days and weeks immediately following the assassination. It is a view which has remained consistent in historical references to the assassination of the President, appearing annually each year on the anniversary of the attack on President Kennedy on November 22, 1963, in Dallas, Texas.

The Official View

The finding of Oswald as the sole assassin of the President did not become "official" until the issuance of the report of the President's Commission on the Assassination of President Kennedy (more commonly known as the Warren Commission) in September of 1964, almost a year after the events of November 22, 1963. However, the view of Oswald as a dangerous, "lone nut" assassin gained semi-official status almost immediately, with the leaking of the FBI report on the assassination, and its conclusions, to elements of the media early in December 1963.

Preparation of that FBI investigative finding—with its conclusion established from its inception—had begun as early as the afternoon of Oswald's murder by Jack Ruby only two days following the murder of the president. That same afternoon, FBI Director J. Edgar Hoover advised presidential aide Walter Jenkins that it would be necessary for the incoming Johnson administration to participate in the effort to "convince the public that Oswald is the real assassin."[2]

That direction was reinforced the following day, on November 25, with another memorandum—this one from Assistant Attorney General Nicholas Katzenbach, to presidential aide Bill Moyers, reading in part: "The public must be satisfied that Oswald was the assassin; that he did not have confederates who are still at large; and that the evidence was such that he would have been convicted at trial."[3] That direction was officially sustained for days, weeks, and in perpetuity. Yet we know that behind the scenes, information suggesting a foreign conspiracy, specifically Cuban or Russian, continued to come to both the FBI and CIA. The CIA's own Mexico City station staff strongly advocated stories of Oswald being a paid Cuban assassin. Officially and for the public none of that mattered—it was going to be Oswald, and Oswald alone.

In retrospect such an obvious rush to an official judgment seems more than questionable. Yet historically there are numerous examples of those in charge during national crises desiring to "capture the narrative," ostensibly in the interests of national security but pragmatically to ensure control over the national response. In such crises there is also a consistent desire to minimize rumor and gossip, and to preempt potential questions about the administration in power as well as the actions of the agencies (or military services) involved in the incident.[4]

As an example, less than five years after the president's murder, both Director Hoover of the FBI and the nation's Attorney General would announce that a single individual had shot and killed Dr. Martin Luther King Jr., with no evidence of others being involved and with no racial motivation—making that declaration within 24 hours of the murder, with absolutely no proof to back up their assertion, no suspect in custody, and the FBI investigation barely having begun.[5]

With Oswald dead, no prospect of a trial, and the FBI's conclusion on Oswald's sole guilt given to President Johnson within only weeks, a good deal of material which might have been challenged in a legal setting ended up simply being handed off to the national media, which accepted it without challenge or question and essentially delivered what would have been the prosecution's case directly to the public—as established fact.

The Media

A political element had been introduced into the attack as motive by the media as early as the day following the assassination, with one Texas newspaper carrying a banner headline "Pro-Castroite Charged in Slaying of Kennedy."[6] Similar copy, and inferences, quickly appeared in newspapers around the nation. "Castroite Held, Charged with Assassination" was the byline in the *San Diego Union Tribune*.[7]

For an ostensible "loner"—as Lee Harvey Oswald would be portrayed by the Warren Commission—extensive details on his background, his time in Russia and his protests in support of the Cuban revolution surfaced quite quickly in the media. We now know that one explanation for that immediate availability of information, especially regarding Oswald's political leanings, had to do with the Scripps Howard News Service, as of 1963 the most prominent news outlet in the nation.[8]

According to Seth Kantor, a Scripps Howard reporter, calls to the Scripps news service desk were referred to Hal Hendrix, the chief Latin American reporter for the *Miami News*. When Kantor reached Hendrix, he found him to possess an extensive knowledge of Lee Oswald, not only background on his time in Russia, but more recently about Oswald's activities in New Orleans—demonstrating for Cuba and the Castro regime, his connection to the Fair Play for Cuba Committee, and even information on Oswald's radio appearances.

New Orleans was not on Hendrix's normal news "beat," but apparently he had gone so far as to call Scripps himself to make the news service aware that he had extensive information on Oswald's activities there the previous summer, and was ready and willing to share it. That might seem a bit mysterious at first; it becomes less so given that Hendrix was later found to be a media resource close to the covert CIA Cuban operations station in Miami (JM/WAVE).[9] Hendrix's special access to Cuba-related information may well have been a contributing factor in his detailed coverage of the events related to the landings at the Bay of Pigs, for which he had received a Pulitzer Prize for his news "scoops." According to former CIA officer Frank Terpil, Hendrix was also a family friend of CIA propaganda specialist David Phillips.[10]

Hendrix's insider relationship with the CIA continued for years, with his reporting of a coup in the Dominican Republic (David Phillips' assignment at the time) through the Scripps Howard news service a day before it actually occurred, and into the early 1970s during the CIA's anti-Allende project in Chile (a project headed by David Phillips). Hendrix was identified as having provided International Telephone and Telegraph with highly confidential information on the Allende government. When questioned on the matter by a Congressional committee, Hendrix was later shown to have lied in order to cover his CIA source.[11] Some three years later a CIA cable revealed that his source had indeed been a CIA officer, and that the CIA was aware that he would protect their association with him in his testimony to the committee.

The information Hendrix was providing through his Scripps Howard connection was only one element of the ongoing development of Oswald's image as a politically radical presidential assassin within the general media. That media coverage fixed the public perception of Oswald following the leaking of the FBI report, certifying him as the lone criminal actor well before the Warren Commission Report solidified it all on its release in September 1964.

Beyond the immediate media impact of Scripps Howard's available background information on Oswald, the significance of the CIA/Hendrix/Phillips connection will receive further attention as we proceed. It is only one of several clues revealing the extent to which the CIA was aware of Oswald and his pro-Castro activism prior to the assassination. It is also one of several indications that the Agency was itself using that knowledge of Oswald in its own activities (in progress and in planning) at the time of the assassination.

Decades later, it was discovered that the CIA-supported positioning of Oswald as a political radical had already been underway well before the assassination. It was being conducted in a propaganda campaign being carried out via the CIA-funded and sponsored Cuban Student Directorate (the DRE). A DRE warning campaign about Oswald had begun as early as August 1963, and had involved letters to Congress, warnings to Cuban exile groups, and local journalists in Miami—all raising the flag about the dangers of Cuban subversion of naïve Americans, especially through the work of the Fair Play for Cuba Committee. At the time of the assassination, recordings of Oswald's radio interviews supporting the Cuban revolution were being circulated from several private outlets, and an anti-Castro propaganda record containing elements of the interviews was packaged and ready for distribution.

The media coverage of Oswald as a political radical and possibly instigated by communist beliefs was also fueled by a series of ongoing leaks of materials out of Dallas, materials which had been originally collected for the prosecution of Oswald, but remained in police custody. Over time, materials including Oswald's personal diary as well as photos (held by both the Dallas Police and in the Dallas District Attorney's office) were shared among Dallas police officers, and several items ended up with the press. Similar leaks occurred throughout the length of the Warren Commission inquiry; such behavior would have been both illegal and embarrassing in any normal criminal prosecution, but with Oswald dead there was no trial, no challenge to the accusations against him, and standard legal practices were essentially out the window.

At one point the Commission itself became concerned, especially over the leaking of the diary, and asked the FBI to investigate. The investigation led to Assistant District Attorney Bill Alexander. Alexander had initially prepared charges against Oswald, presenting him as part of a communist conspiracy, but the conspiracy element had been dropped from the official charges based on calls to Dallas from President Johnson's aide, Cliff Carter. The FBI questioned Alexander about the leak on July 10, 1963, and the *Dallas Morning News* reported that Alexander had been interviewed but strongly denied releasing anything. The FBI's report on the interview notes that, in addition to a simple denial, "Alexander also...made a statement that Lyndon B. Johnson, J. Edgar Hoover, the FBI, and the 'Warren Commission could kiss my a--.'" The FBI report noted that he had been strongly admonished concerning those remarks.[12]

The Warren Commission

As the leaks and popular media coverage of Oswald continued, the Warren Commission proceeded to build its own presentation, one strictly in line with the Katzenbach memo—Oswald's guilt was a certainty, he had no confederates and acted completely independently; with the evidence in hand, he would certainly have been convicted if he had lived to be brought to trial.

Yet despite the extensive and detailed background work done by the FBI on Oswald, one sticking point which had emerged was the question of motive. The investigation had been able to produce no evidence of Oswald's animosity, hatred, or even negative remarks regarding President Kennedy. In contrast, people who did know and talk with Oswald were found to report that if anything he had a positive attitude towards JFK, generally supporting his global policies and thinking that Kennedy was the type of leader who might at least be able to open a positive dialogue with Premier Khrushchev.

In terms of actual evidence, the investigation produced none of the material that might be expected if the attack on the president had been driven by either an aggressively political or personal agenda. There was no written manifesto (yet Oswald had been writing on several political and geopolitical issues in 1963, and that writing was in evidence), no trace of a warning letter or call to the media—or anyone else—before the attack, no written note stating a reason of any sort. Oswald himself consistently denied while in custody being involved in any way in an act against the president. He had been given multiple opportunities to make remarks to the press, and in none of them offered the least sign that he was trying in any fashion to "make a name for himself." There was simply nothing to demonstrate that Oswald was either a firebrand radical pursuing a cause, or someone propelled to kill over some perceived personal issue with the president.

Ultimately the Commission would be forced to construct an image of Oswald which would support the view of him as an assassin based on personality and character issues rather than a specific, actionable motive. That lack of a clear-cut motive alone left many skeptical regarding the official view of Oswald as the assassin. This book will detail solid reasons for that skepticism.

However, motive was only one of the "trust issues" which emerged regarding the Warren Commission Report. In sum, those issues led to the development of a community of skeptics which over time came to reject virtually everything about the case against Lee Harvey Oswald, including the evidence placed into the official record, the construction of the Commission's report—and virtually all the sources used by the Commission in its profiling of Oswald.

Warren Report Criticism

Criticism of the Warren Commission's work began early, largely based in two fundamental issues. The first objection was that there was no legal challenge to any of the evidence used by the Commission in its work. In contrast to due legal process, investigative material (including testimony and statements) was simply entered into the Warren Commission record and collected in 26 volumes of minimally indexed documents which were published separately, two months later than the report itself. Key evidentiary materials were stored in highly restricted access at the National Archives. Attorney Mark Lane made a highly public challenge to that Warren Commission's process and attempted—unsuccessfully—to insert some aspect of challenge into the Commission's work.

In December 1963, Lane wrote to Chief Justice Earl Warren proposing that the Commission appoint a counsel for Oswald who could advocate in his defense—and attached a "brief" which contained certain assertions related to Oswald which had been made by Dallas County District Attorney Henry Wade. The "brief" was published in the *National Guardian*, a politically left New York City weekly newspaper. Lane visited Oswald's family in Dallas and was officially named as counsel by Marguerite Oswald. The Committee's general counsel, J. Lee Rankin, pushed back, notifying Lane that it was not felt "useful" to have an attorney representing Oswald participating in hearings or to have access to investigative materials. Yet following the response to Lane, Chief Justice Warren released a statement that the president of the American Bar Association would be designated to represent Oswald's interests.

Contrary to the Warren press release, the ABA chief did not

personally nor actively participate in Commission activities, instead designating Charles Rhyne to represent him. Rhyne—Dean of the Southern Methodist Law School—was also identified by Warren as representing the Attorney General of Texas to the Commission.[13] Rhyne does not appear to any extent in the Warren Commission inquiry transcripts, and there is no record of any active representation of Oswald's interests in its meeting records.

Mark Lane did independently testify before the Commission in March and July, 1964. His appearances resulted in what were described as heated exchanges with Warren, who made it clear that Lane had no official position and did not represent Oswald's family in any fashion—and that the Commission challenged the truthfulness of certain of Lane's statements. In response Lane published a critique of the Commission in a book titled *Rush to Judgment*; the book became a number one bestseller (it spent 29 months on the *New York Times* bestseller list in 1966) and was turned into a documentary film in 1967. It seems fair to say that Lane's work laid the foundation for what became significant, broad-based public skepticism over the Commission's final report.

Lane's research was supported by Sylvia Meagher, who worked as a research analyst at the UN's World Health Organization. She was one of the first to not only read but study in detail the twenty-six volumes of hearings and exhibits that were published in support of the Warren Commission Report. As a trained, experienced analyst she was "appalled" at the inconsistencies between that material and the summary report and began to collect what proved to be an extensive list of deliberate misrepresentations, omissions, and distortions which she felt demonstrated instances of dishonesty in the Commission's report on the assassination.

In 1965 Meagher published a full name and subject index to the twenty-six volumes—which had been distributed by the Commission with no "working" index. She followed that in 1967 with what became a highly significant critique of the Commission's work; *Accessories After the Fact* became a mainstay of Warren Commission critics and was published in six editions over time, impacting the work of follow-on assassination inquiries, including that of the Senate Select Committee on Intelligence. Senator Richard Schweiker in the preface described the book as being "a meticulous and compelling indictment of the Warren Commission Report," with a significance that "could not be overstated."

Over the years, successive generations of citizen researchers, initially known simply as "skeptics," would follow on with Warren Commission critiques, eventually gaining access to internal Commission materials on its own workings and decision-making. That information solidified the skeptical view by revealing the extent to which Commission staff, and even senior members, had been driven to produce a report which was in line with the initial position defined only days following the assassination of President Kennedy and the murder of Lee Harvey Oswald. Oswald was to be presented as the sole actor in the assassination, there were no others involved, and he certainly would have been convicted if he had gone to trial.

The contemporary work of JFK researcher Pat Speer provides one of the best summary insights into the extent to which the Commission's deliberations and the work of its staff was "channeled" towards that conclusion—and the internal sensitivities regarding the crafting of the report so as not to expose it to criticism or raise public doubt.[14] Speer begins his summary with an example from August 1964, when the Commission was deep into work on its final draft.

> Commission counsels, staff and advisers were active in the process of draft revision and on August 8 the chief Justice Department liaison to the Commission (Howard Willens) wrote a memo suggesting that the report should not include a finding addressing Oswald's capability as a shooter. Willens wrote: "I think our case remains the same even if Oswald had limited or negligible capability with a rifle. In a way, we are emphasizing an argument we don't really need, which

> prompts controversy and may tend to weaken the stronger elements of our proof."[15]

At that late date, the representative of the Justice Department was asserting that it was best to avoid the entire issue of whether Oswald actually had the ability to make the shots that the Commission was going to assert killed the president and wounded Texas Governor Connally. Speer points out that Willens, an attorney for the Justice Department, should have been focused on how strong the case that Oswald was able to make the shots that killed the president actually was, rather than avoiding one of the most fundamental issues of the entire inquiry in order not to offer a subject that might leave doubt in the public's mind or offer opportunities for critics to question the strength of the Commission's conclusion.

Internal Dissension

As it turned out, Willen's concerns about the section of the report dealing with the actual shooting were well considered; it was indeed quite debatable. By early September, Counsel Wesley Liebeler was given a copy of the current draft report to review. Given that Liebeler viewed the report as essentially being the prosecution's "brief" in a case against Oswald, he was shocked by numerous statements which he felt to be incorrect or at best simply unsupported. The result was a 26-page memorandum to the General Counsel J. Lee Rankin on September 26.

Speer provides a blow-by-blow detailing of Liebeler's points—primarily related to Oswald's rifle capability. Item 16 on Liebeler's list provides an example of his concerns:

> "Item 16. The present section on rifle capability fails to set forth material in the record tending to indicate that Oswald was not a good shot and that he was not interested in his rifle while in the Marine Corps. It does not set forth material indicating that a telescopic sight

> must be tested and sighted in after a period of non-use before it can be expected to be accurate. That problem is emphasized by the fact that the FBI actually found that there was a defect in the scope which caused the rifle to fire high and to the right. In spite of the above the present section takes only part of the material in the record to show that Oswald was a good shot and that he was interested in rifles. I submit that the testimony of Delgado that Oswald was not interested in his rifle while in the Marines is at least as probative as Alba's testimony that Oswald came into his garage to read rifle—and hunting—magazines. To put it bluntly that sort of selection from the record could seriously affect the integrity and credibility of the entire report."

In a following item Liebeler was even more outspoken—"Why don't we admit instead of reaching and using only part of the record to support the propositions presently set forth in the galleys. Those conclusions will never be accepted by critical persons anyway."[16]

Counsel Rankin was not at all happy with Liebeler's memorandum. According to author Edward Epstein, Liebeler himself had told Epstein that Rankin's actual response was that no more such memoranda/internal critiques were welcome—the report had to be published, immediately. Liebeler was apparently not one to back off from issues that deeply concerned him, and Rankin allowed Liebeler to present his issues to Norman Redlich. Speer notes that Redlich was Rankin's top aide and the man responsible for reviewing and re-writing both the chapters on the shooting and those on Oswald's likely guilt. According to Epstein, Redlich heatedly objected to all Liebeler's criticisms and closed the discussion by stating that "The Commissioners judged it an easy shot, and I work for the Commission."

Speer's work on the internal activities of the Commission is extensive, and deserves a read by everyone interested in this subject. Those who wish a further exploration of issues with the Commission's work should also consider Gerald McKnight's 2005 book *Breach of Trust.*

Speer calls out one particular point that by itself serves to cement issues of trust with the Commission's report. In 2013 (the 50th anniversary of the assassination), Justice Department liaison Howard Willens' book *History Will Prove Us Right* was published; the book presents an assertive defense of the Warren Commission's work and proceeds chapter by chapter describing who worked on what sections and even who raised certain issues. Yet even in his defense of the Commission, Willens' remarks raise issues of trust—he notes that as late as August one of the lead counsels was very sensitive to any public access to the materials collected by the Commission:

> "Mr. Rankin also told me that he had raised with the Commission the problem of Archives handling of Commission materials. There is apparently a feeling among the members of the Commission that it would be desirable if all the material of the Commission were not available to the public for a year or two after the report comes out. They suggest that the organization and the screening of these materials will take this long, but of course the principal interest here is making sure that sufficient time elapses before any real critics can get access to material other than those which the Commission desires to publish simultaneous with its report. Apparently, the Chief Justice intends to talk with the National Archivist on this subject."[17]

Issues of Trust

As anticipated by its own staff, and quickly identified by the earliest generation of Commission critics, there clearly were an extensive set of open issues with the Warren Commission Report—as well as with the case for Lee Oswald as the assassin. Many of those issues became visible even with the publication of the Commission's own 26 volumes of testimony and exhibits. Counter to Liebeler's proposal, none of the issues had been discussed or acknowledged in the final report of the Commission. His observation that on a number of points the report "was a stretch," and that the open issues should be transparently presented had been ignored, and "critical persons" most definitely did not accept its conclusions.

Over time, with additional inquiries, congressional committee investigations, and ultimately with the JFK Records Act and the work of the Assassination Records Review Board, the criticism only became more extensive and more adamant. With access to original Dallas Police reports, statements from witnesses, autopsy materials, and internal Commission study documents, a considerable number of the interpretations and analyses of the Commission were subjected to challenge. The official shooting scenario and the case for Oswald as the single individual firing from the Texas School Board Depository was found to be have been brought into serious question by the Commission's own expert ballistics/wound panel, convened at Edgewood Armory.

There had initially been considerable doubt, based on the condition of the bullet itself, that a single shot could have both wounded the president and seriously wounded Governor Connally. However, the shooting scenario developed by the Commission—necessary to find Oswald as the sole shooter—required that a single bullet (Commission Exhibit 399) do just that. To deal with that issue, the Commission convened a special panel of experts in ballistics and wounds, working under the aegis of the Army's Edgewood Arsenal.

Yet the technical report of that panel's work on the wound ballistics of Mannlicher-Carcano 6.5 mm. ammunition contradicted the Commission's conclusion. After extensive testing the panel's chairman and all the professional members of the panel concluded that, given the damage to CE399, the Warren Commission's conclusion was not forensically possible.[18] The only participant in the panel's review to dissent from that finding was Commission staff member Arlen Specter—himself the originator of the Commission's shooting scenario. Despite the conclusions of the Edgewood panel experts, the Commission's report presented the technical study as supporting its conclusions on both CE399 and its overall shooting scenario.[19]

A host of similar evidentiary issues have surfaced with the Commission's report, and readers are referred to Pat Speer's balanced work on a number of them, in particular his work on events in Dealey Plaza, and the shooting of the president.[20] As Liebeler had noted, and Willens had rightly feared, the detailed case presented by the Commission in its report has indeed raised serious issues of trust with the Commission's work.

What neither man could have anticipated was that a second major weakness with the Commission's work and in the official presentation of Lee Harvey Oswald would subsequently be revealed—a weakness based on the obfuscation and actual suppression of information by the Central Intelligence Agency. Those actions not only undermined the work of the FBI in its investigation of Oswald (especially regarding his appearance in Mexico City in October 1963), but also prevented both the FBI and the Commission from developing a reliable picture of the CIA's actual knowledge of Oswald prior to the assassination—and its probable use of his identity and activities in propaganda and political action operations.

One of the earliest examples of CIA misinformation related to Oswald involved the CIA's Mexico City station's support of a series of reports which presented Oswald as a paid assassin, hired by Cuba to kill President Kennedy. Originating not with the CIA itself, but rather with a walk-in to the American Embassy, Ambassador Thomas Mann first aggressively promoted a belief in Cuban sponsorship of the assassination to both the Mexico City station and to the FBI. Within 24 hours, the Ambassador had begun to express strong suspicions of Cuban involvement, suspicions which were met skeptically by the FBI Legat (Legal Attache) in Mexico City as well as by FBI headquarters. These suspicions became a major factor as early as November 27, when Mann brought the claims of Gilberto Alvarado to the attention of the FBI and the CIA, claims which were enthusiastically supported by CIA station Chief Winston Scott and his counterintelligence chief David Phillips.[21]

While the FBI and Director Hoover were skeptical of the Alvarado story of seeing Oswald taking a large sum of money from the Cubans to kill President Kennedy, it created a virtual panic at the highest government levels in Washington. The story contained a seemingly incredible amount of detail.[22] Alvarado stated that he had observed, apparently in a public area, Oswald talking with a tall thin Negro with reddish hair and a young woman named Maria Luisa, who was blonde and carried a Canadian passport. Alvarado even provided the precise address on the passport, and described the woman kissing Oswald. The Negro had stated that he wanted to "kill the man" and Oswald had responded that he wasn't man enough to do it, at which time the man had given Oswald $6,500 in cash.

The Mexico City CIA station affirmed the "wealth of detail" provided by Gilberto Alvarado, first reported as a "well-known Nicaraguan communist underground member"—only later did it acknowledge that Alvarado had himself been working against the Cuban Consulate for the Nicaraguan security services. That relationship should either have been already known to the Mexico City CIA staff, or quickly determined, given the strong pre-existing CIA ties to Nicaraguan intelligence.

It seems odd that intelligence professionals such as Scott and Phillips would have credited the level of detail provided by Alvarado, especially when reported from a very public area of a Cuban diplomatic facility—in a conversation apparently observed at very close range by Alvarado. Yet the story and its details were all forwarded to Washington DC without corroboration. In Washington it was treated as a national security matter with respect to the assassination, and produced discussion and concerns at the highest levels of government.

In responding to those concerns, the FBI first determined that Alvarado could not have been at the Cuban Embassy on the date he asserted. However, over some 48 hours, the Mexico City CIA station continued to advise Washington that "Alvarado is telling the truth in general outline but mixed up on his dates." Years later, following retirement, Phillips would go so far as to repeat the details of Alvarado's claims in his own books—including a statement that Oswald was a paid assassin and had carried thousands of dollars in cash back to the United States with him.[23]

The FBI responded by sending a special agent to Mexico City to pursue the matter. However, prior to the agent's arrival, the CIA station had handed Alvarado over to the Mexican Federal Police (DFS) for questioning. Following what was reportedly an intense interrogation, Alvarado simply recanted his story. While that settled matters for the FBI, it left open the obvious questions that the Mexico City CIA officers should have been asking Alvarado before supporting his story to Washington D.C.

Why would a Nicaraguan security agent on a penetration mission against the Cubans not have reported such an incident to Nicaraguan intelligence at the time it occurred? Why would this information not have been immediately passed to the CIA, given that the CIA itself had extremely close connections to Nicaraguan security? Nicaragua had played a key role in anti-Castro actions throughout the CIA's Cuba project. Such questions were never pursued with the Mexico City personnel.

In itself, the Alvarado incident provides an early indication that in many instances the Mexico City CIA station appears to have pursued its own interests regarding Lee Harvey Oswald. And, as we will see, Mexico City would not be the only part of the CIA which proved to be less than open, and less than trustworthy, in regard to its knowledge of—and interest in—Oswald prior to President Kennedy's assassination.

Unfortunately, the FBI itself also appears to have been concerned about details of its own pre-assassination contacts with Oswald, and willing not only to suppress but to alter and destroy items related to those contacts. The work of the Senate Select Committee hearings in the mid-1970s confirmed that the FBI had totally retyped a page of Oswald's personal notebook while in its custody and had substituted the altered page for the original. The retyping removed an attempted contact by a Dallas FBI agent with Oswald, a contact which instead led to the agent interviewing Oswald's wife Marina at Ruth Paine's home, were she was staying.

Alteration of a primary piece of evidence to suppress information was a serious matter, and an extensive inquiry was made, involving the Bureau and with testimony from several of its agents—resulting in the official position by the House Committee that it "deemed the incident regrettable, (but) found it to be trivial in the context of the entire investigation."[24]

The notebook incident becomes even more interesting when considered along with the fact that at least in one instance in New Orleans Oswald had indeed voluntarily met with the FBI. The idea that Oswald had been a source of information for the FBI had been alleged in the earliest days of the Warren Commission inquiry and it had been briefly investigated, yet in later years we have learned that even the Commission staff doubted that the FBI would disclose such a relationship to them. Counsel Rankin is on record as remarking that it would be very difficult to establish any such relationship—"I am confident the FBI would never admit it, and I presume their records would never show it."[25]

More Issues of Trust

Given what has been learned over the years, the totality of information now available shows that the Bureau did knowingly conceal information about its association with Oswald and suggests that it suppressed interest in him as a potential source very much as Counsel Rankin had suspected it would. For example, in 1975 a House Committee took testimony from FBI agent James Hosty that immediately following the assassination, he had been ordered by office chief J. Gordon Shanklin to destroy a note left at the Dallas Bureau office by Lee Harvey Oswald.[26]

Furthermore, a co-worker of agent Hosty related to a Senate Select

Committee that Hosty had privately told him that the first agent to interview Oswald after his return from Russia, John Fain, had considered Oswald as a potential security informant (PSI)—and that Hosty himself had admitted that he was considering him as a PSI as well.[27] In Fain's case that would be reasonable enough, given that Fain had reported Oswald agreeing to inform the FBI of any attempt by communists/subversives to approach him. With respect to Hosty, such an interest would certainly explain Hosty's visit to the Paine house where Marina Oswald was staying—and the alteration of Oswald's daybook recording Hosty's visit.

Both the Warren Commission and the Senate Select Committee (Church Committee) did examine allegations that Oswald had been either an informant or at least a source of information for the FBI. The allegations were of particular interest with respect to the New Orleans office as Oswald had indeed voluntarily requested a meeting with the FBI there. Allegations of a potential "source" relationship explored by the FBI had come second-hand from a former Bureau agent in that office, personally via an aide to President Johnson. The source, hospitalized and under doctor's care, declined to be named to the Committee; one element of his claim was plausibly verified, but without his testimony (even in confidence) the Committee was unable to go further. The FBI also notified the Committee that it had no intention of pursuing the matter on its own.[28]

In another instance, a former FBI office clerk in New Orleans named William Walter reported seeing Oswald's name on a folder in a special filing cabinet reserved for security matters, including source and informant files. However, the Committee was more interested in his associated report of having seen a warning telex concerning a threat to President Kennedy only weeks before the assassination. In the end it focused on technical issues with his reconstruction of the telex, and failed to pursue or take testimony from individuals Walter named who might have corroborated his story. The Committee also ignored the fact that Walter had pointed out that all the individuals in the office has been pressured to sign a special document affirming that they would not disclose information related to the incident in question. No explanation was given to the agents on the need for the special nondisclosure procedure other than that the matter was being treated as a security issue.[29]

Given that it was a known practice of the FBI to recruit potential sources and informants on both security and criminal matters (offices were rated on their monthly production of both), and that the record shows that Oswald voluntarily contacted the FBI on at least one instance in New Orleans, it does seem strange that the office would not have had some interest in at least considering him for a source relationship. This is especially true since he provided them details in regard to the Fair Play for Cuba Committee, the existence of a chapter in the city, and (falsely) the name of at least one other member of the group.

The FBI and its New Orleans office had targeted, and begun conducting intelligence collections on, both Cuban exiles and the Fair Play for Cuba Committee, as early as December 1961. An internal FBI memo from the Special Agent in Charge (SAIC) of the office dated July 27, 1962, summarized its activities, and the first item noted was the lack of any FPCC group in the city at that time; but the report noted that the office was investigating three individuals suspected of pro-Cuba activities.[30]

The memo also noted having several sources and PSIs in place, reporting on both pro- and anti-Castro activities. Two of them, Arnesto Rodriquez and Carlos Bringuier, would be the first individuals contacted by Oswald when he began inserting himself into Cuban affairs there in the summer of 1963.

Given that the FPCC was officially considered a subversive entity by the FBI and was under investigation and surveillance by multiple agencies as of 1963, the lack of follow-up on Oswald is hard to credit—yet that is what the official record was found to reveal. Given Oswald's demonstrations in support of the FPCC, and his contacts with that organization, as well as his claimed membership in an active chapter, it is hard to accept the New Orleans office's apparent lack of active investigation, contact with, or surveillance of Oswald immediately following his hour-long interview.

Admittedly, it is difficult to fully assess that lack of follow-on activity, given that we do not have a copy of the actual field office reports on Oswald prepared by the local agents regarding the initial Oswald contact (Quigley/August 15 and Kaack/August 31). The record we do have is a series of pages out of an FBI Headquarters file on Oswald, apparently excerpted from Quigley's actual report.[31]

The information does detail the interview at length, with biographical data on Oswald, the materials taken into possession when he was arrested, and his description of activities and individuals with both the national Fair Play for Cuba Committee and its local chapter. Unfortunately, that still leaves us with nothing to tell us how the report was processed at the local office or to verify its distribution within New Orleans or at FBI headquarters. It also leaves open the question of how thorough and accurate the headquarters excerpt is. Researcher Greg Parker has pointed out that Quigley's own testimony contradicts the headquarters excerpt with respect to his actually having seen and examined Oswald's identification cards during the interview.

Agent Quigley was questioned about his time with Oswald and his report, but rather than providing the Commission with a copy of the report, Quigley referred them to excerpted material which he stated had been used in Kaack's report.[32] Rather than asking for either report, the Commission proceeded to ask Quigley about the notes he had taken in the interview. Quigley replied that he had destroyed the notes, presumably after writing his official report based on them. No further questions were asked about the report itself, any office response to it, or what follow-up (if any) was done regarding Oswald's information about the previously unknown Fair Play for Cuba Committee group in New Orleans.

It should also be noted that in Dallas on February 10, 1964, Agent Quigley signed an affidavit that he had not attempted to recruit

Oswald as an informant—which would not have been his job, given that separate individuals handled recruiting as well as the management of sources and of paid informants. That affidavit was part of a whole series of affidavits of FBI agents in Dallas and New Orleans, affirming that Oswald had not been a paid informant. However, no statements were made that Oswald had never provided information to the Bureau or been considered as a potential source of information (PSI), especially with respect to security/subversive matters—a completely different matter than his being a paid informant.[33]

Some years later, the Senate Select Committee also obtained testimony from FBI agents that in the recruiting of sources and informants, it had been common practice to make initial contacts and even conduct outreach without extensive paperwork, but only with the verbal approval of the agent in charge of the office. During the period of decision-making and prior to completing the recruitment, there would be nothing more than a single sheet of paper in a security file—and that would not be cross-referenced to other office files on the individual (a match to the situation described above by FBI office clerk Walter in New Orleans).[34]

We are left with the fact that the FBI destroyed a note left with its Dallas office, and later removed and rewrote a page from his notebook which referenced an FBI interview of Oswald's wife. In New Orleans, the Bureau had apparently carried out no serious investigation of his detailed report about an unknown Fair Play for Cuba Committee group revealed by Oswald. And when the individual agent in the New Orleans office who would have had the most information about that office's contacts with Oswald was subpoenaed by District Attorney Garrison's inquiry, he was allowed by the Justice Department to claim Executive Privilege in regard to answering questions about Oswald. Given that history, it is little wonder that Warren Commission critics came to view the FBI as equally as untrustworthy as the CIA regarding its pre-assassination knowledge of Oswald.

Critical Reactions

Even a brief summary of issues related to the work of the Warren Commission and the actions of the CIA and FBI leaves us with ample reason for mistrust and skepticism of its conclusions. Abundant serious issues have been raised not just by citizen critics, but by the Commission's own staff members and by follow-on Congressional inquiries. These issues relate both to the Commission's position on the assassination as well as its portrayal of Lee Harvey Oswald.

Over the decades following the assassination, an ongoing stream of revelations about the work of the Commission as well as activities of both the CIA and FBI led to the development of a critical community which totally rejected the official story of the assassination, and the Commission's view of Oswald. Essentially a new dimension formed, one in which Oswald was viewed in several competing perspectives—Oswald as a naïve, unwitting individual who had been set up as a total patsy, alternatively as someone recruited by mob figures as an actual participant in the assassination, or in another variation as a knowing accessory to an action against President Kennedy.

Multiple versions of the second two views emerged, but several of the more sensational scenarios viewed his role in Dallas as being one more assignment in a long series of covert intelligence missions. In that view, the basic scenario saw Oswald as a radically committed anti-communist who from his earliest years had volunteered for a series of tasks and missions for federal agencies including the Office of Naval Intelligence, the CIA, the FBI, U.S. Customs—possibly even for a Congressional Committee working on gun control.

One of the issues with many of the conspiracy scenarios developed by the critical community is that while they overlay a complex mix of characters and connections onto Oswald's activities, the scenarios still present Oswald as basically one-dimensional. In virtually all those views, Oswald does not act on his own initiatives or agenda, but rather serves as a consistently willing and compliant tool for other parties—from his teenage years up until his death. The scenarios extend virtually no free will to Oswald, presenting him as so politically committed to the anti-communist cause and worldview that he served as nothing more than a tool of others, recruited by multiple agencies and seemingly serving some of them concurrently, especially by 1963.

In one such scenario Oswald is viewed as being managed as a voluntary CIA asset from his earliest formative years in school, molded into being a cooperative figure who would take a changing intelligence mission right up to the time of his death—including serving as a knowingly sacrificial figure to tie the blame for President Kennedy's death to Cuba.

Other scenarios begin with Oswald as a patriotically motivated teenager, recruited to join the military, and then used as a voluntary "dangle" with the intent of exposing communists or other subversive characters serving with him in the military—subversive agents attempting to co-opt American servicemen overseas or inside the United States.

In an extension of that scenario, he is seen as working for the Navy Office of Special Investigations in Japan and then recruited by the Office of Naval Intelligence (or the CIA) and sent into the Soviet Union on a targeted mission. The nature of that mission varies, ranging from a simple test of Soviet intelligence and recruiting practices to something far more strategic, possibly involved with leaking information about American U-2 reconnaissance flights.

Contrary to the official Warren Commission story of Oswald—a "lone nut" acting spontaneously and in an emotionally charged state in the attack on President Kennedy—virtually all the intelligence-related conspiracy scenarios which involve Oswald as a knowing participant in the attack (even in those in which he was not aware of the intent to actually kill JFK) rather than simply as a "patsy," view Oswald as a compliant actor, under the control of others. He is presented as an individual willing to take a series of orders from a variety of different individuals and agencies over several years, with his activities consistently explained by compliance with these orders rather than as an individual who might have more often been independently acting on his own agendas and personal initiatives. Yet as we will see, a serious examination of Oswald's personality reveals a person consistently questioning authority, an individual quite unlikely to be a witting tool of anyone.

One exception to the "intelligence connected" scenarios are those which assume Oswald to be essentially little more than a young man with a limited future, linked though family connections in New Orleans to criminal figures, and recruited for an apolitical act—serving as a low-level and naïve actor in a Godfather-related conspiracy against the president.

Quandary and Challenge

The quandary in dealing with the historical Oswald is that we begin in a state of dissonance. We face media coverage which presented him from the outset as the president's assassin. But the numerous issues with the Warren Commission's findings challenge the credibility of that portrayal. Beyond that, it seems clear that various actions of the FBI and CIA may have added questions rather than clarity in regard to Oswald's motives and activities. The various conspiracy views offer alternatives, but many of them not only conflict with each other, but require quite different assumptions about Oswald and his role (or non-role) in the assassination. Even the traditional approach of neutrality leaves us in a state of uncertainty in regard to the competing views of Lee Harvey Oswald.

Of course, the same thing can be said regarding many of the more frequently discussed and "popularized" figures in both contemporary and ancient history. It is not uncommon to find wildly divergent views of such figures coming from differing biographers, popular authors, and even historians with sometimes wildly varying positive and negative views—with each picking their own sources and content from available material to support their presentations.

Given the dramatic differences in the many existing views of Oswald, any attempt to provide an independent and objective view of him will face serious objections, many of them based on what are or are not acceptable sources of information. Readers preferring the official view will challenge any source other than those used by the official investigations and inquiries, considering them to have been fact-checked and effectively defended against challenge. Priority in testimony will be given to official interviews and transcripts; in particular testimony from agencies or law enforcement will be accepted, given that lies or misstatements would be legally actionable.

As a counter, critics of the official view sometimes react by essentially throwing out any government document as being potentially suspect, especially those from the Dallas Police, the FBI or the CIA. Those critics often apply the same standard to individuals who would normally be considered primary and secondary witnesses—in the case of Oswald, his wife, his family, and even individuals he himself identified as his closest friends or associates. The problem with that approach is that it eliminates virtually all normal legal and historical sources and leaves no data at all—leaving only avenues for pure speculation.

In the following work on Lee Harvey Oswald, we will examine him as an individual, with his own character and agendas, as an historical figure in the context of a presidential assassination, and as an individual "entangled" with the overall Cold War history of the period. In doing so we will endeavor to apply standard historical practices in evaluating source data. Those practices include consideration of situational context of Oswald's remarks, assessment of Oswald's purported beliefs and views through references to documents or other verifiable sources, and consideration of the consistency and fact-checking commentary contained in previously published research and writing on Lee Harvey Oswald.

Of course, even with the best intentions and practices this study will also be subjective to some extent, but with every effort to make it transparently so, differentiating known facts from the authors' own—and others'—speculation. In the interest of that transparency, it is necessary for the authors to declare that they are both Warren Commission critics, skeptical of the official history of the assassination, and have previously researched and written on aspects of the assassination dealing with elements of conspiracy.

Chapter 2

Character and Development

"There was nothing that would lead me to believe when I saw him at the age of 12 that there would be seeds of destruction for somebody."
—John Carro, probation officer, Warren Commission Hearings, Volume 8, 212

Opposing Views

The Warren Commission Report, in Chapter 7, offered a view of Oswald as being unable to establish meaningful personal relationships, perpetually discontented with his own life, a communist in his political views, and moved to action by an overriding antipathy towards America and his own surroundings: [35]

> "Oswald was moved by an overriding hostility to his environment. He does not appear to have been able to establish meaningful relationships with other people. He was perpetually discontented with the world around him. Long before the assassination he expressed his hatred for American society and acted in protest against it. Oswald's search for what he conceived to be the perfect society was doomed

> from the start. He sought for himself a place in history—a role as the 'great man' who would be recognized as having been in advance of his times. His commitment to Marxism and communism appears to have been another important factor in his motivation."

In the years following the Warren Commission's report, a broader exploration of Lee Oswald's history and personal relationships has brought the Commission's characterization into serious question, including the contention that Oswald sought "a place in history" for himself—something that literally no one associated with Lee Oswald had ever heard him actually express in public, or indicate in any of his own relatively extensive views on social and geopolitical issues written circa 1963. In essence "seeking a place in history" became a place filler, a fallback response in place of any substantive motive for what was seemingly a spontaneous decision to kill the president of the United States.

The search for a more objective, historical characterization of Oswald, one including his history as well as his own remarks and writings, begins with Oswald himself. In that respect the Warren Commission's 26 volumes contain a huge amount of relevant information, the majority accumulated from FBI research into his family background, his education, and his time in the Marines.

While some critics literally trust no information provided by the FBI, a good deal of the material in the appendices to the Warren Report has been corroborated and is internally consistent. In addition, the information in the background collection is also at odds with the Commission's summary report in a great many areas, providing a useful illustration of the extent to which the Commission chose to "cherry pick" and load its language to build its case against Oswald.[36]

Additional information, critical for corroboration, includes remarks from Oswald's personal friends (he did have friends, and lovers), individuals who did socialize with him, whom he liked and talked with at length. There are also factual sources, including his own press and media interviews, his documented reading preferences, and his own writings. That writing, which was extensive during 1962 and 1963, was collected by the Warren Commission but placed into the appendices, escaping those who did not venture beyond the Commission's summary report.

A combination and cross check of these sources allows the development of a totally independent image of Oswald—as well as a critical baseline in which to judge both the continuity and evolution of his very personal interests and worldviews, from his teenage years through the months immediately prior to his own death.

Viewed chronologically, and with multiple sources, the details of Oswald's life reveal considerable consistency in both his character and behavior over time, while demonstrating that as much as anyone, he was apt to act "situationally" at times. Situational behavior is neither unusual nor mysterious—much less conspiratorial—regardless of how it may appear at any single point in time.

As an example, over a year after the assassination, the press carried stories based on Marina Oswald's just-released remarks to the Commission.[37] In her testimony she had described Oswald changing after their move from Russia to the United States. She had described him as a caring and affectionate father, helpful but far less attentive to her than early in their marriage. He seemed more irritable, bothered by what she considered trifles, and did not like the Russian friends she had made in the Fort Worth/Dallas area.

Those remarks, and others, were leveraged by both the press and the Commission to infer that Oswald had dramatically changed, becoming reclusive and dangerous by the fall of 1963. Yet what is missing from the media story is the element of "context." With additional sources and background research it becomes clear that Oswald's change in attentiveness (and romantic interest) towards Marina had begun well before the move, noted even in KGB monitoring of the Oswalds following their marriage. The fact is that Oswald himself consistently demonstrated a tendency towards becoming bored with jobs, affairs, and even special interests such as astronomy or photography.

Equally relevant context for Marina's remarks comes from the couple's time in Dallas and Fort Worth after their return from Russia. Over some 16 months the Oswalds had developed a repetitive pattern of behavior—Marina repeatedly separated from Oswald as he moved through a succession of jobs, she relied increasingly on Russian speaking friends and lived with her young child June in several different homes. In return, as Oswald found new jobs or simply began to miss his family he consistently returned to Marina, on occasion literally pleading for her to rejoin him in a new apartment.

That pattern had begun again in Dallas following the birth of the couple's new baby in the fall of 1963. And in totality, Marina's remarks about her husband's frustration during his visit on the eve of the assassination were much less sinister than the newspaper coverage implied—directly related to yet another effort by Oswald to get her to reunite the family, with promises that with yet another new job he would immediately get an apartment, and they could be together again as a family. As Marina herself said, she had agreed to bring the children and join him, but with a young child and new baby she was being much more pragmatic—demanding that she would bring the children and join him after the holidays, when he had gotten the apartment—and a washing machine.

A study of Oswald over time certainly does reveal situational behavior, but it also makes him more "real," subject to basic human weaknesses and with his own particular personality flaws. The following chronological view is an effort to present Oswald as an individual, driven by his own beliefs and personality, but with his attitude and actions at any moment in time influenced by who he was with and what was going on around him. Tracing Oswald's personality and character though his school years, his time in the Marines, his service in Japan, and his experiences in Russia is also key to evaluating the consistency and continuity of his basic behavior. A great deal of the writing about Lee Harvey Oswald has been focused on the year 1963 and his actions immediately before and after the death of President Kennedy. Yet without a comprehensive (and unbiased) picture of his past, specifically focused on personal attitudes and character, it is impossible to judge whether the picture of Oswald painted by the Warren Commission, or even by its skeptics, reflects the real Oswald. It is useful to study the Oswald that developed during his school years and military service. To find that Oswald, it is mandatory that we explore both the details the Warren Commission presented—and those it ignored.

School Years [38]

We see an early example of Oswald's situational nature in the differences between his behavior (and his grades) in elementary and secondary education. Oswald's academic performance in elementary school was mixed, likely due to the ongoing problems with his home life, problems which were quite real and involved his mother's divorce, remarriage, and growing discord within her second marriage.

In the first grade, Oswald's academic performance in Fort Worth, Texas schools (initially at Covington Elementary) was a combination of A's and B's. His attendance was at best only acceptable, with 82 days in school and 15 days absent (he received A's in physical education and health). Given his absences he did not complete all the elements of first grade. He was enrolled in Clayton Public School for his second year of school, but due to a further breakdown in relations between his mother and stepfather, was withdrawn before completing the second grade there, with no grades recorded.

Lee Oswald entered the third grade at Arlington Heights Elementary School and remained at Arlington Heights for the entire school year, completing the third grade with a satisfactory record. He scored A's in social studies, citizenship, elementary science, art, and music, and a D in spelling, something that would become something of an Achilles heel given that writing would become a major interest for him.

In September 1949, he transferred to Ridglea West Elementary School, where he remained for the next 3 years. His record at Ridglea is not particularly remarkable; in the fourth and fifth grades he received mostly B's, while in the sixth grade a mix of B's and C's. He had learned to read relatively well; however, his spelling and writing skills may have suffered due an undiagnosed problem, possibly dysgraphia, which is known to affect either spelling or handwriting or both. Oswald would become an inveterate and prolific reader, yet continually had difficulties with both his handwriting and especially his spelling.[39] In the fourth grade his IQ was recorded at 103; on achievement tests in each of his 3 years at Ridglea, he did best in reading and worst in spelling.

The Warren Commission quotes his early elementary teachers as describing him as a "normal boy," but with a tendency to keep to himself and not outgoing in socializing with other children. As a counterpoint, a classmate of Oswald's in the fourth grade recalled playing with him often at school and walking together with him on their way home from school. The same teacher whom the Warren Commission recorded as describing Lee as a quiet and shy boy also remarked that he was given a puppy for Christmas in 1949 and brought the puppy to her home to show it off and to talk with her and her family.

Time in New York City

Given that Oswald had attended three different schools in his first three years of elementary education, it seems no surprise to find him without a series of close childhood friends during that period. Yet he did make individual friends both in elementary school and later in high school; something the Warren Commission chose not to elaborate on. Instead, they continually presented him as asocial, and even antisocial, based largely on an extended detailing of events in New York City. The move to New York was a sudden one, and placed Lee and his mother in a room in his brother's apartment. The brother, John Pic, was serving in the Coast Guard (assigned to duty at Staten Island), and he and his wife were living in his mother-in-law's apartment.

Whether or not the move was announced to his brother in advance remains a matter of debate; the spare room was only temporarily available because John's mother-in-law was visiting another daughter. Oswald's mother stated that she and Lee had been invited, but John's remarks suggest that their arrival may have been a surprise. In either event the move, sharing a relatively small apartment with his mother, brother, and brother's wife, certainly added to the chaos of Oswald's home life and has to be considered as an element in his personal problems when he and his mother lived in New York City.

There is ample evidence to confirm that Oswald's mother's appearance at her son's apartment created a stressful and challenging situation for all those involved. Entering the New York City schools in the seventh grade also proved especially challenging for Oswald. His southern accent and even his clothing made him stand out in class, and once again he was a new kid with no local history. His response was to simply avoid the situation, ducking out of school to become involved in a pattern of truancy. His behavior became extremely situational during that period, very much dependent on what was going on around him both at home and at school at any point in time.

Initially Lee Oswald attended school in New York regularly, but his conduct was recorded as unsatisfactory. Teachers reported that he did little work, and seemed to spend most of his time sailing paper planes around the room. At the same time, neither his mother nor Lee appear to have gotten along at all well with his brother's wife. There were constant conflicts with Mrs. Pic and even hostility towards her from Lee. The situation reached a point where it became clear that Mrs. Oswald had to leave her son's home, and she did so, finding work at a dress store and moving Lee into an apartment in the Bronx.

With his mother working, Lee's truancy only increased. At the time of their move from the Pics', he was in junior high, obviously an especially challenging time for any young person, and having a particularly hard time "fitting in." His problems were not a matter of his intelligence—by then he was testing with an IQ of 118, the upper range of "bright normal." Teachers found him courteous, but with problems of dependability and self-control. Happier by himself, one of his favorite interests was the Bronx Zoo. When he was caught there by a truant officer, the officer stated that Lee was clean and well-dressed but was surly and referred to the officer as a "damned Yankee." That led to an appearance in Children's Court.

Following that experience with the legal system in New York, his mother moved the two of them again, having found a new and better-paying job with Martin's Department store in Brooklyn. It should be noted that Lee's own work experience would later reflect the same pattern as his mother's, with an inability to hold any single job for an extended period, and the tendency to simply jump from place to place and job to job.

In her newest job, Lee's mother had a long commute to work, resulting in her leaving home early and returning late—that made further truancy all too easy for Lee, who had been enrolled in yet another junior high (his third school in seven months in New York). Professionals who evaluated Oswald over his truancy and behavior commented that his mother was not spending enough time with him, and that he had become "socially maladjusted"—not surprising given the situation of his constant moves between schools and a minimal family environment.

Lee's continuing truancy problems led to school probation, to counseling, and even time in a special Youth House, where professional personnel noted that he was well-endowed mentally, but that he was withdrawn. They evaluated his problems as largely due to his lack of a real family life, and insufficient attention from his mother—who was described as "self-involved and conflicted."

Perhaps the most insightful remarks on Oswald during that period came from his school probation officer, John Carro. Carro had several exchanges with Lee regarding his truancy. Carro found him to be bright, but tired of being teased by classmates over his accent and clothes. Oswald did not think he was learning anything in school and that it was a waste of time; this early "boredom" in school would evolve into a major element of Oswald's personality. His mother worked, and he stayed home and read by himself—even at that point in time expressing a desire to go into the Marines.

When Carro made it clear to Oswald that his choice was either to stay in school and adapt or face some sort of ongoing state commitment—such as a youth farm or children's village—Oswald immediately replied, "In that case I'll go back to school."[40] It appears that Oswald's mother did become more personally involved with her youngest son at that point, and school authorities are on record as stating Lee's overall behavior quickly improved, although he still showed signs of being quick-tempered with classmates.

With improved attendance, Oswald completed the seventh grade with low but passing grades in all academic courses; he did receive a failing mark in Home Economics. His conduct in the classroom improved significantly, with his being rated as generally satisfactory. In contrast to the image created by the Warren Report, Oswald's final period in the New York City schools demonstrated that he was not intrinsically a "loner;" his school evaluation rated him as "outstanding" in Social Participation. He even began to demonstrate more personal interests, joining a model airplane club and even (seemingly inexplicably, but possibly as joke by his classmates) being elected president of his class.

The improvement in Lee's behavior and attitude was significant enough that when Oswald's brother Robert visited New York on leave from the Marines, he found that Lee did not appear to him to be unhappy or to be acting abnormally—nor did Robert observe any strained relations between Lee and his mother. Lee's truancy the previous fall and winter was apparently discussed only in passing, when Mrs. Oswald mentioned that Lee had to appear before a judge.

Oswald's sixteen months in New York City received an exceptional amount of attention and focus in the Warren Commission's overview of Oswald's personality; it highlighted his school problems and displays of temper, and noted purported instances of threats against family members. Its summary overview gave little note of the fact that Oswald's behavior substantially improved during his last months in school and in the city. Even less mention was made of the dramatic improvement in his school attendance following his mother's moving the two of them back to New Orleans, to a more familiar environment.

Back in New Orleans

While in New Orleans and in his ninth school in ten years, Oswald continued to develop into an omnivorous reader, moving on from comic books to a broad range of fiction and non-fiction books. Although his school attendance problem virtually disappeared, his actual class performance is recorded as "mediocre but acceptable;" one placement/achievement test showed he was capable of better than average performance in both English and in his vocabulary knowledge. In a personal history form, Oswald wrote that he enjoyed outdoor sports, especially football, and reading. In terms of classes, he liked Civics and Science best, and Art and English least. As in New York, his stated career goal was to either join the military or possibly work as a draftsman.

Oswald also socialized to a greater extent in New Orleans; he made school acquaintances such as Edward Vobel, who helped Oswald after Lee was punched by a guy while they were on the way home from school. Oswald didn't hesitate to fight back and received a badly cut lip out of the exchange. Vobel remarked that Oswald would never start a fight, but that because he was something of an outsider, he would get picked on and was never afraid to fight back. In one instance a group of boys beat him up for sitting in the rear/Negro section of a bus.

Vobel talked about he and Oswald having a common interest in astronomy, and spending time together throwing darts and shooting pool near the French Quarter. Vobel also related that Oswald once showed him a toy pistol and talked about how they might get a real one—Vobel talked him out of any thought of stealing one from a pawn shop. Oswald would continue that interest in guns, later disciplined in the Marines for having a pistol in his barracks locker, and joining a factory hunting club in Russia.[41]

Between the ninth and tenth grades, a schoolmate of Lee and Edward invited them both to join a student aviation group sponsored by the Civil Air Patrol. That excited Oswald to the extent that he got a job as a paper delivery boy to earn money for a uniform; he eagerly joined in CAP activities including cookouts and other group events. One of the CAP officers recalled Oswald as quiet, but serious about the Civil Air Patrol activities. Photos show him smiling and joining in the fun at CAP activities, including a cookout with CAP officers among whom was an adult leader named David Ferrie, at the time a commercial airline pilot.

During his school days in New Orleans, Oswald developed a pattern of social behavior which would remain consistent throughout his short life—outgoing at times and in individual situations, but only becoming close to a limited number of associates who shared his personal interests and views. It seems fair to say that if the Commission had chosen to publish or emphasize the photographs of Oswald's life available to us now[42]—showing his clowning in a school classroom, laughing with girls at the water fountain, showing off and smiling widely in various poses in the Marines, socializing with Russian families and fellow factory workers (and particularly with a variety of young Russian women) not to mention the courtship, wedding, and family photos with his Russian wife and child—it would have been hard to sustain the image of a fundamentally bitter and antisocial Lee Oswald presented in its summary report. Such images are not to be found in the report or in the 26 volumes supporting it—nor did they appear in the post-assassination media coverage of Oswald.

Yet while not at all antisocial, Oswald clearly remained inner-directed and somewhat asocial, consistently spending more time with books and other printed materials than in socializing with others. Reading, rather than his peers, shaped his personal attitudes and opinions. And he was never bashful about sharing those with others, from his teen years onward. That assertive behavior had developed during his teenage years and remained a consistent behavior for Oswald—whose personal opinions were quite often at odds with the majority of those around him.[43]

Of course, Oswald's certainty about his worldview and beliefs is not unknown in teenagers, but Oswald tended to take it a notch or two beyond most, having no concern over the consequences of expressing himself. The president of the astronomy group which Vobel and Oswald were involved with, William Wulf, described Oswald as being highly interested in communism and talking about its importance for the working class. Oswald complained about nobody being interested in such ideas, and Wulf argued with him about it—in the end Wulf's father overheard them and essentially kicked Oswald out of his house, describing him as loud-mouthed and argumentative.

Oswald's forceful ("loud-mouthed") expression of his own views on government, social issues, and geopolitics is classic inner-directed behavior; inner-directed people tend to be rigid, but also more confident—consequently, their gain in confidence comes with a loss of broader social acceptance due to not being in harmony with the opinions generally expressed around them. As he grew older, Oswald continued to display similar behavior, not the violent or antisocial behaviors focused on by the Warren Commission, but more accurately the tendency to be argumentative, sometimes aloof and affected, and at other times simply perceived as conceited and annoying.[44]

Oswald's basic character and behavior appears to have become quite consistent from his teen years onward; his political worldview seems to have jelled during his teenage years in New Orleans and to have become firmly established following a final move with his mother, back to Texas. It is during this period that the record begins to show clear and consistent indications of Oswald's thinking and beliefs regarding political and social systems.

World View

In the fall of 1956, before starting his junior year in high school, Lee's mother withdrew him from school in New Orleans, ostensibly due to her planned move back to Texas. In reality, she was attempting to facilitate his early, underage entry into the military (Marines)—she had done the same for his older brother. In Lee's case his true age was discovered and his initial enlistment effort failed. At that point Oswald convinced his mother that he was bored with school and was learning nothing new—she accepted that and left him to his own devices. His response was to begin spending much of his time at the library. Years later his mother's only comment was that he appeared to have begun bringing home a considerable number of books, including books on Marxism and socialism.

During the remainder of their time in New Orleans, Lee had worked for a couple of months as a messenger for a freight forwarding company, then worked part time for another, and followed that by working as a "runner" for a dental company. That sort of transitory work history would become something of a standard for Oswald; he seems to have become bored with jobs just as easily as he had become bored with school. Boredom would become a basic element of Oswald's character and a major factor in his behavior during the years that followed.[45]

Oswald's early reading and later his own writing both reflect a fundamental interest in the issue of economic justice for the working classes. That interest developed while he was in New Orleans and continued following his mother's move to Fort Worth—in a letter to the Young Socialist League he described having studied socialist principles for some fifteen months and declared his desire to join the socialist movement. In his correspondence, he also inquired about any local chapters of the youth league he could join—or the possibility of starting a chapter on his own.[46]

At the end of summer 1956, his mother moved the two of them to Fort Worth, Texas, and Lee was again enrolled in school. In a new environment, with no local friends and increasingly independent (he even refused to take orders from the football coach when trying out for the B team) he made no real effort to fit in at school and stayed on his own up to the point where he turned seventeen and was able to successfully enlist in the Marines. Oswald told his mother he wanted to drop out of school and enlist in order to "do something different." Years later, when asked why someone as obviously independent as he was would sign up for the military, Oswald responded that he saw the military as an opportunity for travel and adventure.

Oswald's school years, both in and outside of class, reveal a great deal about his basic personality during that period. We can observe how he reacted to others, his tendency to be a contrarian—more than willing to assert his own views over the adults around him—and his strong streak of independence. As we have seen, Oswald could play "inside the box" if he had no other choice. He could understand and follow the rules, but following the rules needed to be his choice. An important question that follows from that is whether such behavior would prove to be consistent as he grew older and went out on his own. His Marine Corps experience provides us with the details needed to evaluate whether the behavior of his school years was just a phase—did he fundamentally change during his time in the Corps?

Chapter 3

Expanded Horizons

"For better or worse, the average young American male in that age is interested in saving enough money to go buy another beer and get another date. This I don't believe would characterize him [Oswald] at all. He read a great deal."

—John E. Donovan, Marine officer, Warren Commission Hearings, Volume 8, 292

Entering the Marine Corps

At the time he entered the Marine Corps, Lee Oswald can objectively be described as bright, but easily bored, opinionated, and contrarian in his many of his personal views. He was very much interested in socialism and Marxism (which he often referred to as communism, especially prior to his own experience with the Soviet version of communism during his time in Russia), inner-directed and largely asocial (not anti-social). His character combined a mix of strong personal enthusiasms with the tendency to be assertive and annoying to those not sharing his opinions. He can also be characterized as excessively independent. A look at his time in the Marines shows a continuation and consistency in all those elements—along with a significant development of his political worldview, largely brought about by his time and contacts while being stationed in Japan.

Oswald's time in the Marines illustrates both the most positive and negative aspects of his personality. Although younger than most of his fellow trainees, Oswald successfully completed both Marine Corps boot camp and Advanced Infantry Training. During boot camp he received a "sharpshooter" award, shown in his military photo—his final marksmanship rating in the Corps would fall to "marksman," the lowest rating to qualify as a passing score. During that rigorous, heavily disciplined and demanding training there were no notable incidents other than his reportedly being "ragged on" for being a mediocre shot on the rifle range during the advanced training.[47] We have no details on his career placement process, but records do show Oswald had listed aircraft maintenance and repair as a career choice, and he was assigned to a technical career field within the Marine Air Corps.

Possibly his earlier time and training in the Civil Air Patrol student unit helped Oswald in the career field testing and placement, and in the initial technical training. Certainly, Oswald performed satisfactorily in a series of technical schools—first in aircraft electronics, and then at Kessler Air Force Base during his training in radar systems. As he had shown on school tests, Oswald was "bright" and quite capable of learning—if the subject interested him. Yet on a personal basis, Oswald brought along his propensity to continually talk about politics (championing the cause of the working man), not something of any immediate interest to his fellow trainees. He was routinely argumentative and could take either side of a question just for the sake of debating. He was described by others in the technical school training as a "good talker," with an exceptional vocabulary.

Still, his propensity for being outspoken and argumentative led Oswald into the same sort of social situation he had faced in high school, which meant he was often simply avoided and left on his own by most of his fellow trainees. In California, when his squad was given leave and went across the border to Tijuana, Oswald simply left the others, venturing off by himself. On other squad leaves it was the same; Oswald would travel with his squad on the bus to Los Angeles—and then be off by himself, only to show up again at the bus station.[48]

Oswald's personal behavior continued to be much the same throughout his first year in the Marines. He was remembered by a Private First Class in his group as "younger and less mature" than most, staying largely to himself, spending his personal time at the base libraries and in barracks—rather than "horsing around" wrestling, working out in the gym, playing cards or talking about women, as was typical of his barracks mates.[49] Oswald also stood out in his choices of reading material, even reading poetry (Whitman's "Leaves of Grass") on board ship, headed to Japan.

Oswald had expressed to family and acquaintances that he had joined the Marines to go off on his own, to search for new experiences and for adventure. He quickly began to experience both via his Marine Occupational Specialty (MOS), which led to an assignment with a Marine air squadron in Japan. On the way, he was able to spend time in Hawaii (taking pictures, as he would routinely on his travels) when his troopship stopped there on its way to Japan. While in the Far East he was not only stationed in Japan, but traveled with his unit to a deployment in the Philippines.

Upon arriving at his assignment, like most new personnel at any military installation, he was subject to a basic level of hazing and harassment. Oswald's tendency to remain a loner might well have drawn him a few extra servings of each, yet no reported incidents or problems appear to have occurred during that initial period. Serving in Marine Air Control Squadron One (MACS-1), he performed his regularly assigned duties, which involved airspace radar surveillance and guidance of interceptors against unidentified aircraft.

His job performance and ratings were sufficient to gain him a promotion to Private First Class, and he became eligible for promotion to Corporal. As on previous occasions, when Oswald was interested in something and applied himself, he demonstrated that he could be competent and perform well. A Marine officer, Lt. John E. Donovan—who supervised Oswald during his service on a radar crew at Santa Ana, California (associated with the El Toro Marine base) towards the end of his time in the service—spoke well of his job performance. Donovan found him "competent in all functions," and observed that he handled himself calmly and well in emergency situations. Donovan also felt that Oswald was not a natural leader, but that on occasions when he did serve as senior man present, effectively as crew chief, he performed competently in that role.

Oswald's work in radar illustrates his intelligence and his capabilities—when he chose to apply them. It has also given rise to considerable speculation regarding his later decision to go to the Soviet Union, particularly regarding his statements at the time that he was prepared to offer information on U.S. military radar to the Soviets.[50] Oswald did have experience with such systems in Japan, and most importantly, in southern California during his assignment to a radar unit supporting the strategic El Toro Marine Corps air base near Irvine, southeast of Los Angeles.

His radar duties would have given him a solid working knowledge of radar system operations (including Identification Friend or Foe protocols), and he did work with one of the newer generations of mobile radar units, the MP 16 height finder radar, an advanced system with a range of just beyond 200 miles.[51] In addition to equipment capabilities—including range and height limitations—his time at El Toro exposed him to classified tactical information regarding West Coast air defenses. That would have involved the radio frequencies used for communication with interceptor units, call signs for units and installations, and the identification codes for aircraft entering and exiting coastal air defense zones.

Beyond his knowledge of one of the newest advanced radar sets—the MP 16—Oswald had also been trained on an especially critical piece of equipment, the TPX-1. That device transfers radio and radar signals from a receiver placed miles away from the actual radar site, a vital function which prevents homing attacks on the radar transmitter. Following Oswald's arrival in Russia, his friend and co-worker Nelson Delgado described the appearance of a group of unidentified individuals in plain clothes who questioned all radar personnel as to exactly what types of information Oswald had access to, making transcribed records of their statements.[52]

The investigators did not identify themselves, as would have been routine for the Office of Naval Criminal Investigations (NCIS), suggesting that most likely that the group was from ONI, the Office of Navy Intelligence—essentially performing a potential damage assessment should Oswald compromise elements of the West Coast air defense network. That view seems confirmed by the fact that, according to Oswald's unit chief, extended time was indeed spent changing communications frequencies, call signs and identification codes. No document related to such a security investigation appears in Oswald's ONI file; however, given its strategic nature it would have most certainly have been classified, and perhaps never actually associated with Oswald's own personnel records.

U-2 Realities

Oswald's Marine radar experience has led to extensive discussion and speculation regarding a potential covert element associated with his "defection" to the Soviet Union. The fundamental premise of that speculation is that Oswald had certain special knowledge of the American U-2 high-altitude reconnaissance aircraft, gained though his radar assignment at Atsugi. The speculation assumes that Oswald would have had critical information unknown to the Soviets, knowledge about the U-2's operational altitude or mission profiles which could have allowed the Soviets to bring it down. Some have even proposed that senior CIA officers opposed to any Eisenhower administration compromises dispatched Oswald on a mission to provide that information to the Soviets—resulting in the downing of a U-2 aircraft and the covert sabotage of a possible Eisenhower/Khrushchev detente dialogue at an upcoming summit meeting.

There is little doubt that Marines at Atsugi, Oswald included, were aware of the unconventional and distinctive U-2 aircraft, watching it take off and land at the base. Marines in the radar unit were also aware of its ability to reach exceptional altitudes, well above the range of their height finder radar. Radar personnel saw the planes on the ground, tracked them departing and returning to base, and communicated with them at times to verify their identity. Gossip at the base was that they were performing reconnaissance over Soviet territory.[53]

Given the maximum range of the newest M-16 radar (estimated at 230 miles under ideal atmospheric conditions) the radar operators might well have noted the U-2 heading in the direction of Soviet territory as it gained altitude—but even the closest such territory (the Russian-controlled Sakhalin islands) was hundreds of miles beyond the operating range of that radar unit. Chinese territory is even further from the Philippines, where Oswald's unit was stationed for a time—and there is no record of ongoing U-2 operations out of either Clark AFB in the Philippines or from Taiwan during the 1950s.[54] In short, there is simply no way that Marine radar operators at Atsugi could have directly observed the U-2 moving at its operational altitudes "over China" or truth to the premise that Lee Harvey Oswald spent hours "tracking U-2 missions over the People's Republic of China."[55]

More importantly, as far as Oswald having carried critical information and previously unknown information on the U-2's altitude and operations to the Soviets, we now know (as the American intelligence community knew well before Oswald's travel to Russia) that the Soviets had known the details of both from the very first U-2 reconnaissance flights in 1956. Those flights were made from Wiesbaden, Germany—first over eastern Europe and then over Russia itself, as far as Moscow and Leningrad.

During the initial flight the U-2 crew observed some 20 "snap up" attacks by MIG interceptors trying to get high enough to make their air-to-air missiles reach the U-2. The U-2 flights were being fully tracked by Soviet radar and several SA-1 missiles were launched against the flights, failing to bring them down because that generation of anti-aircraft missiles could not reach the U-2's altitude.[56] Yet given the radar tracking and the failed attacks, the Soviets knew what would indeed be needed to bring down the U-2 and immediately began working on a new generation of missiles to do just that.[57]

The CIA had been shocked by the experience with those first missions. In test flights, American radars had been unable to consistently track the U-2's, yet the Soviets not only were consistently tracking the new planes, but were able to effectively vector fighter aircraft to attempt to intercept them and to engage them (both unsuccessfully) with missiles. Study of the U-2 photography showed dozens of Soviet interceptors desperately trying to get high enough to engage the U-2's. The CIA also had direct information on that from intercepts of Soviet ground radio communications with the interceptors. Signals intelligence was carried out as part of the U-2 missions.[58] NSA radio intercept operators also monitored the Soviet air defense network transmissions related to the tracking and attempts to attack the U-2 in real time.[59]

As early as 1956, the Soviets knew the altitude and mission profiles of the U-2 aircraft—and the United States knew that they knew. The CIA made several attempts at fixes to make the aircraft less detectable but none of them proved successful; the Soviet radars continued to be able to detect and consistently track the aircraft being flown out of Japan (Atsugi), Turkey (Incirlik), Pakistan, and Alaska. Worse yet, a new generation of SA-2 anti-aircraft missiles began to go into deployment in 1957.[60] Only sporadic U-2 flights were made during 1958 and 1959, months apart. By 1960 the risk to the U-2 missions had become critical; pilots observed Soviet interceptors continually tracking and attempting engagements. On several occasions, the new SA-2 missiles came dangerously close to the American aircraft.

The CIA leadership, as well as President Eisenhower, knew the degree of risk in the U-2 missions; Eisenhower ordered the overflights suspended, then gave into a request for two final flights, one of which was to go all the way across the Soviet Union. That flight launched from Turkey, and after an hour and over solid cloud cover the pilot entered clear sky, only to immediately see a Soviet fighter below, tracking him. Ultimately a series of SA-2 batteries began launches with at least 14 missiles fired—the concussions from one damaging the aircraft enough to bring it down.[61] Nothing Lee Oswald knew or could have provided had to do with the loss of the U-2 aircraft; it had been simply a matter of risk and the new Soviet aircraft and missile developments, which were already in progress since their monitoring of the very first U-2 flights in 1956.

New Experiences

Oswald's time in the military had started on a positive note. He had done well in infantry and technical training, had been placed in a technical career field and had no performance problems with his radar assignment and duties, and he received a promotion to Private First Class. His officers and fellow marines appeared to have felt Oswald to be competent in his job—but lacking in discipline and in attention to details such as his barracks duties. One of his barracks mates recalled that after a number of bad inspections, the other members of Oswald's Quonset hut complained about him and secured his transfer to another hut.

In general, he was regarded as intelligent, appearing to be better educated than most of the men on base.[62] Fellow Marines noted that he stood out in his knowledge of world affairs, knowing more than many of their officers. But Oswald's tendency to be arrogant in his knowledge could also be annoying, especially so when he displayed it during conversations involving senior NCOs or officers.[63]

In general, Oswald showed little interest in socializing with his fellow Marines; it seems he was simply avoided by most—unless his lack of attention to barracks or kitchen detail got him noticed. But while

Oswald was not becoming more social with his fellow Marines, he was moving into new contacts and experiences outside the service, both socially and politically. One PFC in the barracks later claimed that not long after his arrival, some of the older Marines had taken Oswald to a brothel, stayed to listen in on his session, and rushed back to the base to greet him and share intimate details with all and sundry. From that point on, Oswald would revert to a practice of visiting bars and clubs on his own and finding his own company off base.[64]

Up to his time in Japan, Oswald's social life had been limited and his personal sexual experience seemingly nonexistent. His tour in Japan offered him opportunities he had never had before, and Oswald appears to have taken advantage of them. There are numerous reports from Marines in his unit that Oswald did indeed date and otherwise fraternize with Japanese women. He also began drinking—another new experience for him. Oswald reportedly returned to base quite drunk on occasion, and ultimately drinking appears to have been a factor in serious disciplinary action against him, related to an incident in a bar with a sergeant in his direct chain of command.

Oswald himself stated that he had ongoing conversations with Japanese locals whom he met, and that they had significantly developed his own political views, including his interest in Russia. It is a matter of record that while stationed in Japan, Oswald did begin to exhibit an interest in learning the Russian language, something he would pursue at length upon his return stateside. A fellow Marine gave a statement to the Warren Commission that Oswald was able to speak "a little Russian" while he was overseas, and he also observed that Oswald had become more assertive in Japan—very possibly because he likely had a Japanese girlfriend.

Initially Oswald appears to have been enjoying his time in Japan, performing his radar duties effectively—if not his routine military chores in barracks. He was socializing with locals on his own, very likely had one or more girlfriends, and even indicated his intention to extend his tour of duty in the Far East. Yet on base Oswald continued to be annoying and argumentative at times, especially with officers—and willing to bend or break rules he did not like, including having a personal weapon in his locker. While handling gear in that locker, he dropped a loaded derringer .22 caliber pistol and shot himself in the arm—resulting in his being hospitalized. He was charged with the possession of an unregistered, privately owned weapon, in violation of general orders.

Oswald's unit was deployed to the Philippines following the pistol incident, and he reportedly ended up on permanent Kitchen Police duty until his unit returned to Japan. At that time his general orders violation (personal weapons possession) resulted in a formal court martial, a sentence of confinement with hard labor for 20 days, a fine, and a reduction in rank from PFC to Private. That demotion was effectively a double reduction in rank for Oswald, who otherwise had passed a test for promotion to Corporal while his unit had deployed to the Philippines. In the fall of 1958, Oswald's unit was deployed for a short time to Taiwan, during the Taiwan Straits crisis. It was a temporary assignment of only three to four weeks and there are conflicting accounts of whether Oswald was sent with his unit, at least for part of the deployment. What is not open to question is that in his next semi-annual evaluation, he was given lowered ratings for both conduct and job proficiency.

Not at all happy with the disciplinary actions against him, and frustrated with his loss of the pending promotion to Corporal, Oswald continued visiting clubs off base, and apparently continued his drinking. Within two months he ended up in a confrontation with a Technical Sergeant in his unit, a confrontation in which Oswald, admittedly drinking, had spilled a drink on the sergeant, and been pushed away (likely with remarks). At that point Oswald had called the NCO a name, made his own remarks, and invited him outside, suggesting a fight. The sergeant filed a complaint, leading to a second court martial for Oswald—resulting in more confinement, and the cancellation of his request (which had been granted) for extended overseas duty.

In addition to spending time in confinement (the Brig) Oswald had earlier gone through a series of medical problems, with an initial diagnosis of a urethral discharge as being gonorrhea (venereal disease). After some six visits to sick call and a treatment of antibiotics, which had no effect, the flight surgeon changed Oswald's diagnosis, and a new medication cleared the problem. Years later, researcher Jack Swike (himself stationed at Atsugi shortly after Oswald's time there) contacted the flight surgeon and reviewed Oswald's medical records. The surgeon told him that the unit had experienced problems with a non-specific urethritis associated with the water supply at the base; the problem did not respond to standard antibiotics. Several Marines had suffered from the same symptoms and been cured with alternative treatments—resulting in their records all being annotated that the medical problem had occurred "in the line of duty."[65]

Swike had served as an intelligence officer at the Atsugi base, assigned to MAG-11. He noted that the squadron intelligence section did conduct surveillance in bars and clubs frequented by servicemen. Lists of potential radicals or communists (students or hired "talent") were developed and maintained. If Oswald had been observed talking with individuals known or suspected to be connected to Soviet intelligence—or even student members of the communist party who were known to be active in the areas which Oswald visited off base—it would have drawn attention.

While low-key warnings about certain clubs might be given off the record, ongoing contacts with the wrong people would produce official security reports. Such incidents would have produced reports to the OSI (Office of Special Investigations) being entered in Oswald's records—especially given his job with radar systems. Nothing of that nature has been found in released documents, although there remain numerous open questions as to Marine and Navy internal inquiries following Oswald's later appearance in Moscow.

Given Oswald's job with radar it was also routine for such personnel to either hold a Secret Clearance, if fully cleared, or to be given an Interim Clearance which would not become part of their permanent record once screening was complete. One area of much discussion has been the apparent lack of such a clearance in Oswald's personnel file; Oswald's records show no official secret clearance while in Japan. However, given his own personal experience with intelligence, including at Atsugi, Jack Swike noted that with the disciplinary actions against him, a full clearance might not have been granted Oswald—and any Interim Clearance (a routine practice to keep him on duty) would have been cancelled upon his transfer into a new assignment stateside.[66]

Due to his time in confinement and with his medical problems, Oswald was not involved in a deployment of his unit to Taiwan,[67] and given that the disciplinary actions had resulted in his tour not being extended, his next assignment was back stateside. Upon his return to the United States, Oswald was assigned to Marine Air Control Squadron No. 9 (MACS-9) at the Marine Corps Air Station at El Toro, California, where he had been briefly stationed prior to going overseas.

Oswald left Japan in November 1958 and arrived stateside in December; upon arrival he took leave and traveled to Texas to visit his mother and his brother Robert. By December 21 he was at his new duty station at Santa Ana. There remains some controversy, based on comments from personnel serving with him, as to whether Oswald's radar assignment may have been initially restricted due to his previous disciplinary problems. For some part of his earliest time back in California, Oswald may have been assigned to clerical or janitorial tasks on the base. Some of his fellow Marines later reported that there had been rumors that Oswald had lost his clearance to work on radar crews while in Japan. One Marine recalled having heard that Oswald had once had clearance above the "confidential" level but that he had lost it because he "had poured beer over a staff NCO's head in an enlisted club in Japan"—resulting in his doing time in the brig.[68]

As in Japan, there is no record of Oswald being giving a full Secret security clearance at Santa Ana, although at some point he appears to have been given yet another Interim Clearance which did allow him to go back into radar duty. His own request for an early discharge would have terminated his radar assignment, and an Interim Clearance would have been pulled from his personnel record at the time of his later discharge.

Russian Interests

According to Oswald himself, his time in Japan and his local contacts had broadened his worldview and sparked his interest in Russia and the Soviet system. He appears not to have been especially vocal about that interest while in Japan, certainly not on the level he would be while stationed in California, but there are indications that he had already begun his study of the Russian language while overseas.

A fellow Marine, Daniel Powers, described Oswald as not just reading a great deal, but seeming to be studying from a particular book, which he felt was on the Russian language. Oswald did carry around a blue/black book—the one which Powers felt was a Russian language book—and Power's description does fit that of a book which Oswald still had in his possession at the time of his death, *A Short Russian Reference Grammar.*[69]

It seems that back in the United States, Oswald's study of Russian and his subscription to a variety of publications in Russian became increasingly obvious.[70] Statements on that from his fellow Marines are similar to that of James Anthony Botelho (Warren Commission Hearings, Volume 8, 315): "It was common knowledge that Oswald had taught himself to speak Russian."

- David Christie Murray (8WH319): "When I knew him, he was studying Russian."
- Henry J. Roussel, Jr. (8WH320): "I knew of Oswald's study of the Russian language…"
- Mack Osborne (8WH321-2): "Oswald was at that time studying

Russian. He spent a great deal of his free time reading papers printed in Russian . . . with the aid of a Russian-English dictionary. . . . Because of the fact that he was studying Russian, fellow Marines sometimes jokingly accused him of being a Russian spy."

- Richard Dennis Call (8WH322): "During this time, Oswald was studying Russian. For this reason many members of the unit kidded him about being a Russian spy."

Given his studies, it appears that Oswald felt himself competent enough to take the Defense Language Proficiency Test in Russian at the end of February 1959. He may have been motivated by the fact that scoring at certain levels of proficiency would add to his monthly base pay (or possibly he just wished to test himself). The language test was intended to determine how well a person could function in real-life situations. Oswald got two more questions right than wrong, however his overall rating on the test was "Poor." His best performance was in reading and writing Russian, but that was undercut by his performance in "listening" to spoken Russian. Oswald scored -5 for "understanding" (listening), +4 for "reading" and +3 for "writing." Those scores suggest that he had been teaching himself Russian from a book up to that point in time.

It seems clear from the various recollections of those who knew him in California that by the time Oswald returned to the United States, he was looking beyond the military and the Marines. He had found a good deal of the adventure he originally sought in Japan, and his experiences with women had indeed made him surer of himself and more assertive. But Oswald's propensity to become bored with anything after some four to six months was once again overriding his settling into any situation for the long term.

Marines who were around Oswald in California provided anecdotes about Oswald's being open and eager to express his liking for all things Russian, sometimes in good humor and sometimes seriously. Some of his fellows called him "Oswaldskovich," apparently to his pleasure. He was said to have had his name written in Russian on one of his jackets and to have played records of Russian songs "so loud that one could hear them outside the barracks." He frequently made remarks in Russian or used expressions like "da" or "nyet," addressing others as "Comrade." In one instance he was reported to have come over and said jokingly, "You called?" when one of the Marines played a particular record of Russian music.[71]

Along with an obvious interest in and liking for things Russian, anyone who was curious found Oswald more than willing to express his interest in Russian political views, and to at least some extent in Marxism and Communist ideology. That led to some serious discussions including one with Lieutenant John Donovan, a graduate of the School of Foreign Service at Georgetown University. Donovan evaluated Oswald as having a higher intelligence level than the average enlisted man—even though he could be a troublemaker with officers. He also observed that Oswald's voracious reading, including works like *Das Kapital* and *Animal Farm*, set Oswald apart from most of his fellow Marines.

Donovan also felt that Oswald was reading some material, including a Russian newspaper, because it "presented a very different and perhaps equally just side of the international affairs in comparison with the United States newspapers." But aside from his interest in Russia, Oswald never claimed that he had even thought about becoming a communist himself—nor would Oswald show any enthusiasm for the Communist Party when living in the Soviet Union.

Donovan viewed Oswald as being "truly interested in international affairs," and "very well versed" with the general facts of the foreign situation. He later noted, as did one of Oswald's few close enlisted friends, that beyond Russia, Oswald had a particular interest in Latin America and knew a good deal about Cuba in particular. Oswald openly expressed his support and sympathy for the Cuban revolution against Batista and for Fidel Castro.[72]

A fellow enlisted Marine, Nelson Delgado, had met Oswald soon after his arrival at El Toro; they were the same age, and Oswald became interested in learning Spanish and attempting to speak it with Delgado (a fluent Spanish speaker). It was clear to Delgado that Oswald felt there were serious issues with the way of life in America, but Delgado never felt perceived Oswald as a communist.

Both Delgado and Oswald supported the Cuban revolution, and talked about Cuba and Latin America rather than Russia. The two of them even fantasized about joining the Cuban Army or the new government in Cuba—even the possibility of leading expeditions against dictatorial regimes in the Caribbean and Central America which would "free them too." At one point Oswald told Delgado that he was in touch with Cuban diplomatic officials, and had expressed his interests to them. At first Delgado thought that was a just a tale, but after seeing materials mailed to Oswald from the Cuban Consulate, he accepted it as a fact.

Chapter 4

Breaking Away

"Just remember above all else that my values are very different from Robert's or your's. It is difficult to tell you how I feel, Just remember, this is what I must do."

—Lee Oswald writing to his mother on September 19, 1959, just prior to departing for Europe and the Soviet Union. Warren Commission Exhibit 200.

Looking Beyond the Marines

While stationed at Santa Ana, California, near the large El Toro Marine Air base, Oswald did have a few acquaintances including Delgado (who invited him to join him on a trip to Tijuana), and a few others who joined him in chess games. But generally, his social life with barracks mates was not much changed from the days of his technical training or his overseas duty in Japan. He did not leave the post as often as most, preferring reading or study. He rode on the train with Delgado to Los Angeles, but they separated there and went their own ways. It appears that by the time of his arrival in California, his club hopping and drinking had become a thing of the past, with a turn to reading and his own studies.

Oswald did play squadron football for a time, but his coach described him as having little team spirit and even trying to call plays—he had eventually either just quit or been thrown off the team for not following the coach's orders. Beyond that he also seems to have reset his work attitude, as he had beginning during his last days in Japan. His January and July performance ratings at El Toro show him with a 4.0 in conduct and a 4.2 in job proficiency; a maximum score would have been 5.0. He was described as skilled and proficient in his radar duties and promoted to Private First Class for a second time in March.[73]

Yet in a concrete sign that he was already thinking about the future, and looking for opportunities beyond the Marine Corps, in March Oswald applied for admission to studies at Albert Schweitzer College, a very small and relatively unknown liberal college in Switzerland. Albert Schweitzer had been created and operated as a non-denominational center of the International Institute of Religious Freedom. It had initially offered only summer conferences, but in 1955 expanded to year-round operations. The college received financial support from the Unitarian Church, and Unitarian Church members were involved with promoting it within the United States.

Albert Schweitzer College described itself as a liberal arts school and that is reflected in its curricula and course descriptions. The college literature also describes it as having changed its original name to reflect an admiration and dedication to Schweitzer's moral and philosophical beliefs—beliefs given much media attention through his widely reported relief work in the Congo and by his very active opposition to atomic weapons.

Oswald's connection to the college has been a subject of extensive inquiry and research; even recovering a paper trail for his contact with the college proved challenging to the FBI in its initial investigation. His decision and purpose for enrollment at Albert Schweitzer has remained a matter of contention and suspicion within the skeptical community. Researcher and author George Michael Evica conducted extensive work on the subject, beginning with Oswald's registration for study at the college, accompanied by a $25 payment.[74] Evica determined that although Oswald had registered in March 1959, his actual attendance was only due to begin in spring 1960. That timing would have been in line with the end of his regular enlistment in the Marine Corps, with his term of service set to end in December 1959.

Evica's research also determined that while the college was aware of Oswald, and expected him for the spring session, it had received no further communication from him following his initial application. Despite Evica and others' work, the question of exactly when and where Oswald learned of the college remains a mystery. What can be said is that Albert Schweitzer himself was discussed and reported on in the types of periodicals and media that Oswald followed in his reading—Schweitzer's opposition to imperialism was very much in line with Oswald's views. Schweitzer, with his public stands against the traditions of European colonialism in Africa, was not well-received by the Eisenhower administration. That, along with his fervent opposition to atomic weapons (expressed in his "Declaration of Conscience" in April 1957), led him to be considered by the Eisenhower Administration, and U.S. State Department, as having come under the influence of Soviet Communism.

The source of Oswald's knowledge about the college, including his possession of an application form, has been extensively researched—unfortunately with no firm conclusions. If it is still possible, a comprehensive search of the magazines and newspapers he was reading at the time might reveal articles on or references to the college, suggesting how it might have come to Oswald's attention. Unfortunately, that was one area Evica did not pursue in his own extensive research. The only individual whose name can be directly linked to Oswald's application was a Marine officer in California who endorsed Oswald's application. When questioned years later, he had no specific recollection of signing it, and only commented that his duty would have included routinely endorsing applications for continuing education by any Marine personnel.[75]

Oswald's Albert Schweitzer college application outlined his intended course of study, including ethics, literature, and science—all very consistent with his documented personal interests. He stated that he had finished high school through correspondence (correct given his GED completion while in the Marines), that he was interested in philosophy, psychology, and ideology, and that he had studied the Russian language and had a proficiency equivalent to 1 year of schooling. He also stated that he wanted to write short stories on "contemporary American life" (he would later pursue that goal in 1962/63 with a series of stories and monographs, as well as taking a course in typing). His reasons for attending the college were described as a primary desire to study philosophy, to meet with Europeans, and to broaden his scope of understanding.

Oswald's college goals were no special secret; he shared his plans with his friend Delgado (telling him he would be attending a Swiss school to study psychology), and Delgado knew of his application to Albert Schweitzer. At least one other Marine (Richard Call) also described hearing Oswald speak of his college plans. However, there is no indication Oswald shared any specific plans with his family after his return from Japan.

His sister-in-law related that Oswald had generally talked of wanting to travel, go to college, or write a book.[76] He appears not to have talked about his future with his mother or have been routinely in touch with her after his visit to Fort Worth during transit leave on his way back from Japan in early December. He only seems to have learned about her work injury during a second leave visit in July, 1959. Shortly after that visit, in August, Oswald filed paperwork for a voluntary allotment of part of his Marine pay to his mother and listed her for a dependency allowance—payments of which were made in August and September.

In September, 1959, Oswald filed for a hardship/dependency discharge based on his mother's need for support; his filing was accompanied by affidavits from his mother, a doctor, a lawyer and two of his mother's friends. It was also supported by the finding of the Fort

Worth Accident Review Board which had awarded his mother $934 in compensation for her work-related injury. While his mother had received compensation for the injury, there are also indications that it was relatively minor, and that by the time Oswald visited her in person it was clear that she was going to be able to return to work, and that long-term support was not going to be necessary. Objectively, it seems fair to say that Oswald, tired of the Marine Corps and eager to move on to new adventures, had likely used his mother's injury as an opportunity for obtaining an early out from the service.

The Marine review board approved Oswald's application (he was only four months short of his regular enlistment at that point in time), and on September 4 he was transferred from his radar assignment in MACS-9 to a headquarters unit for administrative purposes and discharge. On that same day Oswald applied for a passport in Santa Ana, California—stating that he planned to attend the Albert Schweitzer College in Switzerland, as well as to travel to Cuba, England, France, Germany and Russia. His passport was issued six days later.

Oswald's passport application stated the purpose of his anticipated travel as attendance at Albert Schweitzer College; that was important to the granting of his passport. As researcher Greg Parker determined, it would have been illegal for Oswald to immediately travel overseas given that he was required to remain in the Marine Corps Reserve for the three months remaining on his original enlistment. Travel for educational purposes was viewed as a legitimate exemption and ensured approval of his application and his ability to travel with the issuance of the passport.[77]

However, during his mandatory three-month reserve period, Oswald was eligible to be called up in any activation of his reserve unit or general mobilization. Oswald was officially placed in a Marine reserve upon discharge, and his failure to request/obtain permission for his trip overseas was officially a factor in the eventual downgrade of his discharge.

There is no indication that Oswald communicated with or changed his status with the Albert Schweitzer College following his initial registration—the college continued to expect him for class late the following spring (April—July sessions). And there is some suggestion that, at least for a time, Oswald had been serious about going to Switzerland for college studies. As with his interest in Spanish, there is at least one report from a fellow Marine that Oswald had spent some time in the study of German, and a set of German language flash cards are listed among his belongings in the Federal Register. Even following his appearance in Russia, there is a suggestion of an ongoing interest in learning German—the German alphabet was written in his notebook, which also contained the address of a German language teacher in Moscow.[78]

Removing the Ties

Oswald's college application had been accepted for the April-July 1960 session at Albert Schweitzer, a timeframe which would have fit well with what would have been his normal discharge date from the Marines in early 1960. Instead, he appears to have responded to his mother's earlier work injury and disability claim (or perhaps simply taken advantage of it for his own purposes) by requesting and being given an early discharge from the Marines. Following his separation from the service he had gone directly to his mother's home in Fort Worth, arriving on September 14, 1959, but clearly with no plans to stay with her or even in Fort Worth. He told his mother that his immediate plans were to go to New Orleans, and get a job on a ship or in the "export-import business." He had worked for a couple of those types of businesses, including with a freight forwarding company, after dropping out of school for a time before his mother's move from New Orleans to Fort Worth.

Oswald gave his mother the impression that going to New Orleans was his best chance for earning the money which would allow him to continue supporting her the way he had started with his Marine pay distributions. He also gave his mother $100 at the time he left Fort

Worth. While he was in Fort Worth, he registered his dependency discharge and entry into the Marine Reserve with the Fort Worth Selective Service Board. He also took the time to visit his brother Robert and his family.[79]

After that, Oswald proceeded to New Orleans, not to find work but rather to take a ship bound for Europe and for Russia, rather than Switzerland. Dealing with Oswald's motives in traveling to Russia, as well as his overall experience inside the Soviet Union, is challenging—bringing us back to the dueling views of Oswald's motives. The Warren Commission Report simply presents it all as an illustration of Oswald's anti-America, pro-communist beliefs, an effort to realize his ideological ambitions, to totally reject the United States and join in the communist experience.

In a counter view, those who visualize Oswald taking his marching orders from one or more elements of the American intelligence community see Russia as one of his missions—with his entry into the Soviet Union being covertly assisted, and any support for such mission officially concealed after the fact. The most comprehensive arguments for that proposition are covered by John Newman in his work *Oswald and the CIA*. In that work, Newman develops the idea of an intelligence mission related to the U-2 aircraft, and the sabotage of an Eisenhower dialogue with Khrushchev at a scheduled summit meeting. The issues arguing against Oswald having knowledge which would have been mandatory to any such effort have been previously discussed. In his most recent work, *Uncovering Popov's Mole*, Newman focuses on Oswald and Russia in the context of a specific counter intelligence effort by James Angleton.

Irrespective of issues of a specific CIA mission in Russia, Newman's studies offer extensive and invaluable documentation and quotations related to Oswald's interaction with the American State Department in Moscow, remarks and statements made by Oswald to reporters, and a review of communications between Oswald and his family members while in the Soviet Union.[80] As illustrated in the following examples, a composite of Oswald's exchanges with American diplomats, his early remarks to reporters and his notes, and communications with his family members give the definite impression that he was acting strictly in line with his own ideological views, and with a determination to pursue his own personal interests in Russia. These interests had jelled during his time in Japan, and become visible to the Marines around him during his time in California.

We have seen that Oswald never hesitated to pursue his own interests, and pursue goals which he held largely to himself. Not antisocial, but asocial behavior—with Oswald consistently inner-directed, with personal values which stayed largely the same from his teen years on. Consistent, but redirected based on what had seized his attention at any particular point in time. That type of personal independence is expressed in a final note sent to his mother prior to departing for Europe:

> "Dear Mother:
>
> Well, I have booked passage on a ship to Europe, I would of had to sooner or later and I think it's best I go now. Just remember above all else that my values are very different from Robert's or yours. It is difficult to tell you how I feel, just remember this is what I must do. I did not tell you about my plans because you could hardly be expected to understand."

Poor spelling and grammar aside, that brief note illustrates Oswald's independence, his contrarian beliefs, and his willingness to act on his own agenda and personal decisions.[81]

Later, after obtaining an entry visa to Russia and while in a Moscow hotel, Oswald delivered a similar message in a note to his brother Robert:

> "I have chosen to remove all ties to my past, and so I will not write again, nor do I wish you to try and contact me. I'm sure you

> understand that I would not like to receive correspondence from people in the country which I fled. I am starting a new life and I do not wish to have anything to do with the old life. I hope you and your family will always be in good health...Lee" [82]

By September 17, 1959, Oswald was in New Orleans, booking his travel to Europe on a freighter with a local travel bureau, Travel Consultants. The freighter, the SS Marion Lykes, was sailing the next day. Oswald gave his occupation as "shipping export agent" and noted that he would be abroad for two months on a pleasure trip. He paid $220 for his fare, but was stuck in a hotel in New Orleans for two more nights as the ship's sailing was delayed to September 20.

While much is on the record (via State Department communications and media remarks) as to Oswald's arrival in Russia, what is not on the record are his exchanges with Russian diplomatic personnel in Helsinki, Finland, nor his personal exchanges with their respective counterparts in Moscow. In Helsinki, he was issued a limited entry tourist visa for the Soviet Union, with his occupation listed as "student." We have only Oswald's remarks about those dialogues, and later official statements from Russia. In addition, we cannot know for certain why Oswald picked Helsinki as a point of entry.

The "intelligence agent" view of Oswald views him being assisted in his travels to Russia, with guidance that the Soviet staff in Helsinki were known by both the State Department and the CIA to be more receptive by granting entry permissions. The source given for that view is a State Department Moscow counsel officer, John McVickar. Despite McVickar's remarks, the Warren Commission was unable to confirm any exceptionally quick processing times at the Soviet Helsinki office.[83]

A counter view would be that Oswald himself would have been concerned that traveling through Berlin and crossing the border via East Germany would have involved going through both American and East German military checkpoints—which might have resulted in questions and very possibly an effort to challenge him, by either country.[84] Travel to Germany and Berlin, through East Germany and on to Russia would have involved more border crossings, more check points, and potentially American surveillance on Russian installations as well as embassies or consulates.

It is true that Oswald's tourist visa for Russia was granted relatively quickly in Helsinki, but as noted previously, that was not particularly exceptional for that location.[85] Oswald was simply issued a standard tourist visa. We do know that Oswald appears to have received no special treatment following his appearance at the Soviet Embassy in Finland, and his train travel and arrival in Moscow were strictly in line with routine tourist practices of the time. The train trip lasted some thirteen hours, and was perhaps the quickest—and definitely the cheapest—way to travel into Russia. Given Oswald's limited funds and frugal nature, that also may have played into his selection of Helsinki as a point of entry.

The Cold Shoulder

Upon arrival in Russia on October 15, Oswald was met by his assigned tourist guide, Rima Shirakova. She would serve as his constant companion during the period of his time as a "tourist" (his tourist visa was good for October 15–21). Shirakova drove Oswald to his hotel, and following a standard routine, asked if he would like to begin with a sightseeing tour. He surprised her by responding that his actual reason for coming to Russia was to obtain Russian citizenship.[86]

Upon contacting her office, she was advised to allow the American to proceed with his intentions, and assisted Oswald in preparing a letter to the Supreme Soviet, asking to become a Soviet citizen. The application cited political motivations and referred to a "decadent capitalist society where workers are slaves." The letter also noted that due to the limits of his tourist visa, Oswald was appealing for quick action on his request.

In response, Oswald got only a meeting with an agent of the Russian Passport and Registration Office on October 18, a meeting in which a very unresponsive official told Oswald that he was being foolish and should just return home, and that his stay would end as scheduled on October 21. Afterward, Oswald described himself as "devastated," virtually in shock. His next official step was to be a final meeting with the Passport Office on October 21, with his train passage out of Russia already booked.

When Shirakova knocked on his door at the scheduled time on the 21st, she got no response and ultimately Oswald was found in the bathtub, with blood in the water and superficial cuts on his left wrist. Instead of a train trip out he was to spend time in a hospital, and be given a routine psychiatric interview.[87] The wrist cutting appears to have been a dramatic gesture on Oswald's part in response to the total lack of interest in him on the part of the Soviets.

It can be judged as a non-serious attempt at actual suicide, since he cut his wrist lightly only moments before the scheduled time for Shirakova's arrival. Oswald's action quickly turned him into a public relations problem for Russian officialdom—an American so enthralled with the Soviet system he wanted to abandon the United States to join it, only to be rejected and so distraught he had to be hospitalized. It was not a good "look" for the Soviet leadership and Russian public relations.

For context, it must be noted that Oswald's Soviet reception was totally unlike some of the higher profile American "defectors" of that era. While Oswald did, some weeks after his arrival in Moscow in November 1959, make strong and derogatory remarks about the American system, his comments were mild compared to other Americans—who were heavily leveraged by the Soviet media, such as William Martin and Bernon Mitchell, who arrived in Moscow the following year, in 1960.[88]

Martin and Mitchell had become friends during their Navy service in Japan, both working at a communications intercept facility. They kept in touch as each returned to school after their Navy service, and once again encountered each other after going to work for the NSA. In December, 1959, both had visited Cuba and in June, 1960 both traveled through Mexico, on to Havana Cuba, and then by freighter ending up in the Soviet Union. In September 1960 Russia hosted a major news conference for them at the House of Journalists in Moscow—both announced that they had requested asylum and Soviet citizenship. They described the United States as being unscrupulous, of spying on other countries, and endangering world peace.[89]

In contrast, neither the Soviet system or its media outlets paid any similar attention to Oswald. Nor did Oswald solicit any such visibility from the press. It was not until after his first exchanges with Russian officialdom and their rejection of him that he even visited the American Embassy in Moscow. Embassy staff pushed back on his intentions during that visit, with an embassy staff member directing American press towards him—exposing his intentions and with the stated intent of discouraging him from his effort to defect.

The Moscow UPI chief was alerted to Oswald's presence by American Embassy staff and approached Oswald at his hotel. Oswald simply sent him away, saying he had no need to talk to the press. In response, the Bureau Chief (Robert Korengold) put the Oswald story on the news wire. Oswald later wrote that the UPI story did put pressure on him to talk. It also elicited a response from his family in Fort Worth, who had no prior idea of his presence in Moscow.

Oswald did bend to the pressure, and in his interview with reporter Aline Mosby he made a number of negative comments about America in regard to racism and social issues. That interview and his remarks were the genesis of the Oswald defection media coverage in the United States—rather than any media exercise by the Soviet press.[90]

From that point on we are fortunate to have extended perspectives and context for what was going on around Oswald inside Russia. Newman's book *Oswald and the CIA* offers the American perspective based on State Department, CIA, and related correspondence, the observations based in views and opinions of American Embassy staff in Moscow. In contrast, Ernst Titovets (who became Oswald's friend and companion in Minsk) presents the Russian view, based in his own interviews and with information from Oswald's Soviet case file (which includes the KGB assessment of Oswald).[91]

Both are essential reading. In particular, Titovets reviews some of the internal Russian debates related to whether or not Oswald should be allowed to stay in the Soviet Union—including the KGB position that he had no military information of special value (they considered that anything he would offer would be "outdated"), nor could he be turned into an intelligence asset.[92] Perhaps not surprisingly, over time speculation did emerge from a number of Warren Commission skeptics that Oswald had become a KGB asset, even that he had acted for the Soviets in the assassination of President Kennedy.[93] Such unsubstantiated claims continued to appear even decades after the attack in Dallas.

Following Oswald's release from medical care on October 28, he found himself once again back in his hotel room, with no official response on his status and the possibility he could be put on a train at any time. The good news was that on that same day he was again ordered to report to the passport office, and Oswald met with four officials there and was advised that decisions were still to be made, but for the present he was allowed to stay in Russia.

Encouraged but still in limbo, three days later on the last day of October, Oswald presented himself at the American Embassy, with the stated goal of renouncing his American citizenship. It is hard not to see that move as anything other than another gesture to convince the Russians of his sincerity and move them to a positive decision on his request for Russian citizenship. The visit and his interactions with the American Embassy staff certainly showcased Oswald's tendency to be assertive—and annoying—when confronted with procedural or bureaucratic obstacles. In the end he was advised that the office was closed and paperwork would need to be prepared, in the form of an affidavit, which he would need to sign. Oswald was advised he could return during normal office hours to complete the formal process—something which he did not do, thereby not legally renouncing his American citizenship, something he never did during his time in Russia.

His appearance and behavior at the American Embassy produced a highly adverse reaction with the diplomatic staff, an attitude magnified by his voluntary remarks to them given that he been a radar operator in the Marines and that "he was going to turn this information over to the Soviet authorities." That was a shocking statement, even though he did not state that such information was classified—if he had, he might well have been detained by security on the spot.[94] Given the strong embassy staff reaction, and the follow-on Navy attaché's cable to the Navy Department that Oswald "had offered to provide radar information" to the Soviets, it's possible that if Oswald had returned to complete his application he might have been held for questioning, given that he would legally be on U.S. soil at the embassy.

Instead, Oswald returned to his hotel and remained simply at loose ends after his abortive approach to the American diplomatic personnel. His next decision (as noted previously), perhaps forced by UPI coverage for the American press and/or possibly to gain more attention from the Soviet system, was to agree to finally talk to at least some American reporters. It may well be that the first personal interview, during some two hours with Aline Mosby, is our best touchstone as to Oswald's fundamental world view at the time of his arrival in Russia.

Miss Mosby reported that Oswald appeared very satisfied with himself, full of confidence, and extremely talkative. He hoped to continue his education in Russia, but certainly he was willing to work. Oswald admitted that his Russian language skills were limited, but was sure that he could quickly improve them. He stated that he disliked life in the United States because of its racism and the contrast between the haves and have nots, illustrated by "the luxuries of Park Avenue and workers' lives on the East Side" of New York, citing his mother's struggles and poverty as an example. He rejected the "exploitation" of capitalism and declared himself a supporter of Marxist ideology.

Oswald also stated he had begun to follow that ideology at the age of 15 in New York City but rejected the idea that he had been influenced by Communists or had been a member of the Communist Party. He also said that he had witnessed American imperialism during his time in the Marines, but that while in the Marines he had saved $1,500 to finance this goal of traveling to Russia. While his intention had not been to become visible to the press, he was concerned that his action and his remarks might cause problems for his mother and his brother.

During the next several weeks Oswald was left to his own devices in the hotel, with his money beginning to run out. He was received in more interviews with Russian officials (several of whom were in reality KGB officers) and was left at loose ends right up to the time in January, 1960, when he was simply advised that he would be allowed to live and work in Russia—but that actual Russian citizenship would not be granted.

The detailed saga of the inter-agency Russian dialogue which resulted in Oswald being allowed to remain, to be assigned to a job, provided financial support, and even assigned to his own private apartment (something very special for a bachelor in Russia at the time), not to mention his own telephone, is fascinating. As would be expected, he was kept under ongoing KGB surveillance, his apartment was fitted with special electronic bugs, and his telephone was tapped.[95] But as Titovets relates, Oswald's personal and work activities proved quite innocuous, and his behavior and interests essentially apolitical—not at all those of a fervent socialist, much less a communist activist.

As noted earlier, Oswald's experiences in different environments—school, the Marines, then inside the Soviet Union—are critical to any evaluation of not just Oswald's personality and behaviors, but also regarding their consistency. We can only truly evaluate his activities during the critical year of 1963 if we can determine whether his behavior radically changed that year, or whether it remained essentially the same as it had from childhood on. And for that evaluation we must delve into Oswald's social life in Minsk and even his work history in a

Soviet factory. In the end the question will be: Did Oswald somehow become someone radically different following his return to the United States from Russia? Or will we find continuity and consistency in his personality, his behavior, and his world view? To answer that, we need yet another objective view of Lee Harvey Oswald, this time with both friends and lovers.

Chapter 5

Russian Saga

"A strange sight indeed is the picture of the local party man delivering a political sermon to a group of usually robust simple working men who through some strange process have been turned to stone. Turned to stone all except the hard faced communists with roving eyes looking for any bonus-making catch of inattentiveness on the part of any worker;"

—Lee Oswald's "Typed narrative concerning Russia,"
Warren Commission Exhibit 92

Exploring Oswald's time and activities in the Soviet Union is challenging, especially as several aspects of his experience overlap in time. During his stay in Russia, Oswald's life proceeded though the following general sequence of events:

- Establishing himself in a job at an electronics factory assignment in Minsk.
- Making a series of Russian friends outside his factory job.
- Socializing with a variety of young women and taking advantage of his unique social position of having a private apartment and significant income for a factory worker.

- Making a series of marriage proposals and ultimately becoming engaged, married, and the parent of a baby girl.
- Becoming dissatisfied with what was essentially a manual labor job in the factory, discontented with Soviet and Communist Party bureaucracy in a daily routine, and generally bored with Soviet life.
- An extended effort to obtain both Soviet and American approval for a return to the United States as well as financial support to allow him and his family to return together.

As in Japan, Oswald's personal experiences in Russia proved highly formative, both socially and politically—especially so given that, according to Oswald himself, it effectively destroyed many of his hopes for how socialism has been implemented in the Soviet system. His time in Russia clearly reinforced his interest in Russian culture, and created friendships that he would continue to sustain even after his return to the United States—those personal connections involve a constant, ongoing exchange of letters.

Yet over time, he soured on the Soviet state and became critical of the nationalism inherent in Soviet geopolitics—he would strongly condemn both following his return to the United States with a Russian wife. His writing following his return to the United States reveals that he was particularly upset by Soviet attempts to use the Communist Party of the United States as a tool of Russian foreign policy.

Beyond that, the details of Oswald's social life inside Russia provide an especially interesting contrast to the image of him presented in the Warren Commission Report—as well as the often brief media references to Oswald being an anti-social loner.

Living in Russia

In the beginning, it appeared that Oswald would become quite satisfied with his efforts to find a place in Russia. While he was essentially assigned to both a location and a job, when he arrived in Minsk (in Belorussia), Oswald was greeted by the Soviet Red Cross and gifted some 7,000 rubles. That allowed him to fully pay off his Moscow hotel bill (some 2,000 rubles) and have considerable spending money to start his new life. Oswald was also personally greeted by the Mayor of Minsk and assigned to a rent-free single person apartment—something quite special for a 20-year-old in Russia.[96]

He was also introduced to two female Intourist "guides," assigned to help him with an introduction to Minsk and to Russian society in general. Oswald took an immediate liking to the younger blonde guide, Rosa Kusnetsova. Rosa was quite attractive and immediately made an impression on him—his notes on Rosa capture what would become an outgoing attitude towards Russian woman—"Rosa . . . blonde, unmarried, we attract each other at once." Rosa and Lee did become quite friendly, and in his early weeks in Minsk they were often together, with her volunteering to take him on walking tours, to movies or the opera. While Oswald might have seen something more in the relationship, it was likely work-related on Rosa's part and once he started actual factory work nothing further developed between the two.

Despite Oswald's stated hope for college studies in Russia, he was given a job with a Belorussian Radio and Television Factory in Minsk (likely based on his Marine electronics training), working under the department head Alexander Zieger. Zieger spoke English, and Oswald became close to both him and his family, even writing to them after his return to the United States. The factory produced electronic parts and systems. Oswald, while trained as a radar operator, ended up not with a technical job, but rather was assigned as a metal lathe operator, along with 58 other workers and several foremen.

His salary was relatively high compared to the overall Russian population, something not uncommon for technical factory workers. He did participate in the factory union, but being Oswald, he complained of being required to attend its boring meetings, describing them as a waste of everyone's time. In that respect his attitude toward regimentation and compulsory activities was little different in Russia than it had been in the Marines.

What was quite different was a significant expansion in his social life, well-documented by both the Warren Commission, his friends inside Russia, and in photographs documenting his dates, family outings, and a series of girlfriends. As an American he stood out both in terms of simply being a curiosity and in having the advantage of being assigned a personal apartment. The apartment, plus a monthly payment from the Red Cross, allowed him a noticeably elevated lifestyle, and supported what came to be an active social life. Oswald himself wrote in his diary, "I'm living big and am very satisfied."

Oswald also began to make friends with a small number of fellow workers at the factory as well as others. He would continue to correspond with several of them after his return to America. During warmer weather Oswald—called Alec or Alek by his Russian friends because Lee was a very strange name to them—joined families and friends in country drives, picnics, and hunting.

He obtained a hunting license and purchased a 16-gauge single-barrel shotgun. His hunting license identifies him as "Aleksy Harvey Oswald" and he joined a local chapter of the Belorussian Society of Hunters and Fishermen, a hunting club sponsored by his factory. Club members hunted in the farm regions around Minsk. In short, surrounded by people whom he viewed as friendly to his own political views, Lee Oswald in Russia presents anything but the image of an antisocial or even asocial "loner." And early in his first summer in Russia, Oswald began a series of romantic affairs, beginning when Oswald met Ella German, a fellow worker at the factory, whom he began to routinely date.

Ella had apparently noticed Oswald as being different from the other young male workers and was intrigued, not initially knowing he was an American. And it appears Oswald continued to be of interest to her largely because of his foreign background—even though certain of his behaviors annoyed her and she began to view him as something of a cheapskate. While Oswald fell deeply in love and proposed marriage, Ella rather brusquely rejected him. She told him that not only did she not love him, but also that becoming too close to an American was far too risky in the Soviet Union. Oswald was crushed, feeling that she had simply exploited him to make other girls envious.[97] His notes indicate that he retained his crush on Ella through a series of later affairs, retaining his obsession with her even after he met the second Russian girl he would propose to—in what would be a final whirlwind romance.

Oswald's social life did survive his rejection by Ella, expanding beyond the factory based on his friendship with Ernst Titovets. Titovets himself was quite familiar with the entertainment scene in Minsk. He introduced Oswald to musical performances, to dances, to the conservatory in Minsk, to Titovets' musical friends—including young women, perhaps most importantly to the girls studying at the Institute for Foreign Languages. The Institute became important in Oswald's social life over several months, introducing him to numerous young women who were curious about an American in Russia and wanted to practice their English skills while he practiced Russian.

Oswald dated several of the girls from the Institute over time, also taking advantage of having his own apartment—something of a rarity for a young man his age.[98] Oswald's social life in Russia was certainly exceptional for him; not only did he meet and have brief affairs with several women, but went as far as proposing to two of them.

Some of the most direct views into Oswald's social life in Russia—including his romantic adventures as well as observations on his likes, dislikes, and personality—come from Titovets, close enough to Oswald that Oswald continued the friendship remotely even after his eventual return to the United States. Over some 15 months Oswald, following his return, he sent Titovets no less than 9 letters and 3 postcards. The last mail Titovets received had been sent from Dallas; it was dated October 28, 1963.[99]

Oswald regarded Titovets as one of his closest friends. While

Titovets spoke and wrote English well, he enjoyed expanding his contemporary English vocabulary with Oswald, at the same time improving Oswald's Russian language skills. They paid special attention to improving Oswald's spoken Russian.[100] The two were close enough to annoy each other yet stay friends, to talk politics, philosophy, and Russian literature and to socialize extensively—not only at the opera but all around town, given that Titovets was very familiar with what entertainment was available in Minsk. That certainly helped with introductions that might have otherwise given Oswald problems in a new city and a new country. Of course, Titovets, knowing the Soviet system, was well aware that Oswald would be under ongoing surveillance by the KGB. He discussed that with Oswald, and they joked about the telephone tap on his phone and where the "bugs" would be in his apartment.

Titovets described Oswald as enterprising, imaginative, ambitious in his goals, and very persistent. He viewed him as self-assured and easygoing with women—but also very susceptible to women who paid any attention to him. Selected for a radio factory assignment because of his electronics work history in the Marines, Oswald faced obstacles due to his limited Russian language skills. Oswald knew some words, phrases, and simple sentences, but nothing like the vocabulary needed to express himself at work—to address that problem, he was assigned to a Senior Engineer who gave him working lessons in Russian.

Oswald was specifically assigned to metal work, where he had no experience—but he did not accept coaching at work easily, and could be quite petty with co-workers. A great number of activities were organized in the Soviet factory. Oswald played volleyball on a factory team—but not enthusiastically—and displayed a lack of team spirit, as he had in Marine football. Another approved activity was at a factory shooting range. Oswald joined in once on the factory range and proved to be a very poor shot with a pistol. The same lack of skill received comment on factory-sponsored hunting club outings. In contrast, Oswald proved much more interested in factory-sponsored social and cultural activities, especially dances.

According to Titovets, Oswald was especially pleased that there was a dormitory of the Foreign Language Institute within a ten-minute walk from his apartment. It offered social connections with Russian girls who were learning some English—he had little concern that it also proved convenient for monitoring Oswald via Institute staff who were KGB informants. The girls at the Institute were themselves monitored because they were learning a foreign language (no doubt those who dated Oswald received special attention), but they also set themselves apart socially by working at being especially stylish, as much as was permitted, and outgoing (in Titovets words, uninhibited).

Being unique as an American and foreigner, Oswald was of great interest to the girls, and he took full advantage of being the center of interest during visits and social activities at the dorm. He would write a good bit about women in his diary, his emotional encounters, and his "conquests": "A growing loneliness overtakes me despite my conquest of Ennatachina, a girl from Riga at the Music Conservatory in Minsk. After an affair that lasts only a few weeks, we part."

Discontent with the Soviet System

But by the start of a new year in Russia, Oswald's propensity for boredom began to show—both at work, where he really had no special skills or interests to attract him, and privately where aside from girls, he was increasingly finding Soviet life to be routine and lacking in recreational opportunities and variety. While his romantic interludes were exciting, beyond that the daily routine of Soviet life had begun to chafe on 21-year-old Oswald's "adventurous" nature.

Overall, Oswald's pattern of behavior in Russia reveals a great deal of consistency with his earlier time in school and in the Marines—including the fact that he displayed an ongoing tendency to become bored in either school or at work, and was consistently a critic of institutions and what he saw as their associated class structures. Unimpressed by the equipment in his factory, he observed that politics was a major factor in its operations, with numerous foremen, "tons of paperwork," and an extensive bureaucracy in its daily operations.

He described factory life essentially built around the "Kollective" with each shop having a Party chief, who maintained discipline, attended party meetings, and ensured that party propaganda was constant and highly visible—with signs and slogans on all the walls. Oswald described the factory meetings as "so numerous as to be staggering." In one month there was one meeting of the professional union, four political information meetings, two Young Communist meetings, one meeting of the production committee to discuss ways of improving work, two Communist Party meetings, four meetings of the "School of Communist Labor," and one sports meeting.

Meetings were compulsory for party members and many were mandatory for all factory employees. Oswald himself passed on both joining the Communist Party, as well as attending the courses on Marxism and Leninism required for Party membership.[101] Marina Oswald testified that her husband did not attend the courses in Marxism and Leninism given in the factory for party members and those who wished to become party members—even though they were scheduled so they did not interfere with work. He also regarded all the routine factory meetings as being far too long, boring, and a waste of his time, but noted that party members posted in the audience monitored individuals for signs of inattention.

In short, Oswald came to realize that the idealized and classless Russia he had hoped for had turned out to be something of an illusion. He not only noted its flaws, but would write about them at length following his return to the United States. His take on the Soviet system was that the average Russian worker was simply co-opted by the state provisions for education and health care, while facing a chronic lack of food products, inadequate housing, and restrictions on personal travel. In contrast, Communist Party members, whom he described as "opportunists," took advantage of the system for their own promotion and privileges, and even factory managers were able to travel to Black Sea resorts.

That emerging view of the Soviet workplace and system led to his becoming increasingly negative at work; in his usual fashion he made no effort to disguise his opinions, and his assertiveness in the factory increased. That led to petty conflicts with co-workers and at one point Oswald even began a one-man strike, refusing to work—something just not done in a Soviet workplace.

He began to complain about any regimented activity, even the mass gymnastics routinely conducted at the factory as well as any other "compulsory" duty such as weekend work at a collective (which he himself was exempted from), writing that maintaining the workers eagerly engaged in such "patriotic" duties was simply a sham on the part of the Party. And Oswald showed no hesitation to express such opinions in his own diary. Titovets's observation was that Oswald had simply had enough of the Soviet system and his life in Russia. Not having been raised in it, he was neither resigned to it nor conditioned to its realities. Once again, Oswald had essentially become bored with what had started as a great adventure. He confirmed that in his own words, in his diary:

> "I am starting to reconsider my desire about staying. The work is drab, the money I get has nowhere to be spent. No nightclubs or bowling alleys, no places of recreation except the Trade Union dances. I have had enough."[102]

Oswald's negative views did provoke some defensive responses from Titovets, but he noted that those tended to evolve into lively arguments on the pros and cons of socialism, capitalism, and of their own countries. He described Oswald as being upset about racism and discrimination in America, but appalled by the degree of government control over the individual in Russia, arguing that people were brainwashed and could not even travel without bureaucratic permission.

Returning from Russia

Oswald was going to receive a great deal of push-back from both the American and Soviet systems regarding his decision to return to the United States—and he faced an ongoing series of struggles with the bureaucracy, especially from the American State Department.

But he displayed his usual persistence and once he had made up his mind, he stayed the course. He even rejected an offer of Russian citizenship—which he had so aggressively sought during his first days and weeks in Russia: [103]

> "One year after I received the residence document, I am called in to the passport office and asked if I want citizenship (Russian). I say no, simply extend my residential passport and my document is extended until Jan. 4, 1962."

By February 1961, Oswald was making his first request to the American Embassy in Moscow, stating that he would like to go back to the U.S., and by March he was anticipating a return. His engineering mentor and friend at the factory advised him not to express that goal in conversations with co-workers or friends. Oswald took the advice seriously and did not even share his plan with his new fiancé, Marina Nikolayevna Prusakova.

It is important to note that Oswald's decision to return to the United States was apparently not affected by the personal fact of his subsequent engagement and marriage to a Russian citizen. While the marriage (and the later birth of a Russian daughter) certainly complicated matters with both governments, Oswald's decision and his personal goals would come first—in Russia and later in the United States.

Oswald had met Marina in March at a Trade Union dance, proposed to her in early April, and following a brief but ardent romance, they were married on April 30. It was some months later that Oswald told his new wife about his intent to return to the U.S. She appeared surprised, but was willing to leave Russia for the United States with him. Titovets notes that Marina had dated foreigners while living in Leningrad and before coming to Minsk. According to friends she had been taken with the idea of marrying a foreigner well before encountering Oswald.

Titovets provides a good deal more information on Oswald's social life and interests during his time in Russia, but one point is especially important as it relates to Oswald's character, and the relationship he would develop with his new wife. Oswald's view of women in general, and a spouse specifically, was quite conventional for his time and upbringing. He felt that a wife should be kind and caring, devoted to her family and children, obedient to her husband, and focused on household duties. He had recalled his time in Japan and with Japanese women as his best time in the service; Japanese girls were very pretty, meek, and eager to please. As he would come to learn, Marina was pretty but most definitely not "meek."

Given the extent to which Oswald's political and cultural views were often so contrarian, his views about women and his expectations for his new wife were quite conservative. Titovets observed that Lee's whirlwind courtship of Marina might well have been too short to appreciate that she was a good bit more emancipated and stronger-willed than he might fully understand, a circumstance that began to cause conflicts between the two even in the months before they departed Russia.

More to the point, he felt that Oswald had quickly become "infatuated" by a pretty and uninhibited young woman whose appearance and behavior gave the image of Brigitte Bardot (a seductive French actress of the time)—and had conducted an aggressive courtship which left little time to surface the simple fact that Marina was not at all interested in the philosophical and political subjects so important to him. Only in time would it become clear that his fundamental concerns in life were not something they held in common; what he wanted to read about and discuss was simply boring to her.

As the months proceeded, Oswald's growing discontent with Soviet life and his initial efforts to return to the United States faced bureaucratic pushback on both the Russian and American fronts. Ultimately, the Soviets proved themselves much quicker to respond to Oswald's emerging desire to leave Russia than the American State Department—the negative impression he had created at the American Embassy in Moscow upon his arrival in Russia remained firmly in place, and his initial appeals were largely met with a cold shoulder, with much stalling and ongoing pushback.[104]

Oswald's quest to get himself and his new wife back to the United States was challenging and lengthy. His February letter to the American Embassy asked for the return of his passport and declared his wish to return to America—if he could do so without legal risk. He stated he was unable to visit the embassy in Moscow, lacking Soviet permission to leave Minsk. The embassy responded that he would somehow have to appear in person in Moscow, but also notified his mother of the contact. By March, Oswald's diary noted he was in a "state of expectation" about returning to the U.S.—however, the Soviets had apparently learned of his plans, and his monthly Red Cross payments were cut off at that point.

In May 1961, Oswald resumed communicating with his family, sending a "friendly" letter to his brother Robert, describing his work and his marriage. The two exchanged more letters and Oswald also corresponded with his mother. According to Marina, during the period following their marriage Oswald met and socialized with several Cuban students residing in Minsk. At the time Fidel Castro was being strongly supported by the Soviet government and presented in a very favorable light. Lee and Marina, as well as many young Russians, found Castro appealing. Marina felt that Oswald would probably meet

Cuban students once every week or so over several months, sometimes going to movies with them. Given his earlier interest in Cuba and Central American, the students undoubtedly reinforced his positive impressions of Castro and the Cuban revolution.[105]

The American Embassy remained adamant that Oswald had to come to Moscow to personally affirm he had not actually renounced his citizenship (even though their records showed he had never done so, or even completed and filed the required form for that). Towards the end of May 1961, frustrated by a lack of response from the American Embassy, Oswald did travel on his own to Moscow, on a weekend so as not to be absent from work. He managed to talk briefly with an embassy staffer, who told him he would have to appear at the embassy on Monday, which he did.

The American Embassy challenged Oswald on several questions, including his position on Soviet citizenship, an oath of allegiance to the Soviet Union, and membership in a factory trade union. Oswald responded negatively to the challenges, although it appears certain that initially he had told the Soviets he desired citizenship, even though they refused to grant it. His exchanges with the embassy are one more example of how Oswald's "situational" behavior sometimes led him to either shade the truth, or commit outright lies when under pressure.

He told the embassy that he had "learned his lesson the hard way," and the staff there felt he no longer displayed the arrogance he had during his earlier contact with them while seeking entry into Russia. Based on their assessments, his passport was stamped and returned—valid only for direct travel to the United States. Following that, Oswald began the procedures required to admit his wife as an immigrant, and he returned to Minsk at the end of a week. Contacts with the American Embassy continued and it was towards the end of June that Oswald told Marina of his plans—his diary notes she was "slightly startled," but agreed to leave Russia with him. At that time, Marina herself began to make inquiries about a Soviet exit visa.

The saga of Oswald's ultimate return to the United States was an extended one, lasting many months and with extensive exchanges within the American State Department (not at all eager to take back an ex-Marine generally, if not legally, viewed as a defector), before a final decision to support his request. Based on related State Department correspondence, in the end the decision to readmit Oswald, and extend a visa to his new wife, appears more a matter of avoiding any embarrassing actions by him (he was considered unpredictable at best) as well as the image of separating a husband and wife.[106] In that regard his return simply seems to have been the easiest way to handle uncomfortable situations with an always persistent Oswald—not unlike the Soviet decision to let him stay in Russia in the first place.

Following the initial embassy experience, Oswald had written to his brother Robert with a greeting for the family, and a remark about writing a book about his emotions and experiences. From that point on, it was a matter of working with local Soviet authorities to get permissions for both himself and Marina to leave the country, a process that drew considerable attention and some level of interrogation and harassment for Marina, both at work and from various officials including those from the Young Communist Party. Oswald wrote the American Embassy complaining of "systematic and concerted attempts to intimidate [Marina] . . . into withdrawing her application for a visa," resulting in Marina developing a nervous disorder. The embassy replied that sort of activity was to be expected and that such applications were "seldom taken rapidly."

Marina herself later testified that when the news of her visit to the American Embassy in July reached Minsk, she was dropped from membership in "Komsomol," the Communist Youth Organization, and a number of attempts were made to discourage her from leaving the Soviet Union. Her aunt and uncle, with whom she lived, stopped speaking to her and she talked to friends about it being a "very horrible time." In context, the Russian departure experience argues strongly for Marina's personal attachment to Oswald and her marriage. It illustrates her seeming willingness to follow his plans regardless of conflicts or discord between them. And it offers a prelude to the relationship the two would further develop in the United States—a relationship which, despite her ongoing issues with her husband (and their separations), would see Marina continually agreeing to follow Oswald from job to job, and city to city.

In another instance of behavioral consistency, Oswald continued to approach and argue for his and Marina's departure with virtually all potential groups whom he felt might influence the matter, showing no concern for the possibility that he might be annoying anyone in the process. He even wrote to Senator John Tower of Texas—who simply forwarded the letter to the State Department. Because, or in spite of, his persistence, some eleven months after he had begun his drive to return to America, the pieces did come into place and, in December 1961, Marina, who was pregnant, was also told an exit visa would be issued by the Soviet Union. For a time, the American Embassy continued to thwart Marina's travel with Oswald, telling him he might have to come alone and send for her, but ultimately his persistence and lobbying persuaded them to grant the proper approvals for both to travel together.

In January 1962, Oswald began an extended series of efforts to obtain travel money, from the U.S. Government, the Red Cross, the International Rescue Agency et al. In the following months he was also forced to deal with the fact that following his appearance in Russia, his Marine discharge status had been changed to "undesirable." A less than honorable discharge posed problems for his return, and although he seems not to have fully realized it at the time, serious prospects for future employment. He began a practice of routinely challenging the discharge which would continue up to the time of his death. An example of his assertions that he was being unfairly treated can be found in the contents of one letter to former Navy Secretary John Connally:

> "I have and allways (sp) had the full sanction of the U.S. Embassy, Moscow USSR. and hence the U.S. government. In as much as I

> am returning to the U.S.A. in this year with the aid of the U.S. Embassy, bring with me my family (since I married in the USSR) I shall employ all means to right this gross mistake or injustice to a boni-fied U.S. citizen and ex-service man. The U.S. government has no charges or complaints against me. I ask you to look into this case and take the necessary steps to repair the damage done to me and my family. For information I would direct you to consult the American Embassy, Chikovski St. 19/21, Moscow, USSR."[107]

His efforts on the discharge classification produced no results; however, the State Department did advise his mother that it would need $900 to make the travel arrangements for her son and daughter-in-law. Within weeks of that letter, Marina had delivered their first child, a baby girl named June Lee. Oswald, still working at his factory job, was gifted with "one summer blanket, 6 light diapers, 4 warm diapers, 2 chemises, 3 very good warm chemises, 4 very nice suits and two toys" for the baby by his co-workers.

In May 1962, Oswald asked to be discharged from the factory. Overall, his work experience in Russia shows a number of similarities to his time in the Marine Corps—reasonably good performance initially, which turned to boredom and ultimately a lack of interest in the work and the job. By December 1961, when Oswald had begun to contemplate leaving Russia, his routine factory work review noted that he did not, "display the initiative for increasing his skill" in his job, that he was "over-sensitive . . . to remarks from the foremen, and . . . careless in his work." Oswald took "no part in the social life of the shop" and kept "very much to himself." This assessment was very similar to those from his final months in Japan or at El Toro.

For his last few weeks in Russia, Oswald's bureaucratic and financial struggles continued, primarily on the American side, as the Soviets seemed to have had no problem with his departing. Eventually Oswald signed a promissory note with the U.S. government, and in June he and his family boarded a ship for the United States.

Chapter 6

Back in the USA

It was not the first time that he mentioned that he was disappointed in the Soviet Union because he did not find there his ideal of justice. "Maybe it does not exist …" he said sadly one day. "And so I came back."

—George de Mohrenschildt, Lee Oswald's closest friend following his return to the United States from the Soviet Union, *I Am a Patsy! I Am a Patsy!*, manuscript posthumously published by House Select on Assassinations, Volume 12, 126

Reentry

While on board ship, Oswald began a series of notes and written pieces documenting his impressions and experience during his time in the Soviet Union—as well as his still-developing geopolitical worldview. That writing would be supplemented by the material in the daybook he had kept during his time in Russia. In total his writing in 1962/63 would offer considerable negative commentary on the Soviet system, reflecting what can only be described as "disillusionment." While continually condemning organized political groups of all stripes, he advocated for a system which would offer a solution beyond either pure American-style capitalism or the Soviet version of communism.

In his notes, Oswald remarked that he had taken support from the Red Cross while in Russia—he would later receive assistance from the Travelers Aid Society and the New York City Department of Welfare upon landing in New York, and accept unemployment payments and other social system support during his months in Texas and Louisiana—yet he was adamant regarding his political independence:[108]

> "I shall never sell myself intentionly (sp), or unintentionly (sp) to anyone again."

That expression has been interpreted as suggesting Oswald had accepted help (wittingly or unwittingly) from the American intelligence community in traveling to and entering Russia. It could also be taken as remorse over his offers to provide military information to the Soviets in exchange for citizenship, although there is no evidence that he actually did provide such information or that the Russians interrogated him in response to his remarks. Yet another view is that he provided information on his time in Russia and on his factory work to the State Department in Moscow, to gain support for his return over their opposition. If nothing else, the remark suggests that from that point forward, he was dedicated to his own agenda, and to totally independent action.

One of the more interesting points regarding Oswald's return, especially with his dramatic change in attitude towards the Soviet Union, is the rather surprising fact that the media in general (including the CIA's press contacts within the media) ignored Oswald. It was a time in the Cold War that negative stories about the Soviets were commonplace, and the return of a "defector" with a list of bad things to say about Russia would seem to have been made to order for propaganda purposes.

Before arriving in the United States, Oswald drafted a series of answers in anticipation of being questioned by the press on his return. Even the Warren Commission was forced to observe that his willingness to engage with the press suggested that Oswald himself considered he had done nothing wrong. In his own view, Oswald had gone to Russia to study the Soviet system first-hand, but in no respect considered himself anything other than a loyal American citizen.

Yet no press approached Oswald following the ship's landing; he was not asked for impressions of the Soviet Union nor given the opportunity to offer what would have been caustic remarks about the Soviet System, the Soviet version of communism or Soviet propaganda. Those remarks would only emerge in written material that Oswald himself produced following his return to Texas. There, Oswald expressed surprise and some disappointment about the lack of any press or reporters upon his arrival in New York or Texas.

Oswald's short stay in New York City further illustrates the point that when he was stressed or under pressure, he could be counted on to express himself adamantly, and at times to simply be a "pain" to those around him. The Travelers Aid Society had found a room for the Oswalds, and the welfare department called his brother Robert in Fort Worth and advised him of Lee's arrival. Robert immediately offered $200 to bring his brother and his family home, but Lee refused the offer and argued that the department should pay his way, otherwise he would simply go as far as he could on the $63 he had himself. Only after a display of obstinance did he finally agree the accept the $200 from his brother, departing with his family for Texas on June 14, 1962. Upon arrival, the Oswalds were met by Robert, who described Lee as having lost weight and picked up something of an "accent" during his travels—but still, basically the "same boy" he remembered.

The "intelligence agent" view of Oswald has consistently speculated that he was "debriefed" by the CIA upon his return to the United States—something to be expected if he was a willing and knowing asset of the Agency. A counter view to his being a witting agent would be that any American returning from the Soviet Union, especially one as visible to and engaged with the State Department, would be tagged for the collection of information about his experience in some fashion—most likely with the information being obtained under some type of cover by the person contacting him. Yet the CIA appears to have passed on using any of its well-documented media assets to conduct what would be called an "open source" debrief of Oswald, or to feel him out for potential propaganda use.

In regard to that issue, one anecdotal report of an Oswald "debrief" comes from Donald Deneslya, a Russian translator working in the foreign documents section of the CIA's Soviet Russia division. His job related to files on Russian technical and industrial facilities, and he recalled having seen a "contact form" in the summer of 1962, relating to a former Marine (either a Captain or Corporal) who was in the process of returning to the United States with a Russian wife.

The individual had lived in Minsk, working at a radio factory there. Within the contact report, there was substantial information on the Minsk factory, apparently the reason the information was routed through his area. He recalled that his office had other information about that factory in Minsk, in the Industrial Registry Office. The origin of the report (such reports routinely had no name associated with them) was New York, meaning that it had come from the New York CIA office, originating either from information collected in New York or "quite possibly" having been passed on from the State Department (pouched directly from the U.S. Embassy in Moscow to New York as a port of entry)—since it dealt with an American returning from the Soviet Union.[109]

Deneslya also stated that he had seen the name "Anderson" on the report. Some years later, author Joan Mellen, after conversations with Deneslya, was able to identify an "Anderson" who worked within the Soviet Russia Division (SR6); "Anderson" was the pseudonym of a woman named Eleanor Reed. There are other examples of women CIA officers using seeming male names, an interesting piece of tradecraft.

One of the simplest explanations for the Deneslya observation—and an explanation for the lack of any need to use media cut-outs or other sources with Oswald in New York—is that the American Embassy in Moscow had collected considerable information on Oswald during his time in Russia; it is even possible that in his ongoing approaches to the embassy, Oswald had offered additional details to encourage them to approve his return. While speculative, the fact that he had offered information to aid his entry into Russia, and the possibility that he had done something similar via the State Department to facilitate his return, would be an alternative explanation for his remark about never "selling" himself again.

In any event, it would have been standard practice for the U.S. Embassy to relay its information regarding Oswald's time in the Soviet Union to the CIA's Soviet Russia division at the time of his return to the United States with a Russian wife. Such a scenario would also explain why the CIA's Domestic Contacts Services was assigned to monitor Oswald and Marina once they arrived back at Fort Worth, Texas. And we do now know that it was indeed Domestic Contacts Services which was tasked with looking into the Oswalds following their return.

Among the first things Oswald did following his arrival in Texas was to begin to put his experiences in Russia on paper. On June 18, 1962 he contacted a public stenographer and asked her to begin typing up a manuscript based on notes from him, as well as material from his daybook. He paid a dollar per page and two dollars an hour; he stayed in her office while she worked, helping her organize the material and translating portions which were in Russian. After two days it appears he had literally run out of money, and refused her offer to postpone further payment or even do the work for free—Oswald left with the work she had done, only some ten pages worth of typed material.

On June 26, Oswald was interviewed by FBI agents in Fort Worth.[110] One of the agents who interviewed him described him as tense and "drawn up"; he said that Oswald "exhibited an arrogant attitude . . . and [was] inclined to be just a little insolent." Oswald declined to say why he had gone to Russia, saying that he refused to "relive the past." He said that he had not attempted to obtain Soviet citizenship, had not been approached by Soviet officials for information about his experiences in the Marines, and had not offered them such information.

Marina's Soviet passport/visa required her to notify the Soviet Embassy in Washington of her address in this country, and Oswald told the agents that he planned to contact the Embassy for this purpose within a few days. He promised to notify the FBI if he were contacted by Soviet agents "under suspicious circumstances or otherwise." Oswald told his brother about the interview, saying that it had gone just fine.

"Friends" in Fort Worth

During that same week, with hopes of finding professional work as an interpreter or translator, Oswald visited a Fort Worth library and was referred to a Petroleum Engineer in Fort Worth who had been born in Siberia and had taught Russian at the library as a "civic enterprise." Oswald contacted the engineer, Peter Gregory, who tested Oswald's Russian reading ability, and after a conversation in Russian, Gregory wrote a letter of recommendation on Oswald's Russian language skills. He also introduced his son Paul to the Oswalds, and Marina gave conversational Russian lessons to Paul two days a week during August and early September. She was paid $35 and the lessons generally took place at the Mercedes Street apartment with Lee present. In addition, Paul Gregory occasionally took the Oswalds shopping; after they became friendly, he had a number of discussions with Lee, some of them politically oriented.[111]

Gregory gave the Oswalds an entrée to a number of people of the Russian-speaking community in the Dallas-Fort Worth area, expatriates who were tied together socially by a common origin, language, and religion. The group was not restricted to people from Russia, but was composed primarily of individuals from Eastern European countries—virtually all of them devoutly anti-Communist. Sometime around August 25, 1962, Peter Gregory invited the Oswalds and several members of the Russian community to his house for dinner. One of the guests was George Bouhe, a Dallas accountant, and a leader in the Russian community. He was very interested in meeting and conversing with Marina, because she had spent much of her youth in Leningrad, which was his birthplace. Mrs. Anna Meller, the Russian-born wife of a Dallas department store employee, was also present at the dinner and would become close to the Oswalds, Marina in particular.

Near the end of August, the Oswalds were introduced to Declan Ford, a consulting geologist in the Dallas area, and his Russian-born wife, at Anna Meller's home. Introductions were also made to Elena Hall, born in Tehran, Iran of Russian parents. Mrs. Hall worked in a dental laboratory and at the time was divorced from her former husband John Hall. George Bouhe made the introductions and took Marina to Mrs. Hall's house to obtain assistance for Marina, who had serious dental problems. In early September, George Bouhe and Anna Meller introduced the couple to other members of the local Russian network, including Max Clark.[112]

As the months passed, this network of Russian speakers came to provide advice and some references for Oswald, but more importantly become a support network for Marina as domestic conflicts developed with Lee—as well as on occasions when Lee moved away searching for jobs.

With no real employment prospects related to his Russian language skills, Oswald approached the Texas State employment agency—as he would do on several occasions over the following months—and in late July obtained a sheet metal working job with a division of Leslie Welding, which manufactured louvers and ventilators. Oswald was forced to face the fact that he had no viable work references other than the Marines, and that his undesirable discharge was a very basic problem. His job applications from that point on reflect an ongoing series of false employment statements—in the Leslie Welding application he stated that he had been a metal worker and machinist in the Marines, and that his discharge had been honorable.

Oswald worked eight to nine hours a day at Leslie Welding. The pay was reasonable for the job, but after a time he began to complain to Marina about the hours and the work. Still, his work record there showed him to have been rated as a good employee, even though it was noted that he kept largely to himself. While the Warren Commission Report accurately positioned Oswald as not making work friends on his various jobs (he was generally not in any specific job for more than a very few weeks or at best a few months), it failed to offer the counter view that he was very outgoing with his friends. Once back in Texas he wrote repeatedly to his friends in Russia, sending them letters and books, and asking to be remembered to various individuals. He described his moves, his job, and the fact that he had subscribed to several Russian publications including *Krokodil*, *Ogonyok*, and *Yunost* as well as a newspaper published in Minsk.

In his letters to his Russian friends, Oswald commented on the fact that it was easy to get the Russian material in the U.S., unlike the restrictions placed on American material which he had experienced while in Russia. His friend Titovets observed that clearly Oswald remained fascinated with the cultural and social life of Russia, in contrast to his lack of interest in the Soviet system or Party politics. Oswald's letters also noted that Marina was having problems assimilating to life in America, largely because of language issues. He wrote that she had not shown any particular interest in learning English, even before their move back to the United States from Minsk.[113]

On August 16, the FBI again interviewed Oswald. This interview took place in the back seat of a car in front of his home and covered substantially the same material as the previous June interview. Oswald once again denied having made any deal with representatives of the Soviet Union. He protested his undesirable discharge from the Marines, and stated that his wife was registered at the Soviet Embassy. He still refused to discuss why he had gone to the Soviet Union, but he was described as less hostile than in the previous interview.[114] But according to Marina, he was upset by the ongoing interest the FBI was showing in him.[115]

After getting the metal working job, Oswald had been able to move his family into a one-bedroom furnished apartment at 2703 Mercedes Street. The apartment furnishing was skimpy at best, and their Russian friends described the Mercedes Street apartment as "decrepit" and with no telephone service.[116] Oswald became upset when his mother bought clothes and a highchair for the baby—things which he could not afford. Oswald apparently decided that he did not want his mother at the apartment anymore, and became incensed when his wife permitted her to visit despite his instructions. After he moved from Fort Worth to Dallas in October, Oswald did not see his mother or communicate with her in any way until she came to see him after the assassination of the president in November 1963.[117]

Outside support for his family became an ongoing issue for Oswald during the next several months. The Russian and Eastern European expatriate community all shared conservative political views—very much in conflict with Oswald's own world view. This increasingly left Oswald as an outsider, uncomfortable in that community but, as usual, never hesitant to express his own opinions. When someone suggested he should thank the person in the community who had helped him get a job his response was, "Why should I thank anyone for getting me a job where I only make $1.25 an hour?" In contrast, an apolitical Marina, with a small child, was received with more sympathy and was given ongoing offers of assistance—something that consistently annoyed Oswald.[118]

Both the politics of the Russian-speaking community, and its ability to offer financial support irritated the always excessively independent Oswald. He increasingly began to avoid them, resenting the gifts they were giving Marina and the baby, and most likely being embarrassed by his own limited financial situation.

Oswald was clearly annoyed with Marina's acceptance by the highly conservative Russian speaking community in Fort Worth, as well as the influence of their homes, cars and material possessions. This was a reversal of his position in Russia, where he was able to offer her an apartment of their own and a relatively substantial income. It was an uncomfortable situation for him, and very likely the major factor in his walking away from his job at Leslie Welding in October 1962—a job where he had been seen as a bit of a loner, but rated as a good worker.

He left Leslie Welding with no notice (he marked "Quit" on his last day's time card), told Marina that he had been laid off, and immediately began looking for a new job in Dallas. In doing so he accepted an offer from Elena Hall to have Marina and the baby in her house until he could find a new job and make arrangements for Marina and the baby to join him. Separation of Oswald from his family, with Marina living with or supported by a series of supportive women friends, became somewhat routine for the Oswalds beginning in late 1962 and continued for much of 1963.

In leaving his metal working job with no notice (he later wrote the company stating that he had moved to Dallas and asked for his remaining wages to be paid to him at a new address), he told George Bouhe that the job had only been temporary (simply not true) and he told his wife that he had been discharged by the company (also not true).[119]

A Friend in Dallas

During the next few months, from October 1962 to April 1963, one of Oswald's few ongoing personal contacts was with another individual, someone who shared Oswald's relatively liberal socio-political views (while also being firmly opposed to Soviet-style communism), someone that Oswald himself would come to see as a "friend"—George de Mohrenschildt. De Mohrenschildt and his wife maintained social contacts with the Oswalds for several months over the winter of 1962/63, until moving to Haiti in the spring to pursue a new business opportunity which had been in development since the summer of 1962.[120]

De Mohrenschildt's first approach to the Oswalds was at their Mercedes Street address, in Fort Worth—which he described as being in a "slummy" industrial area and something of a "shack." As a native Russian, de Mohrenschildt enjoyed Marina's speech, describing it as something of a treat, beautiful and melodious Russian. He found her to have a good sense of humor, but described much of their conversation as somewhat "trite." On the other hand, Lee impressed him as willing to talk about controversial issues and demonstrating the courage of his convictions with a ferociously independent spirit—reminding de Mohrenschildt of his youth and his years as a student.[121] In turn, Oswald appears to have sensed that he could talk openly with de Mohrenschildt, even argue with him on subjects Oswald was passionate about. In one 1963 job application, Oswald listed de Mohrenschildt as his closest friend.

De Mohrenschildt had been born in Czarist Russia, of a family lineage which entitled him to use the title of Baron—he was avowedly opposed to Soviet communism. Socially well-connected (his acquaintances extended to Jacqueline Kennedy's family, the Bouviers) he traveled internationally and did college work at universities in Belgium. Following that he studied at the University of Houston and obtained a Masters in Petroleum Geology from the University of Texas.[122]

As a consulting geologist, de Mohrenschildt spoke six languages, and had worked in Haiti in the 1950s, as well as in several other developing countries including Togoland, Nigeria, Ghana, and Cuba. In Cuba he worked for Three States Oil as well as Charmax, the Cuba-Venezuela Trust. He had worked out of both Dallas and Houston as a freelance, consulting geologist. He was also admittedly a self-promoter, with a history of outreach to those who might help him in his business affairs.[123]

During 1962 and into 1963 de Mohrenschildt renewed his interest in the Haitian oil business and established contact with Clemard Charles, an influential Haitian businessman and political figure. As was his practice, de Mohrenschildt made the rounds in Washington

D.C., making introductions for Charles and attempting to leverage his association with him to obtain government support for his business prospects—even scheduling an appointment with Vice President Johnson in the process.

Earlier, during World War II, de Mohrenschildt had provided estimates of American oil exports to Europe to French intelligence. In post-war years, while working for the International Cooperation Administration, he had been approached by the CIA and volunteered to provide commercial and political information obtained during his travels, especially during his work in Yugoslavia. He was the type of well-traveled business source the Agency was always interested in, and the CIA maintained casual contact with him into the early 1960s—something he himself readily admitted.[124]

De Mohrenschildt made no secret of his contacts with government officials, nor his willingness to provide information to the U.S. government. He openly stated that a government man (J. Walton Moore, Dallas CIA Domestic Contacts Office) had taken him out to lunch and mentioned that a young American and his Russian wife were known to be returning to Dallas.

Moore requested that de Mohrenschildt, well-established in the Fort Worth/Dallas expatriate Russian community, watch for the couple's arrival. In a follow-on meeting, Moore provided an address for Oswald in Fort Worth (suggesting CIA Domestic Contacts had other sources within the Russian expatriate community), and asked that de Mohrenschildt meet the couple and offer his personal observations of them. De Mohrenschildt did just that, but that first contact was some time after the Oswalds' actual arrival in Fort Worth.

De Mohrenschildt himself confirmed that his initial visit to the Oswalds' had been no coincidence. It was simply a follow up on Moore's request to "look into" the arrival of a family whom he had been told was anticipated to appear in the Fort Worth/Dallas area. By that time, both Lee and Marina were already known to several people within the Russian-speaking social community.

The exact function of CIA Domestic Contacts and Domestic Operations circa 1962/63 has been a matter of much speculation over the years, although the general opinion is that it operated under the management of Tracy Barnes, previously a senior officer within the Division of Plans/Operations. Barnes had been a major figure in the Cuba Project and was closely associated with the Bay of Pigs operation. It was known that he had been reassigned after the investigation into that disaster, most probably to Domestic Operations. Based on recent research by David Boylan, we now have a much better insight into what CIA group contacted de Mohrenschildt in 1962. That view comes from a 1962 proposal to reorganize many elements of the Plans/Operations Directorate—with the proposal itself generated as an After-Action response to the CIA's embarrassment in the Bay of Pigs operation.[125]

The reorganization affected many areas of CIA Operations, but specifically called for the creation of a "Domestic Division." That new division was to incorporate the "Contacts Division" which had been operating under the Deputy of Director of Intelligence (DDI) but was to be moved directly under Operations (DDP). Domestic Contacts was to constitute the foundation for CIA domestic operational activities—including the establishment of personal and commercial domestic covers for foreign operations, contacts with domestic organizations in the United States (including businesses and foundations), and the management of CIA proprietary "cover" businesses including CAT (Civil Air Transport / Taiwan) and Fairways (Washington DC).[126]

This expanded view into Domestic Operations in 1962/63 provides useful context in terms of understanding Moore's reporting structure and resolves the issue of where within the CIA Domestic Contacts resided. Unfortunately, up to this point few documents have been obtained regarding Moore, and nothing relating to any contact with de Mohrenschildt or information that might have come from him on Lee Harvey Oswald.

As with many other sources on Oswald, de Mohrenschildt was

interviewed by the Warren Commission, and its questioning was seemingly oriented towards positioning Oswald in the image which the Commission had chosen to project. De Mohrenschildt railed against those interviews later, regretting that he had not been able to talk of the positive aspects of Oswald and had basically been managed in his statements by the questions asked him.[127]

Over the years, largely because of the material which the Warren Report chose to excerpt from de Mohrenschildt's testimony to support the official view of Oswald, and the fact that his initial contact with the Oswalds came from within the intelligence community, de Mohrenschildt's insights into Lee and Marina Oswald have not been well-received by those with a conspiracy-oriented view of the president's assassination.

Yet rejecting him and his wife as sources on the Oswald family essentially discards what would normally be considered some of the most critical historical information regarding the Oswalds' time in Dallas during 1962/63—from the people who were demonstrably the closest individuals to the Oswalds prior to their move to New Orleans. In a historical sense, that would deprive any study of Lee Oswald from the observations of George de Mohrenschildt, someone close enough to be listed as his "friend" by Oswald himself on a 1963 job application (JOBCO, 1963).

There is no doubt that de Mohrenschildt shared several of Oswald's views, including an opposition to racism, and was far more liberal on social issues than others Lee would encounter in Texas. That brought about the same type of relationship that Oswald had established with his friend Titovets in Russia. Oswald and de Mohrenschildt could argue and joke with each other without Oswald pushing him away.

Conversations

Given that relationship, the insights offered by de Mohrenschildt appear to be extremely valuable, especially as they characterize Oswald at the beginning of the seminal year 1963, and are fully consistent with the less detailed remarks from several other sources including Oswald's own writings. The following comments are excerpted from de Mohrenschildt's observations made after he and his wife's first conversations with Lee and Marina Oswald:[128]

> "But I found the ex–marine so much more interesting," I said. My friend, the retired air–force colonel resented Lee, his offhandedness, his ironic smiles and especially his ferocious spirit of independence. All his sympathy went to Marina, the poor Russian refugee.
>
> Since his childhood he [Oswald] was keenly aware of social and racial injustices. Instead of playing basketball or baseball, like any other red–blooded American youth, he read voraciously. Among the books he read was Marx's '*Capital*,' which made a deep impression on him. Ironically, he said, he borrowed this book from the Loyola University library.
>
> I remember concluding this conversation by telling Lee, "If you want to be a revolutionary, you have to be a fool or to have an inspiration. And your actions will be judged by the success or failure of your life."

De Mohrenschildt was also curious about the apparent contradiction between Oswald enlisting in the Marines and ending up in pursuit of becoming a Soviet citizen; what was really behind his seeming fascination with Russia? The two became close enough for Oswald to respond to questions about that seeming contradiction—with the exchanges described by de Mohrenschildt in his writing about their relationship. The following material is excerpted from de Mohrenschildt's writing on Oswald, a manuscript entitled *I Am a Patsy! I Am a Patsy!* Oswald's responses are in quotations:

"I [Oswald] served in the Marine Corps not because I was a patriot but I wanted to get away from the drudgery and to see the world," admitted Lee.

Did you like the service?

"Not particularly. But I had time to study, to read and indeed we traveled a lot."

You told me you lived in Japan. How did you land there?

"Just an accident of the Marine Corps duty. The military duty was boring and stupid. But fortunately I moved around, began visiting places where youngsters meet and established contacts with some more progressive and thinking Japanese. And this," said Lee thoughtfully, "is what led me to Russia eventually. I also learned there of other, Japanese, ways of exploitation of the poor by the rich. Semi–feudal, industrial giants which act paternalistically yet exploiting the workers — proletarians. The wages in Japan were ridiculously low," Lee added.

Lee's mind was of a stoical, philosophical type, that's why, I guessed, he had gotten along so well with the other Russians he met in the Soviet Union. Russians do not mind to suffer and even go hungry if they can spend entire nights talking and speculating on some esoteric matters.

I hoped that the other members of the Russian community would help him also and told him so.

"Thanks a lot, I can take care of myself, I don't need those creeps, I shall find something," he answered gruffly. This was an example of Lee's independence, he refused help, objected even to my help. Rather than to be indebted to someone, he would rather starve on his own.

Lee was serious and did not take life as a joke. But if he happened to be in a good mood, he became an excellent companion, remembered political jokes, told them well, and laughed at yours.

Lee was not jealous of Kennedy's and Bouviers' wealth and did not envy their social positions, of that I was sure. To him wealth and society were big jokes, but he did not resent them.

One evening Lee was in a blue mood and confided that he had not been particularly pleased with his reception in Minsk. Somewhat naively, he had expected to be treated as a special person, a prominent refugee, and nothing happened, there was little difference between his condition in Minsk and that of an ordinary Soviet worker. And so he had become depressed. That evening Lee expressed an opinion that he did not appreciate the Soviet type of government.

Why? I asked.

"It is somewhat too regimented for me," he said. "We were obliged to go to the meeting at the factory after work, dead tired and listened to inflammatory speeches. I was lucky if I was able to go to sleep. Indoctrination of any kind is not to my taste." You are an extremely sincere person, Lee," I told him. "You do not lie even to yourself. Most of the people I know are the opposite of you. They put up a front, they confuse, they deceive, they lie even when thinking."

"I guess it's dangerous to be that way. I know I make a lot of enemies. But what the hell," he acknowledged, "my position is that I am afraid of a very few things in life. I am not cautious. I am not," he smiled, "a turkey which lives only to become fat." And he showed me his non existing belly. He was becoming very thin.

"Lee, your way of life is so un–American, it scares me to think what may become of you."

"It is true," Lee said, "I am probably committing a sin in not being interested in possessions or money. When a rich man dies, he is loaded with his possessions like a prisoner with chains. I will die free, death will be easy for me."

"Life for me," continued Lee, "is like a hungry crocodile. I'd better defend myself. I have to defend myself against the stupidity of this world. It is enormous! Life must be the work of a perfect idiot. Or maybe the stupidity, like breaking of the atom, is self–perpetuating?"

"The philosophers talk but you did it," said Lee enviously. "This trip of yours, what a freedom! 3,600 miles on foot on tough trails of Latin America. This demanded a complete change in life — willingly, suddenly, for this you needed an extraordinary moral audacity."

What I liked about him [Oswald] was that he was a seeker for justice — that he had highly developed social instincts. And I was disappointed in my own children for lack of such instincts.

Next the personalities of Lee and of Gary [de Mohrenschildt's son] clashed. Lee considered Gary a spoiled, rich American, foolish youngster and Gary looked down at him as a supercilious, unpractical lunatic with revolutionary ideas.

Maybe, had he [Oswald] lived longer, he would have fitted better into the scheme of American life, he would have joined the group of love–children, would have grown a beard and certainly would have been among the protesters against the war in Viet–Nam.

"What was most annoying to you in the Soviet Union?" Asked Jeanne who was listening in.

"Those endless, endless meetings we had to attend after work, listening to those deadly, monotonous speeches. You were lucky if you were in the back and could take a nap .... We listened to those bureaucratic outpourings half–dazed, like children during a very boring lesson. Then we voted, rather indifferently, on various trivial issues. Later we would file out, exhausted and would return home. And," Lee smiled, "we never received any extra pay for the hours lost, and we certainly deserved it."

I can visualize him cutting a path of Casanova among the Russian women. And why not? He was a foreigner, he acted freely, he looked pleasantly and his interest in Russian people was warm and genuine.

His own element of self–inquiry, self–denial and self–doubt, mixed with instability worried Lee. But I told him not to worry, in my opinion instability, doubt, constant search were elements of youth and were indicative of exuberant life.

A strong desire for adventure was also one of Lee's motivations. That's why he became a marine, that's why he switched jobs just because he did not like what he had to do so far. And routine was deadly to him. However, his last job at the printing company fitted him well and he seemed fairly happy.

"Why didn't you stay in the Marine Corps?" I asked him one day.

"Oh, I did not care for the military, not much fun, not much adventure either."

"You could become an officer, you are intelligent enough," I countered.

"Oh, no, to hell with being an officer, I don't like to command other guys."

"That Marine Corps was the most miserable period in my life," he said disgustedly. "Stupid work, ignorant companions, abusive officers. Boy, was I happy to have gotten out of it. To hell with the Navy."

One day Lee brought to me typescripts of his experiences in Russia. He was interested in publishing them in a form of an article in a magazine or possibly to develop them into a book. A few typed pages, and poorly at that, in substance could not add much to what he had already told me. And what he had told me was of interest only to me, because I was familiar with the locale, but not to other readers.

Lee was indeed all wrapped up in his work, books, his ideas on equality of all people, especially of all races; it was strange indeed for a boy New Orleans and Texas poor white family, purely Anglo, to be so profoundly anti–racist. "Segregation in any form, racial, social or economic, is one of the most repulsive facts of American life", he often told me. "I would be willing any time to fight these fascistic segregationists — and to die for my black brothers."

We talked pleasantly of his job, of June [the first Oswald daughter] who was growing nicely and we also spoke of the unfortunate rise of ultra–conservatism in this country, of racist movement in the

> South. Lee considered this the most dangerous phenomenon for all peace–loving people. "Economic discrimination is bad, but you can remedy it," he said, "but racial discrimination cannot be remedied because you cannot change the color of your skin." Of course, he greatly admired Dr. Martin Luther King and agreed with his program. I just mention it here, but he frequently talked of Dr. King with a real reverence.
>
> But Lee did not like the communist party either. "In Russia party members are mostly opportunists, carrying their cards proudly in order to get better jobs, or they forced into the party by the circumstances or families."
>
> I remember that Lee did not like any political parties, anywhere. He was just a native–born nonconformist.[129]

As Lee Oswald moved away from the Russian community in Fort Worth in pursuit of work in Dallas, the de Mohrenschildts and other Russian friends were increasingly left as a support base for Marina, especially as there appeared to be increased strain between Lee and Marina. De Mohrenschildt noted that strain was likely exacerbated by Marina, who often talked about the gifts the family was receiving from the Russian-speaking community and how successful many of them had become, owning homes and automobiles.[130]

Those sorts of things impressed Marina, but had never been an interest for Lee. Such a disconnect in interests had not been an issue in Russia, with Oswald having his own apartment, a healthy wage from his factory job—and with home and car ownership simply not relevant to the average Russian worker. Yet despite Oswald's own lack of interest in such things, it is hard to imagine that his wife's remarks would not have annoyed him.[131]

Chapter 7

Lee and Marina

". . . he wanted to see me and he came that evening and he cried and said that he wanted me to return home because if I did not return, he did not want to continue living. He said he didn't know how to love me in any other way and that he will try to change."

—Marina Oswald, testifying about one of the times in which she and Lee were separated, Warren Commission Hearings, Volume 1, 11

Separations

With Lee in Dallas, looking for work, Marina and baby June first stayed with Elena Hall in Fort Worth, then at Gary Taylor's house in Dallas. While there, Mrs. de Mohrenschildt took her to a clinic on three separate days, and Goerge Bouhe provided the money for Marina's dental care.

Oswald did receive advice on his job search. De Mohrenschildt referred him to a friend in Dallas—with no results. In turn, Bouhe suggested the Texas Employment Commission, and Anna Meller provided a connection to a counselor in the Commission's clerical and sales division in Dallas. Oswald visited that office on October 9, stated he wanted to find job outside the industrial or mechanical skills area, and that he had an interest in writing.

At that point Oswald was turned over to the clerical division, and to Mrs. Cunningham, the friend of the Mellers. The general aptitude tests he had first taken at the Fort Worth employment office suggested that he did have some aptitude for clerical work, "outstanding verbal-clerical potential" and a potential for both skilled and semi-skilled jobs, with even some indication that he could do college-level work.

Mrs. Cunningham gave him three special tests: for general clerical work, work as an insurance claims examiner, and drafting work. He scored high on all three. His application form indicated that he did not have a driver's license, and noted: "well-groomed and spoken, business suit, alert replies—expresses self extremely well." He told Mrs. Cunningham that he hoped to develop qualifications for responsible junior executive employment by a work-study program at a local college, but that this must be delayed because of his immediate financial needs and responsibilities.[132]

Mrs. Cunningham concluded that although Oswald would be classified for clerical work, she should try to get him any available job, since he badly needed money. He was referred to an architect for an opening as a messenger, but was not hired. On October 11, he was referred to Jaggars-Chiles-Stovall Co., a graphic arts company, in response to a call from John Graef, head of the photographic department of the company, who had told the employment commission that he needed a photo-print trainee.

Oswald was enthusiastic about his prospects for such a job, and apparently made a good impression; Graef picked him over several other applicants.[133] On the following day he began working in his new position as a trainee, making prints of advertising material. He worked a 40-hour week at approximately $1.35 per hour; his take-home pay varied from $49 to $74 a week. According to Marina, initially "he liked his work very much."

Oswald moved into the YMCA in Dallas on October 15, and stayed there until October 19, paying $2.25 a night. He had used the Taylors' address and telephone number as a place where he could be reached, but on October 9 had also rented Dallas post office box 2915 under his own name at the main post office on Ervay Street. On October 10, he filed a change-of-address form indicating that mail for 2703 Mercedes Street should be forwarded to the post office box. Marina has written that Oswald wrote her letters and telephoned her during the separation while looking for a job in Dallas.[134]

On October 16, Mrs. Hall brought Marina and June to Dallas to have June baptized. Marina apparently did this surreptitiously, because Lee opposed baptism; they did not contact him in Dallas, but left birthday gifts for him at the Taylors. Oswald did not appear very disturbed when he found out about the baptism. Two days later, Mrs. Hall had an automobile accident and went to the hospital, where she remained until October 26; Marina remained in the Hall house. Mrs. Max Clark and Alexander Kleinlerer, a friend of Mrs. Hall, checked up to make sure that she was getting along without too much trouble. After Oswald left the YMCA on October 19, he moved to a room or apartment somewhere in Dallas, which was never located nor documented. It seems likely, however, that during that time he spent several weekends with Marina when she and June were alone at the Hall house.[135]

Four days after Mrs. Hall was released from the hospital, she left for New York to visit friends. By the time she returned, Marina had moved into a three-room apartment at 604 Elsbeth Street in Dallas with Lee, which Oswald had rented on Saturday, November 3. The landlady stated that Oswald had looked at the apartment about a week before. The monthly rent was $68, in addition to which he had to pay several dollars a month for utilities. He paid the rent plus a $5 deposit on November 3, but probably spent that night with Marina at the Hall house. On Sunday the Taylors helped the couple move their belongings to the Elsbeth Street apartment with a rented trailer. Oswald had asked

Kleinlerer to help them move, and Kleinlerer also was present when they departed.[136]

Conflicted

It certainly appears that Lee did want to bring his family together—outside the influence of the Russian community that had been primarily supportive of Marina—and it seems that Lee and Marina had remained attached to each other while separated. Yet once reunited, their marital difficulties started again. While they were moving to Elsbeth Street, Kleinlerer noticed that Oswald slapped his wife for not having the zipper on her dress completely closed. They also argued over his refusal to allow her to smoke. There was another quarrel when Oswald told the landlady that Marina was from Czechoslovakia. Oswald became angry when Marina, who disapproved of this deception, told the landlady the truth.[137]

Reportedly, several people tried to help Marina improve her initially scanty knowledge of English, but Oswald discouraged her from speaking English as he wanted to maintain and develop his own Russian language skills. Virtually everyone in contact with the two described ongoing conflicts, and at one point Marina told de Mohrenschildt that she really should "get away" from Oswald.

When de Mohrenschildt criticized Oswald's conduct with Marina, Oswald replied, "It is my business." Marina herself testified that after they moved into the Elsbeth Street apartment, even with a steady job Lee became "nervous and irritable" and would become angry over "trifles." However, she acknowledged that at times she did things which irritated him and led to fights. Once she had written to a former boyfriend in Russia, saying she wished she had married him—the letter was returned for postage due; Oswald read it and became agitated.[138]

The Warren Commission made much of the couple's marital conflicts, which certainly did exist, and emphasized the idea that Oswald was violent and physical with his wife. Given that both Marina and

Lee could be emotional, it seems likely that things did sometimes get physical (de Mohrenschildt observed scratches on Oswald on at least one occasion). Their relationship became so tense at times that some of those in the Russian expatriate community suggested that Marina leave Oswald. Some even went further, offering their assistance if she chose that course.[139] George Bouhe personally offered to help her if she promised to leave Oswald permanently.

Oswald consistently argued with her over things such as her smoking, and she protested his tendency to be controlling. Other realities set in as well; Marina admitted that in Russia Oswald had been something "out of the ordinary;" he stood out from the average Russian man as being "easygoing, loose and alert," and after their whirlwind courtship they enjoyed a relatively easy life in Russia. But in America, Oswald struggled to find even moderately-paying jobs, and he had little interest in material things—their apartments were always minimally furnished, and they had no car, unlike most Americans.

Because of their constant quarreling, a few of their acquaintances felt that Marina would be better off alone. Finally, in early November, Marina, aided by the de Mohrenschildts, moved into Anna Meller's house with the intention not to return to Oswald. Oswald was apparently quite upset and did not want Marina to leave him. But he did not visit her at Anna Meller's house, and for a short time he had apparently not even known where she was. According to Marina, once he located her, he called, and they met at de Mohrenschildt's house. Oswald asked her to return home. She insisted that he stop quarreling and that he change his ways. He said that he could not change. Marina would not agree to return home with him, and he left.[140]

Marina was uncomfortable at the Meller house, where there was very little room. She moved to Katherine Ford's house where she apparently stayed from November 11 to 17. She indicated that she had decided never to return to her husband; it was Mrs. Ford's impression that Marina was going to stay at other people's houses until a permanent place could be found for her.[141] When Mr. Ford returned from a business trip on November 17, Marina and June moved to the home of Mrs. Frank Ray, where they spent the day. Mrs. Ray, the wife of a Dallas advertising man, was also of Russian origin. Since Mrs. Ray had no baby bed, Marina returned to the Fords that evening. On the next day, however, Marina moved her belongings to the Rays' house. That same day, Oswald called and asked to visit his wife, whom he had been calling and writing. Mr. Ray picked him up and took him to Marina.[142]

Marina testified that at this meeting Oswald professed his love for her. She stated: "I saw him cry . . . [he] begged me to come back, asked my forgiveness, and promised that he would try to improve, if only I would come back." On another occasion she said: ". . . he cried, and you know a woman's heart—I went back to him. He said he didn't care to live if I did not return." That same day she decided to return to him. Mr. Ray packed her belongings and took her back to the Elsbeth Street apartment.[143] The reality in the couple's relationship was that—regardless of the tension, conflicts, and separations—Marina repeatedly accepted Lee's apologies and appeals to reunite the family. After such reunions, it appears that both Lee and Marina would get along together for a time. But inevitably their problems would resume.

Members of the Russian community who had made a special effort to find Marina places to live apart from Oswald felt that their efforts had been in vain. George Bouhe was so irritated that he never again tried to help either of the Oswalds.[144] Contacts between the couple and members of the Russian community largely came to an end during the fall of 1962. George de Mohrenschildt and his wife would be the only ones to maintain any sort of ongoing relationship over the Christmas holidays and into 1963. Lee had accepted a Thanksgiving invitation to a family dinner at his brother Robert's, and the get-together seems to have gone well, with Robert talking about Lee's active interest in June. Yet after a few phone calls and a couple of letters, Oswald once again dropped out of any active personal contact with Robert, although he did continue routine correspondence and the exchange of cards and letters with his and Marina's friends in Russia.

In December Oswald even sent a New Year's greeting card, in Russian and signed Marina and Lee Oswald, wishing "health, success and all of the best" to the employees at the Soviet Embassy in New York City. The card appears to have been a precursor to a new series of contacts with the Soviet Embassy which began very early in 1963.

Despite the Oswalds' break with the Russian community, de Mohrenschildt, knowing that they would be alone during the Christmas season, asked the Fords whether he could bring the couple to a party celebrating the Russian Christmas at their home; the Fords assented. The party was attended by many members of the Russian community. Oswald spoke at length with Yaeko Okui, a Japanese woman who had been brought to the party by Lev Aronson, first cellist of the Dallas Symphony Orchestra; she told Federal investigators that she never saw Oswald again. The Oswalds were not invited to three other Russian Christmas season gatherings which occurred during the next few days.[145]

Marina, by herself, visited with the de Mohrenschildts several times after Christmas. They invited both Lee and Marina to a small dinner party in February 1963; also present were Everett Glover, a chemist employed in Dallas, and his roommate Volkmar Schmidt. On February 22, Glover had a gathering at his house, one of the purposes of which was to permit his friends, many of whom were studying Russian, to meet the Oswalds. They were the objects of much attention.[146]

Marina conversed at length with another guest named Ruth Paine, who had recently separated from her husband, Michael Paine, a research engineer at the Bell Helicopter plant in Fort Worth. Mrs. Paine, who was studying Russian, obtained Marina's address and shortly thereafter wrote Marina asking to see her. Marina responded by inviting Mrs. Paine to visit her. There was likely some foundation for the two women to bond, given Marina's constant problems with Lee and Ruth Paine's own recent physical separation from her own husband.[147]

Disconnected

In an apartment and with at least a regular income (and apart from their former friends whose lifestyles offended Lee and likely contributed to Marina's discontent), the couple settled into something of a routine, with Marina focused on routine family matters, and Lee with new interests that absorbed more of his personal time and to some extent provided some personal "space" between the two. Oswald had always enjoyed taking pictures and both his time in the Marines and in Russia are well-documented in his photos. His new job at the Jaggars-Chiles-Stovall company led to a resurgence of that interest, and he began to devote a good deal of time to developing and working with photographic images.

At that point in time, Oswald appears also to have begun using the name "Alek James Hidell." Alek/Alec is a name found in exchanges with his friends in Russia and even on paperwork from his time there, including on his application to join a factory shooting club. In 1963 the name Alek can be found on identification cards which Oswald may have produced with equipment at Jaggars-Chiles-Stovall. Reportedly one of his fellow employees taught him various photographic techniques, which he could have used to prepare not only these cards, but also the samples of his photographic work which he sent to various organizations.[148]

But fundamentally Oswald's interests were much deeper than any photographic hobby, and he increasingly turned to spending his free time with books, newsletters, and periodicals. It seems that one of the disconnects between him and Marina was simply Lee's overriding interest in books—serious books, literature, politics. Marina noticed a few of the books he was reading, books of a historical nature, including H. G. Wells' two-volume "Outline of History," and biographies of Hitler, Kennedy, and Khrushchev. According to one complaint expressed by Marina, Oswald was much more interested in books and reading than in sex.

While Lee retained an attachment for Marina and appeared genuinely fond of baby June, he was apparently not showing his wife much in the way of regular, ongoing affection, certainly not at the level he had when dating Marina or in the months immediately after their marriage in Russia. Marina complained to de Mohrenschildt's wife Jeanne that even though Lee was working regularly he spent most of his time by himself at home, and generally paid little attention to her, either in conversation or physically. "He comes home tired, hardly talks to me, only to the baby, then reads Russian books and is seldom tender and loving to me."

There is little doubt that the move to America had seriously undermined their relationship, and Marina showed no hesitation in being increasingly critical of Lee—the constant quarrels and complaints resumed:

> "He is so puny, so dull, he never drinks, only works, tires easily, is only interested in books,"—remarks Marina made not only made privately, but directly to Oswald himself. "He goes to bed with me so rarely now. Once in a couple of weeks. He makes me so god–damn frustrated."[149]

De Mohrenschildt also noted that Lee was somewhat obsessed with Russian books, culture, and the language itself. "Incidentally I never saw him interested in anything else except Russian books and magazines. He said he did not want to forget the language—but it amazed me that he read such difficult writers like Gorki, Dostoevski, Gogol, Tolstoi and Turgenieff—in Russian. . . . I taught Russian at all levels in a large university, and I never saw such a proficiency in the best senior students who constantly listened to Russian tapes and spoke to Russian friends."[150]

Yet Marina remained attached to Oswald. She was dependent on Lee for support. Despite their issues, Marina was a mother and homemaker, and for periods the couple appears to have been a functioning as a normal, if relatively poor, family. And Marina did become pregnant for the second time. At the beginning of 1963, after the first of the year, Lee had determined to take advice he had received from George Bouhe back in October 1962, and decided that a typing course would prepare him for better jobs and aid his efforts to become a writer.

On January 14, 1963, he enrolled in a night typing course at the Crozier Technical High School, and started attending on January 28. The class ran from 6:15 to 7:15 p.m. on Mondays, Tuesday, and Thursdays. Although Oswald reviewed a typing textbook at home, he attended the course irregularly and finally stopped going altogether some three months later, around March 28.[151]

Despite some improvements, the relationship between Lee and Marina remained marginal in many respects, and by February 1963 Oswald had begun a series of letters to the Russian Embassy in New York. The correspondence would all be regarding Marina and June returning to Russia; the letters were signed by Marina. In her own testimony Marina stated that at times Oswald would talk about her and the baby going back to Russia, at other times all three of them—but her basic take on it was that he was that he "didn't want her around anymore."[152]

In February 1963, a letter signed by Marina and sent to the Soviet Embassy in New York specifically requested aid in returning Marina, with her baby, to her homeland while "my husband remains here, since he is an American by Nationality."[153] The embassy responded in March that she would have to fill out a formal application and upon receipt it would take five to six months to process and provide a response.

The effort to get Marina (and possibly Lee) back to Russia continued though the spring of 1963, and in July Oswald wrote the New York Russian Embassy requesting urgent action on Marina's application because she was expecting a second child in October—also stating that any return visa application for himself would be a separate matter. It would not be until August that the Soviets responded in writing that Marina's request were being forwarded to Moscow to "begin" its processing, indicating that the Oswalds should expect no return to Russia for Marina, June, and the new baby in 1963.[154]

The effort to return Marina and the children to Russia would be one of two constants for Lee Oswald during 1963, beginning in Dallas at the first of the year, through the family's time in New Orleans, and after their return to Dallas. Oswald would continue to pursue the matter with the Soviet Embassy up until the time of his death—however, the correspondence was all about Marina and the baby. Oswald himself was left as a separate issue, and with highly questionable prospects of an authorized return. The second constant for Lee, though not Marina, would be a growing interest in Cuba.

Even prior to the Oswald's post-Easter move to New Orleans, Oswald himself had become much more focused on Cuba, and according to Marina began to talk about living there, favoring it as compared to his time in the Soviet Union. Marina described Oswald as regarding Fidel Castro as a hero and being very willing to work for Castro and the Cuban cause. It appeared to her that living in Cuba was something which had begun to seriously interest Lee. She also noted that when in New Orleans, Lee asked her to sign the name Hidell; she assumed that he was using it consciously as a variation from "Fidel."

Chapter 8

Marina on Lee

"The main reason is homesickness....one learns it only in a foreign land. My husband expresses a sincere desire to return with me to USSR. I earnestly beg you to help him in this. There is nothing much to encourage us here and nothing to hold us...my husband is often unemployed... Make us happy again, help us return that which we lost because of our foolishness."

—Marina Oswald's appeal to the Russian Embassy in March, 1963, Warren Commission Exhibit 986

As with George de Mohrenschildt, the skeptical/conspiracy-oriented view of Lee Oswald (which most often see him as a "patsy" of some sort in the assassination) has often rejected Marina Oswald as a credible source on her husband's character and behavior. To some extent, that view rests on the fact that Warren Commission attorneys questioned Marina in a manner to elicit and focus on remarks which portrayed Lee Oswald negatively, positioning him as having become increasingly isolated, and even violent.

Approaching Marina Oswald as a source is also made challenging given that little attention has been paid to both the timing and the situational nature of her various interviews and interrogations. Her questioning largely occurred in three discrete sets of interviews, and each had a different focus and agenda for those conducting the questioning. Despite that, her remarks are often lumped together and critiqued as if they had been made at the same time, to the same individuals, and under the same circumstances—which was definitely not the case.

Her first interviews (11/22–11/27, 1963), carried out with her husband in custody and then following his murder, were conducted initially by the Secret Service and then the FBI. Questions were focused on her knowledge of Oswald's more recent activities, contacts with others, and a solicitation of information which would support the initial criminal charges and developing legal case against him. A study of those interviews shows that Marina was quite cautious in her remarks, intentionally withholding information that would have presented Oswald in a negative or incriminating light.

It is also clear that she responded differently to the Secret Service, which was treating her in a protective and supportive manner. The Secret Service Russian translator (Leon Gopadze), whom the Secret Service had brought in from a California office, not only assisted with interview translations and with Marina's testimony to the Warren Commission, but also assisted her as an intermediary when she acquired a representative to handle her personal affairs, business matters, and contracts. The Secret Service openly took the position that its role with Mrs. Oswald was strictly that of a protective nature.[155]

Marina's attitude and dealings with the FBI were of a quite different nature, shaped by negative remarks Oswald had made about that agency over time, beginning with the first interview the FBI had with him upon the couple's arrival in Fort Worth in 1962. Oswald's lack of cooperation and bad attitude was noted in the FBI's report on that interview. Oswald had been annoyed with the FBI's questioning; later he would react to his mail being opened (suspecting the FBI), and most recently had been upset by—and directly protested to the local

FBI office—the approach and questioning of his wife at the Paine residence. He considered that to be harassment; the FBI was apparently sensitive to that issue as well given that, following the assassination, they covered up the visit by altering his personal notebook—the notebook that had recorded the visit and had been taken into evidence.

Oswald had been clearly upset by that approach to his wife, even suggesting in a letter to the Russian Embassy that the FBI was either trying to block Marina's return to Russia or somehow persuade her to defect. Given her husband's attitude towards the FBI and that most recent experience with its agents, it is understandable that Oswald's attitude and remarks would have influenced Marina's reaction to being questioned by FBI agents.

That attitude was captured by a Secret Service agent recording a joint Secret Service/FBI interview on November 27, 1963. That agent (acting as the translator for Marina) noted that Marina was being uncooperative, that she was tired, with a sick child, and that she did not like the FBI as she felt it had caused her husband to lose his job in New Orleans. In that interview she stated that her husband had never spoken against President Kennedy. Oswald had not talked politics with her—he felt women should not be in politics—and she did not know of any of his associates. She described him as strong-willed, stubborn, hot-headed, and with his own opinions about everything (a personal characterization she would consistently repeat during all her interviews and one that seems consistent with his own history). She also affirmed that—based strictly on what she was being told at that time—she accepted he had killed the president.[156]

Some of Marina's earliest statements, made under Secret Service and FBI interrogation, can be shown to have been provably incomplete or false—most specifically regarding photographs of Oswald posing with a rifle and pistol, photographs still in the family's possession at the time of Oswald's arrest. It should be noted that similar false or misleading statements were also made by Oswald himself. At the conclusion of her first round of interviews, Marina certainly had made herself open to charges of obstructing justice, based on the information she was withholding.

In those earliest interviews, Marina herself was clearly under special stress, as a Soviet citizen potentially suspected by the FBI regarding foreign influence over Oswald. There was the possibility that she herself would be presented as a Soviet agent, or an accessory to crimes by her husband. Both Lee and Marina had been monitored by the FBI for signs of communist or other subversive contacts following their appearance in Fort Worth and Dallas. FBI agent Hosty later wrote of being particularly suspicious of Marina as a foreign agent.[157]

Aside from that concern, which certainly would have encouraged her to restrict and be cautious with her remarks, a more situational view suggests that at least some elements of Marina's initial obfuscation appear to have been directly related to questions which might have tied her personally to certain of Oswald's activities. Under questioning, she would have realized certain things she had done could be considered not just illegal, but suggestive of complicity. Beyond that, it must be noted that despite being discussed as a suspect in FBI memos, she was offered no legal advice and received none; in addition, all her replies were filtered through a Russian translator provided by a government agency.

Beyond her initial post-assassination interviews, we now have a much fuller view into the extent to which Marina was later treated as a hostile witness, after a note was discovered in her possessions which was determined by the FBI to connect Oswald to the Walker shooting. The existence of the note, and any reference or remark about what Oswald had told her about his involvement in that, was something that Marina had chosen not to disclose—however, she immediately acknowledged it upon being shown the actual note. From that point on she was repeatedly questioned over some three weeks by the FBI as they conducted their own investigation of the Walker shooting. That investigation and her responses to it will be discussed in the following chapter.

Whatever her motivation—support of her husband, self-protection—as soon as Marina was shown the "Walker note" she would certainly have realized she had placed herself legally at risk for withholding information as well as having destroyed other potential evidence related to her husband's activities. She was further exposed legally due to having placed false signatures on forged documents and having withheld and destroyed evidence in the form of copies of photographs of Oswald with a rifle and pistol. During that second round of FBI questioning, she was at a point in time, lasting over some two months, when virtually anything she might say could be used not only against her deceased husband, but potentially against her.

With that as context, her next round of questioning was of an entirely different nature, in the form of sworn testimony given to Warren Commission lawyers. Marina's Warren Commission testimony has been viewed as especially damning by Warren Commission skeptics given that it did allow her to be quoted in remarks the Warren Commission found useful in its presentation of Oswald in its final report.

Under oath, she admitted that she had indeed signed one and possibly more false documents for her husband (such as Oswald's FPCC membership card); there is reason to believe that he may well have asked her to sign other false identification cards. There is even speculation the she may have signed the money order using the Hidell name which was used to order a rifle—or even collected the rifle from the post office.[158] Her changing remarks about signatures raised Warren Commission staff concerns about her credibility in regard to any items of evidence, even if it was being motivated by her caution and a desire to protect herself.

Marina did admit her knowledge of the so called "backyard" photographs showing Oswald with a rifle and pistol, although her remarks on the photographs were limited and sometimes contradictory. She also provided extended remarks related to the so called "Walker note," including describing a conversation which directly implicated Lee in a shooting attempt targeting General Walker. Those were not responses the skeptical community would later find acceptable; neither was her explanation that she had threatened Oswald with reporting him to the police and on another occasion stopped him from carrying his pistol in public. Still, those remarks under oath were in line with statements she had given to the FBI during their Walker shooting investigation.[159]

Marina's statements to the Warren Commission went well beyond what she had revealed in her very first post-assassination interviews, yet were consistent with what she had told the FBI during their extended investigation following the discovery of the "Walker note," found in her own personal belongings. It must also be noted that in interviews by the Commission she was giving testimony under oath and that she had been informed that she was expected to be honest. She may also have been advised that in so doing she would not face personal consequences for those disclosures which would implicate her in previous obstruction or other illegal acts. That possibility is suggested by in her own remarks, as provided by her translator:[160]

> Mrs. Oswald: Yes. I said before I had never seen it [the rifle] before. But I think you understand. I want to help you, and that is why there is no reason for concealing anything. I will not be charged with anything.
>
> Mr. Gopadze: She says she was not sworn in before. But now in as much as she is sworn in, she is going to tell the truth.

Warren Commission skeptics have tended to reject Marina as a source on Oswald due to her offering information on both the "backyard" photographs and Oswald's involvement in the Walker shooting. In contrast, the Warren Commission staff criticized her regarding instances in which she simply declined having detailed knowledge of Oswald's activities (many of which occurred when they were not living together), or when she remained vague or was inconsistent regarding dates of events—in other words, when she was not providing specifics to sustain points which would have supported an incriminating view of her husband. The committee's own report made much of how disconnected the couple were, yet ignored that issue with respect to her questioning and the details they were attempting to obtain from her.

As an example, Marina offered no specifics as to how or exactly when Oswald acquired both a rifle and a pistol that spring. But the FBI had shown the rifle in evidence to have been ordered by mail, with a coupon from a sporting magazine Marina would have been most unlikely to have ever seen. It is also clear that many of Oswald's own personal interests were not discussed in any detail with Marina, an example being his emerging focus on Cuba—seen in his correspondence with the Fair Play for Cuba Committee, which he began in May while the couple was still in Dallas.[161]

Marina herself explained her apparent vagueness and lack of details regarding her husband's activities with consistent assertions that conversations between the couple were limited to routine daily affairs, and that they did not discuss Oswald's interests or activities (in which Marina admittedly had little interest or even disparaged). Those assertions were sustained in the Commission's own narrative of the relationship between the couple, and numerous other sources describe that as a pattern of behavior that developed between the two following their arrival in the United States.

Issues related to Marina's testimony and remarks related to both the weapons, and the photographs of Oswald holding them will be discussed in more detail as we proceed. However, given her consistency in description of Oswald's personality, his general nature, and specifically his behavior patterns during 1963—and the fact that they are corroborated by other individuals who were directly in contact with him—it would be an error to reject her as a relevant source on his character simply because she said uncomfortable or negative things about him.

In accordance with best practices in historical work, and in an effort to bring in as much balance as possible into characterizing Oswald's character and general behavior, this work treats Marina Oswald as a credible source in regard to her husband when those remarks can be shown to be consistent and corroborated by others—including in Oswald's own writing and statements.

Chapter 9

A Turn to Activism

"...fascism must be abolished, nationalism excluded from everyday life, racial segregation or discrimination abolished by law, dissemination of war propaganda be forbidden as well as the manufacture of weapons of mass destruction..."

—excerpted from Oswald's monograph *The Athenian System*, written during the spring of 1963, Warren Commission Exhibit 98

Reading and Writing

The Oswalds moved out of their Elsbeth Street apartment on March 3, 1963, to an upstairs apartment several blocks away at 214 West Neely Street. Oswald inquired about the apartment in response to a "For Rent" sign; the rent was $60 per month, not including utilities. They moved without assistance, carrying their belongings in their hands and in a baby stroller. Marina preferred the Neely Street apartment because it had a porch and was, she felt, more suitable for June.[162]

Ruth Paine had become Marina's main social contact in the spring of 1963, with Marina having remained somewhat alienated from many of her earlier Russian friends because of their issues with her husband, but also because several of them were simply worn out with caring for her during her separations from Lee, only to find her returning to him. While Marina and Lee had once again reached some level of accommodation (a second child would be conceived during this period) and were living together, they were largely left to themselves.

Ruth Paine and Marina started to exchange visits in March. Mrs. Paine invited the couple for dinner, and on April 20, she took them on a picnic. When Lee was not present, the two women frequently discussed their respective marital problems, and Marina disclosed to Mrs. Paine that she was pregnant. Marina described their meetings:[163]

> "One day we were invited to a friend's house, where I met Ruth Paine, who was studying Russian here in America and wanted to improve her conversational knowledge. We began to see each other. Ruth would come to see me with her children. This was very good for both me and for June. She was growing up alone and becoming terribly wild, so the company of other children was good for her. Sometimes we went out on picnics at a nearby lake. Lee loved to fish, and we would look and rejoice if he caught a little fish. Several times I even made soup out of the fish which we caught by our own efforts. Several times we went to visit Ruth who lived in Irving."

Marina also noted that when they moved into the Neely Street residence Lee had set himself up something of a small office in a closet, spending a great deal of his time at home either reading or writing there. She left him to that, and the two had limited time and communications with each other. While Marina showed no particular interest in either Lee's reading or writing, fortunately we have considerable independent evidence on both—based on materials in his possession at the time he was arrested.

Oswald's reading had always been at the heart of his political world views. His social contacts in Japan had expanded on the geopolitical aspect of those, as had his experiences in Russia with the Soviet system. But a direct personal exposure to the Soviet system had left him disappointed, still seeking answers to the social and political issues that continued to hold his interest.

In 1963, Oswald's reading materials, samples of which were taken into evidence at the time of his arrest, included *The Nation* (a progressive American biweekly magazine that covers political and cultural news, opinion, and analysis), *The Militant* (obtained by subscription from the Socialist Workers Party), *The Worker* (obtained by subscription from the Communist Party of the United States of America), *The New Republic* (an American progressive magazine with commentary on politics, contemporary culture, and the arts), as well as *The Road to Socialism* and *Hands Off Cuba*. Oswald also collected a large variety of pamphlets, brochures, and other literature in Russian.

But in early 1963, Oswald turned from simply reading about social and political systems and geopolitics to writing about those subjects. That writing went far beyond the notes he had put into his *Historic Diary*[164] regarding his time in Russia. It included not only his observations and commentary on the Soviet system but extended on to broader topics such as communism and capitalism, and beyond that to observations on the basic nature of political and social structures.[165] A list of his writings that spring, which were included in the Warren Commission's volumes, is as follows:

- The Collective Life of a Russian Worker
- On Communism and Capitalism
- The Communist Party of the United States
- The Athenian System / Outline and Principles

In his *The Athenian System* monograph, Oswald focused on the elements which he felt were the real driving force behind his views on inequality and poverty. He wanted free education and free healthcare. Capitalism was not something he totally rejected, and individual freedoms had to be preserved—but nobody was to be denied access to such basic needs and services.[166]

As Oswald was returning to his long-term interests in social and political systems, he also appears to have become progressively less interested in the photographic aspects of his job at Jaggars-Chiles-Stovall. There is little indication that his tendency to become easily bored had tempered. During the spring of 1963, Oswald appears to have once again begun to experience the boredom which we find repeatedly undermined his ability to fit into the routine elements of his jobs or even family life.

That tendency towards boredom, and its impact on his jobs and his social life, is something that developed during his school years and would become a constant in his behavior. After a positive entry into the Marine Corps, Oswald had done well in testing and in his technical training and had achieved good performance and job reviews. That continued in his early days in his career field and after his deployment to Japan.

Yet after "settling in" and expanding his social horizons with Japanese locals, Oswald had an accident in barracks with a small pistol, received disciplinary action, and began to increasingly assert himself with both officers and NCOs in his chain of command. The net result was more disciplinary action, the termination of his effort to extend his tour in Japan, and a demotion at the time he was likely to have been promoted to Corporal. Once back in the United States his interest and attention turned from the Marines to prospects of adventure overseas, an interest in Cuba and the Central American revolutions, and then to Russia and the Soviet experience.

Inside Russia, that same pattern of enthusiasm followed by boredom repeated itself. With a relatively good but not challenging job, a superior income, and apartment and an active social life, Oswald eventually became bored with the factory, dismissive of his fellow workers, a challenge for his superiors, and expressed a general dissatisfaction with the Soviet system in general. At one point Oswald even launched a "one man strike" at the factory, a real embarrassment for the factory administration and his supervisors and which once again earned him the reputation of being an oddball at work and the "factory clown."[167]

Back in the United States, that same pattern repeated itself once again. On April 6, 1963, Oswald's employment at Jaggars-Chiles-Stovall was terminated. The reason given was that, in his supervisor's opinion, even though he was trying, Oswald was not effectively or efficiently doing the work he was assigned. In retrospect, Oswald once again had been viewed as something of an "oddball" at Jaggars-Chiles-Stovall; he "barged around the plant" according to co-worker Dennis Ofstein and brought a Russian newspaper into the workplace on one occasion. Yet his oddball behavior did not get Oswald released; once again it was his lack of commitment to the job. The manager of the group where Oswald worked testified that it was routine to give a "trainee" something like six months to measure up to the job, and if they were not judged to be productive in the work, they were routinely terminated. Oswald's termination had occurred at the end of that six months' time frame.

It appears that yet again, Oswald had handicapped himself due to loss of interest in his work, and a failure to commit to advancing in his job while still a trainee. The same thing had happened in the Marines and even in a Russian factory. Promising starts were followed by a failure to fully engage with the job on an ongoing basis. After losing his job at Jaggars-Chiles-Stovall, Oswald immediately began a job search, starting with the Texas Employment Commission. On April 8, he informed the Commission that he was seeking employment but had been referred to no employers. He stated that he had been laid off due to "lack of work."[168]

Boredom, at work or in his personal life, appears to have been Oswald's Achilles heel. Again and again, his enthusiasms gave way to boredom and a need for change—a search for new experiences, new adventures. As Lee had remarked to de Mohrenschildt, he was probably his own worst enemy, looking for something that he was never going to find—but totally unwilling to stop the search. And, bored and uninterested in his job, Oswald's core interests and beliefs appear at the heart of his turn to not just reading and writing, but to action.

Taking Action

In March 1963, Oswald had begun an exchange of letters with the Fair Play for Cuba Committee, inquiring about membership and asking for copies of pro-Cuba leaflets. Given that Oswald was notoriously frugal, it is interesting that his first letter to the FPCC was sent via Air Mail. In that letter he described already having demonstrated for Cuba using a handmade placard. In response the FPCC did send fifty leaflets to Oswald in Dallas, some of which he would use after relocating to New Orleans in late April.

There is one Dallas Police report confirming that a pro-Cuba demonstration had been carried out in Dallas—it was reported to police, but when they arrived at the scene and approached the protester he had fled, with no positive identification being obtained.[169] That incident had occurred in downtown Dallas, at the corner of Main and Ervay, in front of the H. L. Green Variety store. The store was a popular one, in a busy area of downtown, and located along the bus route that Oswald routinely took to work.[170]

Beyond leafletting for Castro, in March Oswald also appears to have begun taking his opposition to racism and the danger of the ultra-right from talk to action. When de Mohrenschildt and his wife visited the Oswalds in mid-April, the two men's conversations turned to a discussion of "the unfortunate rise of ultra–conservatism in this country, of racist movement in the South":

> Lee considered this the most dangerous phenomenon for all peace–loving people. "Economic discrimination is bad, but you can remedy it...but racial discrimination cannot be remedied because you cannot change the color of your skin." Of course, he greatly admired

> Dr. Martin Luther King and agreed with his program; he frequently talked of Dr. King with a real reverence.[171]

As with his support for the Cuban revolution, Oswald's fervent opposition to racist political radicals had been clearly visible in his earlier dialogues, as well as documented in interviews at the time of his arrival in Russia.[172]

Materials recovered from Oswald's possessions confirm a new focus on the ultra-right in 1963. His notebook contains the names, affiliations, and addresses of radical racists—including that of General Edwin Walker of Dallas. The entries included not only Walker's address but also listed other individuals whom Oswald might have regarded as unrepentant "Fascists." The notebook entries list George Lincoln Rockwell and his American Nazi party, the National Socialist Bulletin (known for its excessively violent racism and antisemitism), and the name Burros. Danny Burros was the head of the KKK in New York State, and he had been personally mentored by Rockwell.[173]

Burros had led violent anti-Jewish and anti-integration protests (even targeting the movie *Exodus*), and advocated that the United States declare war on Russia. By July 1963 he was jailed for armed demonstrations against the Council for Racial Equality (CORE) in the White Castle restaurant protests. As David Boylan has noted, it is quite likely that Oswald obtained Burros' name from the American Nazi Party's bulletin, which listed Burros as the American Nazi Party's national secretary.[174]

Of those names in listed in Oswald's notebook, one of the most prominent was General Edwin Walker. Walker had been especially visible in the media in 1963, appearing in headlines because of his violent opposition to school integration, with calls to action in response to communist infiltration of the civil rights movement, and his warnings about Castro's communist hold over Cuba. And Walker lived in Dallas.

The Walker Shooting

The night of April 10, 1963, General Edwin Walker reported that a shot had been fired at him from outside his house. The police did locate at least one witness to suspicious behavior in the area of Walker's house that evening, with reports of two men in a car seeming to flee the scene. However, they found no witness to the shooting itself, no spent shell casing (which might be expected if only a single shot was fired from a manual bolt action rifle), a damaged bullet which they could not link to a specific type of rifle, and no lead to the suspected fleeing car other than a general description. With a lack of hard evidence, the initial investigation included interviews with Walker's political/campaign volunteers, and focused suspicion on a recently discharged Walker employee, William Duff.

Duff was suspected of having a grudge against Walker and was reported by Walker himself as having visited after the attack—individuals close to Walker later speculated that Duff might have even been trying to blackmail Walker regarding his frequent "queer" visitors. Later Duff would use that language during questioning by the FBI. Duff was arrested on suspicion of attempted murder and interrogated. However, the police could find nothing to support actual charges; their investigation found him to be a perennial and effectively compulsive liar, and he was released with no formal charges.

The twists and turns related to the Walker shooting, including the remarks over time from Walker's various associates and political supporters, have considerably muddied the waters about the shooting itself. Some considered that it might have been a hoax, carried out to gain him and his campaign visibility with the press. The Dallas Police themselves suspected the incident might have been "staged;" it was not the first time Walker had contacted the police about harassment or threats.

Readers interested in a comprehensive background survey of the shooting report, the initial police investigation, and comments from

Walker's associates are referred to the research of Dallas author Gayle Nix Jackson and her book *Pieces of the Puzzle: An Anthology*. Her book also presents a detailed study of the post-assassination FBI investigation of Oswald's possible involvement, illustrated with a series of photographs found among Oswald's personal possessions at the time of his arrest—material not available to the police in their initial investigation.

Oswald had not been connected in any fashion to the original police investigation of the Walker shooting; that investigation had simply closed out the case with no solution. It would only be during the weeks following the Kennedy assassination that Oswald would become connected to Walker, and to the shooting. That connection involves several elements, beginning with the reference to Walker and his address in Oswald's notebook, extending to several photographs of Walker's home (from different locations and angles) taken with Oswald's camera. It also included the eventual discovery of a note left for Marina by Oswald explaining what to do in the event that he was arrested or killed, and finally by Marina's own description of what Oswald told her following his return home the night of the shooting.

The note, which led to a full-blown FBI investigation of Oswald's possible involvement, written in Russian, was initially brought to the attention of the Secret Service after Ruth Paine had found it in one of Marina's books, left at her home. The note was a single sheet of paper; the homemaking book was Marina's (*Book of Helpful Instructions*). Ruth handled the book while collecting various items left at her home to take to Marina after Oswald's arrest and murder. When the Secret Service confronted Marina with the note, she revealed that she had found it following an incident in which Oswald had returned home late at night and begun listening to the radio. At that time he had told her he had taken a shot at Walker, but had no idea if he had injured or even hit Walker—or been seen in the vicinity of Walker's house.

Although nothing in the news suggested that Oswald had been seen, she described Oswald as destroying several pieces of paper, information on bus routes, and sketches/maps related to his surveillance of Walker's residence. The contents of the note left for her included references to money she would have had from a pay check on the 2nd of the month, as well as to the payment of their rent (also on the 2nd of the month). That timing suggested that that the note had been made at the time of the Walker shooting, in April 1963.[175] The FBI was notified and initiated an investigation of the note, and a re-investigation of the Walker shooting on December 3, 1963, some two weeks following the assassination.[176]

Skeptics have challenged the authenticity of the note, presenting it as having been created and planted after the fact to confirm the view of Oswald not only as violent, but with a demonstrated history of attempted assassination. Those challenges are based primarily on spelling mistakes in the letter, and what is characterized as poor Russian used in the note. The question has also been raised as to whether it is real but written in relation to some act other than the Walker shooting which Oswald felt might get him injured or in jail.[177]

The Warren Commission did provide a translated copy in English in their published materials, along with an examination of details in the letter which would appear to firmly date it to April, 1963. It also highlighted other points in the note which appear to corroborate Marina's remarks about Oswald and the shooting.[178] It provided no remarks on the spelling or quality of Russian writing, although historically Oswald's Russian reading and spoken language skills have been described as much better than his writing in Russian, which was highly conversational and largely limited to letters. As to spelling, we have seen that was a particular problem for Oswald, even in English.

The finding of the note and another round of questioning of Marina by both the Secret Service and FBI certainly put Marina under a new level of suspicion, with the implication that she might have been an accessory after the fact in the Walker shooting for not reporting it—and raising the question that Oswald might have given her a similar warning before the president's murder which she had not disclosed to investigators. Beginning in February 1964, FBI Director Hoover, using the Warren Commission inquiry as justification, initiated telephone line taps on the residences at which Marina was staying. The FBI continued to conduct surveillance on her, as well as to hold open case files on her within the Dallas office, until 1968.[179]

The FBI conducted its own investigation of the Walker shooting, and as part of that effort a series of photos relating to the Walker residence were obtained. There were two photos of the residence, both from the alley at the rear of the house—one taken from directly behind and facing the house, and the second taken from an angle adjacent to the fence by the LDS Church parking lot adjacent to Walker's residence. The photographs themselves along with the camera had been taken into custody at the time of Oswald's arrest, and the connection between the camera and the photographs was verified by reference to imperfections in the markings on the edges which are unique to the camera lens and which were shown to match the lens/camera to the photographs.

Two other photos were found to have been taken at locations near a railroad track and foot path in an area near Walker's house. The agents had walked the area until they found locations from which the view in the photograph could be matched to the terrain. In addition, through questioning they found that they could date the state of work on a high rise building in the photograph which had been under construction in the background—that date was on the weekend of March 9–10, 1963.[180]

The location of two of the photos was near a railroad track, several blocks away from Walker's residence. The FBI agents did note that from the location, a footpath crossing the tracks was visible and the path could have served as a back route into or away from the area of Walker's neighborhood. It led through an unoccupied area of brush, drainage culverts, and essentially vacant space around Turtle Creek and the railroad track.

Based on that and Marina's comment that Oswald said he had gone to Walker's via a bus, the agents were able to locate a bus route which would have led from a stop well away from the Walker residence, through downtown Dallas and into Oak Cliff, quite close to the Oswald residence as of April, 1963. That route would have been consistent with Marina's remarks that Lee had described taking a bus to and from Walker's home, but via a route that would have allowed him to have boarded the bus well away from the Walker house itself, in a separate neighborhood.

Objectively, the evidence in hand certainly supports the view that Oswald was indeed ideologically dedicated to opposing "Fascists," and had focused his attention on General Walker—as well as other ultra radical racists of the time. Given Oswald's turn to activism in late spring 1963, it seems credible that had decided to focus on Walker and had indeed reconnoitered his residence and made plans to carry out an act against him.

Yet the view that Oswald had specifically shot to kill the General, rather than frighten him or even just to register opposition, comes entirely from Marina's repetition of Oswald's remarks to her. The Warren Commission Report presented Oswald as shooting to kill Walker, giving that as a factual statement when actually it was simply second-hand information from Marina.[181]

Given Oswald's tendency to exaggerate, the question remains open as to what exactly he did at Walker's residence. There has even been speculation that Oswald had been observed by Walker's associates, seen lurking around the property on an earlier reconnaissance, and that they had taken advantage of this during his next appearance to stage a shot for publicity purposes. That view has been supported by the fact that the Dallas Police had initially reported the rifle used in the Walker shooting as a 30.06 caliber, identified as such in the earliest newspaper coverage of the incident on April 10. The FBI's follow-on investigation was unable to match the bullet from the Walker incident to the weapon or the bullets used in the Kennedy assassination.[182]

It seems unlikely that we will ever be certain of exactly what was going on at Walker's residence that night in April 1963. While Marina

Lee Harvey Oswald at age 2, New Orleans, circa 1942. (*Getty Images*)

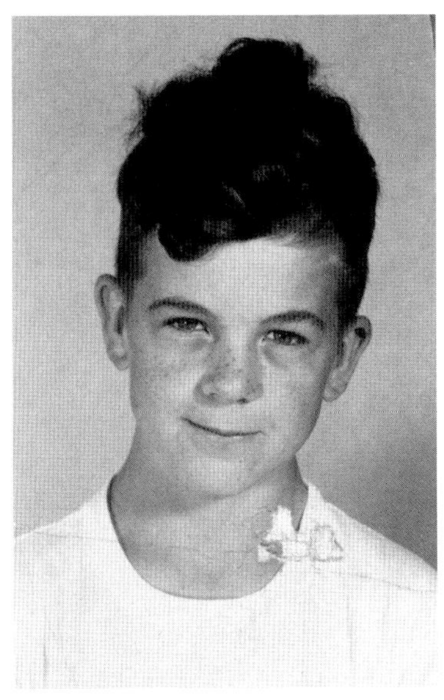

Lee Harvey Oswald, Fort Worth, Texas, circa 1949. (*Warren Commission, John Pic Exhibit 56 via Getty Images*)

Lee Harvey Oswald, New Orleans, age 15, circa 1955. *(Warren Commission, John Pic Exhibit 58 via Getty Images)*

Lee Harvey Oswald at the Bronx Zoo, New York, circa 1953.
(*Warren Commission Exhibit 2893 via Getty Images*)

Lee Harvey Oswald in the 9th grade at Beauregard Junior High, New Orleans, 1955. (*National Archives*)

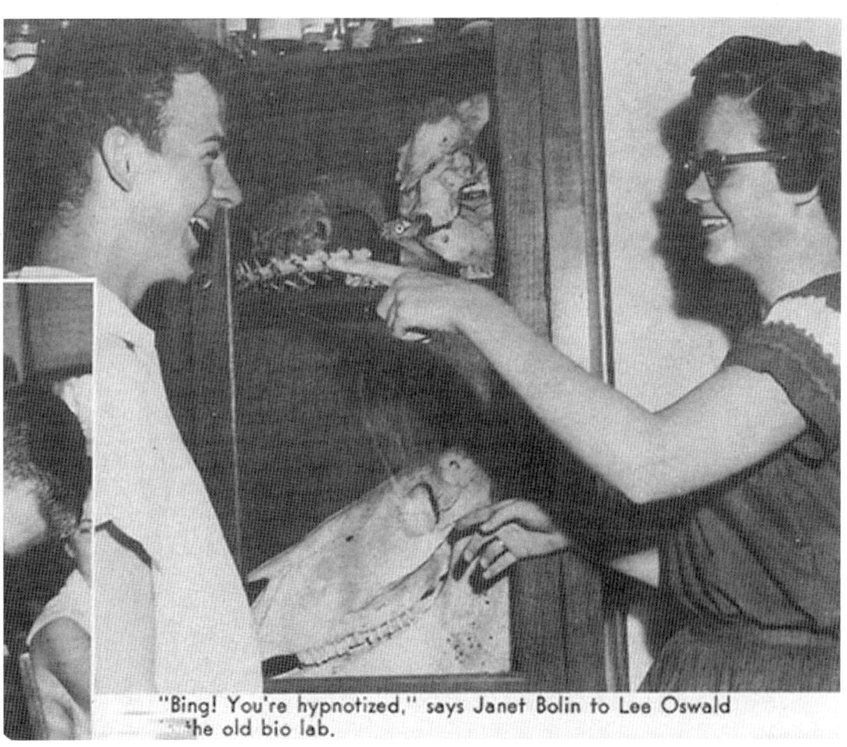

Lee Harvey Oswald in high school biology class in 1956. (*1957 Yearbook of Arlington Heights High School, Fort Worth, Texas*)

Oswald (circled at left) in his marine aircraft control/radar training class graduation photo, 1957. (*United States Marine Corps*)

Closeup of Oswald in graduation photo shown above.

Oswald stationed at Atsugi Naval Base, Japan circa 1958. (*National Archives*)

102

I Lee Harvey Oswald, request that I be granted citizenship in the Soviet Union, my visa began on Oct. 15, and will expire on Oct. 21, I must be granted asylum before this date. While I wait for the citizenship decision.

At present I am a citizen of the United States of America.

I want citizenship because; I am a communist and a worker, I have lived in a decadent capitalist society where the workers are slaves, I am twenty years old, I have completed three years in the United States Marine Corps, I seved with the occupation forces in Japan, I have seen American military imperialism in all its forms,

I do not want to return to any country outside of the Soviet Union.

I am willing to give up my American citizenship and assume the responsibilities of a Soviet citizen.

I had saved my money which I earned as a private in the American M.tary for two years, in order to come to Russia for the express purpose of seeking citizenship here. I do not have enough money left to live indefintly here, or to reture to any other country, I have no desire to return to any other country. I ask that my request be given quick consideration.

Sincerly Lee H Oswald

40583

Oswald's appeal for Soviet citizenship, given to his "flabbergasted" tourist guide following his arrival in Moscow, October 16, 1959. (*Yeltsin Papers, National Archives*)

Lee Harvey Oswald at time of arrival in Moscow, 1959. Oswald never completed paperwork to renounce his American citizenship and was only granted Russian residency. He later rejected an offer of Soviet citizenship during his effort to return to the United States. (*Warren Commission Exhibit 2963 via Getty Images*)

Lee Harvey Oswald assigned to work at the Belarusian Radio and Television Factory in Minsk, Russia (Belarus). (*Warren Commission Exhibit 2892*)

Lee Harvey Oswald with Intourist guide Rosa Kuznetsova, following his arrival in Minsk, 1960. (*Warren Commission Exhibit 2626 via Getty Images*)

Lee Harvey Oswald with Rosa Kuznetsova, Ella German, and Pavel Golovachev, Minsk, October 18, 1960. (*Warren Commission Exhibit 2609 via Getty Images*)

Oswald with Anita Zieger in Minsk, 1960. (*Warren Commission Exhibit 2616 via Getty Images*)

Oswald (right) with Eleanora Zieger and another man, 1960. (*National Archives via Getty Images*)

Lee Harvey Oswald at Zieger family picnic with a Hungarian friend of the Ziegers. Photo found in Oswald's possessions by Dallas Police. (*Dallas Municipal Archives*)

Lee Harvey Oswald with his factory supervisor Alexander Zieger (right), and a friend named Anatole, 1960. (*Warren Commission Exhibit 2624 via Getty Images*)

Oswald with fellow workers at the radio and television factory in Minsk, 1960. (*Warren Commission Exhibit 2625 via Getty Images*)

Lee Harvey Oswald with Marina and her Aunt Lyuba, 1961. (*Warren Commission Exhibit 2610 via Getty Images*)

Marina Prusakova on the balcony of Oswald's apartment in Minsk, 1961. (*Dallas Municipal Archives via Getty Images*)

Oswald and Marina Prusakova on the balcony of the apartment in Minsk, 1961. (*National Archives*)

Oswald and Marina on their wedding day, April 30, 1961. (*National Archives*)

Lee and Marina Oswald, the day after their marriage, with Minsk opera house in background, 1961. (*National Archives via Getty Images*)

Lee and Marina Oswald with baby June in Minsk, spring 1962. (*National Archives*)

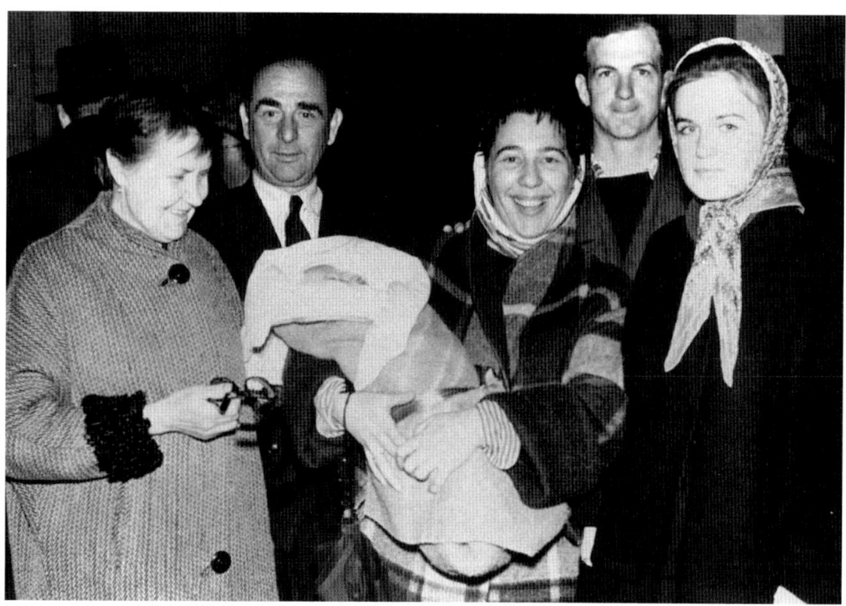

The Ziegers see the Oswald family off to America at the Minsk railway station, May 1962. (*Warren Commission Exhibit 2628 via Getty Images*)

Lee and Marina bound for America, on a train leaving Minsk, May 1962.
(*Warren Commission Exhibit 2629 via Getty Images*)

Marina Oswald on the train leaving Minsk, May 1962. (*Warren Commission Exhibit 2599 via Getty Images*)

Photographs from a scrapbook found among Oswald's possessions after his arrest on November 22, 1963. He kept an abundance of photographs, newspaper clippings, letters, and postcards. (*Dallas Municipal Archives*)

Items and reading material belonging to Lee Harvey Oswald, photographed by Dallas Police and taken from the Paine home after Oswald's arrest on November 22, 1963. (*Warren Commission Document 102*)

described Lee immediately burning notes and papers related to his surveillance of Walker's home, the Walker house photographs were not destroyed, nor did Oswald (admittedly under stress that night, regardless of exactly what had occurred) retrieve and destroy the note he had left with Marina earlier.

Then again, when news of the shooting was broadcast and reported the following day, there was no identification of the shooter, the weapon reported was not his Mannlicher-Carcano, and he may well have simply felt relieved at that point. We also know that Oswald went to great lengths to carry personal souvenirs—especially photos—of his life from his youth, through the Marines, and of his time in Russia. Perhaps at that point the Walker photographs were saved as one more part of his own personal history.

The Backyard Photographs

There is no doubt that Oswald was effectively and publicly "convicted" of an attempt to murder General Walker, both by the media and in the official commentary prepared by the Warren Commission. Once again, a series of leaks and stories from both the original Dallas Police investigation and the later investigations of the FBI were largely responsible for the public's acceptance of his guilt. There was simply no defense against the leaks. The appearance of what came to be known as the so-called "backyard" photos played a major role in establishing Oswald's image as a militant and violent radical, capable of such an attack.

One image from the backyard photo series had been especially effective in establishing the public image of Oswald; it appeared on *LIFE* magazine's cover as the lead for a major story on the assassination published in February 1964. Stories connecting Oswald to the Walker shooting appeared following the FBI investigation, and months before the issuance of the Warren Report the view of Oswald as an armed and dangerous radical had been presented so often and so repetitively that the statement of Oswald's guilt in the Kennedy assassination was essentially anti-climactic.

Yet it was only from a media perspective that either JFK's murder or the Walker shooting were at all connected to the crimes by way of the backyard photographs. When viewed strictly by themselves, during the months prior to the assassination, the photographs emphasized Oswald's new political activism and commitment—following the assassination, they were presented strictly as evidence that he had turned himself into a violent revolutionary. And no motive which would have caused Oswald to focus on or act against General Walker could in any way be extended to President Kennedy, Walker's antithesis in every aspect of social justice and racial equality. While the backyard photographs can certainly be associated with Oswald's turn to a new level of social activism, a thorough examination reveals that their origin and intention was very much removed from any idea of physical violence.

What is often referred to as "the backyard photograph" was actually a series of photographs purportedly taken at the rear of the Oswalds' Neely Street apartment in Dallas—photographs of Oswald dressed in black, with a pistol belt (holding a holstered pistol), and holding a rifle and two newspapers, *The Militant* and the *Daily Worker*. The rifle in the photographs appears identical with or at least very similar to the rifle taken into evidence at the Texas School Book Depository after the assassination of President Kennedy. The man appears to be Oswald, and under questioning Marina stated that Oswald had told her to take the photographs.

The Warren Commission and the media accepted the photographs as real, simply allowing them to convey the image that Oswald was becoming increasingly dangerous—and supporting the idea that he had attempted to kill General Walker months before the attack on the president in Dallas.

Another view is that the photos are real and somehow related to a new intelligence assignment for Oswald, creating and supporting an activist image for him which would be used in an infiltration mission in New Orleans. This view leaves aside the issue that photos could portray Oswald as either supporting the politics of the newspapers—or taking a stand opposing them. An alternative and even more skeptical view is that the photos themselves were total fakes, composites, constructed after the fact and planted to support the image of Oswald as a violent lone nut.

The most often expressed skeptical view of the photographs is that they were faked, either crudely or expertly according to different opinions, but in either case composite images. The origin of this view is Oswald himself—when shown a blow up of one photo, he denied that it was him, and stated that someone had put his head on another person's photograph. The caution to that statement is that at the time Oswald was in custody and charged with murder, the photographs had damning implications regarding the charges against him. As we have seen previously, when placed under pressure it was not unusual for Oswald (not unlike many people) to spontaneously obfuscate, misrepresent facts or tell outright lies. That can be verified in his interviews over the years, including statements made to the FBI in separate interviews during 1962 and 1963.

According to the Dallas police, we have only a single comment from Oswald on the photograph, rejecting it as being faked. Given that Oswald's interrogations were not taped nor transcribed, this leaves us to accept that the police showed him a picture of himself holding a rifle but may not have specifically questioned him about owning the rifle taken into custody at the Texas School Book Depository—which appears the same as the one in the photo?![183]

As the official record stands, we are simply left with the open issue of whether he was directly questioned about three of what would be the most key pieces of crime scene evidence used against him: the rifle from the school book depository, the ammunition associated with that rifle, and the bag which he was accused of having constructed to hide the rifle when he carried it to work that day. It is impossible to say that he was not questioned on these key items of evidence, but if he was, we have no written record of the questions or his responses.

Marina Oswald testified that she had indeed taken photographs of Oswald in the back yard of their Neely Street apartment, but she either recalled few details, or became confused as to the type of camera, number of poses, how she handled the camera which was unfamiliar to her, etc. When shown a signed copy of one photo (signed by both Lee and herself) which emerged years later, she at first identified the handwriting as her own, then backed off and refused to absolutely confirm the handwriting.

The Warren Commission and House Select Committee on Assassinations (HSCA) both addressed the claims of photographic manipulation, but given questions of institutional bias, their negative conclusions have not been generally accepted by the skeptics—several of whom produced their own technical studies highlighting issues with photographs. In contemporary times, advanced photographic analysis studies have addressed skeptics' issues regarding posture—and even the challenge that the position of the figure in the images cannot be correct in terms of stability—concluding that there is nothing technically anomalous about the images. Not surprisingly, even the most recent studies are still not found to be convincing by those who continue to view the all the poses in the backyard photographs to have been faked.[184]

In its work, the House Select Committee on Assassinations collected a copy of a new backyard image pose, one not in the negatives placed in official evidence handed over to the National Archives, but one apparently obtained by a Dallas Police officer at some point in the investigation. The photograph was an 8-inch by 10-inch Dallas enlargement—but the negative itself remains missing from the official record. The photograph itself ultimately made it into the National Archives and is verified by the fact that it is stamped on the rear with the official rubber stamp of the Dallas Police Force. Studies also revealed that the third image contained the same pattern of lens scratches as found on a camera owned by Lee Oswald. That same pattern of lens scratches had already been matched to the other two photographs.[185]

A two-dimensional view of the backyard photos leaves no choice other than to take sides, with Oswald being intentionally victimized after the fact with hoaxed images, or the images being real, but an artifact of an intelligence mission no agency would acknowledge. In contrast, a three-dimensional approach—with Oswald acting situationally on his own agendas—raises another possibility.

In considering the photographs as real and related to Oswald's personal agendas, it is important to acknowledge that finding Oswald in photographs is in itself no surprise. There is an extended history of Oswald having his picture taken—often clowning around or assuming a staged pose—from his school days through his time in the Marines to his years inside Russia. There is a relatively extensive Oswald photo history, most often with other people taking photos of him (something that would be truly exceptional if Oswald had been as antisocial as claimed by the Warren Commission).

And there is no doubt that the newspapers in the photo can be directly connected to Oswald circa 1963. Oswald was in communication with the groups that published both; each confirmed that he was a subscriber, and he had copies of the papers in his possession at the time of his arrest in November. The papers themselves were dated March 11 and March 24 respectively and had been sent second class, putting them in Dallas by March 28. Based on that, and the best reference Marina Oswald could give for having taken the picture, the HSCA estimated that photos were taken on Sunday, March 31, 1963.[186]

In terms of context, Lee Oswald did own a pistol—he was taken into custody on November 22, 1963 with it. He had owned weapons previously, a derringer in the Marines, even a shotgun in Russia, and prior to November 22 there was no significance to a former Marine owning a rifle or a pistol. For that matter there was no particular significance to Oswald reading "gun" magazines or clipping order coupons from them—an order blank from one such 1959 magazine (Guns and Ammo) was found in his personal belongings.[187]

Marina Oswald acknowledged that Oswald had a rifle, but other than being consistent in saying she did not like guns and knew nothing about them, her remarks were uninformative and unproductive in providing any detail on when or where he obtained it or even how it was moved from place to place in 1963—other than it being stored in apartment closets where they had lived. His friend George de Mohrenschildt confirmed he saw a rifle in a Neely Street apartment closet—after his wife had seen it during a tour that Marina was giving her during a visit to the Oswalds' to give June a stuffed animal at Easter.

Prior to November 22, 1963 there also appears to have been nothing significant (nor secret) about the backyard photos to anyone, including Oswald himself. The negatives remained intact and in Oswald's own possession until November, 1963. Multiple copies of the photographs were made, retained by both Lee and Marina and not only shown, but sent to other parties. That certainly suggests that in themselves nothing about the images was considered sensational or dangerous—up to the point when they assumed a much more sinister and incriminating context following the president's murder.

At that point the photos clearly became an issue. Marina and Oswald's mother both testified to the Warren Commission that Marina had become frightened, retrieved two prints of the photographs, hidden one in her shoe the day after the assassination, and then burned both copies the evening of November 23, 1963.

Much of the apparent mystery relating to the photos came from within the Dallas Police investigation itself. Negatives of the backyard photographs were collected (negatives and prints were not individually logged in the DPD collections record), but not all were placed into the evidentiary record itemized by the Dallas Police Department—which officially submitted only one actual negative to the Warren Commission investigation. Ongoing research has shown that prints were made internally by DPD officers of at least three different backyard images, one turning up only years after the Warren Commission work was done.

And at least two Dallas Police officers were found to have obtained copies of prints made from negatives taken into evidence. A print of Oswald holding the rifle in a third image (designated 133-C) was given to the HSCA by the former Mrs. Roscoe White; White had apparently acquired it during his time with the DPD. When questioned on this issue, Dallas police officer R. L. Studebaker testified to the House Select Committee on Assassinations that in 1963, while working in the Dallas Police Department Photography Laboratory, he made numerous copies of the Kennedy photographic evidence for fellow Dallas police officers. Included in the pictures distributed were prints of CE 133-A and CE 133-B as well as of the third image not seen by the Warren Commission.

Yet what stands out from the highly questionable DPD evidence handling is the fact that the Oswald family retained negatives and prints of the backyard photos during the Oswalds' move to New Orleans, and a second move back to Dallas. That fact alone suggests neither Lee nor Marina felt any particular concern about having taken the photos—and that the photos were not some secret elements of a new, covert intelligence mission. They were simply photos.

Another point supporting that view is that Oswald himself apparently made several prints of the poses in the backyard photograph. And he appears not to have been hesitant to share or even use the images in correspondence. One example of that comes from Michael Paine, who that spring was just getting to know Oswald though his wife Ruth's developing friendship with Marina. Interviewed years later, Michael recalled talking politics and world views with Oswald and, during the conversation, Oswald showing him one of the backyard photos.

> "Almost the next thing he does is to pick up the eight-by-ten glossy photo of himself in black with a rifle and a couple of pamphlets [the

> two newspapers] . . .I didn't know what to make of it because it was very different from what I expected to find. I had known communists, and they were mostly intellectually interesting people . . . I'd been told he was a communist and I kind of expected a social idealist and couldn't see the connection between that and this picture of a guy with his rifle in black clothing. It was so different I just did not put the two together. But he was obviously proud of that picture . . ."[188]

Given what we now know, there might well have been a very personal reason why Oswald was indeed proud of the photos, and the fact that they illustrated his new commitment to ideological activism. The explanation could be as simple as the fact that Lee Oswald had just had his first piece of writing published in a newspaper—not just any newspaper, but one that he was holding in the photographs. The March 11 issue of *The Militant*, the issue being held by Oswald in his backyard poses, contained a letter to the editor titled "News and Views from Dallas", with the initials "L H" attached to it.

While it is impossible to prove the letter had come from Oswald, we do know that he subscribed to *The Militant* in his own name. In addition, David Boylan has managed to locate an actual copy of that edition of *The Militant*, and an examination of "News and Views" from Dallas shows verbiage and issues which are entirely consistent with the writing that Oswald was doing at that time—including his call to seriously address the "system" in order to deal with the fundamental social conditions which were producing unemployment, poverty, and ever-growing numbers of people on relief.[189]

The backyard photos may well have been Oswald's personal expression of his new role as an activist; they may also have been used to further his correspondence, and gain increased attention with the groups publishing newsletters, such as *The Militant*. There is some anecdotal indication that Oswald did go as far as mailing *The Militant* a copy of one pose in the backyard photos. That would have been in character for Oswald—assertive to a fault. Something routine, if a bit over the top in March, but something else entirely different by November. The following is excerpted from an interview by Gus Russo:

> "Sylvia Weinstein, who handled the paper's subscriptions [*The Militant*; a publication of the Socialist Workers Party], opened the envelope and thought the man in black was 'kookie.' In her opinion, he had chosen a 'stupid' way to declare his loyalty to the publication."
>
> "Four months later, Weinstein would again hear about Oswald, after his arrest for handing out leaflets for the Fair Play for Cuba Committee in New Orleans. The big worry for *The Militant* office then was, 'Who is this guy? Why is he causing all these problems?' After the assassination, Farrell Dobbs [the editor] directed that the photograph, together with 'every scrap of paper' mentioning Oswald, including his subscription plate, be swept from the files and given to William Kunstler, the well-known civil-rights attorney who represented the publication."[190]

Beyond the photograph negatives and copies that Lee Oswald and Marina kept, verified in the DPD evidence collection and in remarks from Oswald's mother and brother Robert, there is yet one more verified copy of one of the backyard images. That print was signed by Lee Oswald and contained a dedication to his "friend" George de Mohrenschildt. On the reverse side of the photograph Marina had written: "this is the hunter of fascists! Ha! Ha! Ha!"

That copy of one backyard image did not surface until well after the Warren Commission Report had been published. The explanation given for that was that it had been only after George and Jeanne had returned from their time in Haiti, the photo then having been found in a box of English language learning records that Jeanne de Mohrenschildt had loaned to Marina. The box had been stored among the books and furniture warehoused when they had departed for Haiti—possibly put there by a mutual friend who had been using some of the de Mohrenschildts' furniture before finally putting it into long-term storage.[191]

Another, and likely more reliable, version of the handling of that print comes from an interview given by de Mohrenschildt to Edward Epstein in 1977, only hours before de Mohrenschildt's apparent suicide. In that version of the story, Marina had handed the print, with Oswald's dedication signature and her sarcastic note on the rear, to de Mohrenschildt in April—before the Walker shooting. Epstein noted, "two of de Mohrenschildt's friends told me that he had discussed the photograph, and the problems it raised for him, before he returned from Haiti (in November 1966)."

With a recent history of depression, having been committed to a hospital for mental issues, and talk of suicide, it is even possible that admitting his lies about the photo and his failures to fully support Lee (guilt he admitted to in his own manuscript about Oswald, *I Am a Patsy! I Am a Patsy!*) might have helped towards push de Mohrenschildt towards taking his own life. If de Mohrenschildt had a copy of the photograph in April 1963 it would also have explained why during their last visit to the Oswalds' he would have, seemingly out of the blue, asked Lee if he had been the one to shoot at Walker—a question which he intended as a joke but one which seemed to shake both Lee and Marina and might even have triggered Oswald's decision about a move to New Orleans.[192]

De Mohrenschildt may have had some reason to make such a "joke" and later to strongly regret the discussion he had had with Oswald about American racists and the danger they posed. During the FBI's post-assassination investigation of the Walker shooting, he had told the FBI that he (de Mohrenschildt) had described Walker as a "menace to society" to Oswald, remarking that "maybe it wouldn't be such a bad idea if someone took a shot at him."[193] De Mohrenschildt also told the FBI that he certainly had not been serious, but that he was afraid it might have "put the idea" into Oswald's head. During the re-interview of the couple, Mrs. de Mohrenschildt also confirmed that Marina had remarked to her that Oswald had bought a gun during their last visit with the couple in Dallas.

The idea that the backyard photographs were simply part of the new activist role which Oswald was assuming for himself (much like his correspondence with Socialist and even Communist groups, as well as his new effort to support the Fair Play for Cuba Committee), supports Marina's sarcastic comment on the photo—as well as the fact that in themselves the photographs had no special meaning nor presented any risk to the Oswalds prior to the events of November 22, 1963.

At the time, a sarcastic note on the back of the photo would have had little significance, little more than a minor jibe at her husband expressed in private to their mutual friends. Given the implications which would obviously be read into such a photograph following the assassination, and the questions it would generate for her, Marina's post-assassination hesitancy to confirm her signature on the rear of the print is perhaps more understandable—"at first I thought it was maybe my handwriting, but after I examine it, I know it is not." We know from Marina and Oswald's mother that simply having copies of the photo had badly frightened Marina. Following Oswald's arrest, she had hidden two prints. That evening, while both Marina and Oswald's mother were at Ruth Paine's, Marina showed the prints to Marguerite. Both were so concerned by the implications that Marina destroyed the prints at that time. The destruction was later confirmed by both women.

In the days and weeks immediately following the assassination, and with the publication of a backyard pose in *LIFE* magazine in February, knowledge of an armed and seemingly radical Oswald in early 1963 was something for everyone to avoid, if possible. But for Oswald the backyard photographs might have been nothing more—at the time—than a statement of his newly assumed activism and a celebration of having his letter to *The Militant* being in print.

Oswald's views of the world, the opinions and causes which drove him, had remained consistent from the days of his school years' arguments with his friends' parents to the geopolitical commentary he was now putting into his writing. Another point of consistency for Oswald was his ability to "reset" himself to pursue those beliefs. When one door closed for him, he simply looked for another one to open—with no apparent inclination to fault himself over failures but simply to look for new options.

Oswald's reading of *The Militant* may have help been part of another such "reset," a factor in turning his new activism towards a personal involvement in the Cuban revolutionary cause. Cuba and its revolution were a constant theme in the newsletter, with Castro's speeches featured in an ongoing series of articles.[194] *The Militant's* coverage of Cuba and the Castro regime also included endorsement of the FPCC and details of its activism, stressing themes including the Cuban revolution's opposition to racism and its championing of the benefits of socialism for the working class. These topics were very much in sync with Oswald's own personal beliefs and interests. These topics began to appear in his own writing that spring, and they were moving him to take action rather than just read and write about them.[195]

Chapter 10

New Orleans

"Since I am unemployed, I stood yesterday for the first time in my life, with a placard around my neck, passing out fair play for Cuba pamphlets, ect. I only had 15 or so. In 40 minutes, they were all gone. I was cursed as well as praised by some."

—From the first of a series of letters Lee Oswald wrote to the Fair Play for Cuba Committee, requesting pamphlets and informing them of his activities. FBI 105-82555, Section 104, p. 67.

The Move to New Orleans

On April 12, Oswald made a claim for unemployment benefits in Dallas, and four days later the commission mailed him a determination disapproving his claim because of insufficient wage credits.[196] What happened next was a seemingly sudden separation of Lee and Marina, with Marina left in Dallas while Lee traveled to New Orleans and began connecting with family members as part of a job search in that city. In one sense the move seemed straightforward given that Oswald had lived there previously, and still had family connections who might be relied on for assistance. Yet it would become a primary point of contention in regard to all three contending views of Lee Harvey Oswald.

The Warren Commission Report positioned the move to New Orleans as proof of Oswald's violent nature, outlining his likely involvement in an abortive attempt to kill a major right-wing figure, General Edwin Walker. Skeptics of the Commission have either totally rejected any involvement of Oswald with the Walker shooting (presenting all the Commission's purported evidence related to Oswald and Walker as an effort to frame Oswald after the fact) or explained the move to New Orleans in terms of Oswald having received a new intelligence mission.

Oswald's departure from Dallas occurred shortly after the Walker shooting on April 10. Prior to that date, he had registered as unemployed with the Texas Employment Commission on April 8; he filed an unemployment claim on April 12, two days after the Walker shooting. His departure to New Orleans only 4 days later occurred at the time he was notified by mail that his claim for compensation was being rejected due to insufficient wage credits.

What we do know for a fact is that without a job, and with an ongoing failure to find work or get unemployment benefits in Dallas, within two weeks of the Walker shooting Oswald left Dallas for New Orleans. That sort of spontaneous move was nothing truly new for Oswald, not unlike his behavior months earlier in the fall of 1962—leaving Marina and baby June behind to rely on friends while he had gone off on his own to look for a job in Dallas. According to Ruth Paine, when she visited the Oswalds at their apartment on April 24, she was surprised to learn that Oswald was packed and ready to leave for New Orleans by bus.

Oswald explained to her that he had been unable to find employment in or around Dallas, and that Marina had suggested that he go to New Orleans, since he had been born there. Mrs. Paine offered to drive Marina to New Orleans later, and to have Marina and June stay with her rather than at the apartment in the meantime. Oswald helped the women pack Mrs. Paine's car, and the two women moved everything from the Neely Street apartment to the Paine house in Irving.[197] As we will note in the following discussion, there might also have been another occurrence at that point in time which had stimulated the move out of Dallas.

When he arrived at the bus station in New Orleans, Oswald telephoned his aunt, Lillian Murret, to ask if he could stay at her home at French Street while he looked for employment. She had been unaware that he had returned from Russia, or that he was married and had a child, and was surprised to hear from him. She said that she did not have room to accommodate three guests, but that since he was alone, he was welcome.

Oswald had been born in New Orleans, and on his return did show considerable interest in finding out what had happened to the other members of his father's family. He visited the cemetery where his father was buried and called all the Oswalds in the telephone book. By this method he located one relative, Mrs. Hazel Oswald of Metairie, La., the widow of William Stout Oswald, his father's brother. He visited her at her home; she gave him a picture of his father and told him that as far as she knew the rest of the family was dead.[198]

Those sorts of family contacts once again emphasize that, when it was in his interest, Oswald could be quite social, and even pleasant in interpersonal relations. He remained fundamentally neither asocial or antisocial—annoying to many, but personable with people he liked or when he needed to make a good impression.

Following his return to the United States, Oswald's history with job placement bureaus, and in interviews, confirmed his ability to project a good image. In both Dallas and New Orleans, he would be described as neat, well mannered, testing well, and behaving respectfully in job interviews. But a review of his job applications shows the problems associated with his undesirable Marine discharge and his lack of a solid job reference history. It also reveals his need/propensity to lie about his background when necessary.

On April 26, Oswald began his search for employment in New

Orleans. He went to the employment office of the Louisiana Department of Labor and stated that he was qualified as a commercial photographer, shipping clerk, or "darkroom man." The interviewer noted on Oswald's application card: "Will travel on limited basis. Will relocate. Min. $1.25 hr. Neat. Suit. Tie. Polite." Although the employment commission made a few referrals, Oswald relied primarily upon newspaper advertisements and applied for several positions. Mrs. Murret testified that he would spend the day job hunting, return to her home for supper, watch television, and go to bed (very much as his apartment owner would describe his behavior that fall in Dallas). Oswald did write back to Marina in Dallas: "All is well. I am living with Aunt Lillian. She has very kindly taken us in. I am now looking for work. When I find it I will write you."

On May 3, he wrote to both Marina and Ruth Paine: "Girls, I still have not found work, but I receive money from the unemployment office in the amount $15 to 20 dollars. They were mistaken in the Dallas office when they refused, but I straightened everything out. Uncle 'Dyuz' offered me a loan of $200.00 if needed. Great, eh?!"[199]

On April 29, Oswald had filed a request for reconsideration of the Texas employment commission's disapproval of his unemployment compensation claim. His complaint that he had not been credited for his employment at Jaggars-Chiles-Stovall was ruled valid on May 8, and he was granted maximum benefits of $369, payable at the rate of $33 per week. He filed interstate claims again on May 7 and 15, and received $33 in response to the latter; the former claim was filed before the expiration of the proscribed waiting period. Oswald had, in fact, begun working in New Orleans as of May 10; beyond that he had stated on his claims that he had been seeking work, naming fictitious companies as well as companies he had not actually contacted.[200]

Finally, on May 9, responding to a newspaper advertisement, Oswald completed an application for employment with William B. Reilly Co., Inc., at 640 Magazine Street. Reilly's business was the roasting, grinding, canning, bagging, and sale of coffee. On his application form, Oswald listed as references in addition to John Murret, "Sgt. Robert Hidell" (at the time the second known use of that name, in this instance not as an alias but as a reference), and "Lieut. J. Evans." Both the Hidell and Evans names were fictitious. His application was approved and he began work on May 10, at the rate of $1.50 per hour. The job was largely manual labor; his work was lubricating the company's machinery. Initially he wrote to both Marina and Mrs. Paine that he was working in commercial photography.[201]

The same day that Oswald was hired at Reilly Coffee in New Orleans, he managed to rent an apartment (helped by Myrtle Evans, who had known him as a child) at 4905 Magazine Street. Rent was $65 a month. He immediately telephoned Marina and asked her to come to New Orleans. Oswald himself moved into the apartment on that same day, May 9.

Ruth Paine testified that the invitation elated Marina: "Papa nas lubet"—"Daddy loves us," she repeated again and again. Mrs. Paine drove Marina and June to New Orleans; they left Dallas on May 10, spent the night in Shreveport, and arrived on the 11th. Mrs. Paine stayed with the Oswalds for a few days. The three of them, with June and Mrs. Paine's children, toured the French Quarter. On May 14, Mrs. Paine left New Orleans to return to her home.[202]

During their time in New Orleans, the Oswalds and the Murrets visited each other several times, and Marina testified that the Murrets were very good to them. Mrs. Murret's daughter, Marilyn, took the Oswalds on an outing. But, according to Marina's testimony, aside from Ruth Paine and Ruth Kloepfer and her daughters, the Murrets were the only social visitors the couple had. Ruth Kloepfer was a clerk of the Quaker Meeting group in New Orleans whom Ruth Paine had written in the hope that she might know some Russian-speaking people who could visit Marina. Mrs. Kloepfer herself visited the Oswalds, but made no attempt to direct any Russian-speaking people to them.[203]

During their initial time together in New Orleans, it appears the couple's relationship improved considerably. Marina wrote that ". . .

our family life in New Orleans was more peaceful. Lee took great satisfaction in showing me the city where he was born. We often went to the beach, the zoo, and the park. Lee liked to go and hunt crabs. It is true, that he was not very pleased with his job . . . We did not have very much money, and the birth of a new child involved new expenses . . ." As before, Lee spent a great deal of time reading.[204]

But once again, after some three months in a new, but relatively menial job, in New Orleans, Oswald's typical work behavior reasserted itself. It had taken a bit longer when the jobs were more challenging or more inherently interesting—as a radar operator in the Marines or a photographic trainee in Dallas. Otherwise, the result, whether in his Russian factory job, at his sheet metal job in Fort Worth, or even at Jaggars-Chiles-Stovall in basic photographic work, Oswald simply proved to be neither an attentive nor efficient worker. The same proved true at Reilly Coffee.

While the Soviet system could not fire him, there was no such grace with American firms, and on July 19 his employment was terminated. The reason given was simply inattention and inefficiency at work. According to Adrian Alba, Oswald had spent considerable time next door to the Reilly plant, at Alba's Crescent City Garage, talking about guns with him, and reading gun magazines in his waiting room.[205]

Following his dismissal from the coffee company, the following Monday, July 22, Oswald once again visited the Louisiana employment office, to seek new employment and file a claim for unemployment compensation. Thereafter, he collected unemployment compensation weekly and, although apparently making some effort to obtain another job, appears to have listed several fictitious job applications on his unemployment compensation claim forms.

According to Marina he appeared to have given up his search for employment, and began to spend his days at home reading. Oswald may also have been discouraged by the news that the review of his undesirable Marine discharge had resulted in it being upheld—something which was likely to continue to hinder him getting the sorts of jobs he would certainly have preferred in the future.[206]

Returning to Russia

One point of continuity during 1963 was that Oswald continued his communications with the Soviet Embassy in New York. In July he expressed in a letter that a visa for him to return to Russia could be considered separately—Marina's needed to be given priority with a baby arriving in October.

Marina herself had developed doubts that Lee wanted to follow her to Russia—writing Ruth Paine that his "love" had ceased soon after Mrs. Paine had left New Orleans. Mrs. Paine testified, however, that she had noticed friction between the couple even before she left. On July 11, Mrs. Paine wrote Marina that if Oswald did not wish to live with her anymore and preferred that she return to the Soviet Union, she could live at the Paine house.

Although Mrs. Paine had apparently entertained that idea before, this was the first time she explicitly made the invitation. She renewed the invitation on July 12, and again on July 14—attempting to overcome any concern which Marina might have by stating she would be no burden. Marina could help with the housework and help her learn Russian, and she would also provide a tax advantage.[207]

Marina replied to the letter from Mrs. Paine that she had previously raised the subject of a separation with Oswald, and that it had led to arguments. She stated that she was happy enough at present and Oswald's behavior had recently improved and that he was being good to her. She attributed his improved attitude to the fact that he was anticipating their second child. She gratefully turned down Mrs. Paine's invitation at that time, but said that she would take advantage of it if things became worse again. Mrs. Paine replied that she was taking a trip north to visit her parents and would visit Marina in New

Orleans about September 18. She also suggested that Marina come to her house for the birth of the baby.[208]

A Turn Towards Cuba

As early as June 24, Oswald had applied for a new passport, which he received on the following day. Once again, possibly at Oswald's request, Marina wrote to the Russian Embassy, expressing a desire to return to Russia. She explained that she wanted to return because of family problems, including the impending birth of her second child. Accompanying her letter was a letter written by Oswald dated July 1, in which he asked the embassy to rush an entrance visa for his wife and requested that his entry visa be considered separately.

Marina herself later stated that she believed that Oswald had begun planning to go to Cuba and that "his basic desire was to get to Cuba by any means, and that all the rest of it was window dressing for that purpose."[209]

FBI headquarters had become aware of Oswald's new Cuban interests in March, based on his March 21 letter to the Fair Play for Cuba Committee sent from Dallas. In that letter he had pronounced his support for the Cuban revolution and described already having done leafleting for the FPCC in Dallas. His letter to the FPCC was reported by an FBI source inside the FPCC headquarters office.[210] FBI headquarters advised the agents in Dallas who had previously interviewed Oswald, and efforts were made in Dallas to locate and interview Oswald again. But by the time the Dallas office began its efforts to contact him, he had already relocated to New Orleans.

We now know that, through its FPCC headquarters office source, the FBI continued to have access to all of Oswald's correspondence with the FPCC. The FBI had its own asset inside the group's office, an asset who copied correspondence and the FPCC's membership and mailing lists. The FBI routinely prepared intelligence updates on the FPCC and copied the CIA on much of that information. As of July 1963, the

FBI was very much aware of Oswald's ongoing FPCC correspondence. It also had copies of his communications with the Communist Party of the USA (CPUSA), and the Socialist Workers Party (SWP; publisher of *The Militant*) through its covert monitoring of both groups.[211]

By July 7/8, FBI mail monitoring of the *Daily Worker* revealed a letter in which Oswald informed them on June 3 that he had started an FPCC chapter in New Orleans. But even by the end of July, the Dallas FBI office appears to have been still trying to catch up with Oswald, and had not yet located him in New Orleans, much less determined his employment there. It would not do so until mid-August.

The FBI had not placed Oswald on the National Security Watch list at the time of his return to Dallas in 1962 because Dallas Office sources were unable to find any contact between either Oswald or Marina and known, local Communists. But once his ongoing correspondence with the FPCC was discovered, he was placed on the Security Index in 1963 (the FPCC organization was being treated as a proscribed national security risk). The Security Index was reportedly a list of individuals to be "picked up" and detained during any national security crisis.[212]

After losing his job at Reilly Coffee, Oswald displayed no serious, ongoing effort at a job search, and his time became devoted to the Fair Play for Cuba Committee, and his attentions towards Cuba. His only break in the FPCC activities was a speaking engagement, one set up by his cousin Eugene Murret. Murret was studying to be a Jesuit Priest in Mobile, Alabama and had written Oswald about coming to Mobile and speaking to the Jesuit House of Studies about contemporary Russia and the practice of Communism there.

Oswald accepted the invitation, and on July 27 he and his family, joined by some of the Murrets, traveled to Mobile, Alabama. Charles Murret paid the expenses for the trip. Oswald spoke concerning his observations in Russia and conducted a question-and-answer period. He reportedly impressed his listeners as being articulate and forthright. Oswald indicated that he had become disillusioned with Soviet communism during his stay in Russia, and that in his opinion the best political system would be one which combined the better elements of capitalism with the social protections of communism. The group returned to New Orleans on July 28.[213]

While in New Orleans, Oswald continued the FPCC correspondence he had begun while still in Dallas. He wrote several times to the national director of the FPCC, V. T. Lee, expressing his enthusiasm for the group, and proposing that he set up a New Orleans chapter—and even an office. V. T. Lee had responded, cautioning Oswald on the obstacles of recruiting in New Orleans and advising against an office.

Oswald's correspondence with the FPCC had gotten him an initial small supply of leaflets, and he did hold an FPCC membership card in his own name. Yet although Oswald wrote four letters to V. T. Lee during the summer of 1963, there is no evidence that Oswald heard again from him after May 29. There is also no sign that Oswald advised FPCC headquarters that he was recruiting members for a local New Orleans group.

Yet we have indications that by mid-June, in New Orleans, Oswald had begun to do just that, first attempting a limited demonstration in support of Cuba and Castro as early as June 16. A New Orleans harbor patrolman reported responding to a complaint from the Office of the Deck of the USS carrier *Wasp,* docked at the port, that someone was demonstrating in the area near where the USS Wasp was docked.

The individual was passing out leaflets titled "Hands Off Cuba" and "The Truth About Cuba is in Cuba." The incident was recalled as happening on a weekend, with the individual not identified by name—but when asked to leave, responding in a manner characteristic of Lee Oswald in both a physical description and in his attitude. The man asserted that he was in a public area, and adamantly challenged the patrolman's statement that he needed permission to pass out materials to civilians in the area and coming off the carrier *Wasp.*[214]

The patrolman advised the individual that the area around the wharf operated under the authority of the Board of Commissioners of the Port Authority of New Orleans, and that he required written authorization from the Board for the distribution of materials in the wharf area. The individual, described as neatly dressed and well groomed, remained assertive and continued to challenge the patrolman—only leaving when told that the police would be called if he did not desist. Later the patrolman did identity the individual as Oswald, based on photographs he had seen in the paper and on television coverage.

As the weeks passed in New Orleans, Oswald moved to form a "virtual," paper-only, New Orleans FPCC chapter. He did so by issuing himself a membership card in his true name, with the card signed with the fictional "Hidell" name he had used previously—Hidell being the non-existent chapter director. From that point on, Oswald began to leverage the chapter and his role in it as part of his activist credentials, but made no further effort to involve himself directly with FPCC headquarters. As an example of that, on July 7/8, FBI monitoring of the *Daily Worker* produced a copy of a letter in which Oswald informed them that, as of June 3, he had started an FPCC chapter in New Orleans. Oswald did not communicate the same information to the FPCC itself (which would have informed them he was violating its previous advice).

In terms of promoting the FPCC in New Orleans, it seems likely that Oswald may also have been responsible for distributing FPCC leaflets on campus at Tulane University, circa July. A copy of one leaflet carried the name Hidell, and used the joint Oswald/Hidell post office box address which Oswald had set up. That leaflet was reported to have been picked up at the Tulane University library.[215]

Aliases, False Names, and the Hidell Conundrum

Oswald's activities in New Orleans appear mysterious for a number of reasons, and we will discuss the most obvious—his presenting himself as both an anti-Castro activist and an aggressive pro-Castro supporter—at length. However, one of the elements of the mystery, his use of aliases and false names, was not something strictly associated with his new political activism. The use of other names (Alek) is something that began for Oswald while in Russia and became somewhat common following his return to the United States, even in his apolitical activities such as job hunting.

Oswald had faced job-hunting challenges from the earliest days of his return from the Soviet Union. These challenges were largely related to his undesirable military discharge, and his lack of positive references from the jobs which he did get, and which he either left or was let go for poor performance. Family members represented one of his few options in citing true names as job references.

Although he continued to protest the undesirable Marine discharge, he received no satisfaction at all from that effort, which left him with a continuing problem in completing job applications, whether in New Orleans or later in Dallas. Based on a review of the applications he did make, we find that by 1963 Oswald was quite willing to use false names as references, provide false information on his work history, and even lie if he was in a situation where he felt he had no options.[216]

While that is at least understandable in terms of his job situation, what is far more challenging is the question of Oswald's use of false names (specifically the name Hidell) beyond job applications. Especially so regarding the Hidell name, which he used both in applying for jobs (Sgt Robert Hidell being found as a job reference in New Orleans), and for his own personal activities.

He used both the Hidell and Oswald names in authorizing the receipt of deliveries to a post office box in New Orleans (and may have done so in Dallas; the relevant paperwork on that is missing). When questioned about the New Orleans Post Office box, he simply responded, "I don't know anything about that." In regards to Dallas, he did admit to having rented the Dallas box—but denied that he had received a package there under the name Hidell, even though Hidell had been listed as being entitled to receive materials at the New Orleans post office box.[217]

In New Orleans, Oswald repeatedly referenced the name Hidell in association with a non-existent FPCC chapter (including during his voluntary interview with the FBI). Yet at the same time, Oswald carried both the fake New Orleans chapter membership card and a very real national FPCC membership card issued by FPCC headquarters in his own name.[218] As with the use of the name as a false job reference, when he had no viable alternatives, the use of Hidell as a local FPCC chapter leader does make some sense, given Oswald's effort to suggest that others were involved in the non-existent chapter when in fact there were none.[219] While that all seems confusing at a distance, it was so even at the time. The FBI in New Orleans wrestled with the question of whether or not Hidell was a real person.

Beyond being challenged by his own history in job searches and applications, we now know that in the months following his return to the US, Oswald had become aware that mail coming to him from overseas has been opened, including materials he had subscribed to such as *Krokodil*, *The Agitator*, and *Ogonek*—which the post office treated as "foreign propaganda mailings." He had filed a complaint with the post office about the mail intercepts, and added (on the form) "I protest this intimidation."[220]

It is unlikely that Oswald knew the nature of the CIA's foreign mail intercept program, or the fact that the FBI routinely used post office personnel as "sources" for monitoring mail on subjects targeted for investigation, but he certainly had reason to suspect that mail addressed to his true name was "exposed" to being monitored, and that he was a subject of FBI interest. To some extent, it seems that Oswald had begun to realize the "baggage" that his true name carried, dealing with that by simply introducing and using the Hidell name when convenient for specific purposes.

"Hidell" was not a true "cover" in the classic intelligence sense (which includes a standalone identity including job, work, and family connections, all with documents and records to support that identity). At best, it provided Oswald with a separate name which could be used within a particular dimension of activity—allowed him to isolate communications, especially postal communications, as illustrated by his listing Hidell as a separate individual allowed to receive mail at an "Oswald" mailbox.

There is no doubt that Oswald was concerned about his mail, not just in it being intercepted and monitored, but at least to some extent in terms of who might see it if it were delivered directly to a residence. That had apparently happened early on with Russian magazines being delivered to his apartment, and it was an issue even if he took Russian magazines or other "questionable" material to work. That had generated comment at Jaggers and was noted negatively by his manager there when queried as to a referral on at least one follow-on job application.

Oswald was clearly sensitive to his mail having been monitored and opened. In New Orleans, he resorted to the use of a separate mailbox for his FPCC chapter activities. His frequent moves necessitated postal change of address forms, new mailboxes, and at times change notices on mail for his subscriptions. Oswald himself remarked that it was often easier to have mail forwarded than to deal with the changes at the sender's end. This all created a complex mail trail which consumed a great deal of time and energy for the postal service and the FBI to trace during Warren Commission investigations. Oswald's history with his mailboxes, addresses, and other mail issues has also intrigued Commission skeptics and generated speculation on intelligence connections. Readers wishing to explore questions regarding Oswald's postal history will find an extensive detailing of issues discussed in a focused study by Tom Gram.[221]

What is more curious than the use of a separate name for different purposes, is the question of why Oswald would have taken the trouble to create fake identification cards, including a fake photo ID in the name of Hidell. One fake card—the Marine Honorable Service Card—associated "Hidell" with the Marines; the other—a photo ID Selective Service Card—would have provided visual identification of Oswald as Hidell even though real Selective Service Cards did not show photographs. Possession of either card would have been a federal crime.[222]

Oswald held a variety of real identification in his own name—a real Social Security card, a real Selective Service card, and a Department of Defense Service ID Card. They were in his billfold at the time of his arrest on November 22, 1963. Yet he went so far as to create falsified photo identification for the Hidell name. That seems to suggest that he might have anticipated a need to represent himself as Hidell in person.[223] To this point we have no concrete evidence that he ever used a Hidell ID in that fashion—which of course does not mean that he did not, or that he did not anticipate that he might at some point.

The prospect of a commonly agreed-upon solution, acceptable to all views of Oswald, for his motive in having the false Hidell photo identification cards is as unlikely as a resolution to the open issues related to the backyard photographs. Still, it is possible to offer at least one relatively simple explanation—that being that in Dallas Oswald did complete a form which allowed him to receive deliveries at his post office box in the name of Hidell, and that Oswald knew he would need a photographic ID to receive material in the Hidell name. We know that he set up his post office box in New Orleans in that manner; the problem is that the relevant piece of paperwork which would resolve that question for Dallas was never recovered—which simply leaves it as an open question.

If the Dallas post office box had been set up to allow a delivery to "Hidell" it would resolve several open questions related to the skeptical view that Oswald had not actually ordered the rifle connected to him in the assassination. But even if that were not the case, Oswald may have prepared himself to receive the shipment by making Hidell identification cards for his use at the post office, even a photo ID in case that should be required. When Dallas Postal Inspector Holmes was questioned about the delivery of mail, Holmes stated that the general practice of the time was that a card for a package would be placed in a post office box, and even if the name on the package did not match a box holder's name, the package would be handed over to anyone presenting the card at the counter.

All speculative, but having Hidell listed on a Dallas box would be consistent with his known activities in New Orleans—we do have testimony that Oswald was very much interested in purchasing a rifle in New Orleans that summer.[224] That interest was confirmed by Adrian Alba, who was co-owner of the Crescent City Garage next door to Reilly's coffee company where Oswald worked. Alba testified that Oswald had spent considerable time at the garage when he should have been working, just hanging about, and reading gun magazines; he also requested permission from Alba to take magazines away for reading and would return them afterwards.[225]

It was noted previously that clippings of gun-related order forms from different sporting and shooting magazines from as early as 1959 were recovered from Oswald's belongings at the time of his arrest (*Guns and Ammo, Sports Afield*). One of those clippings was an order form for Kleins—which lists a Carcano rifle like that taken into evidence at the Texas School Book Depository. When outdoor sporting magazines were collected from Alba's garage, one (*American Rifleman, June 1963*) was found to have a thumbprint matching that of Lee Oswald.

Researcher Paul Hoch later discovered (verified by the National Archives) that the "tear out" edges of an order coupon from that magazine were an exact match to a coupon recovered from Oswald's belongings (but never tested for prints).[226] This further substantiates the point that Oswald remained very interested in guns during his time in New Orleans, and could extend the mailbox speculation to the idea that he might even have ordered a second rifle in New Orleans, either from Kleins or another reseller.

The Warren Commission was satisfied with Oswald owning a single rifle—recovered from the Texas School Book Depository. Yet there remains ongoing controversy and contention among the skeptics' view of Oswald, which generally does not accept his having ordered or owned a rifle at any time. The possibility that he might have owned (or prepared to purchase) more than one rifle would certainly be far outside either the official or skeptical views of Oswald. A similar long-time question with no concrete answer from either the Commission or the skeptics is why, on November 22, 1963, Lee Harvey Oswald was still carrying fake Hidell identification cards at the time of his arrest.[227]

Tightrope Walking

The Warren Commission gave relatively little attention to Oswald's activism in New Orleans as part of its presentation of his character, possibly because it just did not fit the picture it was painting. His demonstrations for the FPCC were organized and mild mannered; when angrily approached by anti-Castro Cubans, he remained non-confrontational and refused to become violent. In his media appearances on radio and in a broadcast debate, he came across as literate, well-spoken, and not aggressive in his beliefs. He was invited to give a speech on his experiences in the Soviet Union; his remarks were informed, structured, educational, and well-received. All in all, not the behavior of someone antisocial or aggressively militant—and certainly not violent.

The Commission may also have preferred not to deal with the conflicts and seeming chaos of Oswald's activism in New Orleans, an activism which in late July, 1963, saw Oswald walking a tightrope between two violently opposed political factions. From that point on, his activities in New Orleans appear so chaotic that he himself seemed to be living in different dimensions. The explanation for much of that mystery is that in pursuit of his new activism Oswald was doing exactly that.

One of those dimensions involved the Fair Play for Cuba Committee, and his tightrope-walking with the FPCC limited both his relationship with its leadership, and the support he was able to receive from the Committee. His initial efforts related to the FPCC had involved letters, a request for literature and very likely one short-lived public demonstration in Dallas. Once in New Orleans, his correspondence with the FPCC turned to a proposal to form a chapter there, and to rent an office. The FPCC response was discouraging. It noted that there was little popular support for the Castro regime in that area and stated that opening a physical office was not advisable.

That was good advice—if anything, the New Orleans Cuban scene was about anti-Castro advocates and activities. In late July and early August, Oswald would have found the local newspapers featuring stories about anti-Castro Cuban volunteers coming from Miami for military training, and an FBI raid against anti-Castro partisans who had collected a cache of explosives from a location outside the city—for a bombing mission against Cuba.

In the FBI raid on the explosives stash, several anti-Castro fighters from the Miami area, primarily associated with the Student Directorate/DRE (as well as prior CIA military operations against Cuba) had joined an ambitious plan to assemble a large quantity of bombs and stage a two-plane bombing raid on Cuba. Surplus bomb cases were purchased, dynamite was bought from a source in Illinois, and it was all carried to a rural area outside New Orleans (Lacombe, Louisiana) for assembly. Money for the materials had come from Mike McClaney, a former Havana casino operator, and in late July the materials were stored in a trailer on his brother's property near Lacombe / Lake Pontchartrain, Louisiana.

One of the Cubans involved, a pilot who had been taken to Louisiana to assess the bombs, was not impressed by the materials, and opted out of the plan. When back in Miami, he discussed it with another Cuban who proved to be an FBI source. The New Orleans FBI was advised and conducted an intensive investigation (the FBI summary report runs to 112 pages).[228]

A massive amount of material, some 48 cartons of dynamite alone, plus other bomb-making materials had been involved, but none of it was appropriate for building actual aerial bombs. After the raid, the FBI confiscated the collection and relocated it to a military storage depot for explosives. News of the raid appeared in headlines in the New Orleans papers on August 6, 1963. Ultimately, as no specific federal laws had been broken, no charges or other legal actions were taken against any of those involved.

Separately, reports of Cubans arriving for anti-Castro military training had been provided to the local FBI office from its own existing sources; that activity involved Cubans traveling to the area for basic military training prior to being relocated to Nicaragua for what they believed to be military actions against Cuba.[229] It proved to be a complex scenario, perhaps a scam—or possibly just a commercial cover for moving the trainees to Nicaragua.

Initially, more than a dozen volunteers were recruited in the Miami area by the Christian Democratic Movement (MDC) for what they were told was military training and operations outside the United States. The initial recruits were paid to travel to New Orleans, and housed at a rather rundown rural property where they did do some physical and very basic military training over some two weeks.

While the MDC and the Cubans involved believed they were being prepared for military activity, the organizer of the camp, Ricardo (Richard) Davis, had obtained his initial funding from investors who had started a business in Guatemala (Guatemala Lumber and Mineral Corporation), and their position was that Davis was simply recruiting workers for their operations—ostensibly to cut mahogany trees.

The rationale for bringing Cubans from Miami and training them in Louisiana for lumber work seems questionable, but at the time the newly arrived volunteers were reported, the FBI seems not to have pursued the issue—perhaps giving priority to its intense investigation of the bombing plot discussed above, which was going on at that time. In the end everyone had their own story; Davis appears to have told the MDC that he had backers for military training and operations, while telling his sponsors he was recruiting Cuban exiles as laborers.

The MDC camp appears to have first become known to the New Orleans FBI office on July 30, related to the arrival of a second group of Cubans from Miami.[230] On being told that their future lay in working lumber in Nicaragua, they were outraged and refused to continue—leaving them with no money, at loose ends, and ultimately contacting refugee aid groups for support. At that point, the matter began to be reported to the FBI via various unnamed sources. In the end, the FBI raid on the McClaney property on July 31 led the owners of the training camp property to clear the Cubans out, and put them on a bus back to Miami by August 2, 1963.

The McClaney farm dynamite storage "bust" and the reporting of the arrival of out-of-town Cubans for "training" demonstrate that the FBI office had an existing and well-established network of sources inside the Cuban communities in both Miami and New Orleans (both established well before Oswald showed up in New Orleans). In particular, the MDC incident illustrates the extent to which that New Orleans FBI office was networked into the Cuban community, maintaining numerous and well-embedded sources and PSIs. This network included individuals such Arnesto Rodriquez, Carlos Bringuier, and Carlos Quiroga, all of whom would be approached by Oswald himself during the short period in which he was introducing himself into the Cuban community in New Orleans—as a fellow anti-Castro activist.

Oswald's contacts with the anti-Castro community in New Orleans have led many in the skeptical community to view his time there as an intelligence mission, with either the FBI or CIA sending him to the city to serve as a "dangle" to collect information on their activities. One obvious problem with that view (and such an assignment) would be that it was only over some three weeks that Oswald presented himself as being avowedly anti-Castro—he then quickly began his public appearance as a highly public pro-Cuba/Castro supporter.

Such a quick and public turn offered little time for a true intelligence fishing mission. The second issue arises from the fact, as we have only learned over time, that virtually every known individual that Oswald contacted within the anti-Castro community was already an FBI source, an actual FBI security informant, or was already associated with the CIA and its counter intelligence efforts. As previously noted, the FBI had been very active in targeting the Cuban community in

New Orleans. It was routinely getting information on the comings and goings within the Cuban community there, as well as referrals from FBI sources in Miami on anti-Castro activities.

An alternative explanation for such a short "self-directed" infiltration effort might be that Oswald himself optimistically expected he could easily penetrate the anti-Castro community given his Marine military background. That would have allowed him to obtain information that could be used against anti-Castro military efforts by turning any such information over to the government in some fashion—to the FBI, Customs, Immigration? The news he was reading were filled with dialogue about how the Kennedy administration was moving to officially block anti-Castro missions against Cuba. Perhaps he thought he might help in that effort. This is speculation, but Oswald had always been about action, and had never shown any fear in pursuing his goals.

Another alternative might be that Oswald began his New Orleans activism with his own study of the situation in New Orleans, including within the Cuban community. The FPCC had warned him that it was not a good place for a chapter, suggesting there would be opposition. Perhaps Oswald decided to test the situation, exploring matters for himself. We find clues to his new anti-racist activism in his notebook entries (including General Walker's name and address), and we find something similar for New Orleans—with the listing of three different New Orleans stores owned by Cubans.

Beyond those notes, Oswald's first known contact with the Cuban anti-Castro community in New Orleans was through a language school. At the end of July, he approached Arnesto Rodriquez Jr.; Arnesto operated the Modern Language Institute (a Berlitz school) in New Orleans. Along with the possibility of Spanish lessons, Oswald spoke with him about locating anti-Castro military groups whom he might be able to help using his own Marine training. [231] Arnesto would later minimize his own contact with Oswald, but following the Kennedy assassination, a CIA source in New Orleans reported that on November 23, 1963 Arnesto's mother-in-law had remarked during a private conversation that Arnesto had been a "friend" of Lee Oswald. She also discussed his tape recording of Oswald's pro-Castro radio appearance later in August.[232]

Oswald's notebook also contained Carlos Bringuier's name and address as head of the Cuban Student Directorate (DRE) in New Orleans.[233] Bringuier, admittedly, was a close associate of Arnesto Rodriquez Jr. and as noted previously, both men were sources for the FBI—reporting on purported pro-Castro individuals and activities (Arnesto Rodriquez Jr., a.k.a. Ernesto, was assigned FBI source number 1213 S). On August 5, Oswald visited Bringuier at his store, expressing support for the anti-Castro movement and offering his services as a military trainer. He even left a copy of a Marine basic training manual ("Guidebook for Marines") as a reference and offered to donate to the cause by buying some of the bonds the DRE was selling. Bringuier claimed to have told Oswald that he was not connected to any training or military activities, and that Oswald would have to contact the DRE military leadership in regard to volunteering.

And that was it. As far as is recorded, that single visit was the end of Oswald's anti-Castro infiltration—but not nearly the end of the anti-Castro community's contacts with Oswald. That anti-Castro community, and individuals in it in both New Orleans and Miami, would later—after the assassination—become the strongest proponents of the idea that Oswald was some sort of spy in New Orleans. Specifically, a Castro spy.

The New Orleans Cubans (many of them pre-existing FBI and CIA sources) aggressively portrayed Oswald as acting as a Castro agent, effectively infiltrating the anti-Castro community. Some would remark that Oswald had even learned of the new training camp (of which they were all aware) and reported on it. But the timing of both the McClaney raid and the MDC camp incidents precludes that idea—especially given that we now know the true sources of information on each from the FBI itself, neither being Oswald. Of course, following the president's assassination, virtually all of the anti-Castro activists aggressively and publicly presented Oswald as a Castro asset, saying he was either incited by or even paid by Cuban agents to assassinate the president.

Despite the chaos and apparent conflicts of Oswald's activities during July and August, what we can say for sure is that Oswald's overall agenda involved getting to Cuba and working to support its progressive social goals, opposing racism, and providing everyone with the basic services he had been advocating in his own writing. That goal appears to have led him to actions related to both the anti-Castro community in New Orleans and to publicly promoting the Fair Play for Cuba Committee. In the end, very possibly the most significant aspect of all that activity was simply that, in doing so, his actions deeply entangled him with an extended anti-Castro community in New Orleans—one which also reached east to Miami, and to the CIA's own anti-Castro operations.

Chapter 11

Oswald Entangled

Bringuier: "Do you agree with Fidel Castro when in his last speech of July 26th of this year he qualified President John F. Kennedy of the United States as a ruffian and a thief? Do you agree with Mr. Castro?"
Oswald: "I would not agree with that particular wording. However, I and the Fair Play for Cuba Committee do think that the United States Government through certain agencies, mainly the State Department and the C.I.A., has made monumental mistakes in its relations with Cuba."
—Excerpt from a radio debate with Oswald, DRE delegate Carlos Bringer, and Ed Butler

Entanglement

During the Garrison investigation in 1967/68, District Attorney Garrison independently confirmed that Oswald had inquired of Arnesto Rodriquez Jr. about Castro activists in New Orleans, and that Rodriquez very likely had directed Oswald towards Bringuier. In contacting Rodriquez Jr. and Bringuier, Oswald had gained the attention of a group of anti-Castro activists who had been involved with each other since before the Bay of Pigs, at that time members of the Cuban Revolutionary Council which was headquartered in Miami and headed by Antonio (Tony) Varona.

That group included Arnesto Rodriquez Jr. and his father Arnesto Rodriquez Sr. (both authorized to sign checks for the CRC), Frank Bartes, Agustin Guitart (a close friend of Varona who would come to New Orleans to assist with fundraising in the fall of 1963), Carlos Bringuier (who by 1963 had moved on to the DRE), and Sergio Arcacha Smith (separated from the CRC and suspected of donation skimming; he was no longer in New Orleans as of summer, 1963). Those individuals had all been part of a larger local anti-Castro network, and attended meetings which included individuals such as Carlos Quiroga (who appears to have served as a sort of liaison amongst the various different anti-Castro groups in the area) and Guy Banister—at times meeting at homes and other times at Banister's office at 544 Camp Street.[234]

Several of the names from that network of individuals appear frequently with respect to Oswald's time in New Orleans that summer, both in the official investigations of Oswald, and in various individuals' research into his activities in the New Orleans area. Those names and connections are far beyond the focus of this work and have been treated extensively elsewhere—including in Garrison's own writing on his investigation. Interested readers who wish to explore that subject might wish to start with Garrison's story of his own investigation, *On the Trail of the Assassins: One Man's Quest to Solve the Murder of President Kennedy.*

Our attention and exploration of Oswald in New Orleans will focus on specifically those Cubans known to have had contact with and direct knowledge of Oswald beginning during August 1963—Arnesto Rodriquez Jr., Carlos Bringuier, Carlos Quiroga, Agustin Guitart, and Frank Bartes. Two of those names, Bringuier and Quiroga, immediately came into play with Oswald's first contacts in August 1963, beginning with his offer to provide military training for anti-Castro volunteer fighters. While Oswald appears not to have followed up on that offer, we now know that Bringuier immediately began his own follow-up. His first action was to contact DRE headquarters in Miami, seeking direction on what to do about the inquiry from a former U.S. Marine. He received the direction to covertly test Oswald and to expose him if he was not a true anti-Castro activist.

Bringuier would later testify that he was advised to test Oswald, and did so by sending an associate, Carlos Quiroga, to approach Oswald—posing as a Castro supporter. Quiroga was to determine Oswald's true intentions—was Oswald truly anti-Castro or perhaps a pro-Castro infiltrator? Such testing was not all that unusual; even within the Cuban community allegiances were sometimes unclear. In 1961 Quiroga himself had been suspected of being a Castro supporter and was monitored by the CIA. Based on their findings they revised their opinions, and then considered recruiting him during 1962.[235]

It is unclear if Quiroga visited Oswald only once or perhaps more than once. One witness report described him carrying materials, possibly leaflets, to Oswald's residence. After the assassination Quiroga described Oswald as having been fanatically pro-Castro during his contact with him, making vows to defend the Cuban revolution against the United States. District Attorney Garrison investigated Quiroga and conducted a polygraph examination related to details of Quiroga's contact with and knowledge of Oswald. The examination results suggested that Quiroga had apparently lied on several points, including Oswald's contacts with other individuals whom Quiroga refused to acknowledge or name.

Garrison's investigators also found individuals who reported that Oswald had received multiple visits by unidentified individuals, including by two Cubans on at least one occasion. That becomes especially interesting in light of the fact that a former college friend of Quiroga at LSU—Victor Espinosa Hernandez—can be shown to have been in New Orleans from Miami at the time, as a participant in the abortive bombing mission and FBI raid discussed earlier. There is every reason to speculate that Victor would have been in touch with his friend and that either Victor or his friend and fellow traveler to New Orleans, Carlos Hernandez, may have been that second caller reported with Quiroga.

During his brief period of posing as an opponent of Castro and the Cuban revolution, Oswald appears to have had no success in obtaining information on any anti-Castro military activities. However, he had made himself highly visible to the established network of anti-Castro activists in New Orleans. And his contact with Quiroga had revealed his true sympathies to the individuals in that network. These individuals were already either sources or informants for the local FBI office, the CIA and even Customs. He was indeed walking a tightrope, telling anti-Castro factions he wanted to join in their efforts—while maintaining to the FPCC and in personal contact with Quiroga that he was a fervent supporter of the Cuban revolution. Who else may have been in contact with him, or "tested" him during that period, remains an open question.

Ultimately it was Oswald himself who took himself off the tightrope on August 9, with a highly public demonstration of pro-FPCC, pro-Cuba support. Oswald had hired two young men for a couple of hours work, and the three were passing out Fair Play for Cuba leaflets on Canal Street, near the International Trade Mart building.[236] The young men had been hired for a brief stint of work passing out leaflets, with no idea of their content.

One of them (Charles Steele Jr.) later stated that he had been given two dollars in exchange for what was described as fifteen to twenty minutes "work." After passing out leaflets for a time, Steele took the time to read the leaflet and then challenged Oswald, protesting that it was communist propaganda. Oswald assured him that the leafleting was simply intended to be educational, an activity by a group out of Tulane University. At that point Steele had asked for his two dollars and left the area of the Trade Mart.[237] Unlike his earlier demonstrations, Oswald appears to have made a special effort to ensure attention—which he did receive. A local television station deployed a video camera unit to the scene and was already filming prior to the arrival of Bringuier and his friends.

The exact details of the how the television unit came on the scene were never resolved; the station itself explained its presence as simply the result of an anonymous call on a news event in the city. Given that Oswald was media-savvy (New Orleans media and reporters' names show up in his notebook) and claimed in one interview to have previously attempted to contact local newspapers with pro-Cuba information—it is quite possible he himself might have made the anonymous call that brought the television crew out. And when Bringuier and company did appear on the scene, and hotly challenged Oswald, Oswald dared him to throw a punch; the event became even more newsworthy and law enforcement responded. Oswald and the three Cubans were arrested for disturbing the peace. Oswald spent the night in jail and was interviewed the next day by a lieutenant of the New Orleans Police Department.[238]

What came next could have clarified matters with respect to Oswald's overall intentions, but as it turned out, the net result was that it only added elements of confusion by directly involving the FBI with his pro-Castro activities—not so much with Oswald himself, but with a nonexistent pro-Castro faction in the city. Given Oswald's background and the Bureau's previous interest in him, it might have been expected that after his highly public pro-Castro demonstration, he would have been the focus of a new round of FBI attention. Instead, the FBI's attention was diverted from Oswald—by Oswald himself—and focused on a large, previously unknown, and seemingly clandestine FPCC organization within the city of New Orleans. It was apparently a group which the Bureau had no knowledge of at all up to that point, despite their well-established base of existing informants and sources within the Cuban community. The supposed group was led by an individual not only unknown to them, but whom they would be unable to locate or identify during the following months. This was simply because the group and its leader Hidell were a total fabrication, fed to them during an interview carried out at the request of Oswald himself.

The FBI Enigma

Following his arrest, the New Orleans police had initially believed Oswald to be Cuban, either because he claimed to be or possibly because he was speaking so strongly in support of the Cuban revolution. Whether Oswald encouraged that impression or not, the police called an INS officer to determine his true nationality. When later interviewed by the HSCA, the INS officer (Ronald Smith) stated that he was unsure of the confusion at the time, he did not recall Oswald speaking Spanish (or Russian), and within some five minutes his conversation with Oswald had confirmed him as an American citizen.[239]

The NOPD then interviewed Oswald, and afterwards, he then told police that he wished to speak with the FBI. As described previously, an FBI agent arrived and conducted an hour-long interview of Oswald. We do have a secondary record of that interview, from Special Agent Warren de Brueys on August 31, 1963—some two weeks following the interview itself. Interestingly, the report on the interview was not directed to FBI Headquarters or even to the Special Agent in Charge of the New Orleans office, but rather to an Internal Security file within the New Orleans office itself.[240]

That interview was discussed earlier, but upon reexamination it is especially interesting given the amount of time spent discussing the Fair Play for Cuba Committee, not just Oswald's mail contacts with the FPCC's headquarters, but also its purported activities in New Orleans. Oswald identified an individual named A. J. Hidell as the head of the group, and displayed his own New Orleans membership card signed by Hidell, its director. The card had a number 33 on it, which Oswald described as indicating that the local group had that number of members.

He told the agent of speaking by telephone with Hidell several times after becoming a member, discussing the group's activities, and informing him of the group's meetings. He also described meetings at individual members' houses, himself having attended two meetings with some five different people at each—only first names were used in the meetings, no last names were given and he knew none of them by last name (suggesting some level of secrecy in the group's activities). There were no scheduled meetings and members were only advised by telephone as to the time and location of meetings.

Oswald said that he himself had hosted one meeting at his home, as was routine. The meetings involved discussion of current events related to Cuba as well as news of "inside affairs" inside Cuba. A week earlier, Oswald had received a telephone call from Hidell asking him to distribute FPCC literature and he had proceeded to do so, leading to the street confrontation and his arrest. He also described an earlier activity in which he had demonstrated using a placard with "Viva Fidel" on it and passed out FPCC membership applications—which had a mailing address on them for A. J. Hidell. After the FBI interview, Oswald was released on bail, and 2 days later he pleaded guilty to the charges against him and paid a $10 fine.[241]

The August 1963 FBI interviews with Oswald, including his information on the FPCC, were not reported outside the New Orleans office until October 25. It should also be noted that when his arrest and interview were noted on his FBI HQ record, it was copied to Division 5 (Espionage) because that section had the responsibility for the FPCC and Cuban matters in general.[242] [243]

As discussed earlier, there is a possibility that for at least a couple of weeks during the latter part of August 1963 the New Orleans office and Special Agent De Brueys were at least considering Oswald as a source, possibly even a PSI, given that he had described himself as active within the local FPCC chapter. Given the information we reviewed earlier regarding PSI practices, that would have been carried out with only a single sheet in a file, strictly in the local office file.

Aside from that possibility, a review of Oswald's Cuba-related activities in New Orleans and his brief time attempting to infiltrate Cuban groups—consisting entirely of contacts with already existing FBI sources—argues against the view that he had been intentionally sent to New Orleans as an intelligence asset for the FBI. So does his voluntarily providing false and misleading information to the FBI itself. He intentionally misdirected the local office, describing the existence of an unknown and seeming clandestine 33-person FPCC group. According to Oswald, that group conducted rotating private meetings scheduled only by telephone. Furthermore, he had sent them on a wild goose chase after the group's nonexistent leader, Hidell.

Based strictly on information from Oswald's headquarters file, the FBI does not appear to have made an especially strenuous effort to locate such a group, or its leader Hidell. It was not until the third week in September that the local office even began to query their standard sources in the Cuban community about any knowledge of him. And only on October 7 did it begin making general inquiries about Oswald or his possible associates.[244] In the end, Oswald's FBI headquarters documents note that the entire subject of some unknown, possibly clandestine, FPPC group was closed out with a query directly to FPCC headquarters—to which the head of the FPCC responded that they simply had no group or organization in New Orleans.[245] Of course, by the time the issue of an unknown FPCC chapter had been resolved by simply asking the FPCC itself, Oswald had already left New Orleans.

But what about Oswald himself? Why would he do something as risky as volunteer to bring himself directly to the attention of the FBI, and then tell them a series of lies which put him legally at risk? One answer may come from a look at Oswald's decision to become known as an advocate of the Cuban revolution, and if possible, to join that revolution inside Cuba itself.

Initially, first in Dallas and then in New Orleans, his approach had been low key, demonstrating in downtown Dallas but running away when police appeared, demonstrating on the docks in New Orleans with little visibility other than to a security officer who forced him to leave the wharf area. His correspondence with the FPCC, about forming a chapter of his own, only led to a warning that would be a bad idea in New Orleans, where there was little if any pro-Castro/Cuba support.

As we saw in his Russian saga, Oswald was not a person to easily let go of his goals. When his first outreach to Russian officialdom was rejected, he turned to the drama of first offering intelligence on American radar systems—and when that drew no particular interest, to slitting (minimally) his wrist to avoid being put on a train back out of Russia. In Dallas, he may well have turned to something even more dramatic in support of his opposition to racism and ultra-right (Fascist) political agitation. Clearly Oswald was not an individual who avoided confrontation, risk, or drama in pursuit of his beliefs and goals. We saw that earlier in his conversations with George de Mohrenschildt and there appears to be ample evidence for that assessment.

In New Orleans, Oswald moved on from low-key, individual leafletting to staging a large public demonstration for Cuba and the FPCC. He had successfully drawn a crowd, with television coverage and news coverage. All that was in progress before Bringuier showed up; then the confrontation occurred and they were all arrested. In jail, following his arrest in the street demonstration, things might not have looked as hopeful. The FBI had visited him before; he knew he had to be someone of interest to them, and he knew from his readings that the FPCC organization was also a target of FBI investigations.

Oswald had already gotten a new passport; his interest in Cuba and personally going to Cuba is evident, and having the FBI closely watching him could have presented a problem for him. Of course this is pure speculation, but his visit with the FBI did focus them on the non-existent FPCC chapter and on Hidell rather than on himself.

Can we know for certain what Oswald was thinking or what caused him to openly contact the FBI rather than to try and avoid its attention? Obviously not. Would such a risky act be out of character for Oswald? We have repeatedly seen that Oswald was willing to take risks in support of his goals, whether they were physical or legal risks. With that said, what did his approach to the FBI gain Oswald, especially given that he fed them false information? The simplest answer might well be that for Oswald, it was a response to his arrest that represented an opportunity to divert the FBI from any new focus on his personal activities, while he continued to enhance his image as a public activist for Cuba.

Which—given the slowness of the FBI response and its focus on the FPCC rather than Oswald for the following few weeks—was exactly what did happen. There were no visits from the FBI, no summons to the local office, and no interference with the media. By the time he was ready to leave New Orleans, Oswald had built the image of being a popular activist and media spokesperson for the Cuban revolution. He would leave town with a set of clippings, his new activist resume.

Unintended Consequences

Oswald's low key "infiltration" effort in New Orleans was limited in both time and scope, but it did make him visible to key members of the local anti-Castro community. His turn to public pro-Cuba/Castro activities was much more successful. We will never know if Oswald himself had anticipated the quick success he achieved in that effort—but it is almost certain he never fully appreciated its consequences.

The street leafletting confrontation with Bringuier and his friends almost immediately established Oswald as a confirmed pro-Cuba/Castro activist, devoted to a cause virtually guaranteed to generate public attention and comment. Attention from the media, from the anti-Castro community in New Orleans, and especially from one of its largest organized groups, the DRE (the Student Revolutionary Directorate)—visibility not just in New Orleans, but from the group's headquarters in Miami.

Oswald's media attention included both television and radio coverage.[246] His radio sessions consisted of one relatively short interview, and a much more extensive radio debate with hostile anti-Castro speakers (Bringuier and Edward Butler, the head of INCA).[247] Oswald had written to V. T. Lee about his street leafleting, and his arrest. Following the radio interview and debate, he sent a follow-on letter describing the broadcast coverage that he was obtaining for the FPCC story; he also requested more literature.

What Oswald did not describe in his letter was that the host of the show and his debate opponents had obtained information on his time in the Soviet Union and quickly put Oswald on the defensive, forced to protest that he was not a Soviet or Communist mouthpiece. He was specifically asked if the FPCC was a communist front, and Bringuier taunted him by asking if he really belonged to the Fair Play for Russia Committee. Clearly taken by surprise, Oswald had responded relatively as best he could in the face of the accusations.

While Oswald was generally judged to be both articulate and sincere in his interviews and even in the debate, his interview talking points have been viewed as somewhat rote—containing similar language and claims that would have been found in the books, pamphlets, and newsletters he was known to routinely read. It is true that many of his views and remarks, especially on contemporary events, can be found to mirror those in *The Militant* or the FPCC brochures and pamphlets he had in his possession. Yet even in instances where he was taken by surprise, while he did stumble, he was able to come back with responses and rebuttals which were more considered and rational than purely emotional.

His emotional response was held until after the debate. There is little doubt that he realized that his remarks—as well as the FPCC as an organization—had been effectively tainted with the Russian and communist claims and challenges thrown at him. At home he bitterly complained to Marina that he had not anticipated Russia being brought up, that he was unprepared and felt that he had been blind-sided, not having prepared himself for such a situation in advance.

As the DRE chief in New Orleans, Bringuier routinely reported activities in New Orleans to Jose Lanuza in Miami; Lanuza oversaw all DRE's North American chapters. Based on the news and reports coming from New Orleans, DRE headquarters developed a file on Oswald and by late August was beginning to use that information in its own anti-Castro propaganda efforts. The DRE leadership was highly supportive of that activity and aware of Oswald. One of its military leaders, Chilo Borja, confirmed to Jefferson Morley that the CIA also most definitely had been advised by the DRE of its activities with Oswald in New Orleans. He described it as the sort of action that brought them credibility and standing with the CIA; anti-Castro propaganda was the sort of thing they were given CIA money to do.[248]

While this is speculative, there is some indication that the members of the local community that first came into contact with and "investigated" Oswald's claims of anti-Castro support may have decided early on to essentially "preserve" him for their own use, rather than immediately reporting him to the FBI as a suspected spy. That speculation comes from the fact that a number of them served as local sources for the FBI, routinely advising the Bureau on suspected Castro agents or provocateurs. Yet none of them are on record as having filed reports on Oswald with the FBI following their initial contacts, or even after the street demonstration and resulting court appearances.

In fact, Frank Bartes, a local CRC delegate and FBI source, was queried about his knowledge of Oswald by the FBI several weeks following Oswald's voluntary interview with a Bureau agent. Questioned about Oswald on September 10, 1963 Bartes claimed to have no knowledge of Oswald at all—even though he had attended Oswald's court hearing the previous month and argued with Oswald afterwards outside the courthouse![249]

Based on Oswald's initial approach to anti-Castro factions in New Orleans, and Quiroga's testing of him, the DRE reaction to Oswald was to label him not as just some politically naïve young person, but as something more radical and far more dangerous—an actual spy. That was one of the reasons for Bringuier to immediately begin reporting on him to DRE Miami headquarters. Counterintelligence against Cuban sources and agents and propaganda constituted the two major reasons DRE was still being funded by CIA—funded and supported at a time when independent Cuban exile military missions were being actively opposed by the CIA, FBI, and government agencies in general due to Kennedy administration policy decisions following the Cuban missile crisis.

Given the DRE's need for the CIA monies, Oswald represented an opportunity to demonstrate to the CIA that it was actively involved with both tasks—counterintelligence and propaganda. The information the group was accumulating on Oswald in Miami was certainly being copied to the DRE's CIA case officer. Two CIA Special Affairs Staff case officers (George Joannides and Philip Toomey) are known to have been directly in contact with and receiving reports from the DRE organization in 1963.

Both men worked with the DRE from Miami, but documents also show that each of them had also resided in, and worked from, New Orleans for periods of time. The problem with exactly what the CIA Special Affairs staff was being told about Oswald, and what they were doing with the information, is that we lack critical documents from that period of time in 1963. While we know a bit about the DRE-CIA connection from that period (primarily due to the diligent research and legal actions of Jefferson Morley), as of this writing more than six decades later, it has been impossible to obtain the ongoing case officer reports that should have been routinely required as standard CIA practice.

Ongoing reporting on the DRE would have been especially important given its history of unsanctioned activities; the group was characterized in the CIA's own internal documents as especially challenging to control. Instead, the CIA now claims there simply were no monthly reports on the group for a 16-month period which includes all of 1963, no routine assessments of the group's leadership or its propaganda efforts and effectiveness. Claims that there was no routine reporting on DRE, as well as some sixteen key documents identified by Morley's research and still withheld by the Agency, certainly support the possibility that information related to the DRE contacts with Oswald and the CIA's response to them is still being withheld.

The CIA has knowingly and continuously shielded documents which might resolve questions of the DRE/Oswald communications (including the DRE personal meetings with and reports to SAS staff such as Joannides and Toomey) from all Congressional inquiries. Decades after the events of 1963, the CIA was willing to go to court to protect DRE files relating to Joannides, even into the 21st century. That obfuscation and the extreme degree of CIA stonewalling over the DRE and Oswald has proved surprising even to those DRE members formerly involved with the CIA.[250]

Morley's work in this area has included numerous interviews with actual DRE members. Based on his work and that of other researchers, we now have at least part of the story regarding the extent to which Lee Oswald was known within and beyond the Cuban exile community during his summer in New Orleans. It is a story which gives lie to the view that Oswald was a virtual unknown as of November 1963, and an individual not in any way on the CIA's "radar," as propaganda specialist David Phillips would later write.[251] Rather, it appears that Oswald had become entangled with both the DRE and the CIA by acting on his own Cuban agenda.

To fully appreciate Oswald's August 1963 encounter with the DRE, it is important to understand that the CIA maintained its relationship with the DRE largely because DRE was by far the largest anti-Castro organization, not only inside Cuba but extending across Latin America. Because of the youth of many of its members, and its roots within the university community, the DRE also continued to participate in international youth conferences—providing a perfect cover for the CIA to conduct political action and deniable propaganda activities in those venues.[252]

Given Oswald's emerging media image (television coverage of his street leafletting, press coverage, interviews, radio appearances) in support of Castro and the Cuban revolution, the DRE leadership became enthusiastic about leveraging Oswald in its ongoing propaganda efforts. In that respect, Oswald's activities in New Orleans, first as an apparent spy and then as a very public Cuba/Castro/FPCC supporter, provided the DRE with an opportunity they would pursue both prior to and following the events of November 22, 1963 in Dallas. DRE leader Borja stated that the campaign that they had begun against Oswald that August had brought them credit with the CIA; it was exactly the sort of thing they were being paid to do by the Agency.[253]

We know from Morley's work, including his interviews with DRE officers in Miami, that the DRE itself began to aggressively build a propaganda campaign around Oswald, characterizing him as naïve, a dupe, a dangerous radical, and an example of how easily young Americans could be subverted and influenced. They wrote letters warning other Cuban exile and anti-Castro groups in Miami about him. They even sent letters to Congress citing him as an example of the dangers of Cuban influence and propaganda.

But beyond the DRE propaganda efforts, Oswald's activities that August would later be used as part of a highly focused propaganda campaign by others. Oswald's public statements and media appearances would become key content for the work of an aggressive anti-Communist group operating in New Orleans. Ed Butler, the head of that group—INCA/Information Council of the America's—had obtained a tape of Oswald's radio debate with Carlos Bringuier on WDSU radio, and immediately following the assassination began making it available to radio and television outlets, positioning Oswald as a radical supporter of Cuba.

We have no idea when preparations for that campaign had started. What is known is that by early 1964 INCA was using a record, "Lee Harvey Oswald: Self Portrait in Red,"[254] as part of an anti-communist media campaign, a campaign targeted at both the U.S. and Central America. Materials for that campaign were completed and went into distribution early in 1964. The record would continue in circulation until at least 1965. The record itself used translated versions of Oswald's radio interviews, with tape recordings of Oswald and transcriptions provided by Arnesto Rodriquez Jr. The outstanding question is exactly when the idea and development of the campaign, built around Oswald, began and whether it might have been encouraged by the CIA. The extent of the CIA's involvement in encouraging or directing either or both the DRE and INCA propaganda effort also remains unknown.

What is documented is the CIA's association with DRE, and the fact that the CIA itself acknowledged an association with members of INCA.[255] It should also be noted that David Phillips, the CIA propaganda specialist who can be shown to have made a number of false statements in regard to Oswald, was reportedly involved with INCA and Butler in New Orleans as early as 1960—in an abortive attempt to create anti-Castro propaganda prior to the Bay of Pigs landings.[256]

There is no question that Oswald's activities in New Orleans that August were leveraged by both DRE and INCA, both before and following the assassination of the president. Both groups would aggressively promote the idea of Oswald as a Castro-associated killer following the president's murder, either as an actual agent of Cuban intelligence or as a young man under Castro's spell. In fact, virtually all the post-assassination media speculation of Oswald acting under the influence of Cuba and Castro came out of the image Oswald had created for himself the previous summer.

And despite the CIA's successful effort to withhold key documents, research has now provided some specific insights into connections between people around Oswald that summer in New Orleans and the CIA—in at least one instance an amazingly direct family connection. By the summer of 1963, the CIA's JM/WAVE base in Miami (the operations center for covert military and intelligence activities against Cuba itself, as well as the location of the new Cuba project Special Affairs Staff field personnel), and the station's subsidiary operations in Mexico

City, both remained deeply involved in intelligence collections and counter intelligence against Cuba.

One of the CIA Special Affairs Staff members working at the Miami base was the brother of the first known Oswald contact with the anti-Castro community in New Orleans—Arnesto Rodriguez Jr, the head of the language school whom Oswald approached about individuals and groups involved in military activities against Cuba. We previously noted that Rodriquez Jr. was a close personal friend of Carlos Bringuier, involved in Cuban revolutionary activities in New Orleans, and a likely source of the referral of Oswald to Bringuier. Most importantly, we can now document that Arnesto Jr.'s brother Emilio, a CIA Special Affairs Staff political action officer, was a key player in very serious CIA activities targeting Cuban diplomats during 1962 and 1963.

Emilio Rodriquez was tasked with foreign intelligence and counter intelligence targeting Cuban diplomatic officials in both Mexico City and at the United Nations in New York City.[257] Emilio was authorized to establish a residential cover in New York City, and traveled there frequently during 1962 and 1963, in support of efforts against the Cuban staff at the United Nations.[258] One of the primary Cuban targets for CIA political action "dirty tricks" in 1963 was Carlos Lechuga (and his wife); Lechuga had come to his United Nations position from the Cuban Embassy in Mexico City, serving as the Chief of the Cuban delegation at the United Nations.

Other individuals around Oswald in New Orleans in July and August of 1963—in some instances even at his court hearing for charges stemming from the pro-Castro leafletting confrontation with Bringuier—were linked in various ways to CIA activities as well as to reports of Oswald after his departure from New Orleans. As an example, one of the men at Oswald's court hearing was Agustin Guitart, the uncle of Silvia Odio, whom Oswald would reportedly visit in Dallas in late September. Odio's visitor was in the company of two unidentified Cubans who told her they had just arrived from New Orleans.

In 1963 Guitart had been given a provisional operational approval by the CIA as a "cutout" in a field intelligence operation regarding his uncle Rene Guitart, then inside Cuba. Agustin Guitart himself had extended personal connections to very high-ranking and CIA-associated Cuban figures in Miami, including Antonio "Tony" Varona, the head of the anti-Castro Cuban Revolutionary Council (Varona visited Guitart in New Orleans in the fall of 1963).[259]

It is virtually inconceivable to think that CIA officers at the Miami station (JM/WAVE) were not aware of Lee Harvey Oswald as of August 1963—with information which had come by way of DRE case officer reporting, by personal communications with friends and relatives in New Orleans, and more likely both. Miami station DRE case officers and propaganda staff, including George Joannides, certainly should have been hearing about Oswald in August. Unfortunately, actual confirmation of that knowledge is an issue which remains unresolved and in a legal abyss due to CIA stonewalling decades later.[260]

It is even possible that the CIA itself may lack a full answer to the question. As early as 1968, New Orleans District Attorney Jim Garrison's inquiry into the Kennedy assassination initially focused on potential connections between Oswald and anti-Castro Cubans affiliated with the CIA.

In response to Garrison's inquiry, and with great concern over his identification and exposure of CIA assets and personnel, a special CIA team was set up to monitor the inquiry and to frustrate Garrison's access to Agency records. In the second team meeting, the question was raised as to how complete the CIA's own records were as to its Cuban sources and assets. The response was that the records were detailed as regards to individual contacts, but less than adequate about anti-Castro groups. The remark was also made that there were an impressive number of contacts that might become exposed in the Garrison investigation.

Possibilities / DRE and CIA

Were propaganda activities using Oswald's image in play prior to the assassination? The answer to this question is, yes, by the DRE as of late summer 1963. To what extent further DRE or CIA activities were planned or discussed in relation to Oswald remains unknown. We simply do not know due to lack of access to the related CIA case officer files. All we can see is that the major DRE and INCA propaganda effort to tie Oswald to Cuba and Castro influence/control came after the assassination. The DRE post-assassination effort against Oswald was especially aggressive, including a call to Mrs. Henry Luce, the wife of the owner of the TIME/LIFE media empire, offering to provide evidence that Oswald was a paid asset of the Cuban intelligence service and been part of a team sent by Castro to kill the president.[261]

Overall, Oswald's activities in New Orleans appear quite consistent with both his long-term beliefs and political agendas. They are also consistent with his move into a new level of activism and a focus on Cuba. Alternative views see his travel to New Orleans, and his activities there as first an infiltrator and then a protestor, either as part of an actual CIA-directed mission (most likely directed against the FPCC), or even as an early element of a conspiracy to kill President Kennedy and point the blame towards Cuba and Castro.

In evaluating the view that Oswald was being positioned, as early as August, as being potentially dangerous to the president, we have no insight into what either the CIA or the DRE might have been planning as far as ongoing activities related to Oswald, particularly propaganda. We only know that both the DRE and INCA propaganda efforts to paint Oswald directly as a Castro-sponsored actor occurred post-assassination—as did DRE members' efforts to present him as part of an actual Cuban kill team in Dallas. The same can be said for the CIA's Mexico City (Gilberto Alvarado) "walk in" story about Oswald being paid by the Cubans to kill President Kennedy when he visited their consulate in late September, a story supported personally by David Phillips even after the official findings of the Warren Commission.

In neither instance—by either the DRE call or the Alvarado story—were claims of Cuban involvement supported by any actual incriminating material concretely linking Oswald to Castro agents. Certainly, the production and planting of such materials would have been well within the CIA's capabilities in term of creating faked correspondence, tape recordings of calls, or meetings or credible sources for suspicious contacts. All that was standard practice for the Agency, which itself held extensive files on actual pro-Castro agents and intelligence assets.

A much less sensational scenario, one involving the CIA use of Oswald to infiltrate and obtain information to be used in propaganda against the FPCC, is questionable due to the extent to which both the CIA and the FBI had already penetrated that organization. The extent of the FPCC penetration has been documented by Bill Simpich, with his work revealing that FBI informant T-3425-S (Victor Vicente, the social coordinator for the FPCC headquarters office in New York) had been recruited as early as 1961. Vicente was able to provide copies of membership and mailing lists as well as copies of office correspondence—including letters from Lee Harvey Oswald. The FBI also had sources within the Newark, Chicago, and Miami FPCC groups.[262]

The FPCC was well and truly infiltrated, including at its headquarters office where mail was obtained and membership lists copied, well before Oswald came on the scene with them. We have seen that even Oswald's first letters to the FPCC were monitored there and became part of his FBI file. We also know that there was a very real, and very active joint FBI/CIA project (AMSANTA) using FPCC membership as a cover for FBI penetration agents targeted for collecting information inside Cuba itself. That operation had been active and successful well before Oswald even appeared in New Orleans.

Beginning in December 1962 the CIA and FBI had begun cooperating in a new and very sophisticated, intelligence operation built around the FBI's penetration of both the FPCC and CPUSA. FPCC national members (FBI penetration assets) were briefed by the CIA and targeted on specific information to be obtained during travels to Cuba—such travel, if endorsed by FPCC headquarters and communicated to the Cuban Consulate in Mexico City, was accepted by Cuba for the granting of travel visas to the island. We have few details about the operation, although documents show that one asset (traveling via Mexico City and Cubana Airlines) was briefed by the CIA prior to departure and debriefed afterwards. The asset was even able to obtain interviews with Fidel Castro and Che Guevera while in Cuba, based on his introduction by the national FPCC organization. Shortly before his travel, he had also been asked to communicate with and join the Communist Party of the USA.[263]

The AMSANTA project was extremely well-crafted and covert. It was one of the few projects in which the FBI and CIA are known to have effectively collaborated, and aspects of it are strikingly like certain of Oswald's activities beginning in the spring of 1963. In fact, the CIA briefing officer for the project was Anita Potocki, and her name shows up in one HSCA file related to Oswald. Yet beyond the similarities, Oswald's decision not to cultivate ties with the national FPCC headquarters, and the fact (as we will see in actual appearance in Mexico City) that his efforts to get to Cuba were literally at odds with all the practices of the actual AMSANTA program, argue against his being a witting part of it.

On the other hand, given his volunteer contact with the FBI and the provision of information about the FPCC (even though it proved to be false in regard to a non-existent New Orleans chapter), there is at least the possibility that for some short period of time he might have been considered for potential recruitment in such a program. We have no evidence of that, just as we have no evidence that Oswald was considered as an FBI source or PSI—although as with the FBI, such consideration would have been in a local office "soft" file, never actually appearing in any consolidated Bureau or Agency headquarters files until he was officially recommended and began the process of review and vetting as an operational asset. And, as with other documents relating to FBI contact with Oswald or extended interest by either FBI or CIA, examples which we do have suggest that any such soft file documents would be unlikely to have survived long, post-assassination.

Chapter 12

Oswald's Own Agendas

". . . he said he was a friend of the Cuban Revolution. He show me letters to the Communist party, the American communist party, his labor card . . . that he was married with a Russian, and uh, a clipping that he was with two policemen taking him by his arms, that he was in meeting to support Cuba. And a card saying that he was a member of the Fair Play for Cuba in New Orleans...he showed me all of these papers to demonstrate that he was a friend of the revolution."

—Sylvia Duran, Cuban Consulate secretary in Mexico City, interviewed by the House Select Committee on Assassinations, June 6, 1978, Volume 3, 33

Public Remarks

In Dallas, prior to the move to New Orleans, with a regular job and something of a stable if minimal family life (at least from Marina's perspective), Lee Harvey Oswald had engaged with his ideological side again, reading, studying, and writing. He returned to a more activist interest in the subjects—and possibilities—that had begun to occupy his attentions since his time in the Marines. His activism may have been both fueled and focused by the publications he was reading, *The Militant* being a prime example. His dialogues on social systems and geopolitics with de Mohrenschildt may have further stimulated him to action. Certainly, we have concrete signs of his new Cuban activism in the form of his correspondence with the FPCC, and the likelihood of his initial demonstration for Cuba in Dallas.

Oswald's own thinking shortly prior to his departure from New Orleans was captured in notes for remarks he had been invited to make at a small Jesuit school in Mobile, Alabama. It was a short speech with questions and answers about his experiences in Russia. Through the offices of his cousin "Dutch" Murret and his wife (their son was being educated and in preparation to become a Jesuit), Oswald had been invited to address a group of students in Mobile Alabama, at their House of Studies. On July 27, he spoke for some 30 minutes, relating his personal experiences and giving his observations contrasting life in Russia with that in the United States—specifically life under Russian communism as compared to American capitalism.[264]

Oswald's remarks in that address are key to understanding both his thinking and his actions in 1963. He was adamant about things he considered extremely negative about the United States. One of his primary concerns was what he considered the "institution" of racial segregation:

> "It, is, I think the action of the active segregationist minority and the great body of indiffent (sic) people in the South who do the United States more harm in the eyes of the worlds people, than the whole world communist movement."

Oswald made it clear that he personally "disliked capitalism;" he felt it exploited the poor. One listener related that while he did not state it directly, Oswald implied that he had been disappointed in Russia because its foundation was the exploitation of the poor. He implied, but did not state directly, that he was disappointed in Russia because Russia had not truly implemented Marxist theory, and its practices had left him disillusioned with Soviet Communism.

Perhaps most importantly, Oswald asserted that both America and Russia had "major shortcomings" and advantages, but only America allowed the "voice of dissent" and the ability of that opportunity of expression, something he considered critical. Oswald's remarks, recorded in Mobile—some four months before the events of November 22 in Dallas—confirm that Oswald had not found true Marxism in Russia, and that he was still dissatisfied with conditions in the United States, including its continued racism. The speech also demonstrates the continuity and consistency of Oswald's world view—as well as his search for something better.

Preoccupation

By August, in New Orleans, with the loss of his job at Reilly Coffee, Cuba had begun to preoccupy Oswald in much the same way Russia had during his last months in the Marines. But Cuba, and its new revolutionary government, was not just of ideological interest. Given Oswald's demonstrated tendency to follow study with action, the Cuban preoccupation—and the possibility of joining its revolution in person—presented a potential solution to his employment problems, an answer for his boredom, and perhaps most importantly, an opportunity for adventure.

During August, Oswald's public actions had made his name known, and created an image around that name with the local media in New Orleans, but there is no reason to believe he was aware that the DRE was beginning to leverage that name and image for their own propaganda purposes on a larger scale, especially in Miami. In pursuing his own Cuban agenda, Oswald had begun to act, and to act with little regard to consequences, as he had in following his own personal interests to Russia.

Years earlier, he and his friend Nelson Delgado had talked about joining the Cuban revolution and helping carry it on into Central America. But by 1963, Oswald had a wife and child to consider, and the days of going to Cuba simply by boarding a ship or plane from the United States had long passed—the Bay of Pigs and the Cuban missile crisis had put a stop to all travel to Cuba directly from the United States.

Not just put a stop on Cuba in terms of commercial travel, but with the Cuban embargo the Kennedy administration had directed all government agencies (including the intelligence services and even regional military intelligence groups) to monitor and interdict anyone trying to travel to or from Cuba. Even new U.S. passports were being issued with stated restrictions for use in travel to Cuba (that restriction appeared on the new passport Oswald received in June). The only way to travel to Cuba was from overseas—or from Mexico, which still serviced Cubana airlines and flights to and from Cuba. But that sort of travel not only carried financial costs, it required that Cuba grant an entry visa to the traveler. And Cuba had become quite selective with respect to American travelers.

With what has been learned though decades of research, as well as the release of the actual CIA Mexico City station history, we can see exactly how important travelers to and from Cuba were to American intelligence. The massive CIA collections effort in Mexico City revolved around the fact that the only scheduled airline service to Cuba for the entire western hemisphere went through the Mexican capital. Encouraged by the CIA, Mexican authorities had begun photographing the passports of all travelers arriving from or leaving for Cuba—and when possible, photographing the travelers themselves. That intelligence was shared with the CIA and forwarded to interested member nations of the Organization of American States (OAS). Travel control in Mexico City logged some 4,912 legal travelers to Cuba in 1962, and 969 in the first two months of 1963.[265]

Such extensive intelligence collection was only possible due to the very close and personal relationship which developed between the Mexico City CIA station chief Winston Scott (officially First Secretary of the United States Embassy) and the Mexican presidency, in the person of Adolpho Lopez Mateos. That relationship enabled an extended series of joint Mexican/CIA intelligence operations to be carried out in what was the most sensitive foreign capital outside of Berlin. The relationships and networks built by Scott became virtually unique; in senior Mexican political circles the CIA station was sometimes referred to as "the real [American] Embassy."[266] By 1963, Mexico City had become the crown jewel of the CIA's foreign intelligence network within the Western Hemisphere.

The extent of that surveillance—electronic, radio, telephone, photographic, mail opening and intercept, travel document copying—was virtually unique, and is described in considerable detail by Bill Simpich in *State Secret,* using information taken directly from the CIA's own history of its Mexico City Station. The CIA's extensive access to and working relationship with the Mexican president is detailed in *Our Man in Mexico: Winston Scott and the Hidden History of the CIA*, by Jefferson Morley.

In the overall context of Oswald and Marina's 1963 activities, a personal view of Oswald would see him going to Mexico in pursuit of an agenda which included both his family issues, and his goal of reaching Cuba. During the course of the 1963, Oswald had shared his Cuba goals with Marina, but, as with his decision to leave Russia, she appears to have taken that it was his decision to make, and his problem to execute. Her letters and application to return home to Russia either did not include him, or noted that any request involving him would be treated separately. That summer, her most recent correspondence with the Soviet Embassy had renewed her request for permission to return home to Russia—without her husband.

By August, Oswald had begun talking of getting to Cuba in dramatic fashion, with an act which would demonstrate his commitment, and gain him instant recognition as a true supporter of revolutionary Cuba. He spoke to Marina about hijacking a plane, even an airliner (something that would certainly have given him a dramatic introduction), and even asked her to help him—she adamantly declined, telling him it was a crazy plan.

Yet she also described telling him that if he could get to the island legally in some fashion, and send for her, she would come with June and the new baby. Marina felt that Lee had "cooled off" a bit after being arrested during the street leafletting and spending a night in jail. She described Oswald as more cautious, but still focused on Cuba. She also noted that he had begun considering the possibility of going to Mexico as a step towards obtaining permission to travel on to Cuba.[267]

Marina testified that it had been sometime in August when Oswald had first told her of his decision to go to Mexico in an attempt to enter Cuba. He had already gotten a new passport in June, and by September 17 he had obtained a Tourist Card from the Mexican consulate general in New Orleans ("Tourist Card," FM-8 No. 24085)—good for one entry but allowing for a stay of no more than 15 days.[268]

What followed next is, and likely will remain, confusing as to both detail and specific motive. While she was aware that he had talked about Mexico, it appears that Oswald's late August remarks to Marina were limited in any details, much as during earlier separations. He would leave her and the baby, going to look for work elsewhere—possibly back east, perhaps on the Texas Gulf, in the Houston area. And with Oswald once again going off to look for work, and the arrival of a new baby becoming imminent, Marina once again took advantage of the type of offer she had received several times since their return from Russia to Texas.

In mid-July, Ruth Paine had written Marina and proposed that she bring the baby and live with her while she was expecting. Ruth even offered to pay Marina for Russian language tutoring and to pay for doctors' expenses, medicines, and other basic needs of the new baby. She followed that with a letter advising Marina that she would be leaving on a driving vacation at the end of July, which she did, returning by way of New Orleans to visit the Oswalds.[269]

Mrs. Paine arrived in New Orleans on September 20, and spent three nights with the couple, seemingly finding their relations improved, but being told that Lee was going to look for a job elsewhere, in Houston or possibly on the East Coast (Philadelphia was mentioned, and Oswald had also written the Socialist Workers Party and CPUSA about a planned move back East—something he appears not to have mentioned to Marina at all).

During her time in New Orleans, Mrs. Paine found relations between Lee and Marina somewhat improved, but with Lee off to look for work again, Marina accepted Ruth's offer and it was decided that Marina would go back with her to Texas. At that point in time Marina was aware of Oswald's plan to go to Mexico at some point, but apparently nothing of that was shared with Ruth Paine. On Sunday, September 22, Lee and Mrs. Paine finished loading the Paines' station wagon with the family's household belongings, and Oswald was left to himself.[270] Two days later, on September 24, he closed out his New Orleans post office box and completed a form to have his mail forwarded to the Paine residence in Dallas.[271]

It is also a matter of record that before leaving New Orleans, on September 25, Oswald collected an unemployment check for $33 and that he also placed a phone call to Horace Twiford, an official of the Texas Socialist Labor Party. Twiford had earlier received Oswald's name from the party's headquarters in New York, and sent him a copy of its official publication, the *Weekly People*. Oswald told Mrs. Twiford that he was a member of the Fair Play for Cuba Committee, and that he hoped to see her husband for a few hours before he flew to Mexico. Mrs. Twiford told Oswald that her husband, a merchant seaman, was at sea but would be happy to see him at some other time; she offered to take a message. Oswald said that he could not await her husband's return because he was flying to Mexico.[272]

Oswald and Mexico

Given Oswald's preoccupation with Cuba, his failure to find satisfactory work (or any work) in New Orleans—as well as the issue of the false information he had given the New Orleans FBI office—it is no real surprise to find him once again on the move. Using the Mexican travel visa he had obtained in New Orleans, he was next reported approaching both Cuban and Russian diplomatic staff in Mexico City about travel to Cuba. Fortunately, we have a reasonably detailed record of those exchanges with the Cubans and Russians, not only from the individuals themselves, but also from a covert intelligence collection network the CIA was operating in Mexico City.

Given that context, we can turn to our two standard questions about all of Oswald's activities. The first is whether his activities at the Cuban Consulate and Russian Embassy in Mexico City were consistent with the personal agendas Oswald had developed during 1963. The second is to what extent Oswald's remarks and his behavior with Cuban and Russian diplomatic staff is consistent with we have learned about his character and personality.

With respect to continuity, two personal agendas developed in 1963 and run though virtually all of Oswald's activities during that final year of his life. The first agenda began with a December greeting card to the Soviet Embassy in New York, with a follow-on letter signed by Marina in February, 1963—kicking off his effort to get Marina and June back to Russia.

Then, in a February letter to Ernst Titovets in Russia, Marina herself began to complain of missing her old friends in Russia, and being unable to reach them by mail.[273] That was quite consistent with the very personal remarks in Marina's letter to the Soviet Embassy, where she specifically mentioned "returning to the Homeland" and wanting to again feel like a "full-fledged citizen." In that letter she also acknowledged that her husband, as an American citizen, would be remaining in the United States.

In a second letter in March, Marina sent an official application form, and spoke of extreme "homesickness." In that letter, Marina wrote of returning to Russia with her husband. However, a separate enclosure, in Lee's handwriting, speaks of the urgency of responding to Marina given her pregnancy, while stating that his own return visa "should be considered separately."

The only disconnect in what appears to be a campaign to return Marina separately to Russia is found in a letter to Titovets from Oswald in New Orleans—in June—which speaks to the fact that he might well be returning to Russia with Marina. This shocked Titovets, as he realized how difficult that would be for Oswald; personally, he considered it a "naïve idea" at best.[274] Then again, Oswald might simply have recalled that he had been offered Soviet citizenship at one point during his extended struggle to leave Russia and return to the United States.

Based on his ongoing correspondence with the Soviets, Oswald's return was to be considered separately—as a Russian citizen, it was simply more expedient for Marina to be granted permission to return as soon as possible (later an element of urgency would be added, with the request to speed up the process to allow her back before the birth of their second child). But by August, the Soviet Embassy in New York responded to the Oswalds that there could be no expediting the request; it would have to go to Moscow and the process could easily take up to six months for a decision. Given the pace of the exchanges over the previous six months, there was little reason to doubt that even a response to Marina would not happen until after the birth of their second child.

The second theme to emerge for Lee Oswald in 1963 was a return to his interest in Cuba. That interest included a visualization of Cuba offering the ideological and social opportunity that he had once eagerly anticipated in his travel to the Soviet Union. The emergence of that Cuba interest, which became something of an obsession, has been detailed above. But as we saw in his Russian saga, Oswald approached such goals with a great deal of planning, of saving, and of considering options and alternatives. His constant reading fueled both his planning and his preparations.

From a practical standpoint, Oswald's regular newsletter and magazine reading exposed him to articles on Cuba. These would have made him aware that, by 1963, only select American supporters of the Castro regime were being admitted into Cuba, and that one route—the cheapest—was by air travel via Mexico City. However, Americans wishing to take that route had begun to rely on advance written endorsement from the American Communist Party or from the national Fair Play for Cuba Committee. Letters from either could pave the way for Cuban entry visas to be granted.

Whether that had influenced his written communications with both CPUSA and the FPCC is purely speculative, but we do know that during Oswald's visit to the Cuban Consulate in Mexico City, the consulate secretary described Oswald as presenting material showing both Communist Party and FPCC connections. The secretary, Sylvia Tirado de Duran, even asked Oswald why he had not gotten an actual endorsement letter for travel to Cuba from CPUSA. Oswald replied that he had simply not had time to do so, given his wife's impending delivery of their new baby.[275]

More realistically, given Oswald's earlier concerns about his personal mail being monitored (or of all mail to the CPUSA being monitored), he may well have been afraid that such a mail request to CPUSA for aid in traveling to Cuba would have been picked up by the FBI (and rightly so). That certainly could have resulted in more visits from FBI agents, more questioning, and possibly some sort of watch on him. He may have feared that such attention from the FBI might even have resulted in a directive to block his travel to Mexico.

As to his other option for a Cuban travel endorsement, Oswald's relationship with the FPCC was particularly convoluted. Certainly, the FBI knew about that; he had told them himself. However, he would have needed a travel recommendation from its national headquarters, most likely from V. T. Lee himself. Oswald had repeatedly corresponded with the FPCC earlier in the year. He had advised V. T. Lee of his demonstrating for Cuba near the carrier *Wasp* (noting that the officers were interested in his leaflets—true in one sense at least, as described previously).[276] Following that, he had also written of his demonstration in downtown New Orleans, and of his arrest and radio appearances, including the debate in which both he and the FPCC had been tainted with Russian and communist associations.

Yet while Oswald continually tried to impress V. T. Lee, we have no record of any further responses to Oswald from the FPCC during his time in New Orleans—much less any encouragement. He had ignored Lee's negative advice on creating a New Orleans chapter, and he had given false information about the FPCC to the FBI. Oswald may very well have suspected that a request for aid in his quest to get to Cuba would fare no better, especially given that V. T. Lee himself had been indicted for illegal travel to Cuba.

Regardless of his reasons, in passing on a personal appeal for Cuban travel support to the FPCC or CPUSA, Oswald was isolating himself from the most likely source of endorsements that he might have otherwise leveraged to obtain an entry visa for Cuba, even a limited-stay tourist class visa. Without an endorsement from the CPUSA or the FPCC, and with Cuban suspicion of ongoing American counter-intelligence and dirty tricks targeting their diplomatic missions (very much justified), the only real alternative would be to obtain Soviet approval for a Cuban transit visa—traveling though Cuba to Russia.

Given Oswald's prior difficulties in gaining entry to Russia, he appears to have realized that, especially with the U.S. embargo on Cuban travel and Cuban suspicions of American travelers, he would need some leverage to present his case for a Cuban entry visa to the Cuban Consulate in Mexico City. In his Russian effort, he had touted offers of radar system intelligence to the Soviets—and that had not worked. It had only been the drama of his wrist-slitting that had turned the situation into a possible embarrassment for the Soviets, resulting in permission for him to stay.

Oswald may also have decided that he might have to make a very personal appeal for entry at the consulates in Mexico City. This appeal would be based on the urgency for his travel to Russia with respect to his wife expecting a new baby, combined with his own recent history of strong public support for Cuba and its revolution. Perhaps that would be enough to persuade the Cubans to at least grant him a limited entry visa while he pursued his and Marina's petitions to the Soviets.

That speculation appears to be supported by the details of the material that Oswald took on his travel to Mexico City—and the nature of his exchanges with Russian Embassy and Cuban Consulate personnel during his attempt to obtain an entry visa. Items listed for his travel, and those observed/presented at the consulates, included such routine official materials as his 1963 renewed passport, and an earlier passport.[277] But beyond these, in contacts with both the Cubans and Russians, Oswald also presented a limited number of items associating him with demonstrations for Cuba and with the Fair Play for Cuba Committee.

At the Cuban Consulate, Oswald presented a much more extensive set of materials related to his activism, his ideological credentials, and his support for Cuba and its revolution. Those materials included copies of correspondence with the Communist Party, newspaper clippings concerning his arrest for protesting for Cuba in New Orleans, and additional materials illustrating his membership in and support of the Fair Play for Cuba Committee. He even prepared a written personal history which included his early interest in Communist literature, his ability to speak Russian, his confrontation with police authorities in connection with protests for Cuba—and his experience in "street agitation," as a "radio speaker and lecturer," and as a photographer.[278]

Based on statements from staff at the Cuban Consulate, it appears that Oswald did assertively support his efforts to gain an entry/transit visa to Cuba with two main arguments—travel to Russia via Cuba being urgent for his family in order to return Marina to Russia for the birth of their second child, and support for the fact that he was indeed a politically active supporter of both Russia and the Cuban revolution. In its interviews with the administrative receptionist at the Cuban Consulate, Sylvia Duran, and with Cuban Consulate staff, the HSCA investigators confirmed that Oswald's efforts to get an entry visa for Cuba involved these materials, along with the media "resume" that he had built during the summer of 1963. He had taken considerable pains to assemble and take the support materials for that resume with him to Mexico City.

Mexico City Contact Chronology

Numerous open issues remain with respect to Oswald's travel and movements in Mexico City; there remain mysteries regarding that trip that may never be resolved. But strictly in terms of his specific dialogue with the Cubans and Russians, his requests were straightforward and consistent, even if judged as wishful thinking on his part. He wanted to be in Cuba while his family was returning to Russia and he was getting approval to join them. Just that simple. In retrospect, this was not likely to happen, but that is what he wanted and what he asked for from both parties.

In personal interactions with Duran and another official at the Cuban Consulate, Oswald explained that his wife was in the process of returning to her homeland in Russia with their children, and that he wanted a limited duration entry visa to Cuba, so that he could reside there while the process of his family's return was finalized. Such requests were in concert with the ongoing efforts to return Marina to Russia, which had been in progress since the first of that year. His actual Cuban visa application was specifically focused on getting himself permission to travel to Cuba, where he felt he would be better able to support the family's return to Russia. In making that request, he misrepresented the actual state of Russian approval for Marina's request to the Cubans, presenting it as already approved and with the final details of her return being worked out.

The basic chronology of his visits to the Cuban and Russian diplomatic facilities, provided by the CIA, supports that view of his actions. The following working chronology of those contacts, along with details of Oswald's behavior during his various approaches to the Cubans and Russians, is taken from the CIA's description of his contacts and from the statements and testimony of Sylvia Duran and other individuals at both the Cuban and Russian offices.

Oswald's first contact with the Cubans on Friday, September 27, was at their embassy offices, housed in the same building complex as its consulate. There, he stated his goal of getting a transit/travel visa, and was quickly referred to the consulate where such matters were handled. At the consulate Oswald spoke with Senora Duran, a Mexican citizen employed as administrative staff. Duran later made a signed statement to the Mexican police that Oswald had approached her at her desk, and stated he wished to apply for a Cuba transit visa for travel to Russia. Oswald supported his Russian connection with his passport, which recorded prior travel to Russia, with his earlier work permit for Russia (in Russian), as well as various letters in Russian. He also provided proof of being married to a Russian woman.

Oswald added an appeal for special consideration as a strong supporter of the Fair Play for Cuba Committee, illustrated by his work with the FPCC New Orleans chapter, and a plea that he was a very public advocate of the Cuban Revolution. Duran stated that Oswald also mentioned a connection to the American Communist Party (Duran's statement for the Warren Commission states she could not recall if he had claimed to be a member[279]) and displayed documents (most likely correspondence with CPUSA) purporting to be evidence of that CPUSA association.[280]

By the 1960s, membership in the CPUSA was a matter of having paperwork on file with their national office, and "card carrying communist" was an artifact of earlier decades. The term had come into popular usage early in the 1950s during the McCarthy hearings. At that point it had taken on a life of its own in the media. If Oswald had displayed such a membership card it most likely would have been a forgery; no record of his actual membership in the party—despite his correspondence—was ever produced.

We have seen numerous examples from placement office visits and job interviews demonstrating that Oswald could be well-spoken and effective in expressing himself when it was in his best interest—and he appears to have done so initially at the Cuban Consulate. Duran confirmed that he presented himself well and made a positive impression on her. As a result, she did make an effort to assist him with his application rather than simply turning him away, at one point later in the day even calling the Soviet Embassy in order to assess the state of his Soviet entry application.[281] In that call, she mentioned an American wishing to travel to Cuba, but did not give his name. That call, as well as a follow-up call from the Russian Embassy to Duran, is critical in that they were intercepted by CIA telephone monitoring and revealed that an American was trying to illegally travel to Cuba. As standard practice, that prompted a Mexico City station effort to identify the American.

Oswald told Duran that he wished to spend some time in Cuba, at least two weeks, before going on to Russia, and she filled out the visa application. But in doing so, Duran pointed out that Cuba would require proof that he had been accepted by Russia for travel and entry to that country. Duran took down the relevant data and instructed Oswald on what was needed to complete it, including Russian approval of his travel. She pointed out the application would require photographs—at that time Oswald did not have the required photos to attach to the application with him, and he left the consulate to obtain them.[282]

Oswald returned to the Cuban Consulate later that afternoon, bringing the necessary photographs. The photograph from the application has itself caused skeptical comment, because it does not show clothing like that which Duran described Oswald as wearing on his visit to the consulate. That, along with inconsistencies over time in remarks from consular staff on physical description and hair color have become the basis for speculation that it was not Lee Harvey Oswald, but rather an imposter contacting the Cubans and Russians—most likely involved in some sort of intelligence activity.

As a counter to that skepticism, a matching photo, and a sweater identical to that in the photo on the travel application, were recovered from Oswald's belongings following his arrest. While Marina Oswald could provide no information on the photo, she did recognize the sweater and confirm it as being one he owned.[283] The simplest explanation of the photo issue would seem to be that Oswald simply took along photos—something an international traveler applying for travel papers, or even a CIA-prepared impersonator would do—but did not have them on his person during his visit to the consulate. When it was made clear to him that photos were required for the application, he returned to his hotel and retrieved them.

Another counter to the suggestion of physical impersonation is simply that Duran had made it clear that she needed a photo to complete the application. When the American returned with the photo, she had a close view of him along with it—at a minimum the individual would have had to very closely resemble the photo. It has also been pointed out, in the early work of researcher Peter Dale Scott, that with respect to the hair color question, "blond" in Spanish can be translated as including light brown, which was Oswald's hair color.

What we now know of actual CIA operations against the Cuban diplomatic mission in Mexico City also argues against the use of an imposter in what was a relatively minor, low-level contact with Cuban Consulate staff—low-level and brief when compared to other clandestine CIA efforts already well-established and in progress. In separate, much more extensive efforts, the CIA had previously sent Cuban assets to "probe" the Cuban Consulate, both in personal visits and through both business and family connections. Such operations used trusted anti-Castro assets who had well-established social and commercial cover. Most often they were made by individuals who were longtime residents of Mexico City. We will be reviewing a number of examples of real CIA political action operations against Cuban diplomatic staff in the following chapters.

With the question of official Russian approval on Oswald's travel still an issue, Duran then made a call to the Russian Embassy to try to confirm that all the arrangements were in place, and that his travel was or would shortly be approved. [284] She was advised that a request for his wife had been submitted and was being processed—but that it would be some months before it could be approved, and Oswald had no immediate approval for travel to Russia. [285] Duran then advised Oswald that until there was official Russian approval, there was no way that his transit travel could be immediately approved by the Cuban government.

That information led to Oswald's next diplomatic contact on that Friday, an in-person visit to the Russian Embassy. During that visit, he expressed his desire to return with his wife to Russia, reviewed his prior time in Russian, and referenced previous letters to the Soviet Embassy, including his wife's request to return to Russia. At that point, Oswald stated that he wished to join her there and spend an extended time in Russia with her.

He described his problem as one of knowing it would likely take time to get his own travel to Russia approved, and he wished to wait for that approval in Cuba—being a strong supporter of the Cuban revolution and presenting material to support that fact (likely his FPCC membership).[286] The response he received was the same as that which he had previously been given by mail—the applications for his wife's Russian reentry would take months to process; Moscow was involved and matters were in the hands of the Soviet Embassy in Washington.

The calls to and from the Russian Embassy on Friday, September 27 would become especially important to the Oswald story, as they were recorded at the central telephone tap station (LIENVOY). According to the Mexico City station history, that intercept station produced transcripts and call summaries which were made available to the CIA, the FBI, and the Mexican president's office. On that Friday, multiple calls would have drawn attention to the fact that an American was trying to illegally travel to Cuba. And according to CIA personnel, as soon as that was reported to the CIA station chief, he immediately ordered an effort to identify the American.

Following his rebuff by the Russians, Oswald returned to the Cuban Consulate for a third time—only to falsely assure Duran that he had actually been encouraged by the Russians. Given that assurance, she allowed him to proceed with his application. At that point, Duran received a phone call from the Russian Embassy, asking if the American had returned. Duran and the Russian caller discussed the open issues related to Oswald's request and the fact that there was going to be no approval from the Russians for some months.[287]

Duran proceeded to give the bad news to Oswald, making it clear that his request for travel to Cuba was simply not going to be approved at that point in time. Once again, Oswald was being thwarted by governmental bureaucracy—and bureaucracy was one of the things he most thoroughly disliked. The Cuban system was not going to respond to a personal plea for entry into Cuba; the wait for Russian approval for Marina's return to Russia was an unavoidable road block. And, in a pattern of behavior we have seen before, when blocked by bureaucracy and frustrated by process and regulations, Oswald's tendency to become confrontational came into play.

He began to be more assertive with Duran, loud and demanding, and at that point she called in Cuban Consul Eusebio Azcue for support. When interviewed by HSCA staff years later, Azcue described Oswald as both stubborn and confrontational. When Azcue cited rules to him, Oswald became agitated and angry, accusing Azcue of not being a true friend of the Cuban revolution, but simply a bureaucrat.

That was too much for Azcue, who had him escorted out of the consulate building.

According to the CIA's own chronology, the following day, Sept 28, was a Saturday with embassies and consulates normally closed. However, Oswald appears to have made one more attempt to break the stalemate by going to the Russian Embassy, contacting a guard, and managing to get inside for an interview with Russian staff personnel. While there have been objections that an American appearing at the Soviet Embassy on a Saturday would not even have been allowed in—much less interviewed by multiple embassy counsels (including KGB officers) who happened to be on premise—it is important to note that "walk-ins" were not uncommon during the Cold War. There were walk-in defections by Americans to Soviet embassies and Russians to American embassies.[288] One of the major intelligence roles for each side was to make itself open to potential defectors. The idea of an unknown American showing up on Saturday morning and asking for urgent assistance certainly would have drawn the attention of any Russian counsel staff on hand at the time.

Unfortunately, the information that we have on Oswald's Saturday visit and his actual remarks to the Russians came only years later, from interviews and writings of the Russians themselves. Their stories have been received with much skepticism, because they portray Oswald as being agitated, and acting quite dramatically—arguing the urgency of his request in terms of his personal safety. He was described as stating that the FBI was harassing him, and he even feared for his life. To emphasize that point he produced a pistol, which he said he had to carry for his own protection. According to the Russians they wanted nothing to do with such an individual, and once again he was shown the door.

Of course, that level of agitation and emotion is seized on by supporters of the Warren Commission as an indication of increasingly emotional behavior from someone who within two months would murder the president of the United States. Alternatively, it is rejected as totally false by those arguing against the Warren Commission views. What seems to be lost in most commentary on the incident is that Oswald was described as showing the gun only to make the point that he felt himself threatened, and was asking only that the Russians act to allow him to gain temporary and immediate refuge in Cuba, for his own safety. That attitude would later be expressed in a November letter from Oswald to the Russian Embassy in New York City.

In the context of Oswald's personal history, given that a last-ditch, dramatic act of slitting his wrists had managed to gain him a stay in Russia, such an action is actually quite consistent with Oswald's known behavior. When Oswald was stymied, he could indeed be quite dramatic. His Russian friend Ernst Titovets observed that Oswald was a good mimic, with a real ability to do improvisation and throw himself effectively into role-playing as an actor—Titovets had observed those qualities in a series of reading and role-playing sessions he had done with Oswald taking different roles (and even being tape recorded) as part of their mutual practice of each other's native language.[289]

Oswald's attitude towards, if not actual fear of, the FBI may also not have been totally feigned. After his return to the U.S., he would deliver a letter to the Dallas FBI office protesting harassment, and their treatment of Marina, later even bringing up FBI harassment directly with FBI agent Hosty while being interrogated over the murder of the president. Oswald's own description of the dialogue with the Russian Consulate in Mexico City was less dramatic. According to Marina, Oswald later told her that the Soviet Embassy in Mexico City had basically "refused to have anything to do with him."[290]

Oswald's last reported contact with the Russians in Mexico City was a Tuesday, October 1 call. That call was particularly important, because in it the caller asked for the name of the counsel he had met on the Saturday visit, and the Russian staff member identified the person as (Valeriy) Kostikov. The caller also identified himself as "Oswald"—resolving two major questions for the CIA: the name of the American attempting to travel to Cuba and the name of the Russian he had been in contact with at their embassy.

The October 1 call intercept and the official transcript of that call became the foundation for communicating the "possible" identification of the American contacting the Russian Embassy in Mexico City as Lee Harvey Oswald. It became the standard reference in follow-on communications among government agencies during the weeks that followed. It would only become apparent over time, following the assassination of President Kennedy, that there were inconsistencies in how various parties described the October 1 call—descriptions unfortunately only recorded years after the fact. The translators' recollections about the callers would also become blurred regarding which call was being discussed—a Saturday call, the October 1 Tuesday call, or possibly another of some seven calls to the Russian Embassy that the CIA presented as "possibly" being Oswald.

As an example, the CIA translators recalled remarks made during a "long call" they assumed was that of October 1, but which are not on the official October 1 call transcript. CIA officer David Phillips also described similar comments on a "long call" which do not appear on the October 1 transcript. Worse yet, there are annotations and remarks about the caller using "broken Russian" which the translators themselves do not recall having put into any of their transcripts or of annotating onto any transcripts. The origin of remarks characterizing Oswald as using "broken Russian" is totally unclear and could not be identified nor verified by the eventual HSCA inquiry.

We are left with the possibility that one or more transcripts may have been altered, either to add misleading information after the fact, or to sanitize remarks Oswald might have made, possibly in requesting financial assistance from the Russians (which was something Marina had asked for in her correspondence with the Russian Embassy). Both the translators and David Phillips recalled remarks about financial help in the tape they had heard. Beyond that, the reference to "broken

Russian" in the transcripts, something totally rejected by the Russian-speaking translators, becomes highly questionable. We will revisit those and other issues in the following chapter, along with a discussion of why and how the call record became so confusing—perhaps intentionally so in some respects.

The "American" Identified

The CIA's documentary record states that, based on interception (at the LIENVOY central phone tap site) of an October 1 call to the Russian Embassy in which the caller used the name "Oswald," the Mexico City station had "possibly" identified Oswald as the American contacting the Russian Embassy regarding travel. During that call, it was the Russians themselves who had identified Kostikov as someone Oswald had met at their embassy. Based on that information a series of CIA communications followed—communications internally in Mexico City, with CIA headquarters and with other government agencies. Documents show that the Mexico City station almost immediately advised the American Ambassador in Mexico City and the Mexico City FBI Legat of Oswald's presence—including his visits to both the Russians and Cubans and his contact with a suspected Russian intelligence agent (Kostikov) at the Russian Embassy. What they also reveal is that Mexico City informed CIA headquarters only about Oswald's Russian contacts—his contacts with the Cuban consulate and his requests to travel to Cuba were not reported. That lack of communication is certainly questionable, especially given the fact that Anne Goodpasture, a key aide to Winston Scott, would years later explain it by simply stating that headquarters "had no need to know all those other details."[291]

Prior to November 22, 1963, the story of Lee Harvey Oswald in Mexico City would have appeared simple but concerning—primarily to the FBI—as he had apparently been in contact with a Russian intelligence agent. The fact that he had illegally tried to travel to Cuba was in the record, reported to FBI headquarters by the Mexico City FBI Legat—but not by the CIA. It would only be after President Kennedy was killed in Dallas that questions about Oswald's appearance in Mexico City became a matter of serious concern and mystery. And it would be the CIA's own actions, related to its film and tape records as well as its apparent withholding of information, which would fuel questions about Oswald's time there—and immediately after the assassination would raise questions at the highest levels of government about whether he had been impersonated, in person or in telephone calls. And it was the CIA itself that obstructed even the simplest immediate actions which would have resolved the issue of impersonation.

Instead of moving to clarify Oswald's appearance at the Cuban Consulate, after the assassination the Mexico City CIA station quickly and directly intervened with the Mexican Federal police to ensure that Sylvia Duran was taken into custody, harshly questioned, and prevented from being directly questioned by the FBI or by Warren Commission staff, something she offered to do. It would only be years after the fact that the HSCA and others managed to at least interview Duran.

Over time, with follow-on inquiry by the HSCA and released records related to the work of the ARRB, it has also become apparent that the CIA's own records practices have made it virtually impossible to check leads which might have resolved at least some issues. As an example, the Mexico City station's own history stresses the importance of its role in counterintelligence, and as Bill Simpich's research notes, that role included recording all visits by US citizens with Soviet representatives. Yet the relevant CIA station files were purged of all such "visits of US citizens" prior to 1967.

More significantly, details of the operation of the station's listening posts and camera stations were supposedly recorded in detail. Those records should have allowed investigators to determine which stations might have photographed Oswald in his visits. The primary photographic system for the Russia Embassy (LIMITED) began operations at 9:00 in the morning, and on the date of Oswald's reported Friday appearance ceased work by noon. Given that the Oswald visit was late in that day, the lack of a photo from that station on Friday is reasonable enough. However, a second station (LILYRIC) normally operated later in the afternoon, and both LIMITED and LILYRIC operated on Saturday as well. Unfortunately, the HSCA would find the logs for LILYRIC photographic operations to be entirely missing. The CIA's records also show that the Cuban Consulate was supposed to have been photographed on a regular basis in October 1963, yet we have no daily set of photos for that month.

We see the same problems with the station's records of phone taps and tape recordings; it is not even possible to confirm whether Sylvia Duran's phone was tapped by the local LIFEAT listening post at the time of Oswald's visit. Simpich notes that virtually all the LIFEAT records are missing for 1963.

More importantly there are questions about exactly who held transcripts or perhaps even tape copies of the apparent Oswald/Duran call of Saturday, September 28. In the next chapter, the evidence that this call was an impersonation "pretext call" involving neither Oswald nor Duran will be discussed. Regardless, by the time of the assassination, the Mexico City station should have known about and been investigating that call for some two months—especially as it related to Oswald's personal visit to the Russian Embassy. Yet on November 23, the President of Mexico would be the one to call the Mexico City station chief and inform him that the Mexicans had a copy of the transcript (and possibly a tape?) of that call—and were looking into it. Given that the CIA, FBI, and the Mexican President's office were all identified as being provided with information from the LIENVOY intercept program, we are left to speculate on whether the FBI had its own copy of the transcript/tape from the highly suspicious Saturday call.

Once again, the full story of CIA records confusion (or obfuscation) is something beyond the scope of this work. However, in the following chapters we will explore some of the most significant questions—particularly the taped conversations of purported Oswald calls—in order to attempt to add at least a bit more clarity regarding what (and when) both the CIA and FBI knew about Oswald's contacts with the Cubans and Russians in Mexico City.

Chapter 13

Mexico City

"Of course, the Soviet Embassy was not at fault, they were as I say unprepared. The Cuban counsel was guilty of a gross breach of regulations. I am glad he has been fired."
—Lee Harvey Oswald, Letter to Soviet Consulate in New York City, November 9, 1963

Oswald "On the Radar"

During the Warren Commission inquiry, the CIA took the position that Oswald was not a subject of particular interest during his time in Mexico City. David Phillips, responsible for activities targeting both the Cuban and Russian diplomatic facilities in that city, later wrote in his own books about life in the CIA that Oswald was not even "on their radar" in Mexico. Of course, such assertions implied that there were no standing CIA intelligence practices in place to routinely monitor or proactively report on visitors to either the Cuban or Russian diplomatic facilities. It also avoided the issue that special attention was paid to American citizens who might be suspected of illegal travel to Cuba, or perhaps something such as selling information—or even defection.[292]

Given the embargo against Cuban travel, as well as the implications of American citizens going to and from Mexico and contacting Russian Consulate staff in the process, such an assertion seems highly suspect. And, as we have learned and the HSCA confirmed, a CIA/FBI liaison agreement was in place regarding surveillance and counterintelligence practices in Mexico City and was active throughout 1963. It was routine for American visitors to the Cuban or Russian facilities to be monitored and if possible, identified.

We even have evidence of such practices in use during 1963, including with faked "pretext" calls to determine if a visiting American suspect might attempt to provide or sell information to either the Cubans or Russians. "Pretext calls" of various types were standard practice, made to elicit various types of information about Russian and Cuban activities and diplomatic practices. The CIA continued to use them for basic intelligence collections for years after the Kennedy assassination.[293]

In one instance, in July 1963, an American had called the Cuban Embassy, suggesting he had information which he would offer for a fee. The call was picked up on an embassy phone tap, and the officer responsible for counterintelligence at the CIA's Mexico City station—David Phillips—directed that a follow-up "impersonation" call be made. The call was carried out as if from the Cubans, advising the man never to contact them directly again, but setting up a covert meeting. The resulting meeting collected hard evidence of the offer of information for money, which was shared with the FBI. When the individual returned to the U.S., he was arrested and successfully prosecuted.[294]

It is also of note that Jeremy Gunn, an ARRB attorney who was involved in reviewing the Mexico City station's practices, said that in some instances the Mexico City CIA station would work an identification tactic on consulate visitors the opposite way. If a suspect, unidentified caller was detected via telephone tap, CIA clandestine personnel would then make a follow-up pretext call to the consulate or embassy pretending to be the previous caller—and probing to find out if the conversation would reveal names and contact information.[295]

The extent of the CIA's capability to collect all types of information in Mexico City was truly amazing, the result of a working agreement between the Mexican president and both the American ambassador and the CIA station chief. In the following section we will briefly examine activities of the CIA intelligence network in Mexico City—primarily because efforts to protect and conceal the CIA's intelligence collections capabilities there may have led to intentional obfuscation of the historical record related to the assassination inquiry. Those intelligence activities include specific operations being carried out against the Cuban diplomatic staff in the Mexican capital. We now know that certain of those operations directly targeted individuals associated with Oswald's appearances at Cuban and Russian diplomatic facilities; others relate to general CIA station activities in Mexico.

Readers interested in further details of the highly secret CIA relationship between the United States and the Mexican government, arranged through the offices of the Mexican president, and an in-depth description of CIA practices and capabilities in Mexico City, are referred to Jefferson Morley's *Our Man in Mexico* and Bill Simpich's essays in *State Secret* (Chapter 4: Mexico City Intrigue—The World of Surveillance). The CIA's own historical record on the Mexico City station is an invaluable resource.[296] Given that the Mexico City station's interest in Oswald originated in intercepts of telephone calls, it is critical to understand both the details and the extent of CIA electronic monitoring that was in place in Mexico City in the early 1960s. The following overview is based on Simpich's work on the CIA collections network in operation as of 1963.

A Unique Intelligence Resource [297]

The initial CIA phone tap program, LIFEAT, was set up shortly after World War II. LIFEAT used several "outside" phone line taps, at points adjacent to target locations. During 1963, a varying number of taps, ranging from 16 to 24 lines, were monitored from seven listening posts. These listening posts, staffed by local CIA employees, were set up in homes because it made it easier for the operator to avoid sudden entry by phone company inspectors or repairmen. LIFEAT was considered particularly secure given that all the monitoring was carried out by CIA employees, and the information was not shared outside the Agency.

Individual phone call monitoring, tape recording, and some transcription was performed at those sites, with a listening post operator and assistant at each. Because the listening centers tapped into active phone lines (such as the Cuban Consulate line), calls from the centers could be placed as if they were coming from the consulates—care simply needed to be taken to place them during off-hours so as not to have such a call detected by consulate staff. This possibility becomes of particular interest in that one of the suspected Oswald calls, ostensibly involving Oswald himself and Sylvia Duran, was reportedly placed from the Cuban Consulate on Saturday, a day on which the consulate was closed.

The targets of the individual tap program extended to residences (including those of political opponents of the Mexican president) as well as embassy and consulate telephone line taps. Collections at the diplomatic facilities were supported by photographic surveillance, as well as by mail opening and monitoring activities at a central city postal location.

At the beginning of 1959, an additional and more sophisticated, centralized tap operation (LIENVOY) was brought into play. Thirty-two phone lines were tapped within a Mexican central office telephone switching center—with the help of the Mexican Security Police, a.k.a. DFS. The central office tap operation focused on diplomatic embassies, and call conversations were monitored, recorded, and transcribed in a room staffed by Mexican Army officers. Intelligence from all telephone collections were shared with the office of the Mexican president and with the FBI personnel in Mexico City.

The combination of local line and central switching center taps gave the CIA extensive access to communications related to political and military activities in Central and South America. It operated under an extremely covert and politically fragile secret agreement between the CIA, representing the United States, and the president of Mexico. The capability of such a real-time collections system (offering far more detail than photographic surveillance or even mail opening) was considered vital to both the political and national security interests of Mexico and the United States. Its exposure would have been immensely damaging to the foreign relations of both countries.

The "Oswald Calls" [298]

Phone line monitoring is at the heart of the CIA's official story of Oswald's time in Mexico City. And as far as the record goes, that monitoring was on the Russian Embassy, carried out by the Mexican security police personnel (DFS) at the LIENVOY central telephone switch site. Without the monitoring and reporting of the Friday calls between Duran and the Russians about an American wanting to travel to Cuba, the CIA likely would not have undertaken the priority effort at identifying the American which followed. Some 7 different calls to the Russian Embassy—which might or might not have involved Oswald—are noted in CIA records as being potentially related to Oswald's time in Mexico City.

Unfortunately, only many years later would the two translators who worked with the calls be interviewed for the record. A review of those interviews shows that while their personal recollections contain some inconsistencies, they generally raise doubts about certain descriptions of the calls in the CIA's official records. The translators' main contribution was that on at least two of the calls the voice was the same—with one of those calls being the one in which the caller had identified himself as Oswald.

One call, from the Cuban Consulate on Friday, September 27, 1963—by the Cuban Consulate secretary, Sylvia Duran—seems to clearly reference Oswald, although he was not mentioned by name. The October 1 call, in which Oswald's name was used, and a reference is made to a recent visit to the Russian Embassy, appears credible to the extent that it was later supported by the Russian staff. The Russian answering the call acknowledged the visit by the caller and named the Russian counsel (Kostikov) as the person the caller had visited with during his appearance at the embassy.

It is a separate Saturday, September 28 call which has drawn the most attention, in part because it was noted that a woman was involved and that the man speaking used very broken Russian. The call was presented by the CIA as involving Sylvia Duran and Oswald, being made from the Cuban Consulate to the Russian Embassy. Yet the Cuban Consulate was closed on Saturday, as was the Russian Embassy; the call was supposedly answered by a building guard. Beyond the problems of the Cuban Consulate being closed, Duran strongly denied ever participating in such a call. Years later, the HSCA's assessment was that Duran was credible in her denial that she had not been at the consulate on Saturday, nor had she made a call with Oswald to the Russian Embassy on that day.[299] The transcript of this call has the hallmarks of an impersonation—a "pretext" call fishing for information regarding Oswald's visit to the Cuban Consulate the previous day.

The HSCA's reconstruction of the call chronology confirmed that the CIA station's interest in an American wishing to travel to Cuba was triggered by the intercept of the Duran call to the Soviet Embassy on September 27.[300] That call would have been picked up by the CIA monitors at the central switching tap site. It would have drawn special attention due to the mention of an American who intended to travel to Cuba—an illegal act for a U.S. citizen. Under normal procedures, a report on that call would have gone to Anne Goodpasture, in the CIA station's counterintelligence desk area.

The HSCA assessed that is exactly what did happen, and the record shows that the station chief, Winston Scott, placed a note on the call intercept report—asking that the unnamed American in question be identified. According to standard practices, a CIA pretext call, involving an impersonation, might explain the Saturday call—especially as the station chief had just directed that the American contacting both the Russian and Cuban consulates about travel to Cuba be identified. Such a call might have produced a name from the Russians (but did not), especially if the caller had just been at their building, as described in the Saturday call transcript.

In the CIA's Saturday September 28 call transcript, the American talks about having just been at the Soviet Embassy and having left his address (the visit was confirmed by the Russian guard on the call)—but at that point the American (name not given) states he did not have his address (?) at the time he was just at the Russian Embassy and had to go back to the Cubans to get it. The Russian then tells him to come right back to the Russian Embassy and give it to them (again?). The American says he will do so immediately (but did not do so according to the Russians).

Russian staff have confirmed an actual visit by Oswald that Saturday. According to the Russians, in accounts given years later, Oswald was indeed at their building in person—but no second visit occurred. Virtually nothing about this purported Saturday Duran/Oswald call can be corroborated—or found to make much sense, other than in the context of a pretext call in which the callers were fishing for the Russians to repeat the name and address of the American trying to get to Cuba.

With the Cuban Consulate itself closed that day (and the local CIA safehouse site normally unmanned), such a pretext call would have been intercepted, recorded, and transcribed at the central telephone office listening post. That post was staffed by the Mexican Army personnel; the CIA's own translators normally worked Russian and English translations while the listening post staff handled Spanish translation and transcription. David Phillips confirmed this division of labor in his HSCA testimony. He stated that Anne Goodpasture picked up Spanish transcripts from the switching center intercept station; she separately picked up actual tapes from individual building tap listening posts for the station's own employees to translate and transcribe.[301]

The idea that the Saturday call, allegedly involving Duran and Oswald, was in reality a CIA pretext call is purely speculative and not supported in any available Mexico City station documents. Yet records show that the Russian Embassy was monitored on Saturday and an American should have been observed entering that day—any weekend "walk-in" to the Russian Embassy would have drawn special attention.

The incident would have provided the perfect opportunity for a follow-on pretext call to try and surface either the American's name or the identity of any Russians who had met with him. And that would be what should have been expected out of thc sophisticated surveillance system that the CIA had established in Mexico City. This system almost certainly did obtain surveillance photographs of Oswald, as described years later to her children by Greta Goyenechea, the CIA photo surveillance agent designed as LIEMPTY-14.[302]

At this distance in time, when we are fully aware of the extent of the CIA's surveillance and intercept programs in Mexico City—as well as the extent of its counter intelligence practices there—it may be hard to understand why the CIA would have covered up something as simple as a pretext call. But in the immediate aftermath of the assassination, both the FBI and CIA worked hard to project the idea that their pre-assassination knowledge of Oswald was minimal. Explaining a pretext call would certainly have raised many questions. And protecting the surveillance programs was also a high priority—we will see that the CIA even reached out to the Warren Commission to try and prevent publication of a single photograph which disclosed the placement of one of its cameras photographing people entering the Russian Embassy.

As later confirmed by the Russians, Oswald had indeed talked to Russian counsel in that appearance, including to counsel Kostikov. But Kostikov's name only entered the call record on the following Tuesday, provided by the Russians themselves during that call. Finally, given all the material we reviewed, Oswald was a relatively fluent Russian speaker. The transcriber's note that the male speaking in the Saturday call used "terrible, hardly recognizable Russian" would support the idea that the caller was not Oswald, but rather a CIA caller with limited Russian language skill. The fact that such a remark appears, but the official CIA translators had no knowledge of it, also suggests that activities within the Mexico City station were being internally compartmentalized (as well as being at least partially withheld from CIA headquarters), with Station Chief Scott being the only individual in full possession of all the relevant information related to Oswald's activities in Mexico City. Confirmation of that view can also be found in Scott's own memoirs, in which he writes that Oswald was observed during all his visits to both the Cuban Consulate and Russian Embassy, and that the Mexico City station had fully reported all his contacts with both the Cubans and Russians to CIA headquarters—statements clearly at odds with the information now in the official CIA records.[303]

A failure to identify the American in a pretext call would also explain the statement to the HSCA from the CIA staff translators, Boris and Anna Tarasoff, that they were told that any further calls related to the American were to be treated as urgent. They were specifically asked if they could identify the American if he should appear in future calls to the Russians. The Tarasoffs were also adamant that a translation of the next call in the official record, that of Tuesday, October 1, was wanted as soon as possible—and if the American's name was given, senior staff were to be notified.

The caller of October 1 did self-identify as Oswald, and described a previous visit to the Russian Embassy, meeting a Russian counsel who had promised to contact the Russian Embassy in the United States about his request. The Russian on the call advised that a wire had been sent, and identified the counsel involved in the earlier contact as Kostikov.

What is clear from the record is that it was the October 1 call—which entered the name Oswald and a contact with Kostikov into the

CIA station record—that became the basis for advising local FBI staff as well as CIA headquarters that Oswald was in Mexico City and that he had met with Kostikov at the Russian Embassy. What is also clear is that there was never any real resolution of which of the seven calls possibly involving Oswald were in fact him, rather than some other individual calling the Russian Embassy for their own purposes. The CIA never resolved that question, nor did the HSCA.

The Tarasoffs themselves were adamant that they had never heard a caller who spoke in broken Russian, the description of the caller on the Saturday call. Boris Tarasoff was also adamant that he had heard the voice on the October 1 call (where the caller self-identified himself as Oswald) in another call days earlier, but he was unable to say on what day that call was recorded. Given that neither of the Tarasoffs had noted a call including a woman, it is very unlikely that would have been the Saturday call, and more likely it was one of the other seven calls. The HSCA also interviewed David Phillips regarding the Oswald calls, and Phillips's recollections only added to the confusion, agreeing with the Tarasoffs on some points and disagreeing on others.[304]

In that respect, it must be noted that there are several problems with Phillips as a source on anything related to Mexico City—or to Lee Harvey Oswald. It had been Phillips who had been an enthusiastic promoter of the Gilberto Alvarado story, a story in which Oswald was a paid Cuban assassin. Phillips would continue to tout that story (and that Oswald had come back to the United States with money for the assassination) in books written in following years. Yet it was Phillips who officially testified that Oswald was not even "on the CIA radar" during his time in Mexico City.

Beyond that, Phillips was not even in Mexico City at the time of the October 1 call, having been sent to Washington DC and the Miami station as part of his new assignment to the Cuba project under Desmond Fitzgerald. What Phillips really knew about the Oswald calls (or about Oswald in general) remains a major question regarding the total confusion which emerged within the CIA about Oswald and

Mexico City. In that respect, it is also interesting that the HSCA discovered an internal CIA memo which categorized all Phillips' remarks about the cable traffic on Oswald from Mexico City to CIA headquarters as being incorrect and inaccurate. The memo implied that he simply did not know what he was talking about in his statements about Oswald and Mexico City. [305] The fact that station chief Scott would generate such a memo, characterizing the officer who ran all the station's major counter intelligence programs against both the Russians and Cubans as unreliable regarding Oswald's appearance in Mexico City, is interesting—especially since it was Phillips who continually maintained that Oswald was not even a subject of CIA interest at the time. At this distance in time, the disconnect between Scott's story of the station's response to Oswald and that of Phillips is impossible to resolve. It does, however, confirm that a good deal of the mystery regarding Oswald in Mexico City appears to have come from within the CIA, and particularly from within the Mexico City station itself.

The HSCA made a special effort to create a paperwork trail of Phillips's involvement in the Oswald inquiry by the Mexico City station but found that the relevant documents were missing routing slips. In those instances, when records were present for items Phillips should have seen, his name was not on the associated routing slip. Those discrepancies, combined with the negative memo on Phillips, raise the intriguing idea that Phillips might have been intentionally taken out of the official paper trail, possibly to conceal his involvement with an operational interest in Oswald by either a CI/SIG or the SAS Cuba Project.

Confusion, Confabulation or Conspiracy?

As noted earlier, prior to the assassination in Dallas, the story of Oswald's time in Mexico City was relatively clear, complicated only by the concern of the FBI over Oswald's reported contact with Kostikov. Matters became much more complex—and seemingly more sinister—on November 22, when sometime Friday evening a photograph was sent from Mexico City, presented as being of Oswald entering the Russian Embassy there. After reviewing that photo and purportedly listening to a voice recording of Oswald in Mexico, the Dallas FBI Office informed Director Hoover that the individual who had previously been identified as using the name Oswald in Mexico City was not the Lee Harvey Oswald in custody in Dallas. Director Hoover raised that issue with President Johnson, discussing the possibility that Oswald had been impersonated and others might somehow be involved with him or with the attack on JFK.[306]

The issues of the photograph from Mexico City, most definitely not of Oswald (later to become referred to generally as the "mystery man"), and of a tape of someone contacting the Russians, also not Oswald, are at the heart of what became Hoover's immediate concern over impersonation. Although that initial concern disappeared over some 48 hours and never made it to the Warren Commission as a consideration, it did later become a major element of the skeptical view that Oswald might not even have gone to Mexico.

We will discuss that view, and the idea that impersonation in Mexico City was a major factor in the Kennedy assassination, in the following. However, in the post-assassination chaos we first must address the mystery and confusion related to the photograph, the tape, and the CIA's own communications regarding the Oswald in Mexico story. These communications became a mystery in themselves, but they may also reveal something very important about the CIA's own operational interest in Lee Harvey Oswald—as well as their provable post-assassination confabulation of information from Mexico City.

As noted previously, Oswald's reported appearance and activities in Mexico City was consistent with his goals and personal agenda, including his focus on Cuba which had become firmly established in New Orleans during the summer of 1963. Of course, Oswald's pursuit of travel to Cuba was illegal for an American, and would have been officially suspect given questions as to his motives as well as his Soviet history. A CIA effort to identify an unknown American attempting illegal travel to Cuba would have been totally "by the book," and expected.

Given that his name was not mentioned in the first call intercept from the Cuban Consulate, a pretext call to gain more information would have also been standard CIA station practice. Once his identity and a Kostikov contact had been revealed in the October 1 call, reporting of his appearance to the FBI was also standard practice. And that is what we do find in the official record. First the CIA station chief and the U.S. Ambassador were informed, as was the American Embassy Legat (an FBI liaison). The Legat was specifically informed of an apparent Oswald/Kostikov contact.[307]

The next step by the Mexico City station was taken on October 8, via a cable to CIA headquarters advising of Oswald in Mexico City.[308] The cable gave a description of him which matched the "mystery man" photo sent after the assassination, suggesting that the station might well have misidentified the photo as Oswald from the start. It also made no mention of the Cuba-related aspects of his activities. Given that Kostikov was a known Russian KGB officer, suspected of being in contact with agents in the United States, the focus on him in the cable is understandable—but the total lack of reference to Cuba is itself noteworthy and questionable.

On October 10, after receipt of the cable from Mexico City, CIA headquarters sent a cable to the FBI and other agencies advising of Oswald being in Mexico City and contacting the Russians at their embassy.[309] And on that same day, CIA headquarters responded to the Mexico City station's cable—which had asked for background information on Oswald—by sending information from Oswald's general 201 file.[310]

At that point, another round of Mexico City mysteries began, because that file was being held by CIA counter intelligence, specifically James Angleton's CIA/SIG group, and the only information in it related to his time in Russia. Mexico City was thus only given background information related to Russia, and nothing contemporary at all regarding his return to the United States, his activities since that return, or his association with Cuban matters or the FPCC. Later research by the HSCA determined that Oswald's pro-Cuba activities had been placed in a separate, compartmentalized FPCC file.

The CIA headquarters cables provided Mexico City only with the most general background information on Oswald—citing the most "recent" information from State Department being that he and his wife had been approved for a return to the U.S. in May 1962. There was literally nothing about his return, or any of his activities back in the United States. Nothing about his domestic 1963 activities was sent to the Mexico City station, or any other government agency.

However, one thing headquarters did include was a true and accurate description of Oswald, one which did not match the "mystery man" description sent to headquarters from Mexico City. Whether anyone at headquarters or in Mexico noticed that discrepancy, or whether it had some particular use in a CIA/SIG "marked card" activity related to Mexico City, would become—and remain—a matter of discussion and debate among Warren Commission skeptics. The fact that the same officers, on the same day, forwarded the Mexico City station's incorrect description of Oswald in the cable sent to the FBI, State Dept. and Navy adds to the suspicion that games were being played with the Oswald information.

Certainly, the absence of the most contemporary 1962/1963 Oswald information from the CIA headquarters' communications to other agencies, and even to its own station in Mexico City, raises the question of whether information was being intentionally managed for CIA operational purposes. In confirmation of such speculation, years later Jane Roman, a CIA headquarters staff person who had helped prepare headquarters information on Oswald for transmission to the Mexico station and other agencies, was interviewed by researchers John Newman and Jefferson Morley.

In response to their questions about current and critical information on Oswald not being included in cables to Mexico City station, Roman admitted that she had signed off on content that she knew was incomplete and even incorrect. When asked for an explanation, she would only say that compartmentalization of information on Oswald was apparent in the messages, and that such compartmentalization might be interpreted as suggesting an active, operational interest in Oswald within the CIA. Her remarks at least suggest that the more current information on Oswald's activities was being compartmentalized on an operational, need-to-know basis—and was intentionally not circulated to other agencies or even within the CIA itself.[311]

Given the August "visibility" of Oswald to CIA Special Affairs Staff at the JM/WAVE station in Miami, there is certainly reason to speculate on an operational interest by SAS Cuba Project staff—especially given that it was the information on Oswald's Cuban activism which was being withheld from both Mexico City and other agencies. Roman's comments appear to provide corroboration of the idea that Oswald was being viewed as useful for one or more new SAS operations. If true, that would only add to the complexity of CIA records compartmentalization, which appears to have begun with a CI/SIG interest initiated during Oswald's journey to the Soviet Union.

Yet, a possible operational interest is likely only one of the factors leading to the CIA's confabulation of its own collection of information on Oswald during his time in Mexico City. The CIA's intelligence collection and dirty tricks operation in Mexico was the crown jewel in its Western Hemisphere network, extending its capabilities though the Caribbean and Central America to all the OAS member states. There was a clear and present risk that any serious investigation could put on record damaging information about any of the points of contact in which that CIA's Mexico City network might have touched Oswald—phone taps, photographic work, field team surveillance, transportation records intelligence, Mexican DFS activities.

An example of the CIA's concern over revealing even the most minor details of its capabilities in Mexico City can be found in a major effort to suppress the "mystery man" photo from being published in the Warren Commission materials—a concern so serious that the CIA station asked that Allen Dulles intervene with the Commission in order to control the publication of the photograph. The Commission's problem was that a Dallas FBI Agent had shown the photograph to Oswald's mother on November 23, and she had later claimed it to be a picture of Jack Ruby. Ultimately the photo did appear as Commission Exhibit 237 in Volume 16—but the Agency's appeal had been considered serious enough that the photo was drastically cropped for publication, in order not to provide clues as to the location of the camera equipment.[312]

Once in the record and outside CIA control, information about CIA's surveillance programs could have ultimately been leaked, compromised by foreign intelligence groups or even made public by government inquiries. The potential for losing such capabilities at the height of its efforts against Cuba and against Communist groups throughout Central America (many of which were supplied and supported by Cuba though Mexico) was likely an overriding fear. That level of strategic concern can be seen in CIA headquarters communications to the Mexico City station. Headquarters even chided the station for being too aggressive with respect to Duran's confinement and interrogation by the Mexican police. Headquarters' overriding priority was not Oswald and not the Kennedy assassination, it was the fear that "covert surveillance activities might be endangered."[313]

Drawing too much attention to Duran even had its own operational risks. It could have led to the compromise of what was considered an important, active, and ongoing dirty tricks project targeting a number of Cuban diplomatic personnel. Duran herself, it turns out, was a key element in a CIA political action operation against a well-connected Castro regime figure, Carlos Lechuga.

Lechuga had been the head of the Cuban diplomatic mission to Mexico; in the fall of 1963 he was the Cuban Ambassador to the United Nations in New York City. The CIA had discovered that

Duran had previously had a sexual liaison with Lechuga, then her boss in Mexico City.[314] That knowledge became a key element of the CIA's effort to compromise Lechuga's wife. The object was to make her angry enough at her husband to become an asset, developing her as a source on his work at the United Nations, and hopefully inside the Castro regime after his anticipated return to Cuba. Interestingly, one of the SAS officers involved in the Lechuga operation was someone we have encountered before—Emilio Rodriquez, whose brother had been one of Oswald's first contacts with the New Orleans Cuban community.

Mexico City mirrored the Cold War; it mirrored the American effort to subvert the Castro regime, to compromise its revolutionary impact across Latin America. Spy games, counterspy games, multiple CIA operations, individual targets of CIA interest including the FPCC, Kostikov, Azcue, Duran, and Lechuga—all of these added elements of confusion and chaos to Oswald's Mexico City appearance.

Confusion in Mexico City surrounds the call intercepts, tapes, translations, and transcripts of calls—with much of that confusion attributable to the CIA itself, both immediately following the Kennedy assassination and even years later when questioned about those same things by the HSCA. Compartmentalization and confabulation extends to CIA headquarters files on Oswald, and the sending of inaccurate and misleading information to other agencies as well as its own Mexico City station, again strictly attributable to the CIA itself.

So much confusion and confabulation abounds that virtually all aspects of the official Warren Commission / FBI investigation timeline of Oswald's travel to Mexico City, his activities there, and his appearance at the Cuban and Russian consulates, have been brought into question by Warren Commission skeptics. Researchers have identified issues and seeming inconsistencies related to a variety of source materials that the FBI collected on Oswald's travel to and from Mexico City and his lodging there. A full and detailed examination of those issues is far beyond the scope of this study; however, interested readers can find studies available online.[315]

Skeptical concerns about the travel and movements of Oswald in Mexico City were also officially highlighted in the work of the HSCA, which documented a range of problems, including the lack of CIA surveillance photographs of Oswald's entries and exits at both the Cuban and Soviet diplomatic facilities, as well as concerns over CIA tape recordings of purported Oswald telephone calls. The HSCA reinvestigation of Oswald in Mexico City, referred to as the "Lopez Report," was written by staffers Dan Hardway and Edwin Lopez. It is an excellent introduction to the issues with the CIA's own handling of information related to Oswald in Mexico City.[316] The report's information is vital to a full understanding of the extent of CIA photographic and electronic surveillance being carried out in Mexico City and is recommended reading for those wishing a deep dive into such issues.

Following its own re-investigation, the HSCA concluded that it was most probable that Lee Harvey Oswald had personally visited both the Cuban and Russian diplomatic facilities in Mexico City, although it did not entirely rule out the question of some type of impersonation associated with his diplomatic contacts. Specifically, the HSCA raised the likelihood of impersonation regarding telephone contacts. Beyond Oswald's appearances at the diplomatic facilities, the HSCA concluded that it was unable to concretely confirm any other of his activities during travel to/from Mexico City or his activities while in the city.[317]

Beyond that, the HSCA found that while Oswald had been present in Mexico City, it could find no reasonable explanation for the total lack of photos of Oswald, given the extensive surveillance of Cuban and Russian facilities, as well as the fact that the CIA itself reported that Oswald had entered and exited those facilities a minimum of five times during his time in Mexico City.[318]

The HSCA also explored the issue of the so called "mystery man" photograph which had been sent to the FBI the evening of the assassination. Anne Goodpasture of the Mexico City staff was interviewed on the matter, and she stated that that she had advised against sending that photo. Unfortunately, the HSCA interviewer did not ask her to detail her concern. However, it is possible that it may have been related to the fact that, although the Mexico City station had requested contemporary photographs of Oswald to verify the photographs they had of the "mystery man" from the Russian Embassy, they had never received any.[319]

In its initial distribution of information on an American at the Russian Embassy, the CIA itself referred to the "possible" identification of the American as Lee Harvey Oswald. A headquarters CIA cable also notes that confirmation still needed to be done by Mexico City station—confirmation based on the provision to Mexico City of contemporary photographs of Oswald.[320] Given that no such photographs were provided to Mexico City prior to the assassination, the identification of photographs of the American as Oswald could not have been considered as confirmed. Given the excitement and stress the night of the attack in Dallas, the file photograph may simply have been pulled and sent with no warning that confirmation of the individual as Oswald was still pending.[321]

The issue of tape recordings of an individual purported to be Oswald is more complex—and more confusing. FBI documents including communications from Director Hoover on November 22/23 specifically refer to FBI agents in Dallas viewing a photograph and listening to a tape from Mexico City. The agents involved reported that the individual the CIA had identified as Oswald at the Russian Embassy was not the Oswald they had been in contact with earlier and certainly not the young man in custody in Dallas. CIA and later FBI documents both appear to contradict Hoover's remarks, stating that only photographs and transcripts, not tapes, had been sent from Mexico City on 11/22. The FBI documents affirmed later that the Bureau had never had Oswald tapes in its possession; that position was also officially affirmed to the HSCA.

In context, the CIA's statement seems logical, as it was standard Mexico City station practice to erase tapes after transcripts had been prepared—unless tapes were being held for a special purpose. That suggests that any tape remaining in Mexico City as of November 22 was being held for a special purpose, having been retained or copied outside normal CIA practices. Is it even possible that a tape copy had been held by the FBI in Mexico City as part of its local investigations of the Oswald/Russian contact? Or that it had obtained a tape or transcript from the Mexican president's office? The source of the FBI's determination that the living Oswald's voice did not match that of a Mexico City recording was not necessarily a tape delivered by the CIA itself.

Then there is the issue that Warren Commission staff members David Slawson and Coleman are on record stating that they listened to a recording of Oswald during their visit to Mexico City in April 1964. The possibility that Winston Scott might have held back the copy of at least one tape is also reinforced by a 1995 ARRB interview of Anne Goodpasture. When her questioner, Jeremy Gunn, noted the Warren Commission staffers' affirmation of having listened to a tape, Goodpasture could only speculate that "it may have been a tape that Win Scott had squirreled away in his safe."[322] We don't know which of the seven purported Oswald calls this was, but it's possible the CIA station chief had held back a copy of a tape in which a pretext call had been placed to the Russian Embassy. The staffers would not have known Oswald's voice, and the idea of impersonation was not on their radar, having been a closely held secret within the FBI, White House, and Secret Service.

As with both the HSCA and the ARRB, we are left with open questions regarding the warnings about imposture that arose the evening of the assassination. It is clear that those concerns arose out of the fact that there actually had not been a confirmation of Oswald being at the Russian Embassy—a lack of confirmation due to the fact that contemporary photographs had been requested but not provided. The photograph of an American entering the Russian Embassy had been misidentified, and the photographs of Oswald which should have been available from both the Russian and Cuban embassies were either non-existent or suppressed for reasons the CIA never chose to reveal.

In that context, the FBI's confusion (and Director Hoover's later remarks about CIA lies regarding Mexico City[323]) is understandable. While we are unlikely to ever learn the full story behind the CIA's compartmentalization of information, and how its different departments were even lying to each other about Oswald, it becomes easier to see how its actions fueled decades of discussion of events in Mexico City as being directly related to the assassination of President Kennedy.

Conspiracy?

The previous discussion of Mexico City provides ample evidence of confusion, compartmentalization, and confabulation—all coming from within both the CIA's Mexico City station and its own headquarters. Any single questionable action, possibly even all of them, can be interpreted as a combination of standard CIA practices, including its known tendency to prioritize its own sources and operations over virtually anything else. In this instance, possibly CIA's protection of its own concerns overrode an investigation of the assassination of an American president.

But the CIA's actions have contributed to the skeptical view that there was something far more sinister about the story of Oswald in Mexico City—involving impersonation, the connection of Oswald to Kostikov, and the idea of that connection being a "poison pill" which subverted both the FBI and CIA from aggressively investigating the Kennedy assassination.

Aside from the extended questions about the CIA's internal handling of the Oswald call record, the association of Oswald with Kostikov emerged among Warren Commission skeptics as a major point of suspicion regarding the JFK assassination. Kostikov himself was a known Soviet intelligence agent, suspected of contact with covert Soviet assets, including Americans, operating inside the United States. He had been under CIA observation and surveillance in Mexico City, as well as during his travels in Mexico, and was known to have met with a Soviet asset (designated as "Tumbleweed"/a European then living in the United States) that the FBI was monitoring inside the United States. As recently as September 1963, Kostikov had even been placed under surveillance while traveling in northern Mexico.[324]

Given the implications of a contact between Oswald and a Soviet KGB agent only weeks before the assassination, the Kostikov association has been used by those alleging a Soviet conspiracy in the murder of the president. More commonly, though, that reported contact has been proposed as a "poison pill" in the Kennedy assassination. In the "poison pill" scenario, Oswald is generally assumed either not to have been in Mexico City at all—or to have had nothing to do with a visit to the Russians, or to the call in which his name was linked to Kostikov. The assumption is that the visit and call were both impersonations, planted to connect the Kennedy assassination to the Russians and preempt any serious investigation of conspiracy, due to the dire implications of the Soviets being behind the attack in Dallas.

The "poison pill" scenario views the presence of the Oswald/Kostikov contact within CIA and FBI records prior to the assassination as a key element in ensuring that Oswald would have to be presented to the public as a lone actor, thus forestalling any investigation of conspiracy in the attack on the president. The scenario remains the same regardless of whether the planting of that contact originated with a high-level CIA coup (regime change operation) or as the result of a rogue group with connections inside the CIA.

While the logic of that scenario is clear, it must be evaluated in regard other relevant information—including the fact that the Oswald/Kostikov connection itself was well-known to the FBI and agencies such as the INS prior to the assassination, and there is no record of any obvious post-assassination effort to remove or cover up that record. Documents show that the CIA had immediately notified the FBI Legat in Mexico City regarding Oswald, his visit to the Russian Embassy, and the reported contact with Kostikov.[325] The FBI used the cover of legal attaché (Legat), and numerous CIA station chiefs in Mexico City had prior experience as FBI agents. The Mexico City Legat had immediately communicated the Oswald/Kostikov contact to FBI headquarters (directly to Hoover's office) while requesting current information on Oswald.[326]

The Legat advised Hoover about the contact, stating that the CIA had informed him of it, and identified Oswald as a former Marine and Russian defector. The Legat's communication to Hoover occurred on October 18, and was followed other internal FBI communications about Oswald, Kostikov, and Oswald's apparent intention to travel to Cuba. An airtel from the Dallas office on October 19 to Hoover (copied to Mexico City and New Orleans) stated that the Immigration and Naturalization Service had advised the Dallas office that Oswald had been in the Soviet Embassy in Mexico City and had been in contact with Kostikov. We also have Hoover's remarks about Oswald on the day of the assassination, which reveal headquarters' knowledge of Oswald, including that he had either had been to Cuba or was trying to get to Cuba—Hoover remarked only that the Bureau was unclear on his reasons.[327]

And on November 22, it was not the Oswald/Kostikov contact which led Hoover to raise a concern of conspiracy with President Johnson. Instead, as of the evening of November 22 the burning issue for the FBI was the concern that Oswald might been impersonated in Mexico City. And it was impersonation—not Kostikov and Russian sponsorship of Oswald—which was the topic of discussion in Hoover's early Saturday morning telephone conversation with President Johnson on November 23.[328]

What may or may not have been quickly learned about the mismatched photo and the voice on the tape is still unknown; the "mystery man" photo remains a mystery. We only know that for some unknown reason, within two days of the assassination and after the very early, high level concerns, all parties involved essentially dropped the discussion of impersonation.

Does that reflect a "poison pill" in action—possibly. Or does it suggest that there was an impersonation but that it was found to have come from a legitimate CIA pretext call—also a possibility. Was the photograph simply sent by mistake, having perhaps been originally and mistakenly identified as being Oswald? We are left with choosing between serious concerns over a foreign conspiracy or serious concerns about exposing agency practices, inter-agency competition and confusion. The tie-breaker in that choice may be that it was a remark by a Russian counsel which entered the name Kostikov into the Oswald record—not by some unknown caller.

We also know that there was a much more sensational and aggressively supported claim for Oswald as a paid assassin. That claim, one with extensive details, did create concern in Washington D.C, concern over a Cuban conspiracy in the assassination. It was a story almost laughable in its details, but aggressively supported out of Mexico City by the American Ambassador, the CIA station chief, and David Phillips. Yet it too was a story that was not "buried" or suppressed, but rather detailed in a number of CIA and other government documents.

In the end, as far as the Warren Commission and its report was concerned, Oswald's Mexico City trip largely moved into the background. A view of Oswald as being used in some sort of conspiracy was no more welcome than a focus on his increasingly sophisticated 1963 writing on social systems and geopolitics, his effective media appearances in New Orleans, or his well-organized and well-delivered speech to a Jesuit school on his experiences in Russia and his personal political views. None of that fitted well with the Commission's image of a bitter, isolated "lone nut."

It also needs to be noted that, over time, the open issues and questions about Oswald and Mexico City fostered extensive discussions among Warren Commission critics and the emergence of the belief that events there were a major element in the conspiracy which assassinated

JFK. One such view has an Oswald impersonator intentionally contacting Cubans and Russians in a manner that would suggest they were engaged with him, encouraging him, or even paying him to assassinate the American president. In that scenario, the Mexico City activities were designed to directly frame the Russians or Cubans as Oswald's sponsors, allowing those involved in the conspiracy to use the president's murder to force the United States into attacking Cuba and ousting the Castro regime.

An alternative view gives the same role to a witting Oswald, involved in the creation of the same scenario in a prelude to the assassination, but with a different motive. In this version of the scenario, the Cuban and Russian contacts represent the "poison pill" previously discussed, intended to force the suppression of any serious investigation of conspiracy in the president's murder.

All those views and scenarios are dependent on the skeptical belief that Oswald, as a long term, witting intelligence asset, had been sent to Mexico City on some type of intelligence collection mission targeted against the Cubans, Russians, or both.

In introducing our exploration of Lee Harvey Oswald and Mexico City, we noted that strictly in terms of Oswald's own statements to the Cubans and Russians, his limited contacts there were relatively straightforward, and very much consistent with the agenda that he had been developing throughout 1963. Yet given his history and the degree to which his own actions crossed paths with CIA interests and operational activities, it becomes extremely challenging to untangle Oswald from what was going on around him—adding an increased degree of difficulty to the puzzle that the Warren Commission created.

Which of course takes us directly back to Oswald himself—and to the long-standing question of his true relationship to the CIA. We will proceed to address that, and the associated question of "witting vs. unwitting" in the following chapters.

Chapter 14

Oswald and the CIA

"Yeah, I mean I'm signing off on something that I know isn't true…to me it's indicative of a keen interest in Oswald held very closely on the need-to-know basis. The only interpretation I can put on this [the language in the cable] would be that the SAS group [CIA Cuba Project Special Affairs Staff] would have held all the information on Oswald under their tight control."

—Jane Roman, formerly senior liaison officer on the Counter Intelligence Staff of the Central Intelligence Agency, 1994, "A retired CIA officer speaks candidly about Lee Harvey Oswald," Jefferson Morley

Intelligence Collection in Russia

Speculation about an intelligence role for Oswald has been extensive among Warren Commission skeptics, with some having it begin as early as his childhood years. However, the majority of the scenarios presenting Oswald as a witting intelligence asset tend to focus on his Russian experience. When a Russian intelligence "mission" for Oswald is brought up, the three most common roles described for him have been either a) associated with deep geopolitical action (carried out by elements of the CIA, essentially sabotaging a summit meeting between President Eisenhower and Chairman Khrushchev), b) with Oswald operating as a technical/industrial intelligence collection asset, or c) being used in a record-oriented "mole hunt" for Soviet sources within the CIA itself. All those views, although operationally quite different, have on occasion been presented under the umbrella view of Oswald as a witting part of a "false defector" program. All have appeared in books on Oswald over the years, and as with the Warren Commission view of Oswald, each needs to be considered with respect to its own counter story.

Issues related to a purported Oswald "false defection" associated with the U-2 have been previously discussed—that included the Russian detection and tracking of the U-2 aircraft on its very first mission. American intercepts of Russian air defense communications from that flight revealed that the Russians were fully capable of detecting and tracking the U-2. Monitoring their tracking of follow-on flights verified that they had full details of the aircraft's operational parameters long before Oswald's appearance in Russia.

Furthermore, Oswald would have been personally unconvincing as a credible asset for carrying unique U-2 intelligence. Normally that credibility comes from the individual having direct experience or access to highly restricted information. Nothing in Oswald's experience as a radar operator suggested that he might have been aware of anything other than the fact that the U-2 was a special aircraft capable of high-altitude flight. Oswald's limited exposure to the U-2 gave him no special credibility, and as far as dangerous knowledge, he had none. The CIA was already aware that Russia had all the information required to track and bring down the U-2. The agency had known that for some time, aware that a shoot-down could happen on any given mission, and had directly warned President Eisenhower about that risk.

An alternative, sending Oswald as some sort of industrial/technology spy, does not seem to fit his own stated goal in Russia—which was to take up college-level studies. His assignment to a factory job was something of a disappointment for him—and the job itself was randomly assigned as to location and work. Regardless of that, if he had been a technical collection asset we might find clues to such an assignment in a review of his actual factory activities, as well as in the information on his job that he brought back following his return to the United States.

Ernst Titovets points out that Oswald's manuscript documenting his Soviet experience did include a quite detailed description of many aspects of Soviet life, focusing on its political, social, ideological, and even domestic aspects.[329] Oswald's own notes and remarks make much of the "absurdity" of propaganda and the shortcomings of the Soviet factory system management structure. Of course, all those topics were of considerable personal interest to Oswald, and he would later use a good deal of that information in writing his 1963 monograph "The Collective—The Life of a Russian Worker."

However, there is little to nothing in his notes, the manuscript, or Oswald's writing about the actual military work that was connected to the Radio and Television factory. In contrast, we know that the CIA did have a very sophisticated project for recruiting and using Americans to collect technical and technology-related information from the Soviet Union (designated as operation Lincoln) beginning in 1959 and continuing through at least 1963.[330]

That program focused on technical intelligence, specifically regarding rocket and missile developments. Individuals with a knowledge of not just conversational Russian, but language abilities specifically involving terminology related to science and technology, were selected for screening and recruitment. Priority was given to those who were expected to be traveling to some extent within Russia. Some 3,836 travelers were screened, 612 were identified as candidates, 159 were assessed in detail, and in the end 64 passed the screening, volunteered, and were recruited for the program.

In support of the technical collections program, CIA Domestic office staff also required special training and preparation in order to conduct effective interviews upon the volunteers' return, as well as accurately collect and consolidate technical information of interest. A CIA evaluation of the initial years of the operation was positive, noting that it had even collected useful operational information, as with the deployment of anti-aircraft missiles. By 1962 the focus had turned to a more general collection of research and development/technology information, still related to missiles, but more related to development than deployment. During 1962/63, Operation Lincoln moved on to a focus on recruiting scientists and academics who would be involved in studies which would put them in contact with Soviet academics working in areas of science and technology related to rocket and missile development.

Maintaining some level of scientific and commercial contact offered opportunities for intelligence collection—but that came with some risk. An example of both opportunity and risk can be found in the experience of Robert Webster, a former Navy electronics specialist who after the military went to work for RAND Corporation as a materials specialist, working in the application of plastics and fiberglass beginning in 1957. It was an area where United States technology was well advanced over the Soviets, but also one of great importance to rocket and missile construction.

In 1959 Webster traveled to Moscow several times, having been assigned to help set up and staff an American technical exhibition in which RAND was participating. Reportedly while in Moscow, Webster—with a wife and children back home, but with ongoing marital problems—began dating a young waitress during his seven weeks stay; he subsequently married her and they had a child.. The young waitress likely was working for the KGB. After being granted a 20-day Russian internal travel visa, Webster disappeared from the Exhibition with his new girlfriend.

It is known that Webster approached Soviet officials at the Exhibition about becoming a Russian citizen, and apparently offered to help duplicate the advanced materials spray equipment which was being demonstrated by Rand. His offer was accepted and he filled out an affidavit as an "expatriate," but made no public rejection of his citizenship nor media remarks against America. In doing so he appeared to be abandoning both his wife and children; his wife left him in the process and the children ended up with his parents. Yet in January 1960, when he learned that his mother had suffered a mental breakdown and that his father was left to take full financial responsibility for his children, Webster began an effort to return to the United States—initially opposed by the Soviets—but which ultimately, after two years and multiple appeals, proved successful.

Some of what we know about Webster is because his employer, RAND Corporation, did expend considerable effort to support him and even to try and get him back to the United States in the face of the initial Soviet opposition. However, we know considerably more because in their examination of Oswald's Russian experience, the HSCA went so far as to study the entire set of Americans who had been in Russia and who might have been "false defectors" during the period of 1958–1964. Some 380 people were initially identified, and the Committee then worked that list, and ended up with 11 individuals with experiences generally comparable to Oswald's, and which the State Department had classified and treated as defectors.

An extensive set of criteria were then examined for anomalies which might suggest the individual was utilized in some fashion by the CIA.[331] Of particular interest was whether or not the individual did have information valued by the Soviets (in the case of Webster it was determined that the KGB was known to have requested information on fiberglass and plastics though double agents), and to what extent they were actually debriefed by the CIA upon their return to the United States (in Webster's case he was found to have been voluntarily and extensively debriefed by the CIA with Air Force participation).[332]

The HSCA examination made no definitive judgement on whether Webster might somehow have been part of a voluntary collections program (such as those in the Lincoln operation). However, it did note that upon his return, Webster's voluntary CIA debriefing was extensive. And the CIA interest in him contrasted with their apparently random interest in and approach to many of the other "defectors"—several of whom, like Oswald, did not appear to be contacted directly by the CIA upon their return at all. Webster's interviews were more suggestive of an actual intelligence debrief, first involving a voluntary home interview (by a CIA officer and a representative from the Air Force) and then a two-week session in Washington D.C.

American general intelligence collection related to the Soviet Union of the period (commercial, industrial, economic, political) primarily used Americans traveling abroad in business and academic-related activities. Given the types of information being targeted (including such specifics as international banking and foreign exchange information, strategic mineral, and petroleum reserves, industrial capacity and even Russian mapping/topography), volunteers were normally selected from international business firms (firms which in some cases were separately providing operational covers for CIA activities).[333] In the case of academics, specialty knowledge related to the areas of interest was critical. Students were generally selected for similar specialties in studies, or recruited from universities with strong cultural exchange programs. As with the Lincoln project, volunteers were carefully screened and selected, with a focus on obtaining volunteers with strong social and bonding skills.

As CIA practices note, effective collections in such activities depended largely on interpersonal relations, and the conduct of what is known as "elicitation," the ability to carry out casual conversations with colleagues and obtain valued information inductively over time rather than through any sort of direct questioning. Of course, the Soviets were certainly well aware and suspicious of such practices, and at times even called out specific academics, universities, and exchange programs—with strong denials from those accused.[334]

There were also CIA operations of a more covert nature, recruiting and inserting individuals with native language fluency into both Russia and Soviet bloc nations. Volunteers were recruited from the populations who had either emigrated from Russia, fled during the internal conflicts during Russia's occupation of eastern European countries following World War II, or come across to the west as actual defectors. Various activities under programs designated as Red Bird and Red Sox[335] involved intelligence collection, but also political and even military action goals in some instances.[336] In the end these "black entry" programs were evaluated as almost totally unsuccessful, due to what the CIA described as "implacable and ubiquitous" KGB security. Most individuals and even groups were identified by rigid security practices and either executed or imprisoned. The chief of the CIA's Soviet Russia Division described the whole concept as basically having been "strewn with disaster."

In summary, neither the known history of the U-2 nor Lee Harvey Oswald himself fit the speculation that he carried special information to the Soviet Union that enabled shooting down the U-2 as part of a high-level CIA plot to destroy improved American relations with the Soviets. Oswald's own background was a poor fit for any of the known CIA intelligence collections projects being run against the Soviet Union during that era, all of which used far different practices for inserting low-profile assets with credible covers. Even Oswald's personal activities and interests were outside the areas of intelligence collection which are now known to have been targeted by the types of assets the CIA was using in its Soviet collection programs.

High Stakes in Mexico City

In evaluating a possible intelligence role for Oswald in Mexico City, especially given his short time there, his personal impact during his appearances at the consulates was quite limited. If anything, his rejection confirmed that travel through Mexico was only viable with endorsement either from the CPUSA or the FPCC—a fact that the CIA and FBI were well aware of and had actually used in their AMSANTA project. As to any intelligence collection outside the consulates, during the extended inquiry into Mexico City following the assassination, rumors did surface that Oswald had socialized with Duran after office hours, with stories of a "twist party" and even of a sexual encounter.

Yet Duran (who had been recommended for a position at the consulate by Theresa Proenza and was filling in at a staff position previously held by her cousin, who had died in a car crash), as previously mentioned, was already an element of a very sophisticated CIA sexual compromise operation targeting the Cuban ambassador to the United Nations, Carlos Lechuga.[337] CIA counterintelligence officers in the Special Affairs Staff had become aware that Lechuga and Duran had been involved in an extended affair during the time Lechuga was stationed in Mexico City, before his appointment to the UN.

The Cuban government was also aware of the affair, and it appears to have been a major reason for his reassignment. As early as November, 1962 the CIA had also obtained information that Lechuga had offered to divorce his wife and marry Duran; the information was felt to be especially powerful leverage, and rather than directly targeting Lechuga himself, the effort was intended to leverage the affair with Lechuga's wife.[338] The hope was that she could be made angry enough that she would remain married, but become a particularly important source on Cuban diplomatic activities and on high-level Castro administration figures.[339]

So, a CIA political action operation targeting Lechuga, which directly involved Sylvia Duran, was already active well before Oswald appeared at the Cuban Consulate. Anything that would have drawn further attention to Duran (including rumors or gossip about her sex life) or her family, might have exposed her affair with Lechuga—undermining the chances of a potentially high-level intelligence Castro government penetration. If anything, Oswald appearing at a party with Duran, and then seducing her into a one-night affair would have been a very unnecessary risk with the potential of exposing a unique CIA foreign intelligence operation in Mexico City. The exposure of a very high-level sexual compromise operation could have had a disastrous effect on overall Special Affairs Staff (SAS) covert political action operations against the Castro government.

The HSCA investigated each of the Duran rumors and stories in detail; the Lopez report describes their interviews and work—with no positive findings on any of the sources or claims. Readers will find extensive details in the Lopez Report previously cited. One of the reasons the HSCA investigators were able to do that detailed work on Duran was because the CIA itself had previously been carrying out and generating internal memos on its penetration, political action, and personnel compromise operations targeting the consulates in Mexico City, particularly the Cuban Consulate. David Phillips later wrote about the "cat and mouse games" he had been involved with—actively running "dirty tricks" using the model of the Red Cap enticement/compromise practices cited previously. The Cuban Consulate itself had been extensively compromised with electronic bugs and intercepts, by surveillance cameras, and mail opening operations, and by sending in witting agents to interact with personnel.

The political action and dirty tricks operations were enabled, and made more deniable, with Phillips's access to assets from the Cuban Counter Intelligence group (the AMOTs) which had been created at JM/WAVE in Miami. The AMOT group consisted of well-trained, anti-Castro Cubans who were especially skilled in surveillance, infiltration, and electronic collections. Select AMOTs had been detailed to Mexico City to train local listening station and surveillance personnel, and at times operated the equipment themselves. Some were connected socially or even through extended family to Cuban diplomatic personnel in Mexico City. WAVE resources essentially functioned as a "shadow" CIA station supporting Special Affairs Staff operations against Cuba.

Several AMOT operatives were experienced enough to present themselves as supporters of the Cuban revolution, doing business in

Mexico. Those individuals were used to contact consulate and embassy personnel though letters, calls, and on occasion in person. In a few instances those contacts focused on either compromising or "turning" Cuban diplomatic personnel not only in Mexico City, but elsewhere. Such efforts were patient and prolonged, involved continual testing of the personal and political attitudes of diplomatic targets such as Teresa Proenza and Eusebio Azcue.[340]

In 1963, Teresa Proenza was serving as Cultural Attache at the Cuban Consulate in Mexico City. As a long-time Cuban Communist party member, a known Soviet contact within the Cuban government, and with a close relationship to the Cuban Vice Minister of Defense (a hardline Moscow advocate), Proenza had been singled out as an element of a CIA political action operation to discredit the Vice Minister and poison the Cuban relationship with the Soviet Union in the process. That operation was active during 1963. False documents were planted through the Mexico City embassy, and in the end the operation was highly successful. Proenza was removed from her Mexico City assignment in December 1963, ending her long-time career as well as her position of influence in the Castro government (she ended up with a job as a librarian in Cuba).[341]

During the same period in 1963, the Cuban Intelligence group at JM/WAVE, and its AMOTs, were being given an expanded role in supporting the "cat and mouse" game against the Cubans in Mexico City. Based on extensive document research by Bill Simpich, we now know that beginning that summer Mexico City CIA station Chief Winston Scott was focused on turning Eusebio Azcue into a CIA source. In support of that effort,[342] Jose Casas (AMOT-106), with personal connections to several Cuban regime figures, was dispatched to Mexico City. Casas first approached Duran, and then managed to connect with and converse with Azcue on a number of matters over an extended period of time. Those sorts of positive, "elicitation" contacts were far beyond anything Oswald could have accomplished, and based on the reports generated, effective in evaluating the potential changes in politics and regime affiliations of the Cuban staff.

Compared to the depth of the ongoing access the CIA had for information collections at the Cuban Consulate and embassy, and the extent of its already ongoing efforts against Duran, Azcue, Proenza and other personnel, it is difficult to credit that Oswald's brief visit would have or could have added to the body of intelligence work already in progress. Even the story of an unproven social contact or dalliance with Duran after hours would have added nothing significant to the profile the CIA had already developed on her, while potentially compromising an operation already well-developed and being actively pursued.

Unwitting vs Witting

With respect to both his lengthy stay in Russia, and his brief visit to Mexico City, Lee Oswald just does not seem to be a fit as a witting collections asset given what we know of such structured, detailed, and targeted CIA intelligence collection practices. If anything, rather than "fitting in" with some conventional cover, in both Russia and Mexico City he stood out—so much so that he was immediately suspect, so much so that he became a problem, either dealt with politically inside Russia as Titovets describes based on actual Soviet documents, or literally thrown out of two consulates in Mexico City.

That, however, does not mean that Oswald's appearance in Russia, and in Mexico City could not have been of interest—and use—to the CIA, with him in an *unwitting* role. The use of Oswald in such a matter was first proposed by Peter Dale Scott in his essay "Oswald and the Hunt for Popov's Mole," an essay in which Scott detailed how the information and routing of files routinely created around Oswald's Russian activities could have been used internally within the CIA as a "marked card" operation.[343]

Falsified or simply incorrect information in select files can be traced to identify individuals circulating information found in files for which they are not authorized. Scott gives a very useful overview of the practice and his essay is highly recommended. Scott's work on such unwitting use of Oswald has been carried forward by both John Newman and Bill Simpich. In *State Secret,* Simpich examines how Robert Webster might have been unwittingly used in a CI/SIG "marked card" counterintelligence operation.[344]

The use of unwitting individuals and the conduct of marked card file projects was one of the activities carried out by the CIA's special counterintelligence group—CI/SIG (Special Investigations Group)—with such work driven by the focus of its chief, James Angleton. Angleton himself was personally and obsessively focused on the existence of Soviet double agents ("moles") inside the CIA itself. He became known for that obsession, and for the practice of running what were called "mole hunts," compartmentalizing and monitoring documents and files to identify individuals who might be performing internal espionage within the Agency.

A major argument for the unwitting *use* of Oswald, for his being of ongoing interest to the CIA, lies in the fact that from his first appearance at the United States Embassy in Moscow, information related to his personal activities was compartmentalized within the CIA, a compartmentalization which became visible once again during his appearance in Mexico City. Events in Mexico City, and the seemingly chaotic CIA response to Oswald's rather modest activities there, have made visible the fact that, even as of fall, 1963, personality file information on the most basic, contemporary activities of Oswald were being controlled—with selective distribution inside the CIA as well as to other key government agencies such as the FBI.

The existence of file compartmentalization and control suggests a special Agency interest in Oswald, leaving open the question of exactly who might have pursued that interest with actual operations centered around his documents or his activities. One way to answer that question is to ask, as observed by Peter Dale Scott in what can be described as a "negative template"—where would we expect to find internal activity files on Oswald, and where they are missing or probably withheld? The answer that has emerged from the work of Scott, Newman, Morley and other document researchers calls out two specific groups whose records and actions match the negative template related to Oswald in Mexico City. These two are the CIA Counter Intelligence/Special Investigations Group, whose use of Oswald likely began at the time of Oswald's appearance at the American Embassy in Moscow, and the Cuba Project Special Affairs Staff, whose involvement with Oswald began during the summer of 1963 through DRE and case officer contacts at the JM/WAVE Miami Station.

The first sign of compartmentalization occurs within CI/SIG and involves a variety of communications related to the handling of information routed to CIA from State Department sources in Moscow, circulated to the CIA, FBI, Navy, and other agencies. For some two months the expected paper trail of that information within CIA Counter intelligence and its Office of Security is missing or at best chaotic. So much so that even though CI/SIG placed Oswald on its highly classified "watch list" related to mail and communications intercepts, it did not even open a routine 201 personality file on him for a full year.

Given the significance of Oswald's appearance in Russia, especially in the period while he was still being denied an extended stay beyond his tourist visa by the Soviets (and might have left or been forced out at any time) it would be expected to find a 201 file on Oswald being created immediately—but that did not happen for a full year following his apparent defection. And when it was opened, under the incorrect name of Lee "Henry" Oswald, it was created and held under the total control of CI/SIG, the office which would still hold it in its control in the fall of 1963. Ownership of the 201 file suggests a CI/SIG interest in Oswald, and it would be reasonable to expect to find new material being entered into the file on a routine basis, something which appears not to have occurred following his return to the United States.

The situation regarding Oswald's 201 file at CI/SIG resulted in headquarters not only not informing Mexico City of his FPCC and

Cuba-related activities, but also essentially suppressing any information outside of his time in Russia. The latest information noted was a report from May of 1962 relating that Oswald was still an American citizen, but that the State Department had given approval for the return of Oswald, his Soviet wife, and their infant child to the United States. Mexico City was not even informed that the Oswald family had actually returned, much less regarding any of his moves, jobs or Cuba-related activities for 1962/63![345]

Of course, the world of CIA files is a complex one, intentionally so for security purposes, but as with any large bureaucracy, especially one with global operations, it has to rely on certain basic files—headquarters files, with basic biographic information and photographs, if possible, generally available to all regional and country offices. The personality files are just that, general files which contain current information on people whom the CIA offices may become aware of and of possible interest in their ongoing activities. Yet when the Mexico City station urgently requested just that current information on Oswald in October 1963, the "latest Hdqs info" received was dated May 1962, and stated that he and his wife had received permission to return from the Soviet Union.

John Newman writes at length about what he terms a "Black Hole" in Oswald's files. Newman details that hole in his book *Oswald and the CIA*—and notes that the issue even came up during the Warren Commission inquiry into Oswald.[346] The Commission's lead counsel wrote the CIA, requesting confirmation that the Agency had received and was in the possession of several of the earliest messages and communiques relating to Oswald's activities in Moscow, messages originated by the State Department and the Navy. The CIA response was that it could neither confirm that it had received the State Department communiques, nor confirm when and whom had received or handled the earliest Navy messages.

Later, in 1978, the CIA remained unable to answer the same sort of file inquiries from the HSCA. At that point in time, the Agency was able to locate some individual documents from within CI/SIG files, but it simply could not provide a coherent paper trail for them in terms of original receipt or, equally importantly, the internal response to them. Not could it provide a response which would explain why none of them had gone to where they would have been of the most operational interest in Oswald at the time, the Soviet/Russia Division.

In his file research, Newman found that the most recent document releases, based in the work of the ARRB, have illuminated enough of the story to confirm that Counter Intelligence and CI/SIG did indeed hold what would be a "soft file" on Oswald, yet some of the most significant Oswald documents, even those existing in other agencies, are missing from it, as is any explanation of why the Soviet Russia division was not receiving the advisories and updates that would have been expected.[347]

Given the significance of Oswald's appearance in Russia, especially in the period before he was granted entry for an extended stay, the Soviet Russia division certainly had a role to play in monitoring him and the activities going on around him. The Soviet Russia Division did indeed create 201 files on several "defectors," and an Oswald file would have been expected to be among them. But as mentioned above, no personality file was established there, or anywhere else, for a full year.

And when it was opened, it was created and held not in the Soviet Russia division, but within and under the total control of CI/SIG, the office which would still hold it until the fall of 1963. The only official CIA response on the creation of the Oswald 201 file comes from the 1978 HSCA questioning of Ann Egerter. During her interview, she explained what a 201 file was and why it would be opened—stating that a file would be created for those people who CI/SIG saw as being of an intelligence interest or for some reason under suspicion of being a security risk.

Ownership of the Oswald personality file certainly suggests a CI/SIG interest in Oswald, and it would be reasonable to expect to find it updated, with new material being entered to keep it up to date with personal information on Oswald. An additional detail, suggesting a special interest in Oswald, lies in an explanation for why the Soviet Russia division did not play a key role in the record keeping on Oswald—and was instead literally locked out of distribution on materials related to him.

The HSCA never resolved that particular question. But during his decades of exploring the CIA's record keeping system—and the details of materials circulation inside the CIA—one exceptionally diligent researcher revealed what appears to be the most probable answer. It is inferential in nature rather than a single smoking gun type document, but it points directly towards a very early (exactly how early is impossible to say) interest in Lee Harvey Oswald's appearance in Russia by CI/SIG and its head, James Angleton. The likely answer is revealed in the decades-long work of CIA document researcher Malcolm Blunt and explained in a conversation between Alan Dale and Malcolm in their book, *The Devil is in the Details.*[348]

The detail in this instance relates to a discussion of "choke points" inside the Agency, beginning at the CIA's Office of Mail Logistics (within the Directorate of Intelligence). As Blunt describes the system, cables, aerograms, or similar messages came to the CIA at the mail logistics office and from there to the Records Integration Division (RID).

Records Distribution maintained a forwarding list, sending certain types of information or documents relating to designated individuals on to designated departments and divisions. According to standard practice, cables regarding a Russian "defector" would have gone to CIA Security and to the Soviet Operations Division. It would then be up to either group to open working files as well as a 201 Personality file. HSCA inquiries determined that not every "defector" had files opened, but Oswald's offer of radar information to the Soviets strongly suggests that would have occurred.

What happened in Oswald's case is that multiple copies of cables and messages were sent from State to CIA (some 15 copies in at least one instance) suggesting that a wide distribution inside CIA was anticipated. But instead, copies were directed by RID to only two places, the Office of Security, and to one individual (Ann Egerter, Angleton's primary staff officer) inside CI/SIG. The reason for the restricted distribution, as Blunt points out, is that the mail logistics distribution was user-driven. Groups specified categories and individuals they wished to be receiving messages on from other agencies and that drove the distribution.

Yet in this instance, RID was directed specifically to restrict distribution on Oswald-related information. What that appears to suggest is that Angleton and CI/SIG had intervened to essentially capture (along with the Office of Security, with which CI/SIG shared a working relationship) the information coming into CIA on Oswald. And as Blunt also points out, that meant that CI/SIG and Security were the only two "active" offices holding the information. Mail Logistics and the Record Integration Division were strictly passive, administrative functions.

To some extent, this resolves the question of where inside the CIA an active interest in Oswald began, and the likelihood that it involved actual operational activity that would have been related to Angleton's ongoing interest in Soviet moles—and mole hunting through the use of controlled document circulation. It would have allowed him or select staff to follow the path of incoming information on Oswald, and determine if it reappeared somewhere that it should not.

Angleton became well-known for many things during his long tenure with the CIA, especially his work in counter intelligence—where he broke away from the traditional practices of trying to penetrate adversaries' intelligence services, and instead focused almost entirely on Soviet penetration of the CIA. As part of that he became obsessed with what he considered "false" Soviet defectors—during his time he claimed to have "turned back" 22 such defectors. However, in later years both his successors at the CIA as well as the FBI estimated that all of them had actually been quite legitimate. In that respect, he had been responsible for a massive loss of potential intelligence on the Russian KGB and GRU (military intelligence services).[349]

Finding Angleton and CI/SIG using Oswald or any other Soviet "defector" in a file tracing, document routing mole hunt would be standard practice of the time, and certainly no surprise. The question then is why the CIA as an organization would not know that internally, and would apparently be itself confused with what was going on with the Oswald files. It would also leave open the question of why the story of a perfectly legitimate mole hunt would not be somewhere in their own records, at least within CI or CI/SIG records.

The answer to that turns out to be twofold. First, it comes down to the fact that Angleton was allowed to build his own filing system, independent from any other CIA system including the central records files. From a records standpoint, Angleton operated his own agency within the Agency. This gave him the ability to create and monitor document distribution "choke points" for mole hunting, but paper documentation for certain of those activities may well have been restricted to Angleton's own special files. Second, material on Oswald was also going to the Office of Security, which ran its own files independent of the central CIA system (and does not do 201 files), and to Counter Intelligence, specifically to CI/SIG, where Angleton's independent office filing system was located.[350]

Having a totally independent file system meant that Angleton was truly in a very special position within the Agency, and his biographers point out that during his era that meant Angleton was used for a variety of discretionary projects, including the collection and "sanitization" of personal/sensitive documents. That included materials held by deceased CIA officers, including Frank Wisner (an early senior officer who suffered a mental breakdown and committed suicide), and the Mexico City Station Chief's personal papers (which Angleton personally removed from his home safe). Following the president's assassination, he was assigned as the liaison between the CIA and the Warren Commission.[351] Which leaves us with no specific answer as to what

Oswald material might have been personally held by Scott, yet ended up with Angleton.

The full story of the extent of Angleton's obsession with Soviet penetration of the CIA as well as his singular discretionary activities only emerged after Angleton's separation from the CIA (a dismissal related to his involvement with domestic surveillance of American anti-Vietnam war protestors and domestic dissidents). Following his departure, there was much speculation of what he might have held in his own special files, and what happened to those files.

We now have at least some closure, if unsatisfactory, to both of those questions—based on a lengthy memorandum entitled Destruction of Angleton's Files, which describes the dispensation of some 400 feet of files taken from Angleton's personal security storage area by Andrew Briggs. Briggs served the CIA over decades as the master controller of what information was too sensitive for the CIA to reveal, not just to the media or the public, but to Congressional committees and official government inquiries. Briggs' work on the Angleton file collection is described in the memorandum, detailing an effort that required a staff of three people and which took more than three years to complete.[352]

Briggs himself passed away in November of 2015. His obituary noted that he had joined the CIA in 1952 and retired in 1986, only to be immediately brought back as a consultant working for the Agency into the 1990s. His professional specialty was administration, and he held positions in several of the CIA's directorates—serving as Comptroller, Director of Services Staff, Inspector General, Executive Director, and Congressional Liaison. In June 1983, while serving as Executive Director, he had the unique distinction of briefly being designated as the Acting Director of Central Intelligence (DCI) and Acting Deputy Director (DDCI), serving in all 3 positions concurrently.[353]

During his tenure, Briggs became very involved with the CIA records systems, including both administrative and operational files. During the Congressional committee inquiries of the 1970s, he was personally involved with responding to freedom of information requests as well as in clearing documents for the Church Committee inquiry into intelligence practices—and later inquiries from the House Select Committee on Assassinations. Dozens of Briggs-related documents are now available, and they provide insight into routine CIA document actions such as requests for information on Martin Luther King[354] and E. Howard Hunt.[355] Some of the documents simply provide clues to the offices and individuals involved with responding to such requests; others offer more interesting details.

In one instance, during the Watergate scandal, a reporter requested documents pertaining to Howard Hunt's domestic travel while employed by the Agency; Hunt was a prime figure in the scandal, and known to be a long-term CIA employee. At the time one of the major questions about Watergate had to deal with any potential connection between the CIA and Hunt following his "official" retirement.

Briggs' internal response regarding the request for Hunt's travel documents was to confirm that Hunt had indeed been assigned to the CIA Domestic Operations group (DO) for a period of time, but that office held no travel records. Travel documents were available in the Office of Finance, but Briggs offered the opinion that the FOIA request be denied on the basis of protecting Hunt's personal privacy—as well as the practical point that when all information relating to operational data was removed according to standard practice, the resulting documents would be "useless" to the requestor.[356]

Of special interest to our exploration of Oswald and the CIA is the fact that in 1976, following the dismissal of long-time Counter Intelligence chief James Angleton, Briggs inventoried and evaluated CIA counter intelligence (CI) files including those held outside the standard CIA operational records system. That included the files, records and materials personally assembled and controlled by former CI Chief James Angleton. Briggs' memorandum on the processing of Angleton's files describes the collection of documents to have been massive, over four hundred feet in length.[357]

The review, integration, and destruction task was described by

Briggs as requiring three full-time staff and a part-time supervisor to evaluate the files. He initially estimated that something on the order of twelve person-years would be involved in the job. In the end it took four calendar years to complete, and was only partially done as of late 1979. Briggs also noted that Angleton's materials contained information considered to have been sensitive/compartmentalized—too sensitive to have been included in the CIA's integrated filing system. That suggests that Angleton's uniquely compartmentalized files would not have been made available for search and release to the 1964 Warren Commission inquiry on the Kennedy assassination—the Presidential Commission to which Angleton himself served as the CIA liaison. Nor would it have been made available to other Congressional investigations.

An annex to Briggs' report described sections of the Angleton files (which likely would have included internal "mole" hunting operations) that were deemed by Briggs as "too sensitive" to integrate into the consolidated, general CIA headquarters files. The circulation of that annex attachment was restricted even within the counter intelligence group. Beyond that, no "destruction" document listing and authorizing the destruction of sensitive records has ever been located.

It seems safe to say that with the knowledge of the withholding and then destruction of Angleton's sensitive counter intelligence and special investigations materials, we have at least a partial explanation for the chaos and compartmentalization which existed with respect to Oswald's files within the CIA—a situation that even perplexed officers within the Agency itself as well as the HSCA. However, to address the full question of whether or not Oswald was of use to the CI/SIG, we need to go beyond his time in Russia and examine whether or not Angleton had any interest in Cuban affairs, or in activities in Mexico City.

The answer to both questions is a definite yes. Following the disaster at the Bay of Pigs, Angleton had been personally directed to create and train a highly motivated counter intelligence service which could operate against Cuba. In the fall of 1961, Angleton presented his assessment, along with recommendations for the formation of what would come to be called the Cuban Intelligence Service. That group was formed during 1962, largely from the personnel who had been trained withing the Cuba Project (by David Morales). Its personnel were designated with AMOT numerical crypts. As noted previously, AMOT assets out of Miami Station (JM/WAVE) would be used in training and collecting intelligence assess in Mexico City during 1962 and 1963.

Angleton's Cuban interests continued through 1962 and into 1963, first with consulting with William Harvey on a Castro assassinations project in 1962, and then in 1963 with a focus on counterintelligence activities against Cuba. As Bill Simpich points out, a 1963 report from Angleton on Cuban control and capabilities for subversion, espionage, and sabotage—including the use of covert agents—was presented to the CIA Deputy Director, Richard Helms. Angleton's report addressed the use of non-Cubans for pro-Cuba activities, and in a section on "Suppression of travel information," discussed means by which individuals traveling to Cuba could conceal that travel.

A more specific indication that Angleton's personnel might still have been controlling information on Oswald comes from the fact that when the FBI began generating reports on Oswald and the FPCC in 1963, those reports did go to the CIA—specifically to Jane Roman, who had the responsibility for distributing them. That information was sent to Counter Intelligence and entered into the general FPCC file (file 100-300-011)—but not into Oswald's 201 personality file which CI/SIG controlled.[358] Clearly, as Roman told Morley and Newman, information on Oswald was being compartmentalized within Counter Intelligence.

Exactly what CI/SIG was doing, or planning to do, with the compartmentalized information is unknown—and based on the Angleton file destruction, very likely unknowable to any absolute certainty. Unfortunately, the same thing holds for the other group which almost certainly had contemporary information on Oswald which was not being shared internally, and potentially being developed for planned for use in propaganda activities. That group was the Cuba Project's Special Affairs Staff.

We can directly see that the DRE, as a deniable surrogate for SAS, had already been conducting some messaging activities built around Oswald's public activities and media appearances in New Orleans. Any effort planned to expand that deniably via DRE and INCA into a full-scale propaganda campaign, either targeting the FPCC specifically or in broader propaganda efforts against Cuba, would have resided in DRE case officer files which are still being held secret by the CIA—or in field office soft files that once existed in Miami or Mexico City, files associated with SAS and possibly with the new AMWORLD project. What we cannot see is either still being legally withheld, or may have already been destroyed. That is not idle speculation, as we know that certain sensitive Miami station materials were either destroyed or otherwise withheld from the Kennedy investigations, specifically those related to a JM/WAVE inquiry into possible Cuban involvement (pro or anti-Castro Cubans) in the Kennedy assassination.[359]

Given what we now know in regard to the extensive and highly classified intelligence collection and dirty tricks programs that the CIA was conducting Mexico City, as well as the extremely time-sensitive nature of high-level political action operations against diplomatic targets like Proenza, Azcue, and Lechuga/Duran, we can fully appreciate the extreme measures that would have been taken to prevent exposure of all or any of those activities. This raises the possibility that much of what we see in the CIA's obfuscation, obstruction, impersonation, and very likely destruction of evidence related to Oswald's time in Mexico may have much more to do with CIA operations than with Oswald—or the assassination of the president.

Which brings us back to the question of "witting vs. unwitting" and a final assessment of "unwitting" in terms of Oswald being a "witting" and "directed" CIA asset. What has focused previous speculation on a "witting" role in Russia, New Orleans or Mexico City has been the tendency for Oswald's own interests and agenda to become submerged in the chaos of the operations and agendas which were going on within the intelligence community which surrounded him during his own activities. If we focus specifically on Oswald's actual behavior, we find it very much in line with what would be expected from his own agenda and goals of the time. In Mexico City, that meant his goal of reaching Cuba. The materials he carried to Mexico and Duran's description of his presenting not only documents, but items intended to show him as a supporter of the Cuban revolution, argue for the personal appeal we would expect if he were acting on his own.

His attempt to dodge the issue of Soviet approval for a transit visit was certainly consistent with his tendency to try and talk himself past obstacles. So was the shift in personality which occurred when that did not work and Oswald realized he was going to be held to the rules. Finally, his confrontation with Azcue—in which he accused Azcue and the consulate of just being "bureaucrats"—was the typical behavior we have come to be familiar with from Oswald.

And although it might seem strange at first, Oswald's activity in Mexico City outside the consulate and embassy visits was also much like his early days in Russia, a mix of visits to embassies and consulates combined with sightseeing. In Mexico City, Oswald was officially recorded as being out of his hotel by nine in the morning, returning around midnight. His overall activities were very much those of a tourist. He ate lunches near the hotel; Marina testified he had told her that he had seen a bullfight, which would normally have been on Sunday afternoon, and that he had visited museums and done some sightseeing. He apparently saw one or more motion pictures, either American with Spanish subtitles or Mexican with English subtitles.[360] As we know from his past experiences, Oswald preferred to entertain himself and had been a frequent moviegoer, especially in the Marines and later inside Russia.

From notations in his Spanish-English dictionary and the markings on his guide map of Mexico City, it appears that Oswald intended to attend a jai alai game, but may not have done so. He purchased several postcards depicting bullfights and tourist attractions, which he brought back to Marina. She had told him before he left that she would like a Mexican silver bracelet as a souvenir, and he brought her a silver bracelet inscribed with her name. She suspected that the bracelet, which appears to have been of Japanese origin, did not actually come from Mexico (we have seen Oswald was notoriously frugal and certainly he had limited funds). He also did not buy the Mexican phonograph records which Marina had requested, despite the notation "records" which he had placed in his diary.[361] His address book also contained the telephone number and address of a Cuban airline in Mexico City, but there is no evidence that he visited its office.[362]

The issue of this trip to Mexico was raised in his wife's very first interview, immediately following Oswald's arrest. The Secret Service asked Marina about Oswald's travels to Washington D.C. (apparently based on remarks in his letters to SWP and CPUSA), and to Mexico City—at that time she answered negatively, stating she had no knowledge of his travels. As discussed previously, that was one of several of her first-day remarks that was a lie, or at least obfuscation, very possibly with her under considerable fear of personal repercussions, possibly arrest as an accessory to her husband's activities, or charges that she was acting as a Soviet agent (a suspicion expressed by FBI agent James Hosty).[363]

As for Oswald, he himself refused to even discuss Mexico City when he was asked about it by FBI agent Hosty during interviews following his arrest on November 22. His very personal reaction to the question may have also been due to his already being angry at Hosty for the FBI having visited, and in Oswald's view having harassed, his wife while she was staying at the Paines' home.

After his return to Dallas from Mexico City, Oswald focused on his personal concerns, his job and family issues and the imminent arrival of a new child. As we have repeatedly seen, he was not going to abandon his beliefs or his geopolitical agenda. But once again, at least for a time, he moved into reconciliation and reset—unwitting as to the interests and plans of others that his earlier activities had triggered.

Chapter 15

Reset in Dallas

"Whenever she [Ruth Paine] was not at home, he tried to spend as much time as he could with me—he would watch television in the house. . . . He remained with June [while Marina went to the hospital to have their second child] because June was crying and we could not leave her with strangers. He wanted to go with me, but we couldn't arrange it any other way. . . . Every father talks a lot [about the baby]. . . . He was very happy. He even had tears in his eyes."

". . . he called me from work…asked the nurse how I was doing… [after he got his job] Usually he would call me during the lunch break, and the second time after he was finished work, and he told me that he was reading, that he was watching television, and sometimes I told him that he should not stay in his room too much, that he should go for a walk in the park."

"I remember there was one weekend when he didn't come on a Friday, but said that he would come on a Saturday. And he said that was because he wanted to visit another place—he said that this was also based on an ad in a newspaper and that it was related to photography [Oswald had been working at the Texas School Book Depository for approximately a month at that time]—supposedly there was a job open, more interesting

work . . . and he went there in the morning and then on a Saturday he came to us, still during the morning."

—Marina Oswald testimony to Warren Commission,
Warren Commission Hearings, Volume 1, 53-58

Back in Dallas

The next view we have of Oswald is with him back in Dallas and in the same sort of "reset" we have seen previously. In retrospect, his return to Dallas seems fully consistent with his long-term behavior patterns, despite the drama with Azcue at the Cuban Consulate, and the Soviets at the Russian Embassy (with Oswald literally being shown the door out at both). His activities upon returning to Dallas also tend to confirm Marina's testimony that he was disappointed by events in Mexico, but not exceptionally disturbed. Overall, he simply appears to have begun to bounce back—as he often had before when his plans of the moment failed.

Back in Dallas, he immediately turned to job hunting, and then to visits and time with Marina and June at the Paines'. His goal, as it had been on similar occasions, appears to have been a return to a focus on once again bringing his family together, reaching out to Marina to move them all back into an apartment. According to those around him at the time, including Marina as well as Ruth and Michael Paine, Oswald displayed no particular signs of immense or ongoing frustration (other than the quality of the jobs he continued to get), or any extreme reaction to his recent experiences before returning to Dallas. If anything, his activities appear to have been an effort to set the stage for reuniting the Oswald family, a family with a new baby due shortly.

His first move was a visit to the office of the Texas State Employment Commission, where he filed an unemployment compensation claim, and announced that he was again looking for work. He spent the night at the YMCA, where he registered as a serviceman in order to avoid paying the membership fee.[364] On the following day, he applied for a job as a typesetter trainee at Padgett Printing and Lithography. He made a favorable impression on the department foreman and gave Jaggars-Chiles-Stovall as a reference. Unfortunately for Oswald, Padgett did a reference check and Oswald's former manager at Jaggars-Chiles-Stovall passed on the information that Oswald had been known to speak Russian when he worked there and was thought of as something of an oddball. He advised Padgett not to hire him and Oswald did not get the job.[365]

After he had begun his job-hunting, Oswald telephoned Marina at the Paines', and asked her to have Mrs. Paine pick him up in Dallas. Marina refused to ask Ruth to do that and Oswald hitchhiked out to the Paine home, where he spent part or all of the weekend. Marina testified that her husband had "changed for the better," but although he seemed to want to be with her and bring the family together, she did not want to immediately live with him. She was pregnant, close to her delivery date, and thought it would be better "to be with a woman who spoke English and Russian." On Monday, October 7, Mrs. Paine drove Oswald to the bus station, and he returned to Dallas to look for a job and a place to live.[366]

Oswald thought that the YMCA was too expensive for him, and intended to rent a room. He inquired about a room at 1026 North Beckley, where he lived later, but on October 7 there were no vacancies. He next responded to a "For Rent" sign at a rooming house at 621 Marsalis Street and obtained a room, for which he paid the weekly rent of $7 in advance—moving in on the same day. Oswald then immediately resumed his job-hunting, relying partially on referrals by the employment commission.

He reportedly spent much of the time when he was not looking for work in his room, and telephoned Marina daily—"Lee called twice a day, was worried about my health and about June." On Friday, Oswald told his landlady, Mrs. Mary Bledsoe, that he was going to Irving for the weekend, but would return the following week. She then refused to rent the room to him for another week, apparently because she just did not like him—or in some reports because she heard him talking in a language other than English on the house telephone.[367]

Oswald spent the weekend of October 12–13 at Mrs. Paine's home, during which time she gave him a driving lesson. He told Marina that he had received the last of the unemployment checks due him, and that it had been smaller than the previous ones. Mrs. Paine testified that Oswald appeared discouraged because his wife was expecting a baby, he had no job prospects in sight, and he no longer had any source of income.[368]

The following Monday, Mrs. Paine had business in Dallas, and Oswald rode with her into the city. He picked up his bag from Mrs. Bledsoe's rooming house, and later that day rented a room at 1026 North Beckley Avenue from Mrs. A. C. Johnson for $8 a week. He registered as O. H. Lee and moved in immediately. The reason for his use of an alias is unclear; Marina later tried to call him at the North Beckley apartment, was told that no Lee Oswald was a lodger there, and became really upset with Oswald over the matter.[369] While we have no absolute insight into why Oswald had begun to use different names, shielding his personal residence, he certainly knew that he had voluntarily given false information to the FBI in New Orleans. Most recently, he had attempted illegal international travel (for an American citizen) to Cuba. It is certainly possible that he suspected the FBI might have a renewed interest in him—this might also explain why he became so upset when they tried to reach him though his wife at the Paine residence.

According to leads given to the FBI following the assassination, Oswald applied for several jobs in downtown Dallas, including a job as a photographer at the Adolphus Hotel. However, due to demonstrably aggressive questioning by the FBI, those reports were challenged, and do not appear in the official record of his activities in Dallas.[370] Oswald certainly did continue to look for work, continually handicapped by the same problems he had begun to face in New Orleans, and dealing with it in the same way—by falsifying information on his job applications. His October job application for work at the Texas School Book Depository stated that he held an Honorable discharge from the Marines, indicating that the Marines had been his last job.[371]

On October 18, Marina and Ruth Paine had planned a birthday party for Oswald, who was turning 24. They put up some decorations and got a birthday cake and wine. Oswald was so moved by the gesture that he was described as having tears in his eyes. He remained emotional throughout the evening, crying and apologizing to Marina for all the things he had put her through. On October 20, Marina gave birth to a second daughter, Audrey Marina Rachel Oswald, at Parkland Memorial Hospital.

Continuity

On November 1, 1963, Marina Oswald sent a change of address form to the Soviet Consulate in New York City. She also restarted her effort to return to the Soviet Union by sending a letter apologizing for her delay in providing more details on why she had been requesting that she be allowed to return to Russia. She detailed problems with her husband finding work, and related that she would be able to find work as a pharmacy assistant in Russia while she could not do so in the United States.

Marina explained the delay in her response with reference to family issues including the arrival of a second child. Marina had never renounced her Russian citizenship and had been in routine correspondence with the Soviet Consulate on some 15 occasions since July 9, 1962. She had routinely submitted change of address forms, held her Russian passport (returned to her in September 1962), and since February 1963 had numerous exchanges with the Soviet Embassy in New York requesting approval of her return to Russia.[372]

As part of that process, Marina had earlier completed and submitted a questionnaire detailing information in support of her return appeal, advised the embassy of her pregnancy in July 1963, and asked for urgent consideration for her appeal in July. In August the Soviet Consulate advised her that her request had indeed been forwarded to Moscow. Most interestingly, in her November 1, 1963 letter she noted that her husband now wanted to return to Russia with her.

And on November 9, Oswald himself sent an appeal to the Russian Embassy in New York supporting a request for the couple's return to Russia. In that correspondence he argued for Soviet action by stating that both he and his wife had been harassed by the FBI, and that his wife had been approached about defecting to the United States.[373]

Oswald's claims of harassment regarding the FBI may sound "over the top" (and the "defection" claim is likely untrue or an exaggeration); they are fully consistent with Oswald's reported remarks about FBI harassment to Soviet Embassy staff in Mexico City, and very much in line with Oswald's later reaction to FBI agent Hosty on November 22, when he accused Hosty of harassing his wife.

They are also consistent with a now-missing complaint letter which Oswald had delivered to the FBI office in Dallas, reportedly protesting Hosty's visits to the Paines' as harassment of his family. The skeptical/conspiracy view is that the incident is an artifice of some sort, and that the letter may actually have contained intelligence for Hosty, or even a warning about JFK's visit to Dallas. The fact that Hosty was advised to destroy the letter could support either view. In any case documented evidence of Oswald having formally complained of FBI harassment prior to the assassination would not have been a good look for the Bureau—or been something which fit well with the Bureau's report on the assassination.

Over time, the November letter from Oswald has been challenged as a possible forgery, because in it there is also a mention that Oswald was unhappy with his reception at the Cuban Consulate and was happy that the consul he encountered there was being replaced. The question has been raised as to how Oswald could possibly have known that information. In considering that question, it is important to note that Consul Azcue himself later stated that if it had been up to him, he would have blocked Oswald's request for a Cuban visa. Yet the Warren Commission inquiry determined that Oswald's application had been completed with Duran's assistance; it was submitted to Havana and actually approved—contingent on Oswald providing confirmation that the Russians had approved his travel request.

Sylvia Duran also confirmed that she had advised Oswald that his application was being forwarded for evaluation, and she gave him her name and the consulate phone number in order to check on its status or to provide information related to his request. Her statement to the Warren Commission also noted that she could not recall if he had or had not made any follow-on contact about the application. Given her apparent empathy towards Oswald's effort, it is certainly possible to speculate that Duran herself had told Oswald that Consl Azcue was being replaced, and thus would not be a problem with his application. Duran herself remarked in her statement to the Warren Commission that Alfredo Mirabel, the replacement for Azcue, was in the consulate that day and was with Azcue when she asked him to come out and speak with Oswald.

Throughout November 1963, Oswald continued to live in Oak Cliff on weekdays, but stayed with Marina and the children at the Paines' on the weekends. According to Marina, that pattern of visitation continued up to November 21, when Oswald came to the Paines' on Thursday, rather than the weekend. During that visit he once again appealed to Marina and proposed that he would rent an apartment in Dallas so the family could be together. Marina stated that Oswald said he was tired of living alone, and that if she agreed he could get an apartment the next day. He did not want Marina to continue living with Ruth, but rather to bring the children and join him in Dallas.

Marina admitted that she had been very unresponsive to Oswald's remarks at the time, refusing to talk to him at first, and then telling him that she would rather stay with Mrs. Paine to save them money. After all, she had a brand-new baby and a small child, and they needed money to buy a washing machine. As usual, Marina was being far more practical than Oswald, and there was no threat that she was leaving him permanently, just being realistic about their family situation.

She also told Oswald that she wanted to remain at Ruth's until the holidays, but Christmas was coming and they could all be together then. Oswald appeared to accept that, telling her that he would get her the washing machine.[374] Oswald was obviously frustrated during the visit, but the next morning got up early to go to work and talked with Marina briefly. She did not fix him breakfast, which she normally did not when he was there, tending to the two children instead.

In contrast to Marina's actual description of her interactions with her husband on November 21, 1963, the Warren Commission Report positioned her remarks (and Ruth Paine's) to support the impression that Oswald had reacted so strongly to his talk with Marina the evening of November 21st, that their conversation was somehow a factor in his murder of President Kennedy the following day. In that same vein, much has been made of the fact that Oswald left his wedding ring at the Paines', in a teacup in the bedroom with Marina. One interpretation of such a gesture is that Marina's rejection of his pitch for an immediate move to an apartment had moved him into an unbalanced state of mind. Obviously, such an interpretation is simply speculation, and if anything suggests a passive symbolic action by someone the Commission positioned as emotional, irrational, and violent at the time. A counter view—as we will explore in detail below—is that Oswald was considering another option which might have taken him to Cuba, and that he left the ring as a remembrance for his wife should something happen during that effort. More objectively, the tendency to read major meaning into something such as a ring in a teacup suggests how far even the simplest things have been used as evidence to position Oswald definitively as an enraged presidential assassin.

Certainly, the Commission's narrative failed to note that his visit to the Paines' on Thursday evening was quite consistent with previous occasions over the past year—instances in which Oswald had spontaneously rushed to wherever Marina was staying, with a plea for her to "come back" and join him in reuniting their family. From a personal view, his behavior on November 21 was not at all unlike those previous occasions; it was simply a pattern of life (and marriage) that they had both established during their continual separations following his return to the United States from Russia.

In the context of his own history, Oswald's visit to Marina and an appeal to reunite the family was simply a repeat of a constant pattern in their relationship, less dramatic than many that had preceded it, and with Marina being far more conciliatory than on previous occasions—a visit with Oswald still holding a job and demonstrably very interested in his young girl and new baby.

The simple fact is that Oswald's ongoing ideological interests, and his tendency to become bored in any job (or any relationship) worked against what would have been considered a stable, traditional lifestyle. Oswald went from one job to another, one adventure to another—but he was also quite capable of "resetting" himself when the adventures failed, or simply when daily life became boring to him. His marital relationship perfectly illustrates that pattern. He would separate from Marina, only to miss her (and later the children) and return to her and a family relationship. That is exactly what we see following yet one more "adventure" in Mexico City, a return to job hunting, to work even at a menial job, and a return to time with the family at the Paines' and an effort to bring them together again on their own. If that had happened, the cycle would likely have repeated itself once again.

The Warren Commission Report offers a very different view of Oswald the day of the Kennedy assassination—in effect, it offers us two conflicting views. In one, Oswald had become consumed with rage based in his marital and personal problems, and spontaneously retrieved his stored rifle (and four rounds of ammunition) from the Paine garage in order to express his extreme anger by shooting the president of the United States. In that view, Oswald had entered an extremely emotional state but managed to totally conceal that from everyone around him both up to and after the time of the shooting.

But separately and in contradiction to the "spontaneous rage" scenario, the Commission seems to present Oswald's Thursday evening trip to the Paines' as an example of cool premeditation—motivated by his final rejection of the American establishment and a decision to express that rejection, a rejection and frustration which Oswald had turned against the nation's leader. That would mean the exchanges with his wife about moving the family together were simply a cover for his need to obtain the rifle he needed for the attack on the American system by killing its president. In effect, these are two very different views of the events of Thursday evening, November 21—both from the Commission itself.

Chapter 16

November 22, 1963 / Alternative Views

Reporter: "Did you shoot the president?"
Oswald: "I didn't shoot anybody, no sir."

—Recorded late on November 22, 1963 as Oswald was being led down a corridor of the Dallas police station. FBI 124-10370-10011, 410

The Warren Report view of Oswald is that of a witting, lone actor in the assassination. Two alternative skeptical views have presented Oswald as either being totally unaware of a pending attack on the president—or with him wittingly involved in what is most often described as a "false flag" action carried out by the CIA. A "false flag" is a harmful action designed to look like it is carried out by someone other than its actual perpetrator.[375] False flag operations are a historical reality, but not necessarily as common as frequently assumed/discussed in the media. Although the origin of the term is literal and of a tactical nature—ships flying the flag of the target of their attack and only changing (or not) to their own flag at the time of an actual attack—in current usage they are discussed with respect to major events such as invasions, coups, and regime change.

Usage of the term with respect to the Kennedy assassination is specifically in the context of a dramatic and violent incident staged so that the apparent attacker (Cuba) can be immediately connected to the party to be blamed for the attack, providing justification for the actual party behind the attack (United States) to claim the right to respond. In this view, the association of Lee Harvey Oswald, based in his public support of Cuba's revolution and Fidel Castro, is seen as a mechanism to trigger an American attack against Cuba. The idea of a false flag operation being involved in the attack on President Kennedy is most often associated with a series of proposals (Operation Northwoods) which had been produced by the Joint Chiefs of Staff in March 1962.[376] Those proposals were ideas for attacks against the United States which could be falsely attributed to Cuba, and thus used as pretexts for a military response. Although the CIA is often incorrectly connected to the Northwoods false flag proposals, they were actually prepared outside the Agency, at the request of Edward Lansdale (interagency Cuba Project head, appointed by President Kennedy).

Oswald's witting participation in such a mock attack would assume that he was ideologically (and covertly) deeply bound to an anti-Communist, anti-Cuba world view. He would have to be so committed that he would have been willing to carry through and potentially sacrifice himself in such an action, if not by his death, then by agreeing to place the blame on Castro, and accepting a considerable time in prison because of his involvement. The ideology attributed to Oswald in this "false flag" view would be consistent with those who view Oswald as virtually a lifelong anti-communist tool of various intelligence agencies, but fails to explain why Oswald made no supportive remarks which would have pointed towards Cuba and Castro upon his arrest, in front of the media or during his various interrogations.

The problem with that scenario is that in any "false flag" action—with Oswald as a witting and active participant—he would have had ample opportunity to concretely tie himself to the shooting (and to Cuban connections in the attack) even if he had not fired a weapon. He could easily have made himself fully visible at a window on the upper floors of the school book depository, he could have made last-minute negative remarks against JFK at work, or said something sensationally radical in front of witnesses.

If he had been knowingly cooperating in a false flag action targeting Cuba and the Castro regime, Oswald could easily have left a note or a written manifesto declaring his action to have been in support of the Cuban cause—of more specifically to encouragement by Cuban agents or contacts. Alternatively, if he had acted entirely on his own, for other political or personal reasons, he had every opportunity to declare it in writing or to claim a place for himself in history in his remarks to the press following the assassination.

There would have been no reason not to do so in either case, knowing that a rifle which could be traced to him had been left in the Texas School Book Depository, the scene of the shooting. With that knowledge, he would have been certain he would be charged and convicted—claiming responsibility and expressing himself for whatever reason would have done no further harm.

Yet none of those elements are reflected in his actual remarks while in custody; statements which were remarkably consistent give the stress of his situation:[377]

1:45 P.M. Arrest at the Texas Theater

> "I don't know why you are treating me like this. The only thing I have done is carry a pistol into a movie ... I don't see why you handcuffed me ... Why should I hide my face? I haven't done anything to be ashamed of ... I want a lawyer ... I am not resisting arrest ... I didn't kill anybody ... I haven't shot anybody ... I protest this police brutality ... I fought back there, but I know I wasn't supposed to be carrying a gun ... What is this all about?"

4:45 P.M. At a Lineup for Helen Markham, Witness to Tippit Murder

> "It isn't right to put me in line with these teenagers … You know what you are doing, and you are trying to railroad me … I want my lawyer … You are doing me an injustice by putting me out there dressed different than these other men … I am out there, the only one with a bruise on his head … I don't believe the lineup is fair, and I desire to put on a jacket similar to those worn by some of the other individuals in the lineup … All of you have a shirt on, and I have a T-shirt on. I want a shirt or something … This T-shirt is unfair."

6:30 P.M. Lineup for Witnesses Cecil J. McWatters, Sam Guinyard, and Ted Callaway

> "I didn't shoot anyone," Oswald yelled in the halls to reporters … "I want to get in touch with a lawyer, Mr. Abt, in New York City … I never killed anybody."

7:10 P.M. Arraignment: State of Texas v. Lee Harvey Oswald for Murder with Malice of Officer J. D. Tippit of the Dallas Police Dept.[378]

> "I insist upon my constitutional rights … The way you are treating me, I might as well be in Russia. … I was not granted my request to put on a jacket similar to those worn by other individuals in some previous lineups."

7:50 P.M. Lineup for Witness J. D. Davis

> "I have been dressed differently than the other three … Don't you know the difference? I still have on the same clothes I was arrested in. The other two were prisoners, already in jail." Seth Kantor, reporter, heard Oswald yell, "I am only a patsy."

11:20 - 11:25 P.M. Lineup for Press Conference; Jack Ruby Present

> When newsmen asked Oswald about his black eye, he answered, "A cop hit me." When asked about the earlier arraignment, Oswald said "Well, I was questioned by Judge Johnston. However, I protested at that time that I was not allowed legal representation during that very short and sweet hearing. I really don't know what the situation is about. Nobody has told me anything except that I am accused of murdering a policeman. I know nothing more than that, and I do request someone to come forward to give me legal assistance." When asked, "Did you kill the president?" Oswald replied, "No. I have not been charged with that. In fact, nobody has said that to me yet. The first thing I heard about it was when the newspaper reporters in the hall asked me that question … I did not do it. I did not do it … I did not shoot anyone."

Certainly nothing was left in writing to support a false flag scenario, much less for Oswald to implicate himself in any fashion. As we have seen repeatedly, Oswald talked; he spoke to the media whenever possible and consistently wrote and even corresponded with groups such as CPUSA and SWP in support of beliefs and actions. If he had knowingly participated in a false flag action intended to point towards Cuba and Castro, it is hard to understand why he would not have enthusiastically made some sort of remarks that would have carried forward the fundamental reason for a false flag attack—rather than the remarks to the press that he was being made a "patsy"—but only because he had been in Russia.

While the issues with such a false flag scenario are clear, it would be naïve to think that anyone could now describe Oswald's own thoughts immediately before the attack on President Kennedy with absolute certainty. We cannot even be exactly sure of his response to the accusations against him, given that none of his post-assassination interrogations were recorded or independently transcribed and officially notarized at the time. We are left with descriptions of them from handwritten notes (themselves not officially notarized) by interviewing officers, and their own personal recollections after the fact, recollections not examined or challenged in a criminal trial process.

Based on the lack of interrogation recordings, notarized transcripts, and other primary evidence, we cannot even be certain that Oswald was shown and immediately questioned on some of the most fundamental physical evidence from the crime scene. That would include the rifle recovered from the Texas School Book Depository, the ammunition recovered from that building, and the bag purportedly used to carry the disassembled rifle into the building.

Among the few absolutes we have as to Oswald's own responses immediately following his arrest are the brief remarks he made to reporters, captured on film during his movement though halls at the police station and later during an extremely brief press "showing" late that night. In the first instance, Oswald responded that he did work in the building at the scene of the shooting (the Texas School Book Depository) and stated that he was being treated as a "patsy," singled out because he had lived in the Soviet Union. During those remarks to reporters he protested that he had not been given access to legal counsel and requested legal assistance. In his few late-night remarks to the press, he denied having been charged with the murder of the president, stated again that he had not been given access to legal counsel, and again strongly requested assistance.[379]

The best insight into his personal thoughts of the charges against him, his state of mind, and his concerns while in jail may come from actual excerpts of Oswald's conversations with his wife and mother as well as his brother Robert on the day following his arrest and the charges of murdering a police officer and the president of the United States.[380] Readers can judge for themselves if these exchanges support the image of Oswald's state of mind as either presented by the Warren Commission Report or as a witting participant in a false flag attack (somehow gone very wrong):

November 23, 1963 1:10 - 1:30 P.M. Lee Harvey Oswald Visited by Mother, Marguerite Oswald, and Wife, Marina Oswald

(To his mother) "No, there is nothing you can do. Everything is fine. I know my rights, and I will have an attorney. I already requested to get in touch with Attorney Abt, I think is his name. Don't worry about a thing."

(To his wife) "Oh, no, they have not been beating me. They are treating me fine ... You're not to worry about that. Did you bring June and Rachel? ... Of course we can speak about absolutely anything at all ... It's a mistake. I'm not guilty. There are people who will help me. There is a lawyer in New York on whom I am counting for help ... Don't cry. There is nothing to cry about. Try not to think about it ... Everything is going to be all right. If they ask you anything, you have a right not to answer. You have a right to refuse. Do you understand? ... You are not to worry. You have friends. They'll help you. If it comes to that, you can ask the Red Cross for help. You mustn't worry about me. Kiss Junie and Rachel for me. I love you ... Be sure to buy shoes for June."

November 23, 1963 3:30 - 3:40 P.M. Robert Oswald, Brother, in Ten-Minute Visit

"I cannot or would not say anything, because the line is apparently tapped. [They were talking through telephones at the jail.] ... I got these bruises in the theater. They haven't bothered me since. They are treating me all right ... What do you think of the baby? Well, it was a girl, and I wanted a boy, but you know how that goes ... I don't know what is going on. I just don't know what they are talking about ... Don't believe all the so-called evidence." When Robert Oswald looked into Lee's eyes for some clue, Lee said to him, "Brother, you won't find anything there ... My friends will take care of Marina and the two children." When Robert Oswald stated that

> he didn't believe the Paines were friends of Lee's, he answered back, "Yes, they are ... Junie needs a new pair of shoes."

Oswald's remarks while in custody, as well as his demeanor while in contact with law enforcement—and even his minimal contact with the press—simply give us no sign that he was reacting emotionally to the president's death or to his personal involvement. If anything, his emotional reaction is focused on law enforcement, and his personal interests appear to be in legal representation and in his family. If anything, he appears to be confident that with an attorney and a defense, he would easily prove his innocence.

As noted in the introduction, this work focuses neither on the details of the attack in Dealey Plaza nor the controversies over evidence for various conspiracies. Those subjects have been and will continue to be addressed by a plethora of books. Both authors of this work have reached their own conclusion that Oswald did not shoot President Kennedy. Given that conclusion and the implications for conspiracy, the two issues of physical evidence connecting Oswald to the shooting will be briefly discussed in the Epilogue. We feel this deep examination of his character and the consistencies in his behavior over time (including both immediately before and after the assassination) support that view rather than the proposition presented by the Warren Commission.

In this exploration, we have addressed major controversies related to Oswald apart from the actual attack in Dallas, including the long-standing issue of whether or not Oswald was a witting intelligence asset for the American intelligence community—specifically for the FBI and CIA. Our findings on that, presented in the preceding, are that he was not, even if for some brief periods he might have been considered as a potential source or informant for the FBI.

We specifically do not find Oswald to have been a witting asset of the CIA in either his Russian saga or in his brief visit to Mexico City. On the other hand, we find a certainty Oswald was unwittingly being used in propaganda efforts by the DRE, and a likelihood that his activities were being unwittingly used as the foundation for a series of highly compartmentalized propaganda efforts being developed by the CIA's Special Affairs Staff—as well as in ongoing "mole hunting activities" carried out by James Angleton's Counter Intelligence/Special Investigations Group.

Those CIA activities, and others related to Oswald only by propinquity, were kept secret from the FBI and from the Warren Commission. In the earliest days following the assassination, the concealment of those activities (both in Mexico City and as related to the CIA's own internal investigation of the possibility of either pro- or anti-Castro involvement in the attack on the president) fed serious national security concerns at the highest levels of government.[381] Those concerns were fueled by additional claims of Cuban involvement coming out of the Mexico City station and from statements of Cuban involvement with Oswald coming from the CIA's client group, the DRE.

Those national security issues, and the implications of a Cuban or Russian conspiracy, directly contributed to the suppression of any possible conspiracy in the assassination. They also drove the highest levels of the Johnson administration to do whatever was required to seize the narrative of the assassination. That initiative ("damage control" being possibly the most accurate description) included the extensive involvement of President Johnson, and ultimately resulted in the "lone nut" scenario. This narrative effectively preempted a legitimate inquiry into the attack on President Kennedy, and fostered the FBI and Commission leaks to the media which resulted in the public conviction of Oswald over some eight months in 1964.[382]

Loose Ends

After decades of research, the Garrison inquiry, the Church Committee on CIA activities, the House Select Committee on Assassinations, the JFK Records Act, and the work of the Assassinations Records Review Board, we have made great progress in understanding the obfuscation and suppression of information which followed the assassination. We have a far clearer understanding of the extensive issues of evidence, and of leads towards conspiracy which were not effectively pursued. Yet what we do not have are explanations for certain aspects of Oswald's own activities the day of the assassination.

There are elements of Oswald's behavior on the afternoon of November 22 which are anomalous in terms of both his character and standard patterns of behavior. One of those issues is Oswald's decision to leave not just work, but to vacate the Plaza area entirely very shortly after the shooting. Oswald's own remarks state that he did so only after confirming with a supervisor that there would be no more work that day. Yet Oswald's character always included a significant element of curiosity. His not staying around to go back to work would be consistent. But his apparent lack of interest in what might just have happened to the president, including the likelihood of a violent demonstration or right-wing protests (things which had been in the news all week, with the City Council even issuing a proclamation urging citizens to act against such incidents), seems strange.

So does the fact that he not only left the Plaza rather quickly, but that he took either a combination of a bus and taxi (per the official investigation) or was driven away by unidentified parties in a car. Clearly the latter incident (reported by multiple witnesses and noted on television by the Dallas police chief that day) would suggest a serious loose end. But even the official story of a notoriously frugal Oswald, reportedly getting off a bus which was then stopped by traffic, and taking a taxi to a location more than a block away from his apartment, is out of character for Oswald.

Equally strange for Oswald, who was something of a news junkie; Oswald routinely watched television in the evenings, even in the common rooms at rental apartments.[383] Yet on November 22, even having heard from the cab driver that the president had been shot, he made no effort to follow a huge national news story, but rather quickly changed clothes and headed out to take in a war movie at the Texas Theatre.

Leaving work, quickly vacating the Plaza, paying for a cab ride, and choosing a movie over the news are quite personal and situational—only Oswald himself could have provided explanations for those actions. What is arguably not a matter of personal idiosyncrasy is that when taken into custody at the theatre, Oswald did have a pistol in his possession—and that a rifle and shells were found at his place of work.

Given a view that Oswald did not shoot President Kennedy, and that he was indeed framed, some alternative scenario must be offered which would somehow associate an unwitting Oswald with other people, people directly involved with a conspiracy against the president. Such a scenario would have to address the question of whether—completely independently of the attack on the president—Oswald might still have been following his own agenda on November 22, 1963.

This would be an agenda completely outside of the conspiracy to kill President Kennedy, but an agenda that also exposed Oswald to being manipulated and framed with the planting of physical evidence connecting him to the shooting. When Oswald learned of the death of the president, with JFK being shot just outside the School Book Depository where he himself worked, Oswald was certainly quick enough to have realized that "his plan" for the day might not be "the plan." That would have led him to do whatever he deemed necessary to protect himself, including arming himself with his pistol, prepared to use it if he felt threatened—including by police officers. The combination of being initially unwitting and then terribly uncertain would have been a brutal combination of emotions for Lee Harvey Oswald on the afternoon of November 22, 1963.

As it turns out, there is at least circumstantial support for the view that Oswald had become part of a plan unrelated to JFK, a plan related to his own agenda regarding Cuba. There were, from the earliest days following the assassination, leads to other individuals in contact with Oswald, individuals who may have falsely inserted themselves into his Cuban goals, gaining the influence needed to both manipulate and ultimately frame him for their own purposes.

Chapter 17

The DRE and Oswald

"Luce told Glaser that, according to 'Julio Fernandez,' Oswald had approached the anti-Castro group to which Fernandez belonged and offered his services as a potential Castro assassin. The Cubans, however, didn't trust Oswald, suspected he was really a Communist, and decided to keep tabs on him. They eventually penetrated Oswald's Communist 'cell' and tape recorded his talks, including his bragging that he could shoot anyone, even the Secretary of the Navy."

—House Committee on Assassinations summary of a 1975 reporter's interview with Clare Booth Luce, wherein she described a call she received on the night of Kennedy's assassination.

There is no doubt that Oswald was in contact with DRE members and their associates (several of whom were also involved with the Cuban Revolutionary Council / CRC group) in New Orleans in the summer of 1963. There is also no doubt that he was tested by one and possibly more of those individuals who approached him as pro-Castro supporters. When Oswald first contacted the DRE in New Orleans, presenting his Marine background and offering himself as a military trainer, Carlos Bringuier had referred him to the DRE military wing; Bringuier himself was solely involved in fundraising. At that point, Bringuier began to send a stream of "Oswald" reports to DRE headquarters, detailing contacts with Oswald and outlining efforts to collect information that could be used for anti-Castro propaganda. In Miami, the DRE built an extensive file on Oswald, including information on his time in the Soviet Union.

Those activities went much further than simply collecting information and building a file. DRE issued a press release and called on Congress to investigate Oswald and the growing Cuban influence inside America. Letters were written to congressmen, and the press release was distributed to several other exile groups in Miami for their own use.[384]

The CIA itself was forcing the DRE away from military operations, making its funding increasingly dependent on its counter intelligence and propaganda activities; continually discouraging it from any new military initiatives. One of the principal DRE leaders, Manuel Salvat, is on record that by the summer of 1963, he had personally moved from military affairs to being chief of propaganda activities for the DRE.[385]

Because the DRE was being financially supported by the CIA for its propaganda work, the Oswald opportunity was deemed extremely important. As noted previously, one of its leaders, Isadore Borja, described its activities against Oswald to researcher Jeff Morley—emphasizing how critical the New Orleans information was for its propaganda work. That was exactly the sort of thing that gained them credit with the CIA.

Unfortunately, we have neither the DRE's own Oswald files, nor the related CIA case officer records to give us a full view of the DRE's efforts. However, based on Morley's interviews with DRE members, there is no acknowledgement that their contact with Oswald, or any related propaganda work related to him, continued beyond the New Orleans contacts. There is simply an inexplicable gap of some three

CABLE ADDRESS DAIWORK NEW YORK • ORegon 9-9450
23 WEST 26 ST. • NEW YORK 11, N. Y.

Dec 19, 1962

Lee H Oswald
P O Box 2915
Dallas Texas

Dear Mr Oswald;

Mr Jackson is on leave for a few weeks, so permit me to thank you for the blow ups.

Your kind offer is most welcomed and from time to time we shall call on you. These poster like blow ups are most useful at newsstands and other public places to call the attention of newspaper readers that the "Worker" is available.

Best wishes for a peaceful New Year.

Sincerely yours,

Louis Weinstock, General Manager
Louis Weinstock

Letter from Louis Weinstock of the Socialist Worker's Party in December of 1962. Oswald offered to do photo work for the organization. (*Dallas Municipal Archives*)

116 University Place
New York 3, New York.
Dec. 9, 1962

Mr. Lee H. Oswald
Box 2915
Dallas, Texas.

Dear Mr. Oswald:

Your letter and reproductions were turned over to me by the SWP office.

I am familiar with reproductions and offset printing processes. It is clear from your work that you are skilled at blow-ups, reversals and reproduction work generally. Do you do any other phases of the process as well as photography? What about layout and art work?

Top portion of Socialist Worker's Party recognition letter for Oswald's photographic skills and volunteer work offer, December 1962. (*Dallas Municipal Archives*)

Lee Harvey Oswald with rifle and holstered pistol, early spring 1963 at the Neely Street house. He is holding copies of *The Militant* and *The Daily Worker* newspapers. Oswald subscribed to both publications. *(Warren Commission Exhibit 133 via Getty Images)*

Photo taken from the street in front of General Walker's house in Dallas, early spring 1963. Found among Oswald's possessions. (*Warren Commission Exhibit 5 via Getty Images*)

Photo taken from Oswald's possessions, depicting the alley running behind the Walker house. (*Warren Commission Shaneyfelt Exhibit 23*)

Two FPCC handbills in Oswald's possession. Oswald and Hidell names listed as separate contacts at separate locations. New Orleans, 1963. (*Warren Commission Exhibits 2966 A, B [HSCA Exhibit 595]*)

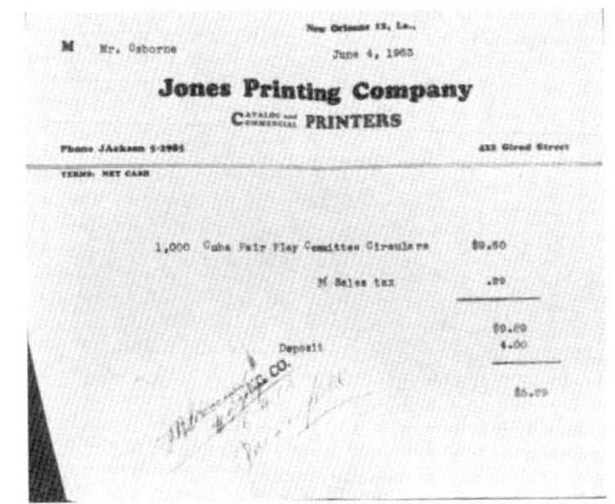

M Mr. Osborne

June 4, 1963

Jones Printing Company

PRINTERS

1,000 Cuba Fair Play Committee Circulars	$9.60
% Sales tax	.29
	$9.89
Deposit	4.00
	$5.89

Receipt for printing of FPCC handbills, found among Oswald's possessions. (*Dallas Municipal Archives*)

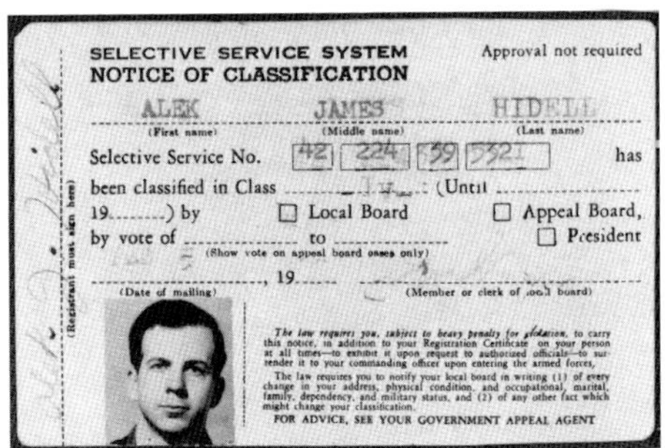

SELECTIVE SERVICE SYSTEM
NOTICE OF CLASSIFICATION

Approval not required

ALEK (First name) JAMES (Middle name) HIDELL (Last name)

Selective Service No. 42 224 39 5321 has been classified in Class ____ (Until ____ 19____) by ☐ Local Board ☐ Appeal Board, by vote of ____ to ____ ☐ President (Show vote on appeal board cases only)

____, 19____
(Date of mailing) (Member or clerk of local board)

(Registrant must sign here)

The law requires you, subject to heavy penalty for violation, to carry this notice, in addition to your Registration Certificate on your person at all times—to exhibit it upon request to authorized officials—to surrender it to your commanding officer upon entering the armed forces.

The law requires you to notify your local board in writing (1) of every change in your address, physical condition, and occupational, marital, family, dependency, and military status, and (2) of any other fact which might change your classification.

FOR ADVICE, SEE YOUR GOVERNMENT APPEAL AGENT

"Faked" Selective Service card for Alex James Hidell. (*Dallas Municipal Archives*)

JESUIT HOUSE OF STUDIES
3959 LOYOLA LANE
MOBILE, ALABAMA

August 1, 1963

Dear Mr. Oswald:

This is just a very brief note to express my thanks for the talk you gave us on Russia Saturday, July 27th. I feel that I came away from your talk with an understanding of the Russian people as a people, with ideals, goals, problems--normal, everyday human beings, something that is quite easy to forget with all the threats of war hanging in the air. I find your talk has helped to make me a broader and deeper person, more universal and sympathetic in my thinking. I hope in the future both America and Russia can draw closer to one another and thereby increase in friendship and understanding.

I also wish to tell you that I greatly admire you search for truth and your living in Russia, and I hope you have or will find it.

You can be assured of a permanent remembrance in my prayers and sacrifices, you, your wife, and your family.

With sincere gratitude,

Paul Piazza, S.J.

Paul Piazza, S. J.

Letter written to Lee Harvey Oswald a few days after Oswald's talk on life in Russia to the Jesuit House of Studies in Alabama, August 1, 1963. (*Dallas Municipal Archives*)

Oswald passing out FPCC leaflets near the International Trade Mart in New Orleans, August 16, 1963. (*Warren Commission Garner Exhibit 1 via Getty Images*)

Oswald and two "hourly hired" young men passing out FPCC leaflets in New Orleans. (*Warren Commission Pizzo Exhibit 453-B via Getty Images*)

Silvia Odio, visited in Dallas by three men in late September 1963. One of those men, who said they had come from New Orleans, was identified to her as "Oswald." (*HSCA "mugbook," record number 180-10124-10172*)

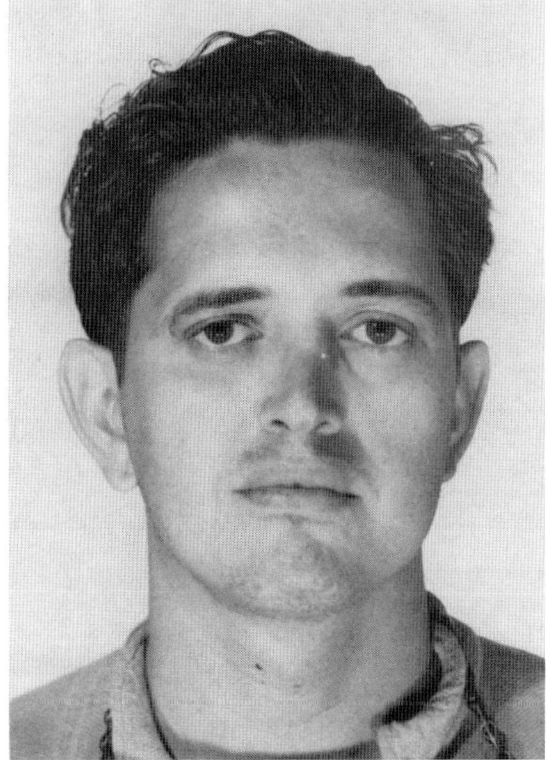

New Orleans anti-Castro activist Carlos Bringuier was charged with accosting Oswald during FPCC leafletting near the International Trade Mart. Bringuier was the senior DRE leader in New Orleans, reporting directly to the Student Directorate's headquarters in Miami. (*HSCA "mugbook," record number 180-10124-10172*)

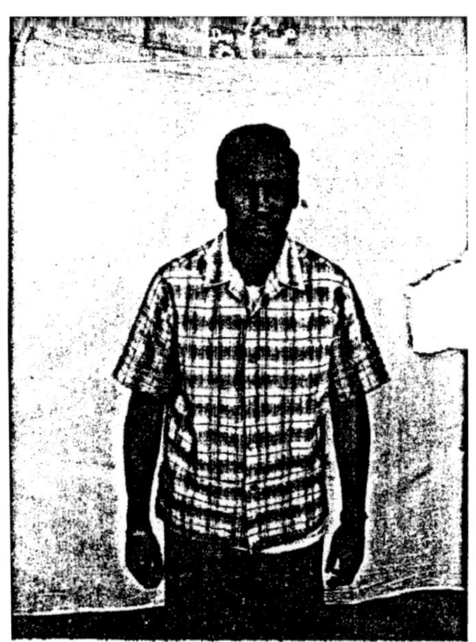

Victor Espinosa Hernandez was a DRE member in Cuba who participated in assassinations of Batista regime figures. He attended Louisiana State University and was an early volunteer for the CIA's anti-Castro operations. Trained for special clandestine operations in Panama and at the Belle Chase camp outside New Orleans, Hernandez was operationally approved for high-risk CIA operations; also independently participated in private military operations against Cuba. Possible visitor to Silvia Odio in Dallas, fall 1963. (*CIA files, record #104-10079-10332*)

Carlos Hernandez, a volunteer for the CIA's anti-Castro operations, was trained for special clandestine operations in Panama and at the Belle Chase camp outside New Orleans. He was operationally approved for high-risk CIA operations into Cuba and also independently participated in both DRE and private military operations against Cuba, and was an early recruit to the new, highly secret CIA AMWORLD project in fall 1963. CIA cryptonym AMHAZE-2523. Possible visitor to Silvia Odio in Dallas. (*CIA files, record #104-10172-10114*)

Sylvia Duran, Cuban Consulate secretary in Mexico City. Processed Oswald's Cuban visa application. (*HSCA Exhibit 433)*

Oswald photo used in Cuban visa application at Cuban Consulate in Mexico City. (*Commission Exhibit 2788*)

Cropped photo of Mexico City "Mystery Man," conditionally identified as Oswald by Mexico City station to CIA headquarters. (*Warren Commission Exhibit 237*)

Copies of passport type photos, matching Oswald's Cuban visa application photo. Taken by Dallas police from Oswald's belongings following his arrest on November 22, 1963. (*Dallas Municipal Archives*)

David Atlee Phillips. CIA career officer. (*Periscope, AFIO, 2005*)

George Joannides, CIA case officer for the DRE. (*CIA FOIA files*)

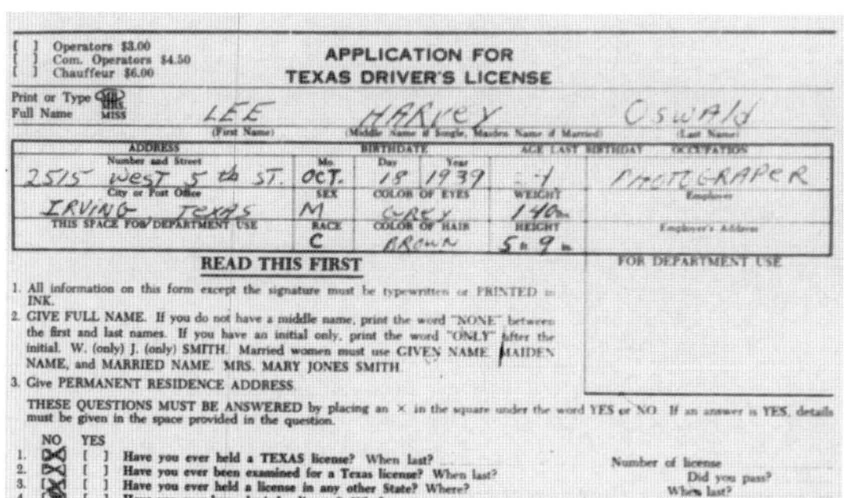

[ ] Operators $3.00
[ ] Com. Operators $4.50
[ ] Chauffeur $6.00

APPLICATION FOR
TEXAS DRIVER'S LICENSE

Print or Type Full Name MR. MRS. MISS — LEE (First Name) — HARVEY (Middle Name if Single, Maiden Name if Married) — Oswald (Last Name)

ADDRESS Number and Street	BIRTHDATE Mo.	Day	Year	AGE LAST BIRTHDAY	OCCUPATION
2515 West 5th ST.	OCT.	18	1939	[illegible]	PHOTOGRAPER
City or Post Office	SEX	COLOR OF EYES		WEIGHT	Employer
IRVING, TEXAS	M	GREY		140 lbs.	
THIS SPACE FOR DEPARTMENT USE	RACE	COLOR OF HAIR		HEIGHT	Employer's Address
	C	BROWN		5 ft 9 in.	

READ THIS FIRST

FOR DEPARTMENT USE

1. All information on this form except the signature must be typewritten or PRINTED in INK.
2. GIVE FULL NAME. If you do not have a middle name, print the word "NONE" between the first and last names. If you have an initial only, print the word "ONLY" after the initial. W. (only) J. (only) SMITH. Married women must use GIVEN NAME, MAIDEN NAME, and MARRIED NAME. MRS. MARY JONES SMITH.
3. Give PERMANENT RESIDENCE ADDRESS.

THESE QUESTIONS MUST BE ANSWERED by placing an × in the square under the word YES or NO. If an answer is YES, details must be given in the space provided in the question.

	NO	YES		
1.	[X]	[ ]	Have you ever held a TEXAS license? When last?	Number of license
2.	[X]	[ ]	Have you ever been examined for a Texas license? When last?	Did you pass?
3.	[X]	[ ]	Have you ever held a license in any other State? Where?	When last?

Top portion of an application for a 1963 Texas driver's license for Lee Harvey Oswald, found among Oswald's possessions after his arrest. (*Dallas Municipal Archives*)

Oswald held for questioning by Dallas police following his arrest, November 22, 1963. *(Associated Press)*

Oswald showing handcuffs at Dallas police station. (*Bill Winfrey, Dallas Morning News, Sixth Floor Museum*)

Lee Harvey Oswald giving remarks to the press at the Dallas police station. While led through the hall and bombarded with questions from reporters, Oswald responded "I don't know what this is all about . . . they are taking me in because of the fact that I lived in the Soviet Union . . . I'm just a patsy." (https://www.youtube.com/watch?v=IhmAHlcZHt0). (*AP*)

Dallas "jail booking" photo, November 23, 1963. Taken after Oswald's capture, initial police questioning, and comments to reporters. (*Dallas Municipal Archives*)

Men used in "lineups" on November 22, 1963; Oswald as dressed during those lineups. Oswald was positively identified only regarding travel by cab and bus the day of the assassination. One witness claiming to have seen the actual shooter refused to positively identify Oswald during the lineup; that individual's claim proved highly questionable. (*Warren Commission Exhibits 1054, 520*)

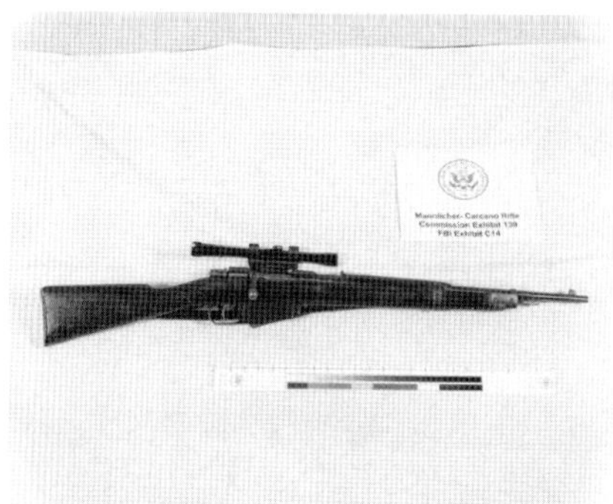

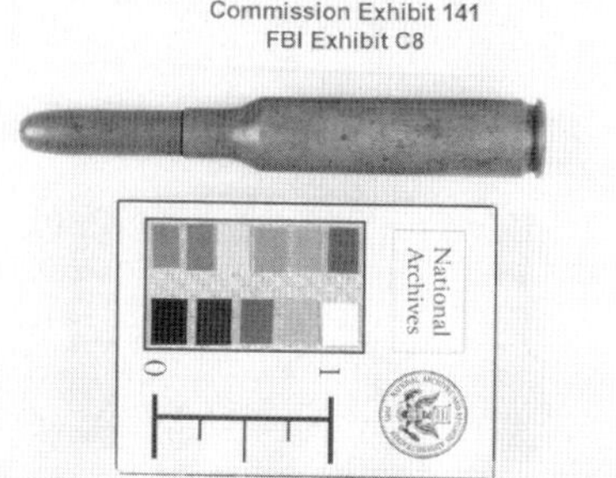

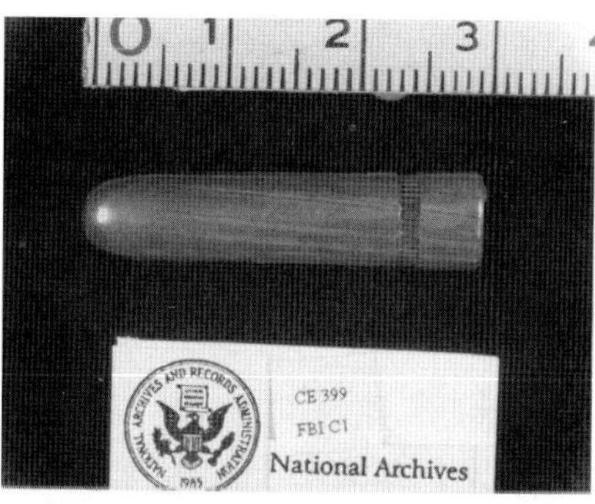

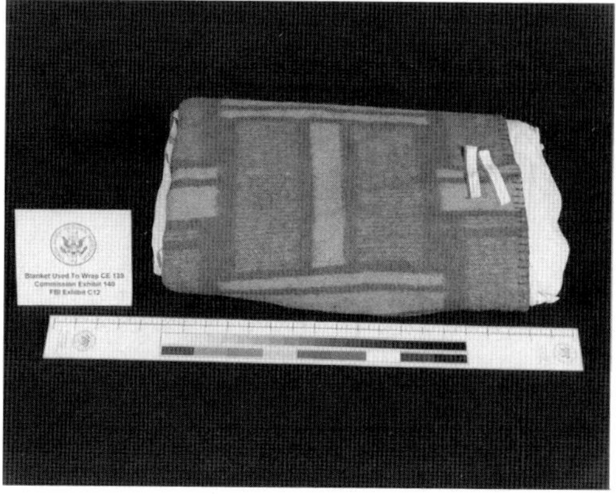

Physical evidence offered to prove Lee Harvey Oswald to be the assassin of President Kennedy (see facing page for discussion). (*National Archives evidence photographs*)

Descriptions of items on facing page:

(Top left) CE 139—Mannlicher-Carcano rifle, serial No. C2766, hidden among boxes near a stairwell on the sixth floor of the Texas School Book Depository (TSBD). Oswald was not observed in possession of a rifle by anyone on the day of the assassination.

(Top right) CE 141—6.5mm Mannlicher-Carcano cartridge found in rifle; three cartridge hulls were found on the sixth floor of the TSBD. The mail order connecting Oswald to the purchase of the Mannlicher-Carcano rifle did not include ammunition, nor could the FBI ever prove that Oswald had ammunition in his possession at any time, nor determine the source of the ammunition recovered in the Texas School Book Depository.

(Middle left) CE 142—Bag made from wrapping paper. This item was not photographed at the crime scene. The only witness to Oswald having a paper sack the day of the assassination testified under oath that what he saw did not match the sack in evidence. He had been shown this sack the night of the assassination and stated, verified as truthful under polygraph examination, that it was not the same as the smaller lunch-sized bag Oswald had taken to work that same morning. CE 142 also exhibited no oil traces, which would have been expected had it been used to transport a "well-oiled" rifle.

(Middle right) CE 399—The undamaged and clean "Magic Bullet" found on a stretcher in Parkland Hospital. No legally verifiable chain of evidence exists for this bullet. The Warren Commission's own ballistics panel reported that it could not match the bullet either to the reported wounds it was presented to have caused, nor to the Commission's shooting scenario. The bullet exhibits markings matching the Mannlicher-Carcano's barrel, but the bullet could have been fired from the rifle at any time.

(Bottom left) CE 567 and CE 569—Fragments of nose and base of a bullet said to have been recovered from the Presidential limousine, and linked by the FBI to the rifle discovered in the Texas School Book Depository. Later research disqualified the key forensics technique used in that identification.

(Bottom right) CE 140—Blanket found in the Paine garage, said to have stored the rifle. The FBI found fibers in the paper bag (CE 142) but could not determine whether they had come from this blanket. No oil traces were found on the blanket.

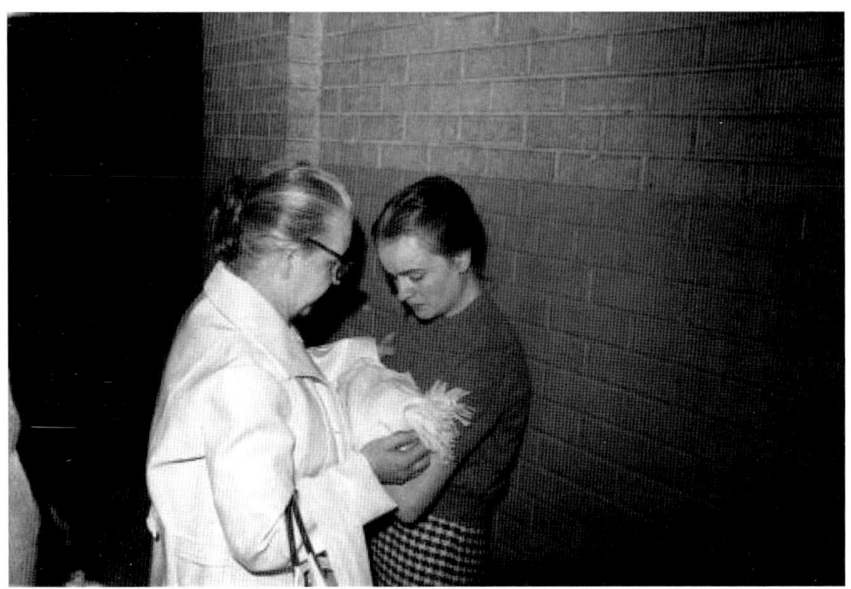

Marina holding baby Rachel with Lee's mother Marguerite, standing in the hallway at Dallas Police Headquarters, November 22, 1963. (*Darryl Heikes, Dallas Times Herald. Sixth Floor Museum*)

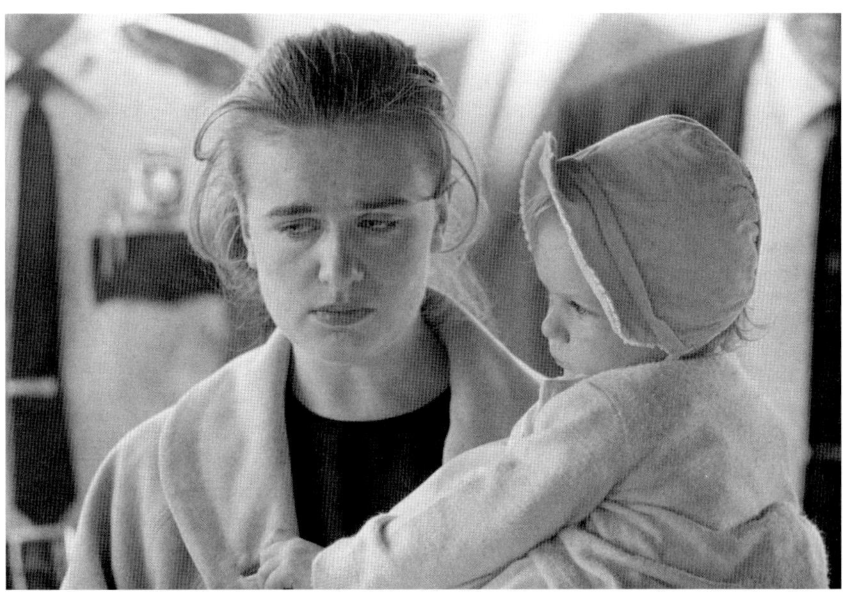

Marina Oswald at Lee's funeral, holding June, November 25, 1963. (*Bettman Archives via Getty Images*)

months, in which the DRE members maintain that they just gave up on using Oswald in an aggressive propaganda campaign and paid no attention to him following his time in New Orleans. Yet, they returned to a major media outreach effort trying to link him to Fidel Castro and Cuban sponsorship of the attack in Dallas immediately following the president's murder.

On the evening of November 22, a series of telephone calls from DRE leaders began to alert the press to Oswald as being a Cuban agent, and to Oswald having acted under Cuban influence or specific direction. In one sense such calls can be viewed as strictly opportunistic, associating a figure known to DRE, now in police custody and being touted as the assassin, with Oswald's support for Cuba already documented in its files.

However, one particular call stands out from the more generic claims, a call made from DRE-affiliated individuals to Mrs. Clare Booth Luce, who had previously offered financial support for DRE boat missions against Cuba. The call to Mrs. Luce offered very specific information, including information not in the media nor known to the general public at the time. The caller stated that Oswald had been in Mexico after leaving New Orleans, that he had been under observation, and there were witnesses prepared to describe having heard him talking about killing JFK and making threats against him. Furthermore, they had proof that he had become part of a covert Cuban hit team operating out of Mexico.

There is no doubt that Luce took the call seriously—she reported it and the details to the FBI—or that she had indeed provided money for Cuban exile maritime missions against Cuba. Her involvement in that was summarized in a report by investigator Gaeton Fonzi to the House Select Committee on Assassinations concerning his own investigation of the DRE:[386]

> "Luce said that after the failure of the Bay of Pigs invasion, her friend, William Pawley, persuaded her to help sponsor a fleet of

> motorboats for a group of anti-Castro Cubans who, Pawley envisioned, would be Cuban 'Flying Tigers,' flying in and out of Cuba on intelligence-gathering missions. Pawley had helped start Gen. Claire Chennault's original Flying Tigers in World War II. Luce said she agreed to sponsor one boat and its three-man crew. She said she met with this Cuban boat crew about three times in New York and, in 1962, published a story about them in LIFE magazine. Following the missile crisis in October 1962, Luce said that the Kennedy administration clamped down on exile activities against Cuba, and the Pawley-sponsored boat raids were discontinued. Luce said she never saw her 'young Cubans,' as she called them, again."

Sources (McCarthy and Ayers) suggest that at least two of the individuals who initially met with Luce, known to her and known by their "war names," were Isadore Borja (known as Chilo) and Juan Francisco Blanco (known as Julio Fernandez). Manuel Salvat may have been the third; all had been DRE military leaders circa 1962, with Salvat being the coordinator of the boat mission that led to Pawley's referral to Luce. Luce stated that her post-assassination caller had been a student lawyer when he was in Cuba, which as noted earlier, would point toward Manuel Salvat—a law student before his exile to the United States.[387,388]

Luce went to considerable effort to report the call to the FBI, and to provide them with information about the caller, whom she described as known to her.[389] The call had come from an individual she had talked with the year before. For some unspecified reason, she felt the call was from New Orleans. He did not give a name and, in her interviews, she simply stated that she would refer to him as Julio Fernandez. She said the Cuban told her he was calling because he wanted to tell her about some information that they had on the president's killer, Lee Harvey Oswald.

The caller said Oswald had approached the individuals, and offered his services as a potential Castro assassin. The Cubans, however, did not trust Oswald, and suspected he was really a Communist, and decided to keep tabs on him. They eventually penetrated Oswald's Communist "cell" and tape recorded him, including his bragging that he could shoot anyone, even the secretary of the Navy.

It was also learned that Oswald suddenly came into some money, had gone to Mexico City, and from there back to Dallas. Her caller stated that his group possessed tape recordings and photographs of Oswald, and well as samples of the handbills he passed out in New Orleans. Most important, the surveillance of Oswald revealed that he had actually became a "hired gun" for a Cuban communist group that had contacted him in New Orleans, and that he worked for them in the attack in Dallas. Later, during the Garrison investigation, Luce contacted her caller again and was told the group had contacted the FBI, offering all their information, but were warned never to talk about it or face deportation.

Luce's caller did not identify himself by name during the call, and her DRE contacts appear to have used "war names" with her rather than true names. What is most likely is that Luce's caller had at some point been with the military arm of the DRE and involved with the boat missions she had supported. The most likely candidates would be either Fernandez or Salvat. Determining the true identity of "Julio Fernandez" is more difficult, but we do have information suggesting that it was Blanco Fernandez. We find this in a firsthand report from Captain Bradley Ayers, who was an Army trainer detailed to the CIA at the JM/WAVE Miami station during the summer of 1963. Ayers writes that one of the most active DRE military leaders, Blanco Fernandez, still operational with the CIA in the summer of 1963, had used the alias "Julio Fernandez."

More significant, in terms of the "others" being in contact with Lee Oswald, specifically aware of his movements beyond New Orleans, it seems significant that DRE-affiliated individuals were already aware the night of the assassination that Oswald had been in Mexico, and were prepared to offer witnesses who would support the idea that he had threatened JFK, and/or support the idea that he was a potential assassin. Given the perceived importance of Oswald to the DRE for its propaganda efforts, an ongoing effort to monitor and possibly even contact and manipulate him would be quite consistent. What seems much stranger is that they would have so easily abandoned further opportunities related to him—even if they were only laying the groundwork for a more dramatic propaganda campaign beyond the one they had started in August.

It also seems quite strange that, according to Salvat himself, when he traveled to Dallas in the fall, he personally heard talk from local Dallas contacts that Oswald was there, and had been seen attending exile group meetings. Given the contacts, interest, and resulting DRE propaganda related to Oswald only months before in New Orleans, it is more than strange that Salvat would not have alerted local DRE members to Oswald or reported his presence to DRE headquarters—or his CIA case officer.[390] Yet he makes no mention of warnings or communications about Oswald turning up in Dallas, where a new round of DRE meetings and covert weapons purchase activities were in progress. What would explain Salvat knowing of Oswald in Dallas, but taking no action to pursue what had been considered a major new opportunity no more than three months earlier?

Given the demonstrated DRE interest in propagandizing Oswald, and using him as an example for touting the dangerous Castro influence inside the United States, it seems reasonable to speculate that some level of monitoring/tracking would have occurred, with information about Oswald's travels and activities at least shared among DRE members. That at least might explain the accurate references to Oswald's movements in the call to Luce. Otherwise, there is no explanation for the reference to his being in Mexico or in contact with possible Cuban agents there. At the time of the call, there was simply no public information circulating regarding his travel to Mexico or his contacts there. Any knowledge of Lee Oswald in Mexico City existed only within the intelligence community at that time.

When Ruth Paine was questioned about Oswald and Mexico, she

stated that before the assassination, neither Oswald nor Marina had said anything about Mexico nor talked about Oswald having been in Mexico before coming to Dallas. [391] There is also no indication that Oswald had ever discussed Mexico with any of his co-workers or with Michael Paine. This suggests that if DRE members had information regarding Oswald and Mexico, they had either obtained it by being in covert contact with him or in some sort of joint effort with the CIA.

Beyond the DRE knowledge of Oswald having traveled to Mexico, the remarks to Mrs. Luce contain two other points that are found nowhere else in the media or public record at the time of the call. The callers offered the knowledge—and evidence to support the claim—that Oswald was not just a Castro-Cuban political activist, but potentially known to be an actual danger. They claimed to have heard him speak about killing people (and possibly even to have recordings of that, but Luce's remarks on the call are not definitive on that point). In addition, they claimed he had been contacted by Cuban agents in New Orleans and in Texas, and had become actively associated with individuals from a Castro "hit team"—implying that an armed group under Castro's orders had carried out the attack in Dallas.

Of course, if the DRE had actual evidence of such things, it would have been obligated—and seemingly eager—to have reported it earlier to the CIA and, in turn, the CIA to share it with the FBI. In several instances, DRE members, as part of their counterintelligence role, had indeed identified suspected Castro intelligence agents who were in turn investigated by the FBI. One such individual was in Dallas and actively being investigated in the fall of 1963.

If the DRE had indeed reported individuals merely suspected of being Castro agents or intelligence sources in contact with Oswald to its case officers, certainly they (and CIA/SAS counter intelligence) should have been interested in monitoring and reporting on Oswald beyond New Orleans. Moreover, the claims made in the Luce call would have required action long before the assassination, unless of course either the DRE, the CIA, or both were engaged in some activities of their own with Oswald which are missing from the record—or unless independent actors affiliated with the DRE had decided to move forward with their own more radical agenda (as they had in unsanctioned boat missions and air attack plans).

The DRE had developed a very vested interest in Oswald. Did they really just abandon it—and him—for no reason after promoting him as a singular example of Castro and FPCC subversive actions inside the United States? Or are there indications DRE-affiliated individuals may have been in contact with Oswald beyond New Orleans? To deal with that question, we first have to examine the DRE backstory and then explore what its members were doing in 1963.

Chapter 18

The DRE Backstory

> *"For not only does the AMSPELL [DRE] leadership fanatically believe it has the right to dictate conditions for collaboration with KUBARK [CIA], but it displayed in this and subsequent discussions a flagrant disregard for the recent months of patient efforts in which we have sought to foster AMSPELL programs along lines of mutual interest—during which time KUBARK has been the sole and generous supporter of a consistently intractable AMSPELL."*
>
> —AMSPELL Progress Report for October 1962, CIA record number 104-10170-10028

Members of the DRE (the Cuban Student Directorate) had first opposed the Batista regime, playing a significant role in the struggle that put the Castro regime in power in Cuba. During that effort, the urban student revolutionaries had concentrated their efforts in the Cuban cities, as well as on the assassination of Batista regime figures. Those actions contrasted with Castro's own July 26 movement, which carried out armed insurrection in rural areas and smaller towns. After the revolution and following the students' turn against Castro, the student network conducted covert anti-Castro regime activities. Over time, many of its members were forced off the island and ended up in the United States, either joining the initial CIA Cuba project or continuing their own independent anti-Castro activities.

Following the disaster at the Bay of Pigs in the spring of 1961, the CIA began a relationship with a newly organized student group (DRE/DR) headquartered in Miami and with a significant membership inside the United States. The new group maintained extensive contact with former associates on the island, making it prized as an intelligence and counterintelligence source. The DRE/DR was valued for its intelligence gathering, its potential in propaganda work, and the intense commitment of its members.

Many of the most committed members were primarily interested in active involvement in military operations against Cuba. Those individuals included recent exiles from Cuba, such as Manuel Salvat (originally designated for propaganda, but who became primarily interested in military activities), as well as paramilitary trainees and maritime operations personnel from the earlier Cuba Project, such as Carlos Hernandez, Victor Espinosa Hernandez, John Koch Gene, and others.[392 393 394]

Government agencies interested in the DRE's potential included not only the CIA, but also the Defense Department, which approached exile groups though the Army and Army Technical Field Intelligence. The military was focused on using major Cuban exile groups—especially those with active on-island networks—to collect information about Soviet units, weapons, and other activities inside Cuba. Given remarks by the DRE military group leader Juan Francisco Blanco, it appears that the Pentagon was also interested in using the DRE on-island network, and also showed an interest in its maritime operations as having the potential for intelligence collection efforts.

While the Department of Defense and the Army primarily viewed the DRE as a tool for collecting information on Soviet activities and weapons inside Cuba, the CIA pursued a broader use of the group—ranging from propaganda to actual military operations. Those efforts were pursued though the CIA's Miami Station. CIA officer Phil Toomey at the Miami station (JM/WAVE) was involved in organizing the new DRE/DR relationship with JM/WAVE, and would become an early and key case officer for the group. David Morales served as its military liaison, and case officer for the DR military element from 1961 to 1962. For simplicity, and because many available documents and sources do not contain the differentiation between the DR and the DRE, we will use the generic "DRE" in our discussions of the group.

Morales was operationally involved with DRE leaders, including Jose Maria Lasa, Manuel Salvat, and Juan Francisco Blanco. Some of these individuals continued to be involved with CIA maritime missions from 1961 through 1963; some were even taken into the new Artime AMWORLD project as it became active later in 1963. Contacts between Salvat and Morales, using the pseudonym Dr. Menza, appear in CIA documents related to Miami Station. Morales served as the liaison/case officer for the DR military element beginning in 1961 and was directly involved in initial attempts by the CIA to direct and focus its activities.[395] [396]

As described in CIA working documents, any semblance of actual control over the DRE activities remained largely a matter of the confidence and personal relationships developed with CIA case officers. In return, the DRE directorate demanded total control over its own propaganda activities, and was equally independent in military activities as well. The CIA's difficulties in controlling and directing DRE activities is exemplified by the events of August 1962, initially arising from a highly confrontational series of events held by DRE delegates at an international student conference in Helsinki, then followed by a sensational and highly publicized two-boat mission into Havana Harbor, which included the shelling of the Blanquita Hotel.[397]

Both were described in CIA documents as DRE agitation-propaganda activities (agitprop), with the boat raid designed to obtain both U.S. and international attention on the Soviet presence in Havana. While the DRE attack in Havana Harbor is often discussed and received much media attention at the time, the aggressive DRE activities in Helsinki are interesting in that they demonstrate a degree of independent action far beyond the role the CIA had intended for the individuals sent as delegates.

On the fourth day of the World Festival of Youth and Students, an event attended by some 18,000 participants from 137 countries, four of the DRE attendees (Manuel Salvat, Carlos Hernandez, John Koch Gene, and Enrique Beloyra) broke through a crowd of spectators and proceeded to wave a sign demanding "Freedom for the 15,000 young prisoners in Cuba." At that point, Salvat and Beloyra proceeded to vocally berate the Communist youth delegation from Cuba while Anna Diaz-Silveira took photographs of the protest. Finnish police intervened, seized the sign, and took John Koch Gene and Beloyra in for questioning. In response, Salvat, Diaz-Silveria, and Hernandez held a special press conference to protest the actions and conduct of the Finnish police.

According to the DRE attendees, from that point on their group was constantly followed and kept under watch by the Finnish police. That surveillance resulted in the arrest of both Koch and Beloyra—and the discovery by the police of two .38 caliber automatic pistols hidden in luggage inside the station wagon that the DRE delegates were using.

The Finns were unhappy that DRE youth conference attendees not only conducted aggressive and vocal protests against other attendees, but also with the fact that members of the DRE delegation were armed during the conference. The CIA internal report on Helsinki indicates that the DRE delegation was enthusiastic and aggressive, but that DRE members presented a serious challenge with respect to being directed and controlled by the CIA case officers involved.[398, 399]

Names from the DRE delegation to the Helsinki youth conference continued to appear in DRE domestic activities inside the United States, including in Dallas in the fall of 1963. As an example, Manuel Salvat, who functioned as a key figure in DRE propaganda activities, was accompanied in his domestic American travels by a DRE member and staff secretary, Anita Diaz-Silveira (also known as Mirta Dortico).[400] Both were in Dallas during the fall of 1963.

The couple traveled to Dallas on one occasion, confirmed by Salvat himself, and the possibility of another visit in November was suggested by a statement from a local Dallas DRE member.[401]

There is no doubt that DRE members were prepared to act independently of the CIA in the areas of both propaganda and military action, with a special interest in using both to gain national and international media coverage, and they did receive special attention from major print publications such as *LIFE* and *TIME* magazines. The DRE's increasingly independent action seriously concerned the CIA, and in August 1962 a joint meeting led by Morales was convened. The meeting covered DRE military, political, and propaganda activities"; the CIA summary report of the relationship was less than positive:

> "When AMHINT-2 [Salvat] finally returned, a meeting was held with him on 17 August. ZAMKA [David Morales], NOEMAYR [Ross Crozier] and NELANDER [likely Calvin Thomas] represented AMHINTS [DRE military group], AMSPELL [DRE political leadership] and AMBARBS [DRE propaganda group], respectively . . . *the meeting could not be considered a success*...AMHINT-2 was adamant in retaining control of AMBARB funding of at least one official delegate in each country. He refused to even consider LCFLUTTER (polygraph testing) for himself..."[402]

As time passed, Blanco Fernandez and Manuel Salvat became more influential in DRE activities, and the group became increasingly dismissive, distrustful of, and hostile toward the CIA—as reflected in this quote from the marginalia found on the CIA draft of its own DRE history:

> "Salvat had written to friends in Miami about this state of affairs (i.e., CIA not providing adequate support to DRE), and threatened

> to kill CIA personnel involved should anything happen to Muller (AMHINT-1) as a result of Agency bumbling."

As 1962 was ending, following the peaceful resolution of the Cuban Missile Crisis, the conflict between the unrestrained DRE demand for autonomy and the routine CIA mantra about control became increasingly visible. In October, an internal CIA progress report discussed conflicts with control of both DRE propaganda and military activities. DRE press releases were issued independently of CIA consultation, in a relationship described as "contempt" for CIA policies. JM/WAVE station chief Shackley (pseudonym Andrew Reuteman) noted their refusal to even consider any CIA involvement in their use of CIA funding, noting that in October, a DRE CEDAR infiltration team aborted a mission due to dissatisfaction over arrangements for their standby craft.[403]

Matters quickly became even worse when JM/WAVE station personnel in Miami became aware that DRE leadership had bypassed it entirely, meeting with CIA personnel at headquarters to register complaints and discuss the viability of the relationship. DRE leadership refused to discuss the talks with JM/WAVE, and went even further, stating it could participate in no further paramilitary operations until the situation was resolved. JM/WAVE also learned that DRE paramilitary personnel had been directed to look for jobs in the event a full break with the CIA eventuated. As a final note, DRE stated it was fully prepared to break with the CIA over issues of American policy, including any sign that the United States was prepared to reach some sort of compromise with the Castro regime.[404]

During 1963, the DRE military group continued to move away from the CIA to find its own sources for funding and weapons, turning both to familiar names from the Batista revolution and to new sources, including virulently anti-Communist Americans. In a search for weapons, it even turned to former Castro revolutionary era figures such as Frank Sturgis (who had his own connections to right-wing weapons and equipment dealers).[405]

Salvat himself had been politically active inside Cuba (when he was a law student), both in the revolution against Batista, and afterward in early opposition to the emergence of a strong communist element within the new Castro regime. Once in the U.S., Salvat had affiliated himself with the new DRE organization, and despite his CIA operational approval and sanctioned military missions into Cuba, became a significant public figure in DRE efforts to oppose CIA control and conduct independent DRE military activities. He became especially well known as the coordinator for the DRE's most successful (and highly visible) two-boat attack on targets in Havana harbor.[406, 407] Ironically, while Salvat remained largely uncontrollable, he stayed on the CIA payroll until 1966.

That DRE boat mission, and the shelling of targets in Havana, were reportedly made possible by the acquisition of a 20 MM cannon, obtained by DRE member Carlos Hernandez. While the mission itself was presented as totally independent and "unsanctioned" by the CIA, both Salvat and Hernandez had engaged in both operational and propaganda activities for the CIA's Miami station immediately before and after the raid.[408]

The Havana attack received extensive American media publicity and gained the attention of prominent anti-Communists including William Pawley (of World War II Flying Tiger fame) and the Luce family, owners of a major media empire including *TIME* and *LIFE* magazines. Intermediaries already working to supply the DRE with funds and weapons put Pawley in touch with its leaders and persuaded Mrs. Luce to become a contributor toward future DRE missions. Both Pawley and Luce offered financial support to the group; however, the resolution of the Cuban Missile Crisis of October 1962 resulted in the Kennedy Administration's moves to block further raids on Cuba by exile groups.[409 410]

During 1963, new Kennedy administration policies, which had evolved following the Cuban Missile Crisis, directed Federal agencies to suppress independent exile group military efforts. This led to the virtual ending of CIA support for the DRE military wing activities.

Some personnel did remain on call for CIA missions, and some DRE associates actually remained operational with Miami Station. However, many others were left with no sanctioned option for military action against Cuba.

CIA case officers were still routinely meeting with DRE leaders during the summer and fall of 1963, with Joannides trying to maintain close personal relationships given the Agency's rocky relationship with the group as well as its ongoing intransigence in terms of control over its membership. There were case officer meetings with DRE leader Fernandez-Rocha every couple of weeks, sometimes as often as three times a week.[411] Yet regardless of such personal engagement, there was a continual conflict between CIA and DRE agendas—a conflict so strong that it was well-recalled in an interview of Manuel Salvat by Jefferson Morley even decades later. Salvat was adamant that DRE had strongly stated that it was simply not going to take any orders from either the CIA or the United States in regard to military activities directed against Cuba and Castro.

And as noted previously, during 1963 DRE military leaders such as "Chilo" Borja and Manuel Salvat had become increasingly frustrated and bitter about the new Kennedy administration restraints. In interviewing individuals willing to speak on the subject, Morley found that by the summer of 1963 attitudes inside the DRE were "extremely bitter" towards the CIA and the Kennedy administration. Morley's interviews with former DRE members and CIA personnel support that assessment; when talking with SAS officer Ross Crozier he was given the impression that attitudes inside the DRE towards JFK were "scarcely less hostile" to the president than to Castro. Even in official JM/WAVE memos to headquarters, station chief Shackley described the attitude within the DRE for administration policy makers as nothing less than sheer "contempt."

Chapter 19

Independent Action and Miami Cubans in New Orleans

"U.S. CUSTOMS ADVISED THAT SAM BENTON, AN AMERICAN, AND FOUR CUBANS, RENE JOSE ESPINOSA HERNANDEZ, VICTOR ESPINOSA HERNANDEZ, EVELIO ALPIZAR PEREZ, AND CARLOS HERNANDEZ SANCHEZ, WERE ARRESTED. . . . ALSO TWO THREE HUNDRED POUND BOMBS, THREE BOXES OF EXPLOSIVES WEIGHING ABOUT FORTYFIVE LBS. AND AN UNDETERMINED AMOUNT OF GASOLINE WERE SEIZED."

—SAC Miami to Director, FBI, reporting on arrests of June 15, 1963, FBI record number 124-10206-10397

By the summer of 1963, individuals affiliated with the DRE, previously used by the CIA in covert military actions against Cuba, had become personally frustrated by the changes in policy that appeared to be slowing down the tempo of CIA maritime operations. Several of them had become highly skeptical of the Kennedy administration commitments to "freeing" Cuba; others were no longer even being called on to participate in the few new CIA maritime missions that were occurring. For some of the most well-trained and intense members of the special infiltration cadre (such as Carlos Hernandez and Victor Espinosa Hernandez) that had been prepared for missions into Cuba, that frustration meant turning to opportunities outside the CIA, to anyone who could come up with the financing and equipment to organize a maritime mission or propose some type of attack on Cuba.

If necessary, that meant joining in efforts which were not officially DRE-sponsored or managed, but which still offered the opportunity for military actions against the Castro regime. Matters were also complicated because certain of the more independent actors affiliated themselves with multiple groups and totally independent operations. As an example, Carlos Hernandez' original anti-Castro affiliation was with Manuel Artime's MRR. Hernandez had been a member of Artime's Comandos Rurales (Rural Commandos) along with Nestor Izquierdo and Rafael Quintero. He would later train together with Quintero, Izquierdo, Artime, Victor Espinosa Hernandez, Humberto Solis Jurado and Miguel Alvarez Jimenez. The latter two, along with Carlos Hernandez, would go on the become members of the AMHAZE team that would train Nino Diaz's men at JMMOVE in the New Orleans area prior to the Bay of Pigs invasion.

Quintero, Espinosa, Hernandez, and Alvarez all became members of the highly-trained infiltration teams that were being sent on missions into Cuba prior to and following the failed landings. All were successfully exfiltrated from missions prior to the Bay of Pigs and were not among the members of the Brigade that were captured and held prisoner in Cuba. By 1962, Carlos joined the DRE as Military Advisor to train new members of the DRE in military and infiltration tactics. He had trained with DRE leaders Manuel Salvat and Luis Fernandez in the camps as part of the invasion force.

By spring 1963, Carlos Hernandez had left the DRE and was going on missions to Cuba with Laureano Batista Falla, who headed the MDC, Christian Democratic Movement. [412] Batista's MDC would set up the short-lived training camp just outside of New Orleans in July 1963 which was previously discussed. By the late summer of 1963, Carlos Hernandez and Humberto Solis had left the MDC and joined forces with the chief of supply for Manolo Ray's JURE group, Carlos Zarraga Martinez. Zarraga led his own loosely organized JURE maritime operations affiliate Cuba Libre, and Carlos Hernandez was named Military Coordinator for Cuba Libre while Solis served as its Operations Coordinator.[413]

While Zarraga was involved with Cuba Libre, he remained quite active in JURE activities, supplying both weapons and men for JURE military missions and infiltrations into Cuba. Zarraga worked closely with both Manuel Ray and JURE's head of military operations, Rogelio Cisneros.

Later, in the spring of 1964, Zarraga and Cisneros set up a camp for training groups of JURE infiltration teams that would accompany Manuel Ray in his effort to land in Cuba and declare a government in exile, with Ray as the leader. This camp was located in Polk City, Florida on the ranch of Weir Williams and was headed by JURE member Luis Posada Carriles.[414] Ray's attempt to infiltrate Cuba failed, causing both Cisneros and Zarraga to ultimately quit JURE. Zarraga would later join forces with friend Herminio Diaz-Garcia. Both Zarraga and Diaz-Garcia had been members of the old UIR in Cuba.[415]

The tendency for multi-group connections and independent action makes it quite challenging to identify individuals who may have come into contact with Oswald, concealing their true alliances and ultimately coming to manipulate him in accord with their own agendas. Answering that challenge means focusing on others who can be documented to have been in the New Orleans area while Oswald was there in the summer of 1963—and demonstrating connections that might have brought them into direct contact with Oswald.

We briefly discussed one such activity earlier during our exploration of Oswald and his time in New Orleans. That operation involved an attempt to set up bombing missions against Cuba, with the missions to be flown out of Florida. However, with the extensive Federal agency focus on halting anti-Castro activities out of Florida, and the intense monitoring of the Miami area in particular, the initial plan for the bombing mission was uncovered and broken up by the FBI.[416]

Instead of abandoning the bombing effort entirely, a far more ambitious plan was developed—one using two aircraft out of Texas, a transit air field outside New Orleans, and bombs made with explosives from Illinois. Military surplus practice bomb casings were purchased, and dynamite was bought from a long-standing source in Illinois, and transported to a rural area outside New Orleans (Lacombe, Louisiana) for assembling into live bombs. When the bombs were ready, two B-26s were to fly in (reportedly from the Houston Texas area), stop only briefly for the bombs to be loaded, and then fly on to carry out the attack.[417, 418]

The bombs were to be assembled from war surplus practice bomb casings (designed only to hold sand as a filler), using dynamite purchased from an established Minuteman weapons dealer in Illinois, Richard Lauchli. Lauchli had long been a supplier to Cubans, from the revolutionary years to the anti-Castro efforts. The FBI summary report on the Louisiana bombing plan states that Carlos Hernandez Sanchez, Acelo Pedroso, and two others went to New Orleans together. There, they met Victor Espinosa Hernandez, who had transported the bomb casings and dynamite.

A pilot recruited for the mission later informed the FBI that he had seen two planes, which he believed to be B-26s. He did not state specifically where he had viewed the aircraft, but said he had been told the bombing effort was a DRE project. In further conversation, he stated the aircraft were not based near New Orleans, but located further away, in Texas, perhaps in Houston.

He had been told they would be flown in and loaded for the attack only when the bombs were ready. The planes would not remain on the Louisiana airfield for more than four or five hours before departing on the mission. He also told the FBI he had judged that the bombs being prepared were totally unsuitable to the aircraft in question, and that whoever was organizing the effort did not understand the technical issues involved in the planned attack.

The Lacombe phase of the bombing plan involved several DRE-affiliated military personnel, including Carlos Hernandez and Victor Espinosa. And it brought them into the New Orleans area at the time when Oswald was in his initial stage of contacting and interacting with Bringuier, presenting himself as an anti-Castro activist. It was at the point in time when DRE headquarters had directed Bringuier to "test" Oswald by having individuals contact him representing themselves as Castro supporters or covert Cuban agents.

Chapter 20

Oswald and Cubans from Miami?

". . . on or about November 1, 1963, an unidentified male made remarks to an employee of the Parrot Jungle . . . this unidentified male was said to have made reference to President Kennedy, and "shooting between the eyes," and that he had a friend who was an American, a Marxist, and was a sharpshooter and could speak several languages, including Russian . . . referred to his friend by the name 'Lee,' and remarked that his friend was either in Texas or Mexico."

—Report of FBI agent James J. O'Connor of April 3, 1964, Commission Document 829

As it turns out, the FBI had indeed received several reports about Oswald being contacted, and in the company of mysterious Cubans while in New Orleans. The individuals were unknown to the local Cuban community—they appeared for a time, left, and were never seen again. FBI sources reported it, and we have information directly from Orest Pena and Arnesto Rodriquez. Harold Weisberg wrote of their experience in great detail in *Oswald in New Orleans* and *Whitewash,* including the strong FBI pushback that Pena received after reporting it, after bringing the issue up again following the assassination.[419]

Oswald's contacts with unknown Cubans in New Orleans were locally discussed, and of such interest that they were one of the first leads pursued by District Attorney Garrison in his investigation, significant enough that he sent his investigators to Miami to try and identify them. Unfortunately, that effort was aborted by his initial contacts with the Miami exile community (in the person of Bernardo de Torres), and diverted by the exposure of his inquiry to the press.

Most importantly, we can now document that there were new Cubans from Miami in New Orleans at the time of Oswald's appearance there, individuals affiliated with the DRE's military wing (Carlos Hernandez, Victor Espinosa Hernandez, and John Koch Gene)—all CIA maritime mission veterans with ongoing mission service in 1963. Carlos Hernandez had been a key figure in the DRE Havana Harbor attack and was considered one of its military leaders; he originally fought with Manuel Artime's group against Batista and then joined Artime in the Movement to Recover the Revolution (MRR) opposing Castro.[420] [421] As noted above, he had become something of an independent actor in 1963, even working with a JURE-associated group in order to remain involved in military missions against Cuba.

An indication that those individuals might have independently carried information on Oswald back from New Orleans comes from a separate report from Miami, made to the FBI, and describing an incident prior to the assassination. A young Cuban had made some fascinating remarks while attempting to "chat up" cashier Lilian Spengler at the Parrot Jungle restaurant on November 1, 1963.[422]

The young man had bragged about his own shooting skills in chatting up Ms. Spengler at the Parrot Jungle restaurant in Miami—as well as those of his friend who hated Kennedy as much as he did and who could "shoot Kennedy between the eyes." He and his friend Lee were both sharpshooters, Lee spoke Russian and, at the time, Lee was living in Mexico or maybe Texas, he was not sure which. Other restaurant employees heard the exchange, verified the story, and even the identity of the young man, Jorge Soto Martinez. In the end, the FBI pushed back as hard against the Spengler report as they had against Pena's report of out-of-town Cubans with Oswald in New Orleans. She was effectively told just to drop it and stop talking about it.[423]

While Soto Martinez was no DRE member himself; he had worked at the Fontainebleau Hotel in Havana, managed by Mike McClaney. And Soto Martinez had arrived in Miami not long before the Parrot Jungle exchange. At the time, he was living at Mike McClaney's estate, and it was McClaney who had funded the abortive DRE air raids from Miami, and then from Louisiana. Carlos Hernandez himself confirmed that he and Victor Espinosa Hernandez had visited McClaney on more than one occasion, including following their trips to and from the New Orleans area.

It is certainly possible, if speculative, that Soto Martinez's information about Oswald—including Oswald being in either Mexico or Texas at the time—may have come from Carlos Hernandez or Victor Espinosa Hernandez. Soto Martinez's gossip about "Lee," his shooting abilities, and his residence in Mexico or Dallas may be far more critical than the FBI could ever have realized at the time it was reported.[424] In retrospect, the implication that individuals associated with the Lacombe FBI raid and abortive bombing mission had brought back details not only of Oswald's background, but of his movements following his time in New Orleans, appears to be highly significant. It might also suggest that individuals such as Carlos Hernandez and Victor Espinosa Hernandez had begun to confabulate Oswald's image into something far more than a naïve young Castro supporter.

The question that emerges is whether we can trace unknown Cubans associating with Oswald who might well have been in the position to have some sort of influence on him in Dallas—influence that would extend to events during the week of the assassination. We can document reports of such individuals being in contact with Oswald in

New Orleans. We can also potentially identify them as independent DRE-affiliated members of the group visiting the New Orleans area during the period in which Oswald had become known to the Cuban exile community there.

Maintaining covert contact with Oswald, and introducing themselves as Castro supporters, would have been quite consistent in context of either element of the DRE's CIA-sponsored tasks of counter intelligence (identification and monitoring suspected Cuban intelligence assets) or propaganda. Covert testing of Oswald by Quiroga, posing as a Castro supporter, had been the first response following Oswald's initial contact with Bringuier. Whether or not DRE leaders were encouraged to continue that effort by their CIA contacts is a question the documents in their case officer files might answer. Yet those documents have been withheld from all interested parties for decades. Even at the time of this writing—following years of legal action—it is still impossible to determine to what extent they may have been destroyed and may be lost entirely.

Of course, there is also the possibility that individuals affiliated with the DRE might have pursued contact with Oswald on their own, especially as they have demonstrated to have increasingly begun to act on their own initiative. Both scenarios leave us with the question of whether or not there are ongoing indications of contact with Oswald by unidentified Cubans after he left New Orleans.

As it turns out, reports of just that did emerge—but only after the assassination. The nature of those reports, and the image of Oswald they convey, is especially interesting given that they support the post-assassination messaging of Oswald as being involved in suspicious activities with Cuban associates and capable of violent acts, including assassination of political leaders. The reports describe him as perfectly capable of violent crimes, including murder. Yet, as with the reports out of New Orleans, the FBI pushed back against those later reports, in one instance fabricating information given to the Warren Commission, as well as undermining the credibility of the source.

The exact dates of those incidents, both in Texas with one outside Houston and another in Dallas, remain unclear. But both appear to have occurred shortly after Oswald had left New Orleans, during a period in which he was on his way to Mexico City, with the intent of obtaining a transit visa which would have allowed him into Cuba on his way to Russia.

The first incident involved an approach to a former gun runner, Robert McKeown, who had purchased and transported weapons for the revolution against Batista, supplying revolutionary groups on the island by smuggling the materials by boat and sailing out of Louisiana through Mexican ports to Cuba. He had been charged with and convicted of weapons violations, but later become the subject of much media attention when Fidel Castro personally visited him following the revolution. On his boat trips to Cuba, McKeown became acquainted with numerous Cubans involved in the revolution. One of them, Jorge Sotus, (a fellow revolutionary and friend of Carlos Hernandez) was arrested and convicted along with McKeown.[425]

McKeown told the FBI and stated in testimony to the HSCA that in August or September 1963, two men had approached him at his home, stating that they knew he dealt in weapons. They made offers to purchase weapons for a revolution in El Salvador.[426] At the time, Cuba was suspected of having a major role in leftist revolutionary activity in Central America, including in El Salvador. In later years, Cuba would be viewed as a major instigator in the El Salvadoran civil war. Objectively, such an approach to McKeown could be viewed as a contact by Cuban agents involved in covert Central American activities. And it would have appeared very consistent with Oswald's own interests—while still in the Marines, Lee Oswald had talked of going to Cuba and joining either the revolution against Batista or against similar corrupt regimes in other Central American countries.

When McKeown declined to even consider the weapons sales proposition, the two men—one of whom he identified later as Lee Oswald or someone closely resembling him—kept pushing, even making a ridiculously high offer to buy a single, scope-equipped, high-powered rifle. McKeown also rejected that offer and the men left, not realizing that McKeown had recalled one of them from his gun running to Cuba, a man known to him only by the name "Hernandez."

That name is especially interesting given that Carlos Hernandez and Victor Espinosa Hernandez were the individuals involved in the earlier Lacombe FBI raid in the New Orleans area, and very possibly might have been the mysterious, "out of town" Cubans seen in contact with Lee Oswald in New Orleans.

A New Orleans connection between Lee Harvey Oswald and Carlos Hernandez is strictly speculative. Yet it becomes plausible given that records show that Jorge Sotus, convicted for weapons smuggling along with McKeown, had been close to Artime and his group during the revolution against Batista, operating in the Sierra Maestra. Sotus was among many in Artime's circle who had turned against Castro's new regime, going into exile and joining the CIA's Cuba Brigade (listed as Jorge Sotus, "Marina Escalon Retaguardia").

Carlos Hernandez followed the same path as Sotus, from being an Artime supporter, rejecting Castro, and then joining that same CIA Brigade. The two men were together in the Brigade, and both Hernandez and Sotus received special infiltration training. Both men went on to become operational in a variety of maritime missions for the CIA, under the overall AMHAZE project umbrella. One particular mission of record, Operation Yeast, was led by Sotus and involved Carlos Hernandez among others.[427]

Given Sotus's revolutionary experience with McKeown, and his extended operational association with Carlos Hernandez, McKeown's identification of "Hernandez" as the individual accompanying Lee Oswald outside of Houston certainly raises the possibility that the Cuban was indeed Carlos Hernandez. It also suggests the possibility that Carlos Hernandez was one of the "mystery Cubans" who had contacted Oswald in New Orleans, one of the individuals who may have covertly established contact with him, representing themselves as Cuban regime supporters or possibly even Castro agents.

If the FBI had pursued the details of the DRE information given to Clare Booth Luce, and aggressively followed up on the New Orleans and Houston reports of unknown Cubans in the company of Oswald, they certainly would have found at least a suggestion that the man charged with killing President Kennedy might indeed have associated with suspicious unknown parties prior to the assassination. This explosive connection might well have been taken to suggest a conspiracy involving a Castro team of covert operators inside the United States.

Beyond that, a successful purchase of one or more rifles from Robert McKeown in Houston could have had a major impact in connecting the assassination to Cuba. The effect of a rifle found anywhere in the vicinity of the attack on the president, subsequently traced to a known Cuban gun runner and friend of Fidel Castro, can hardly be underestimated. Given McKeown's testimony regarding the rifles being purchased for revolutionary activities in Central America, Oswald could have been further positioned as a radicalized recruit committed to Cuba and its socialist revolution.

Of course, the McKeown incident alone would have added nothing to specifically support the claim that Oswald had become part of a Cuban assassination team, certainly not as an actual shooter. Nor would the McKeown report directly have confirmed him as a direct threat to the president. Something more would have been needed to support the story presented in the call to Luce, something to characterize Oswald as a person who hated Kennedy, and who was a marksman capable of "shooting the President though the eye"—as Soto Martinez had said in his own words in Miami.

Chapter 21

Oswald with Cubans from New Orleans?

"He wanted me to introduce this man. He thought that I had something to do with the underground, with the big operation, and that I could get men into Cuba. . . . When I had no reaction to the American, he thought that he would mention that the man was loco and out of his mind and would be the kind of man who could do anything like getting underground in Cuba, like killing Castro. He repeated several times he was an expert shotman."

—Warren Commission testimony of Silvia Odio, Volume 11, 377

Just the sort of description of Oswald given by Soto Martinez at the Parrot Jungle—as radical, violent, and a potential assassin—did make it into an FBI report, associated with the appearance of more "mystery Cubans" in Dallas. The description of a radical and "dangerous" Oswald came in a telephone call following a visit of two men who were accompanied by a young American introduced as Leon Oswald. Ultimately, the entire incident became so controversial and explosive that the FBI literally had to lie to the Warren Commission to explain it away.[428]

The appearance of the two newcomers in Dallas in late September was noted in a letter from Amador Odio (a prominent figure in Cuba, who was also a trucking company magnate and an early opponent of the Batista regime) to his daughter Silvia in Dallas, Texas. When Amador began to oppose the Castro regime over its increasingly communist leanings, several of his children, including Silvia and her sisters, were sent away from Cuba. In his letter to his daughter, he warned her that the unknown visitors she had written to him about in her recent letter had not been sent by him, were not known to him, and should not be trusted—he had no friends who should be in Dallas, and unless she could supply a name, she should have nothing to do with them.

Silvia, with her husband and four small children, had initially entered the United States through Miami and then moved to Puerto Rico, where she was essentially deserted by her husband, who went to Europe on business and abandoned her. She then left Puerto Rico and moved to Dallas to join two brothers and two of her younger sisters (Annie and Sarita), who were already living there. Her sister Sarita was a student at the University of Dallas at the time. Silvia herself had attended school in Philadelphia and had graduated from Villanova University with a degree in law.

Amador continued his opposition to Castro following the departure of his children, but he and his wife were charged, convicted, and imprisoned for harboring individuals on his estate outside Havana who had been involved in an attempted assassination of Fidel Castro. Amador wrote Silvia from the Cuban prison, noting that her visitors were especially suspect since they had used his confidential "war name" in introducing themselves, and that information was known only to a handful of people in Cuba.

The men who had appeared at the apartment of Silvia Odio, seen by her and her sister Annie, had claimed to have just arrived in Dallas, saying they came from New Orleans and were associated with the Cuban

Revolutionary Council and with JURE. They asked for her help in preparing fundraising materials. That seemed especially strange since Silvia was personal friends with JURE leader Manolo Ray, had visited him and his family in Puerto Rico during the summer, and discussed anti-Castro activities, including weapons purchases with him. Moreover, Ray had previously sent his chief military leader (Rogelio Cisneros) from Miami to Dallas to meet with Silvia and discuss potential channels for weapons.[429] In that context, Silvia had every reason to suspect the purported JURE supporters who showed up with no advance notice or introduction from the JURE leadership.

On the other hand, the presence of the Odio family in Dallas was no secret. Silvia and her family were well known within Cuban exile circles in Dallas and New Orleans. Her uncle lived in New Orleans and was himself aware of Lee Oswald, having personally attended Oswald's court appearance for the leaflet incident along with Carlos Bringuier.

At the time of the visitors' appearance, Silvia had a good job, and was working on moving into a larger apartment. Her sister was helping her pack when the men arrived. While employed, Silvia had remained active in the JURE movement and maintained a social life in Dallas. She was also an unmarried mother and pregnant at the time. There is also no doubt she was under stress and was receiving medical treatment for an elevated nervous condition. Her doctor had diagnosed her with stress symptoms, but without other physical or psychological issues.

The visit of the two men concerned Silvia, especially as to how they might have obtained confidential information about her father. At the time, she had only exchanged a few words of greeting to the American who was with them. She was also puzzled because one of the men had called her the following day. She thought he was trying to "chat her up," but in doing so, he had described the young American in words almost identical to those used by Soto in his remarks about his friend "Lee" at the Parrot Jungle incident in Miami. Silvia's caller described the young American as an ex-Marine, an expert marksman, and a tremendous asset for anyone who might use him.

He was also described as extremely critical of President Kennedy, asserting that the anti-Castro Cubans should have killed JFK over the Bay of Pigs, and they "had no guts." He could do anything, he could go "underground," go to Cuba, kill Castro—except you never knew how to take him or what he might do next. Odio also noted that one of the areas discussed was the possibility of getting the young man into Cuba.[430] We can only speculate as to whether or not that possibility had been shared with Oswald as one reason for the visit to Odio.

At the time, those remarks were simply part of the phone conversation. Silvia was not sure why the American was even mentioned, possibly just something to keep her on the phone and talking. Other than writing her father, she appears not to have thought too much more about it, since other Cubans had approached her for help with translations and solicitations.

But on the afternoon of November 22, she began hearing news about the attack on the president while she was at work and she fainted. Later, the name Oswald and images of him made it even worse, convincing her he had been the man with the suspicious men. She talked to her sister Annie, who had been at the apartment and briefly saw the men, as well as to a friend—who took her story to the FBI, much to Silvia's dismay.

From that point on, the Odio story and the FBI's investigation of it becomes mired in personalities, agendas, and controversy. What seems evident is that she was approached by strangers from New Orleans, and that someone named "Leon Oswald" was part of the contact. It also suggests that in at least two instances by October 1963, Oswald was being introduced to others and in both cases described as a loose cannon, dangerous, and capable of assassination.

In pursuing leads between Oswald and unknown "others," a closer look of the interaction between Silvia Odio and her visitors certainly seems warranted. Following the assassination, she told the FBI on December 23, 1963 that:

> ". . . in late September or early October, 1963, two Cuban men came to her house and stated that they were from JURE. They were accompanied by an individual whom they introduced as LEON OSWALD. Miss Odio stated that based upon photographs she had seen of LEE HARVEY OSWALD she is certain that LEON OSWALD is identical with LEE HARVEY OSWALD. Miss ODIO stated she is not certain if she misunderstood the first name of LEON or if the two Cuban men who introduced OSWALD as LEON had misunderstood him. Miss ODIO stated that the purpose of their visit was to ask her to write some letters to various businesses in Dallas and request funds for JURE."
>
> "Miss ODIO stated that both her parents are presently in prison in Cuba and for this reason she declined for fear that her parents would be possibly harmed."[431]

When asked to describe her visitors she said that they were "Mexican" looking, but Cuban. The taller one used the war name of Leopoldo. She was unsure what name the shorter, stocky visitor used but it may have been "Angel" or "Angelo" although she said she may have been mistaken. She described the shorter man as "five feet seven, something like that." And when asked his approximate weight, she replied "170 pounds, something like that because he was short, but he was stocky." For reference, Carlos Hernandez was five feet seven-and-one-half inches tall and 185 pounds.[432]

When asked to describe Leopoldo she said "he was very tall and slim, kind of,"[433] and was around "165 pounds," and "he must have been 6 feet." Victor Espinosa was five feet eleven and 170 pounds.[434] Espinosa was questioned by the FBI after he was detained for coordinating the aborted McLaney raid. They described him as "swarthy, high cheek bones, somewhat long, flat nose; slight Indian appearance."[435]

When Odio was asked by Wesley Liebeler of the Warren Commission about where her visitors had come from, and how they knew how and where to contact her, she replied "they came from New Orleans" and they knew her "family."

Odio's family in New Orleans was her uncle Agustin Guitart. Guitart was the assistant delegate of the Cuban Revolutionary Council (also known as the Revolutionary Front, Frente or CRC) in New Orleans. The official CRC delegate was Francisco "Frank" Bartes. Both Guitart and Bartes were CIA assets.[436, 437] And, as mentioned earlier, both Bartes and Guitart were at Oswald's court appearance in New Orleans—along with Arnesto Rodriguez, Carlos Bringuier, and Celso Hernandez. After the court appearance, Bartes argued with Oswald outside the courthouse.[438]

Were Carlos Hernandez and Victor Espinosa the two companions of Oswald at the Odio visit? Both men were extremely active in both covert and overt military operations, having first volunteered for and then been selected for special training in CIA covert missions prior to the Bay of Pigs landings. Both were members of infiltration teams successfully infiltrated and then exfiltrated from Cuba together prior to the invasion.[439] They were skilled and experienced in operating independently and clandestinely. Carlos Hernandez had been a member of the DRE delegation that went to the World Festival of Youth and Students in Helsinki, in a sanctioned CIA political action operation in the July 1962. All nine team members of that group had CIA Provisional Operational Approvals as part of an "Agit/Prop" operation run out of JM/WAVE by Ross Crozier and Philip Toomey.

Prior to the Odio visit, Carlos Hernandez had been given another Provisional Operational Approval by the Special Affairs Staff / Special Operations (SAS/SO) for the AMWORLD project, where he would become a member of the "Quintero's Commandos" team that was run by Rafael Quintero. All were seasoned in guerrilla and infiltration tactics. Carlos Hernandez was one of a handful of AMWORLD recruits that were exfiltrated "black" (under deniable cover so his actual identity and origin was concealed) outside the United States on December 1, 1963.[440 441]

Testifying later about the call from "Leopoldo" she received after work the day after the three men visited, during which "Leopoldo" made the comments about Oswald, Silvia Odio stated that "he was trying to get fresh with me that night. He was trying to be too nice, telling me that I was pretty, and it started like that."[442] The record shows that Victor Espinosa Hernandez considered himself a ladies' man and included in his CIA personnel file his occupation as "student/playboy."[443] He was close to Rolando Cubela (AMLASH-1) and would go clubbing with him in Cuba. His nickname was "Papucho" which is roughly translated to "hottie."

One of the key questions in regard to the Odio visit is how the unidentified Cubans from New Orleans would have known her address and phone number. Silvia's address and phone were not publicly listed, because she had only been at her current address for less than a few months and was in the process of moving to a new apartment that was closer to her work. However, it is a matter of record that her uncle, Agustin Guitart in New Orleans, was in close touch with Silvia and the two talked weekly. Guitart was well-connected within the anti-Castro Cuban community, close to both Frank Bartes and the head of the CRC in Miami, Antonio Varona. Varona stayed at Guitart's house on November 14, 1963, on a fundraising visit for the CRC.[444]

The Guitart/Odio connection is of particular interest given that Guitart's close friend Frank Bartes was a friend of both Victor Espinosa Hernandez and his brother Rene. Rene, in turn, had been in the truck with Carlos Hernandez when they were stopped by US Customs[445] during the first summer bombing attempt on Cuba, and was close to Bartes's daughter Moppie (Maria) Bartes.[446] He visited her when she was in Miami and would call her often when she was in New Orleans.

Bartes also met Victor Espinosa when both were at Armand Peirdro's house in Miami, in June 1963. Victor told Bartes about the first aborted raid but related to the FBI that he didn't know anything about "having dynamite and explosive material in Louisiana, but did mention that they would like to try to bomb Cuba again."[447]

Silvia Odio's formal interview by Commission staffer Wesley Leibeler on July 22, 1964 differed slightly in regard to her description of her visitors' purpose. She told Leibeler "…the second Cuban, took out a letter written in Spanish, and the context was something like we represent the revolutionary council (which would be the CRC, with Bartes as the primary delegate in New Orleans), and we are making a big movement to buy arms for Cuba and to help overthrow the dictator Castro, and we want you to translate this letter and write it in English and send a whole lot of them to industries to see if we can get some results."[448]

In summary, while no absolute proof can be given, several elements of Odio's descriptions of her visitors match the physical descriptions of Carlos Hernandez and Victor Espinosa as well as Victor's known personality. Both men can be shown to have been in New Orleans in the summer of 1963 and, as noted earlier, Carlos Hernandez was well acquainted with Carlos Quiroga, who is known to have covertly contacted Oswald in the guise of a Castro supporter. Both Carlos and Victor also had the personal connections to individuals in New Orleans, such as Bartes and Guitart, who could have provided not only the location of Silvia Odio—in Dallas, where Oswald's pregnant wife was due to have her second child—but the JURE and CRC contexts for remarks made to her during their appearance at her apartment. This included her father's "war name," known to Guitart, and other on-island connections of both Carlos and Victor from the revolution against Batista.

As to a motive for the Odio visit, we are faced with a variety of possibilities. The visit certainly could have been associated with an ongoing DRE or DRE/CIA propaganda operation using an unwitting Oswald—with the two Cubans representing themselves as Castro supporters or agents to him. Perhaps it was part of a longer-term CIA "Agit-Prop" campaign aligned with the DRE's initial use of Oswald in anti-Castro propaganda following his activities in New Orleans. For that matter, it might have been a "sanctioned" propaganda operation, but with an extra element introduced by the participants. Might an approved op be piggy-backed with a conspiracy-related goal of planting the image of Oswald as being violent, dangerous, and a potential assassin—the same message the DRE caller delivered to Clare Booth Luce the night of the assassination?

Chapter 22

Framing Oswald

"Mr. John Thomas Masen, owner, Masen's Gun Shop . . . advised he handled 6.5 ammunition. . . . The photograph of Lee Harvey Oswald was exhibited to Mr. Masen and he advised he was unable to identify this individual as being a person to whom he had previously sold 6.5 ammunition."

—FBI report of March 13, 1964,
Commission Exhibit 2694

We have discussed two specific conversations relating to Oswald being reported as either dangerous or as an activist and clandestine Castro supporter in Texas—McKeown in Houston and Odio in Dallas—following his departure from New Orleans. Others certainly may have occurred and gone unreported. Given the FBI propensity for pushing back against such reports of Oswald with others, some suggestive reports, such as the one from the Parrot Jungle in Miami, may never have entered the record at all.

By themselves, the Houston and Dallas incidents suggest that unknown parties were circulating the image of Oswald, not just as a highly public advocate for the Castro revolution, but someone increasingly covert, much more radical, and dangerous. This portrait of Oswald is someone who associated with Cubans not known in the local communities, men who praised Oswald for his shooting skills, and portrayed him as out of control and potentially dangerous. And the incidents suggest that Oswald was in personal contact with those individuals, very possibly following their lead with a hope that it would support his goal of reaching Cuba.

Interestingly, once Oswald was back in Dallas, Cubans from Miami began appearing in that city. By October, the DRE had also become increasingly involved in Dallas, both in fundraising and in a variety of activities related to illegal weapons purchases.[449] In mid-October, DRE representatives Manuel Salvat, Anna Diaz-Silveira (aka Anita), and Joaquin Martinez de Pinillos all arrived in the city. Ostensibly, their time in Dallas was to be spent on creating visibility for the organization and for fundraising. However, during the visit, some effort was also made to source weapons for an expanded offshore military effort. That was something the CIA most definitely did not and had not been supporting, and the DRE had no obvious source of funding to purchase new weapons.

The DRE had proposed such an initiative to the CIA in October, even listing the weapons and support it would need for a new military project. In retrospect, it appears that proposal was possibly a last-ditch effort to compete with the new Artime/MRR/AMWORLD project, which was being strongly supported by Robert Kennedy, the Cuban Coordinating Committee, the Special Group, and CIA/SAS chief Desmond Fitzgerald.

By early fall, the DRE was already being encouraged to send its action-oriented volunteers to work with Artime and his MRR group (a cover used in recruiting for the AMWORLD project). The likelihood of gaining support for a competing initiative was virtually nonexistent and, by early November, the chief of JM/WAVE communicated that fact in no uncertain terms to the DRE military leaders.

Yet despite the CIA's ongoing opposition to DRE military

action—which it had been adamant about throughout 1963—the DRE continued its search for weapons (with no obvious source of money for them) in both Chicago and, for the first time, Dallas. In Dallas, it did not turn to a well-established, long-time weapons supplier such as Lauchli in Illinois, but rather to an individual who had only entered the business in 1961. In 1963 that individual, John Thomas Masen, primarily worked as a local gunsmith, operating largely out of his home and performing gun repairs and upgrades such as re-barreling rifles and mounting scopes.

Masen was especially interested in custom ammunition and worked with black powder and other specialty cartridges.[450] He had also become suspect by the FBI for his contacts with ultra-right radicals, including members of the Minutemen. When he was approached by the DRE, he was already the object of a serious ATF probe, focused on his converting weapons to fully automatic firing and possible sales of military class weaponry.[451]

It is Masen's connection with ammunition and rifles, as well as his ongoing contacts with DRE members in Dallas from October through November, which needs to be considered in the long-standing mystery related to the primary evidence that was used to tie Oswald directly to the assassination of President Kennedy. That evidence included both the rifle and the shell "hulls" recovered from the Texas School Book Depository. Yet the shells presented a problem, in that the FBI could find no evidence that Oswald had purchased ammunition for the Carcano rifle—or even that he had ever had such ammunition in his possession. The only ammunition of record was the three expended hulls (shell casings) found at the Depository, and one additional round officially reported found in a six-round clip recovered in the rifle—in total four shells supposedly having come from a six-round clip.

There are numerous evidentiary issues with that clip—as well as the logical question of why anyone would buy a box of ammunition and then not have enough to fully load an ammunition clip. Anyone familiar with rifles knows that such a magazine when not fully loaded may not function properly when shooting the weapon.[452] What turned out to be a massive ammunition investigation by the FBI, in which more than 1,300 expended 6.5mm cartridge cases were recovered from shooting ranges and other local places where target practice routinely took place, resulted in the failure to recover a single empty shell casing which matched the 6.5mm WCC rounds represented as being used in the assassination of JFK.[453]

That in itself seemed to suggest such cartridges were something of a rarity, especially in Dallas, and that did indeed prove to be the case. In the end, the FBI was only able to identify three potential sources for the cartridges that Oswald was supposed to have used—two in Dallas and one in Louisiana. One of those two sources in Dallas was none other than DRE weapons contact John Thomas Masen, who claimed he traded for and sold at least two boxes of those particular cartridges, yet claimed to have no memory of who had bought the relatively rare ammunition.[454]

Moreover, the FBI determined Masen had even reworked some of those cartridges from full metal jacket rounds to soft point rounds to be used in hunting. That is especially interesting because at least some observers have suggested that certain of President Kennedy's wounds have the appearance of being created by soft point rounds rather than the purported full metal jacket, penetrating, military ammunition Oswald was officially alleged to have used in murdering the president. It is intriguing that Masen would have had both types of ammunition available for sale.

When questioned, Masen was unable or unwilling to reveal to whom he sold the Carcano ammunition; he only admitted that he was selling it in 1963. What is absolutely certain is that one of only two sources of such ammunition in Dallas was in frequent contact with individuals from the DRE in the days and weeks immediately before the assassination. While it appears the DRE members were unable to acquire their "shopping list" of weapons, we know they were "dealing" weapons in

Dallas. Did they purchase a Carcano from Masen—we know he sold them—or was it perhaps just a few rounds of ammunition?

Is it possible that at least some independent actors affiliated with the DRE might have gone as far as joining in a conspiracy against President Kennedy, at least to the extent of using ongoing contacts with Oswald to connect him to the attack—to position him as violent, a loose cannon, out of control? Or to do more, such as planting evidence to frame him at the scene of the crime?

As we noted early on in this work, there are serious questions regarding the handling and processing of virtually all the crime scene evidence that the Warren Commission presented as directly connected to Lee Harvey Oswald. Those issues have been discussed extensively in other works, but in regard to the concept of "framing" Oswald by planting material at the Texas School Book Depository without his knowledge, certain evidentiary issues need to be highlighted.

As noted previously, the actual record of witnesses placing a rifle in Oswald's possession becomes quite limited following his departure from Dallas for New Orleans. Marina alone recalled seeing a rifle (assembled in New Orleans; disassembled and in a blanket in Dallas). Yet, Oswald was actively reading magazine advertisements and discussing purchasing a rifle during his time in New Orleans.

The Warren Commission dealt with the issue by asserting that a disassembled rifle was transported to Dallas and stored in the Paines' garage, wrapped inside a blanket. Yet a forensics examination of the blanket in question revealed a total lack of gun oil traces—traces which would be expected from wrapping, handling, and transporting a disassembled rifle which the FBI determined to have been well-oiled.[455]

The issue of gun oil traces came up again with respect to the Commission's description of how the rifle was carried into the Texas School Book Depository on November 22, 1963. That scenario required the disassembled rifle to have been placed inside a large paper sack, carried to the book depository, and covertly reassembled at work by Oswald. Researchers have pointed out several problems with that assertion, beginning with the reassembly of the weapon. The Warren Commission stated that the assembly work had been done with a small coin. Yet at four different locations where screws would have to be inserted and tightened (including on metal surfaces) there is not a single indication of the scratching that would have occurred if a coin had indeed been used. Furthermore, a reassembled rifle must be "sighted in" to obtain even a basic level of accuracy in aiming the weapon for shooting a target at a distance—such "sighting in" after reassembling the weapon is done by firing live rounds with the weapon. This issue was totally ignored by the Commission in its shooting scenario.[456]

The Commission's solution for getting the weapon into the Texas School Book Depository also faced other issues. Buell Wesley Frazier drove Oswald to work that day and had a relatively close view of the paper bag that Oswald brought to his car. Frazier repeatedly stated that the large sack in evidence was not what he had seen Oswald carrying, and that Oswald's bag was too small to contain even a disassembled rifle. An FBI report relating information from the Dallas Police confirms that as early as the evening of November 22, Frazier was shown the large, heavy wrapping paper bag which had been taken into evidence the evening of the assassination. He declined to confirm it as the bag Oswald had carried—it was too large and not made of the light, "crinkly" paper Frazier recalled seeing from just that morning. Frasier's remarks were verified as truthful by Dallas Police polygraph testing, yet neither the polygraph interview nor Frazier's first-day statements were noted by the Warren Commission.[457]

In one sense, the idea that Oswald was framed with a rifle planted by individuals who had begun associating with him as early as his time in New Orleans is a simpler explanation than the scenario offered by the Warren Commission. The trained and experienced individuals we have discussed would have had no problem in obtaining Oswald's rifle, with or without his knowledge. Entering the Book Depository (itself left open into the evening so that the various book company personnel had access to their officers) would have been no challenge. And placing an assembled weapon along with spent ammunition (bullet hulls) would resolve the issues of oil stains and a large paper sack (which had not been photographed at the crime scene as the spent bullet hulls had been).

But would it be enough simply to plant a rifle and hulls—with Oswald not involved, he would likely be somewhere else, certainly not in the sixth-floor window firing a weapon. Yet even simply planting his rifle would have certainly have led to charges as an accessory—and with his time in Russia and public support for Cuba, Oswald's protests would have gained little consideration. Which leaves the question of whether it was even necessary to fire the planted rifle from the building.

The Warren Commission asserted proof positive that the weapon in custody had not only been fired, but that the rounds that had hit the presidential limousine had all come from it. That claim was supported with a variety of ballistics assertions, all claiming to match recovered bullets to the rifle and ammunition found on the sixth floor of the book depository. But, as with a great many of the Warren Commission assertions, follow-on research has led to questions and issues with virtually all the initial "proofs" that the recovered bullets had to have been fired from "Oswald's rifle."

One of the first "proofs" to fall was the claim that neutron activation analysis provided proof positive that the recovered bullets from the shooting matched the unfired ammunition recovered from the book depository. Years later, extensive chemical studies would disprove that premise—to the extent that the neutron activation matching technique was disqualified from further FBI use in criminal cases.[458]

The FBI's initial ballistics testing of the rifle as compared to CE399 (the "Magic Bullet") was presented as totally conclusive, yet when reexamined by the HSCA that testing was at best found to have shown inconsistencies in the results obtained by the FBI, as compared with those of the Commission's own ballistics panel.[459]

We previously noted that the Commission's ballistics panel's own tests of CE399 had led it to reject the shooting scenario the Commission had developed around that bullet. Later studies have raised even more issues with the Warren Commission's assertion of an incontestable match between the TSBD rifle and CE399.[460] Worse yet, independent study of eyewitness observations of the bullet recovered at Parkland Hospital (CE399) and issues with its legal chain of possession have surfaced the question of whether the bullet officially identified as CE399 was indeed the bullet initially taken into Secret Service possession in Dallas.[461]

Which leads back to the basic question of whether Oswald could have been framed simply by placing a rifle traceable to him hidden under cases of books by a stairwell doorway, along with hulls of fired rounds by the depository sixth floor window. Certainly, that would be the simplest, lowest risk option. Recruiting someone to fire the weapon at JFK's motorcade would have involved far more risk, but cannot be ruled out—nor accepted as a certainty, given the issues with the Commission's work matching the recovered rifle to the largely undamaged round presented as CE399.

In the end, we can only offer speculation on how easily Oswald could have been framed, as well as a possible lead involving the source of the specific Carcano ammunition that would have been required for such an act. The FBI's initial investigation found no indication that Oswald himself had purchased Carcano ammunition in New Orleans, or somehow transported it to Dallas. What they did find were sources for the ammunition in Dallas—and one specific source which is of special interest with respect to the individuals of interest we have identified, individuals directly associated with the DRE and its activities in Dallas in the fall of 1963. Those individuals were provably engaged in purchasing weapons and ammunition from gun dealer John Thomas Masen.

And Masen was admittedly stocking and selling the specific Carcano ammunition in question in 1963. He admitted to that—what he would not provide were any specifics on the customers for his Carcano ammunition.

While the Masen-DRE contact is suggestive, we are left to face the fact that with Oswald dead, and Masen not talking about who he sold what to that fall, there is literally no way to prove that Oswald was indeed framed with the planting of a rifle and bullet hulls. Such a possibility was never even considered as part of the criminal investigation of the president's murder, nor by the Warren Commission inquiry or the House Select Committee on Assassinations.

The most that can be done at this distance in time is to explore the context in which such a thing could have occurred—a context in which people who had been in contact with Oswald for months could have taken advantage of that association. Certainly, if DRE-affiliated individuals representing themselves as Castro supporters had been influencing Oswald after he left New Orleans—with offers of carrying the Cuban revolution on into Central America, or even going directly to Cuba—then speculation in regard to the possibility of his being framed becomes even more interesting.

And that takes us back to certain questions regarding Cuban visitors to Dallas in October/November, as well as the reports of unidentified anti-Castro (and outspoken anti-JFK) activists from out of town who suddenly appeared on the scene and engaged in speaking activities.

In one such speaking engagement, the unnamed speaker made extremely hostile remarks about President Kennedy, stating that something was going to be done to deal with him.[462] After the speech, and upon learning he had been taped, the speaker took the tape by force—warning that he held a black belt in martial arts. It is impossible to identify that speaker. The speaker's identity remains unknown, but for reference, Carlos Hernandez is described in CIA documents as being both a black belt in judo and regarded as a sharpshooter.

While the identities of some of the Cubans appearing in Dallas are unknown, we do have records of at least some "official" DRE activities.

According to Anna Diaz-Silveira, two meetings were held on October 13, 1963. The first one was at 1:00 PM for Spanish-speaking people at the Dreyfus Club, attended by more than 70 persons. A second meeting for English speakers was at 8:00 PM in a conference room over a bank at a shopping center. General Edwin Walker attended the second October 13 meeting and donated five dollars. A third meeting was on October 20 at a bank in Fort Worth on the expressway running from Fort Worth to Dallas.

According to Joaquin Martinez de Pinillos, the DRE also had meetings at the University of Dallas (where Sarita Odio was a student), at Southern Methodist University, and at a high school in Dallas. Pinillos, Diaz-Silveira, and Manuel Salvat spoke at these meetings. While there is no concrete evidence that Lee Oswald attended any of these meetings, Manuel Salvat told HSCA investigators that he heard a rumor that Oswald was at one the meetings, but he did not see him.

Given the specific report of a young man and woman at Red Bird airfield, a story we will explore in the next chapter, and the relatively limited number of Cuban women involved with the DRE (or with the more active exile military groups in general), it is important to document that there was at least on such woman active in Dallas in the fall of 1963. One source on that is found in the statement of Cuban exile Colonel L. Robert Castorr and his wife Trudy.[463]

The Castorrs had been unable to attend the public DRE meeting on October 13, but later met two unidentified members of DRE who were speaking in small meetings at both Sarah Castillo's apartment and Ed Twilly's house. Castillo was a Dallas fund-raising delegate for the DRE. Trudy Castorr described the DRE meeting as quoted below. Given the previous discussion of Manuel Salvat and Anita Diaz (aka Mirta Dortico) representing DRE on visits to Dallas, it seems likely that the Cuban girl was Anita Diaz.

> "These two men came to the Twilly home in the company of a very attractive Cuban girl who represented this student group and also

Dean Perkins, whom I know very well, Dean and his wife Jan; I believe they are from the St. Bernard Parish and they were interested in the resettlement of the Cubans long before I ever became interested. And also, Sarah Castillo came to this meeting."[464]

Chapter 23

Under the Influence?

"Two days before the assassination, on Wednesday November 20, Wayne January was in his office when a car drew up in front of his window. Wayne January was a partner in a small aircraft company operating out of Red Bird (airport). . . .It was a 1947 four-door black Dodge, identical to one he owned . . .as he looked across at it two of the three occupants of the car, a man and a woman, knocked on his door and came into the office. They asked if he could arrange for them to charter a light aircraft to take them to Yucatan. They asked intricate questions of the kind that were unusual for people planning a vacation. They asked about fuel consumption, the number of hours in the air, the total distance. . . . They did not look like the types who could afford the charter they were asking for and he wondered whether, in fact, they were headed for Cuba rather than Yucatan and whether if they asked him to pilot the plane, he would ever come back again . . . January said they should look elsewhere . . . .Interested in the car, he escorted them and had a look at it. He also had a look at the young man sitting in the passenger's seat. . . .

> *Two days afterwards he recognized the man who had been sitting in the car. It was Lee Harvey Oswald."*
>
> —*Say Goodbye to America*, Matthew Smith

DID LEE HARVEY Oswald come under the influence of anti-Castro Cubans posing as pro-Castro supporters? We know of one such approach in New Orleans, and we have no idea how long it might have actually lasted, or whether it was restarted. There were reports of Cubans with Oswald, implicating him in buying weapons for revolutions in Central America, in Dallas with inquiries about how it might be possible to covertly get him into Cuba—to kill Castro perhaps; he was a loose cannon and could kill Castro, or JFK.

And then, following the assassination, an intriguing report was made to the FBI—another report from Dallas, of Oswald with unidentified Cubans. Following the president's death, air services manager Wayne January at Red Bird Airfield, just outside Dallas, contacted the FBI to report that only days before the assassination, a man and a woman had approached him with the intent to charter an aircraft for a long-distance flight—they mentioned Mexico, possibly to the Yucatan. They asked several questions about the range of the aircraft, and he had become concerned that they might be interested in hijacking it for a flight to Cuba.

They had arrived in an old-model car, were not well-dressed, and seemed unlikely to have the funds to pay for such an aircraft charter, including the pilot fee. He also noted that they were accompanied by a third individual who remained in the car. After the assassination, January felt that individual looked a great deal like Lee Oswald.

A lack of FBI interest in his report, but a high degree of interest by the FBI officers in connecting January to Jack Ruby, discouraged January from pursuing the matter further with the Bureau.[465] January was also amazed when he was later shown an official copy of his interview with the FBI; they had recorded the incident with the man, the woman, and the third individual closely resembling Oswald as having occurred months earlier, not the week of the assassination. Yet January was certain that he had specifically given the FBI the date as being only two or three days before President Kennedy's Dallas visit, and noted it was only the proximity to the attack on the President which had caused him to report the incident.

While it is impossible to fully corroborate January's report or Lee Oswald's presence at the scene, it is interesting that we do have a report from a waitress that Oswald showed up late for his regular breakfast at the Dobbs House restaurant on November 20—and that he was in an unusually ill mood. That mood might have been because he had not been allowed to participate in the conversation about chartering the aircraft, or that plans for a flight to Cuba were still in flux.[466]

While the restaurant report itself is anecdotal, it is true that the Texas School Book Depository did not use a time clock for its workers. Instead, the supervisor would circulate during the day, and note if anyone was not there for work. Given the size of the building, and the storage on the upper floors, a late arrival by Oswald likely would either not have been noticed, or he would have received only a verbal remark about a late arrival.[467]

If it had been Oswald with other individuals at Red Bird airfield, it certainly would not have been the first time that he was reported in the company of unidentified persons. The first such reports of his being seen in the company of others had come during his time in New Orleans. As noted previously, the reports of Oswald in the company of individuals unknown to the local Cuban community had been one of the first areas of investigation during District Attorney Jim Garrison's JFK assassination inquiry.

However, Garrison's investigators were stymied in their attempts to trace the individuals back to Miami. Not only did his effort to resolve the identity of the Cubans fail, but his investigation was exposed to the press though a Miami contact—a well-connected anti-Castro activist, Bernardo de Torres. Garrison's investigators had sought help from a private Cuban investigative firm owned by de Torres' brother and de Torres prematurely exposed the investigation to the media, ending any further attempts by his investigators to collect information from the Cuban community in Miami.

While Garrison's interest in unknown Cubans reported to have been in contact with Oswald in New Orleans was essentially sabotaged by de Torres, numerous similar leads were given short shrift by local FBI offices—either obfuscated or preemptively rejected in Miami, in New Orleans and in Dallas. Director Hoover had ordered a report presenting Oswald as the lone assassin; suggestions of conspiracy were not welcome, and the FBI already had its own internal problems with Oswald—some agents were disciplined, some were reassigned.

All we can say for certain is that there are multiple indications of Oswald being in touch with unidentified Cubans following his time in New Orleans. These Cubans appear to have been maneuvering him for their own purposes while appearing to him to be helping him with his own goal, and with what had become something of a Cuban obsession for him. Did those individuals take advantage of their knowledge of Oswald and set him up as a Cuba/Castro-connected patsy? Did they tempt him with a plan to hijack an aircraft and appear in Cuba as a hero to the Cuban public? Was that on Oswald's mind the week of the assassination, on the day of the assassination?

As noted earlier, Oswald had raised the possibility of hijacking either a commercial airliner or smaller plane with Marina during their time in New Orleans. He had even discussed her participating and their both using pistols. Marina had been adamant that she wanted nothing to do with anything like that, and Oswald had dropped the subject. At the time, such a dramatic action might have seemed the most direct route for him to fulfill his Cuba goal—arriving in a hijacked aircraft of any worth would certainly have brought him the attention he desired, and confirmed his commitment to the Cuban revolutionary cause.

Inside Cuba, aircraft hijackings had been a major element of the Cuban revolution, a practice encouraged and touted by Che Guevera.

Hijacking aircraft for flights to Cuba first became a form of political statement in 1961. In May of that year, a small plane with eight passengers flew out of Miami to Key West. During the flight, a passenger drew a pistol and first used the phrase that would become all too familiar during the 1960s—"Let's go to Havana."[468] While commercial aircraft hijackings could be dangerous (there were deaths in such attempts), forcing a chartered airplane—with sufficient fuel and flight range—would have been far safer for all involved.

Such a plan would indeed explain many of the apparent anomalies in Oswald's behavior that day in November. It would have been something entirely apart from an attack on the president. It could explain his rush away from work, the pistol, even his strange behavior at the Texas Theatre where witnesses described him approaching different people as if he were looking for someone. It perhaps explains even the Hidell identification card in his billfold—a connection to his pro-Cuba activities in New Orleans. And based on our study of Lee Harvey Oswald, it would have been very much in the nature of his character: never give up, always look for another option, even if it involves a risk—no fear.

Yet those actions—along with a rifle planted by those he thought were his friends, his comrades—would leave him under arrest, fully convinced of his innocence, and with no idea of how much trouble he was truly in during the short time before his own murder.

It takes us back only a few days, back to Red Bird airfield, a young man and a young woman in an older car, making inquiries about the rental of a private aircraft—one with the specific capability of long-range flights. Something about the pair made Ray January think of Cuba and the possibility of an aircraft hijacking. At the time, those thoughts were based on the couple's questions and their behavior. Only after the assassination did January connect his suspicions to the individual waiting in their car—a young man whom he felt resembled Lee Harvey Oswald.

Given his Cuban goals, it is certainly possible to visualize a scenario in which Oswald, frustrated by repeated efforts to get to Cuba on his own, agreed to involve himself in a plan to hijack an aircraft (something he had even floated in conversation with his wife during the past summer in New Orleans). It would have the element of drama, and allow him to arrive as a persecuted political exile (something he had gone so far as to claim in Mexico City).

Could just such a plan—supported by individuals he had been in contact with since New Orleans—have been on his mind the week of the president's assassination? Could it have been a new, if risky, option for him on November 22? Could it even have caused him to make one more appeal to his wife before pursuing the offer—and was he even fully committed to the idea?

Perhaps more importantly, would it have given his new associates access to Oswald? Access and at least some level of control over his actions, even to the point of positioning him as an unwitting patsy in the attack on President Kennedy? We have seen that after Russia, Oswald had vowed never to let himself be used—but had his Cuban obsession once again led him to the point of being exploited?

The Red Bird incident with January could be viewed as an effort—possibly not even fully appreciated by the actual participants—to manipulate Oswald, and control his movements the week of the assassination, specifically on the day of the president's visit to Dallas. The control might only have been general, something on the order of having him leave work after lunch, or perhaps something more specific in terms of where to meet to proceed to the airfield. Although we know that the effort to rent the aircraft from January failed, we simply cannot know what Oswald himself might have been told about the visit to the airfield. Beyond that, we can only speculate as to what the couple at Red Bird were aware of at the time of their visit. They themselves may have taken it to be only a part of some evolving anti-Castro propaganda initiative involving Oswald, carried out by the DRE with or without CIA knowledge. Of course, with or without their knowledge, there may well have been something far more sinister in play.

There is a case to present Oswald as being involved with "others," specifically unidentified Cubans, following his time in New Orleans. Was he expecting to fly out of Dallas that afternoon, with all local attention on the president's activities in Dallas? We can only offer speculation, but such a scenario would explain the apparent anomalies in Oswald's behavior the day of the assassination. Given the insights into Oswald's character, his beliefs, and his preoccupation with Cuba—which had emerged during 1963—such speculation would also be consistent, conceivable, and worthy of consideration.

It would also be very true to Oswald's character—never give up, always have options, "reset" as necessary, and if an option involves a risk—no fear. It would also explain Oswald in custody, knowing he had not shot the president, that he was innocent. He just needed legal counsel and he needed to remain calm and reassure his family, which is exactly what he did. "Be sure to buy shoes for June," Lee told Marina on Saturday, November 23. The next day, he was murdered.

Epilogue

> "It was a stage trick, complete with accessories and false mirrors, and when the curtain fell the actors, and even the scenery, disappeared."
>
> —*Farewell America*, James Hepburn (pseudonym)

In retrospect, the fact that Lee Harvey Oswald has remained such a controversial historical figure is due in part to the Warren Commission's one-dimensional portrayal of his character—and in large part is also due to the unresolved issues with its final report on the assassination of President Kennedy. The Commission's simplistic image of Oswald was necessitated by the basic fact that it could offer no specific motive for Oswald to murder JFK. Its report had failed to document even a single instance of Oswald making a negative statement about the president, nor could it identify any criticism of JFK in Oswald's writing. What was documented was Oswald's public opposition to racism and his constant calls for racial and social justice—views which were quite consistent with JFK's own personal positions and with his administration's actions. The Commission's problem with motive was further reinforced by reports that Oswald had actually made positive remarks about the president.

Further investigations, decades of document releases, and an overwhelming amount of citizen research has revealed the extent to which both the White House and the Warren Commission literally forced the historical portrait of Oswald into that of a radical, rage-driven assassin. Which leaves us with an obvious question: Why was it so important to officially conclude that Oswald was the lone actor in the assassination of an American president?

Those who did not live through the period before the Berlin Wall fell may not appreciate the intensity of the Cold War in 1963. The Cuban Missile Crisis, which very nearly resulted in all-out nuclear war, was just a year in the past. While that event is remembered as a great Kennedy success, many in the military and certainly among Cuba's foes regarded it as yet more weakness. Nuclear war was in the air, and a finding that foreign actors (Russian or Cuban) were behind Kennedy's death was all too likely to lead a stampede. On the ride home from Dallas, LBJ told his aide Bill Moyers, "I wonder if the missiles are flying." Later the following week, he strong-armed Senator Richard Russell and others onto the Commission, saying "we've got to take this out of the arena where they're testifying that Khrushchev and Castro did this and did that and kicking us into a war that can kill 40 million Americans in an hour."

Despite statements from those involved, truth was not the "only client" of the Commission, and the timidity of its investigation allowed the FBI and CIA to protect their own interests and maintain their own priorities. To quash the idea of conspiracy in the assassination, the Commission pictured Oswald as radical and "violent," offering that characterization in support of its "lone nut" assassin conclusion. The contention of this work is that the Warren Commission's summary report painted an incomplete and biased picture of Lee Harvey Oswald, intentionally avoiding aspects of his life which would have challenged its basic finding. Our broader and more inclusive exploration of Oswald's character offers an alternative view, providing a more complete picture of the complexity of Oswald's personality.

But aside from the issue of an incomplete historical portrayal of Oswald, the final Warren Commission Report left history not just with the puzzle of Oswald, but the mystery of the assassination itself. As we have shown, even those within the Commission were aware that there were significant issues with certain of its positions—including Oswald's basic ability to have carried out the shooting, as well as myriad problems with the firing sequence of three purported shots from the Texas School Book Depository, including the infamous Single Bullet Theory. We now know the Commission's own ballistics panel disagreed with the shooting scenario, and the extent to which the Commission forced its solution has only become more obvious over successive decades.

Of equal concern is the knowledge that even Warren Commission members and staff understood that they had virtually no resources for investigation outside those of the FBI. Released documents confirm that understanding, as well as the internal Commissioners' view that under Director Hoover, they might be given limited or even false information. We have noted instances of just that happening with respect to Lee Harvey Oswald, including the destruction of a note Oswald hand-delivered to the FBI office in Dallas. Perhaps even more damning in regards to the overall puzzle of the assassination is that there were clearly instances in which the FBI failed to seriously pursue leads which might have pointed towards potential suspects in contact with Oswald. Among these incidents is the report from Wayne January at Red Bird airfield outside Dallas.

One of the most revealing examples of the FBI's pattern of closing down rather than opening up leads came with the report of two Latinos who appeared at Silvia Odio's residence in Dallas. These individuals stated that they had just come with from New Orleans, and identified the young and "loco" man with them as Leon Oswald. The Odio incident appeared serious enough that even with most of its report written, the Warren Commission requested that the FBI further investigate and resolve it.

The FBI did so, with Director Hoover informing the Commission that it had identified the parties involved as three men from Miami. It was all a misunderstanding by Odio, Hoover declared, and the issue could be dropped from further consideration. It would be years later, with new records releases, that FBI investigative documents out of its Miami office revealed that Hoover's remarks were false, and that the FBI was very much aware internally that nothing had been resolved. There was no confirmation of Odio's visitors as Hoover had claimed. Actually, the FBI's field office in Miami had interviewed the three men, and had determined that they were not in Dallas at Odio's apartment. For confirmation, the three men's photos were also shown to Silvia Odio and her sister, who stated that they were not the men who had visited her. That negative identification was not shared with the Warren Commission.

If the FBI had continued to proactively investigate the Odio incident, there is at least a chance that would have led them back to New Orleans, to Silvia's uncle Agustin Guitart, and to his connections to the network of anti-Castro Cuban exiles which we explored earlier in this work. Guitart was himself very much aware of Oswald and his activities in New Orleans. Of course, any such truly open-ended FBI investigation of that nature would have required extensive cooperation and support from the CIA, which was in itself problematic.

The abundance of leads not truly followed and other "missing pieces" of the assassination mystery suggests that the popular skepticism regarding the Warren Commission's solution to JFK's assassination—which continues to this day—is indeed justified. It is beyond the scope of this work to deal with all the motives and decisions which led both the FBI and CIA away from proactively and aggressively pursuing leads connecting Oswald to unidentified individuals, and not sharing all of what their internal inquiries had suggested. The directive laid down in Assistant Attorney General Katzenbach's memo from the day after Oswald's death—declaring that "the public must be satisfied that Oswald was the assassin; that he did not have confederates who are still at large"—was a whole of government project.

The passage of time has revealed more details about highly relevant information that was shielded from the Warren Commission. Some of that—such as the Castro assassination efforts—was revealed in the work of the Church Committee and the House Select Committee on Assassinations. But beyond that oft-cited example, we also know that very specific JFK assassination-related investigations were conducted, and that their findings were then held within the CIA itself.

Only in recent years have document releases revealed that the CIA itself, at its headquarters in Washington, D.C. and at JMWAVE in Miami, fully understood that the attack on President Kennedy might have involved either pro- or anti-Castro Cuban actors. Members of the CIA's Special Affairs Staff, including personnel at the Miami station, were aware that Oswald's contacts with Cuban exiles in New Orleans had exposed him to anti-Castro Cubans who were on record as considering President Kennedy to be a traitor to their cause. The CIA had even been called on by the Secret Service for assistance in pre-empting potential anti-Castro Cuban violence against President Kennedy during his visits to Miami and Tampa in the fall of 1963.

Documents show that in the weeks and months following the attack in Dallas, the CIA itself internally investigated the possibility of a Cuban element in the murder of the president, either by pro- or anti-Castro Cubans. Material taken into evidence by the HSCA revealed a JMWAVE station inquiry into the possible involvement of Cuba-associated actors. That information was recorded in a documented titled "1963-1964 MIAMI STATION ACTION TO AID USG INVESTIGATION OF THE MURDER OF JFK."[469] The JMWAVE inquiry was a result of a communication from CIA headquarters, and was signed off on by JMWAVE station chief Theodore Shackley.

Shackley directed that the inquiry make use of personnel resources of the station's Cuban counter-intelligence group called the AMOTs. That authorization was confirmed by the group's head, Anthony

Sforza. The House Select Committee on Assassinations files provide a description of what was to be a very detailed inquiry, including the movements of Cuban exiles who were out of the Miami area (or whose locations were unknown) at the time of the assassination. Focus would also be put on individuals who might have been in possession of significant funds, weapons or vehicles—all potentially needed for the attack in Dallas.

The CIA inquiry was also to investigate anti-Castro Cubans with the motive and capability to have carried out the attack in order to provoke American action against Cuba. Thanks to a related document, we also know that CIA staff in Miami, Tampa, and Mexico City were briefed (but only orally) on questions and lines of inquiry for the investigation.[470]

It must be noted that any credible list of Cuban exiles for such an inquiry would have included several of the CIA's own special anti-Castro Cuban military operations assets. Some of these were working in current autonomous maritime operations; some had been laid off due to a downturn in missions; some were being recruited into a very secret, compartmentalized operation known as AMWORLD. That operation, ordered to be entirely deniable and operate outside the United States, was headed by CIA officers Carl Jenkins and William Harvey, who had headed ZR-RIFLE, the CIA's "executive action" assassination program. The AMWORLD operation was under the operational direction of Cuban exile leaders Manuel Artime and Rafael Quintero.

Only a handful of CIA officers, including Ted Shackley, David Morales, and David Phillips, were read into the AMWORLD program. JMWAVE personnel such as David Morales and Tony Sforza were informed of the project strictly because they were required to support its initial activities including training and recruiting. David Phillips had also been directed to support the project, including via the establishment of special safehouses outside the United States, initially in Mexico City. Cubans recruited for the AMWORLD operation, such as Carlos Hernandez, were being deniably moved outside the

United States in the fall of 1963. Hernandez would have been of special interest, since he had been in the New Orleans area while Oswald was active there in the summer of 1963.

Based on the information obtained by the HSCA, both CIA headquarters and its Miami field office were very much aware of the possibility that anti-Castro exiles would have had an obvious motive to strike at JFK, and do so in a manner which would have thrown suspicion on Cuba and Castro. Fulfilling the latter motive would have required some sort of link that would have tied the attack to Cuba. The implication that Lee Harvey Oswald, with his highly public media resume of Castro support in New Orleans, might have provided such a link is unlikely to have escaped professional intelligence officers at either location.

Yet while such suspicions did exist and a CIA internal inquiry did occur, there is no evidence that a report of the inquiry was compiled, or that findings related to anti-Castro exiles was ever provided to the Warren Commission—or to any of the follow-on U.S. government assassination investigations. The documents we now have at least put the lie to remarks by JMWAVE Chief Shackley. Shackley declared that the JMWAVE station had done nothing proactive in response to the assassination; he maintained that there had been no investigative role for the CIA in the assassination investigation—that was the FBI's job.[471] The HSCA was unsatisfied with that response, officially noting what appeared to have been a failure regarding pursuing information and leads.

This leaves us with the question of whether the CIA's internal Cuba assassination inquiry raised questions and concerns which were considered safest not to explore further, much less report. Did intelligence officers simply choose not to pursue certain leads—or did they suppress findings—to protect ongoing, secret projects such as AMWORLD, or active JMWAVE covert military operations against Cuba? The CIA certainly seems to have chosen "protection" as its priority with respect to Oswald's time in Mexico City. Was the same decision made following the CIA's own internal inquiry into possible anti-Castro Cuban involvement in the murder of President Kennedy?

Over time, leads to Cuban exile involvement, and even leads to specific people with information about that involvement, did emerge. They came from people directly involved with anti-Castro efforts in 1963, in some instances individuals directly involved with CIA covert maritime operations of Florida, as well as with individuals directly involved in the AMWORLD project.

One of the first such leads came from two close personal associates of John Martino, a former Castro prisoner and someone personally associated with Cuban exile efforts in 1963. Martino had been publicly involved in anti-Castro activities and was committed enough to have personally participated in an extremely secret mission into Cuba. That mission involved him with a Cuban exile paramilitary team, a former ambassador to Cuba—William Pawley—and CIA operations personnel from JMWAVE.[472] It also brought Martino to the attention of JMWAVE station chief Shackley and Operations Chief David Morales, as well as several of the most activist anti-Castro figures in Miami.[473]

Martino had initially been among the anti-Castro figures working to connect Oswald to Cuba and Castro in the aftermath of the assassination. Yet following his death, one close friend and another business partner both contacted the HSCA, first anonymously and then with their true names, John Cummings and Fred Claasen. Both independently related remarks from Martino shortly before his death. In those remarks, Martino described having been aware of and even having served as a courier for anti-Castro activists involved in the attack on President Kennedy in Dallas. The HSCA took the report seriously, even documenting Martino's travel to Dallas and New Orleans. However, at the time, his family refused to confirm that Martino had ever spoken about such a thing. Only much later would both his wife and son confirm that Martino had spoken about JFK being attacked in Dallas, including on the evening before it occurred.[474] "Flo, they're going to kill him. They're going to kill him when he gets to Texas,"

Martino told his wife about President Kennedy on the morning of November 22.

Later, there would be other leads pointing to the involvement of Cuban exiles. Perhaps one of the most interesting was given to the Assassinations Records Review Board by Gene Wheaton in the 1990s.[475] Wheaton contacted the ARRB with a two-page fax, describing conversations he had heard in sessions with two individuals. One of the two was a business employee of Wheaton named Carl Jenkins. Jenkins had been CIA chief of project AMWORLD operations, and the case officer for the project's senior Cuban military officer, Rafael Quintero. Quintero himself was a long-time friend of Wheaton, and the second individual involved in the JFK assassination talk that Wheaton reported to the ARRB.

At the time of the conversations, all after business hours and clearly social in nature, Wheaton and Jenkins (sales manager for Wheaton) were seeking business doing air transport for the CIA-backed Contra effort against the Sandinista regime in Nicaragua. Quintero was acting as senior Contra support field officer, working in the field with Carlos Hernandez. Hernandez and other AMWORLD alumni had joined in the Contra anti-communist effort against the Nicaraguan government.

In the after-hours conversations, remarks were made about the attack on JFK, about a conspiracy, and about certain of the individuals involved being known to both Jenkins and Quintero. When Wheaton had first become aware of that information, he offered to work with the two men to arrange for Congressional immunity for their information. They had adamantly rejected that idea. Wheaton was cautious in his outreach to the ARRB, only proposing that it contact the two men and attempt to interview them.

In response to his outreach to the ARRB, Wheaton was sent a standard form letter signed by John Tunheim, the ARRB Chairman, thanking him for his interest and advising that a staff member would be in touch with him. In the end, there was limited contact and Wheaton supplied information confirming his relationship with Jenkins and

Wheaton. But ultimately the ARRB failed to take any further action and simply thanked Wheaton for his interest in their work—with another standard form letter.

Our focus with this book has been on Lee Harvey Oswald, and the issues which developed around his beliefs, his activities, and his personal life. In doing so, we moved beyond Oswald himself to explore how his own goals might have brought him into the position of being framed for the attack on President Kennedy. Proposing that Oswald was unwitting in the assassination, but that he was implicated by his own history, is one thing, but asserting that he was actually framed as the shooter leads us to the issue of evidence. There would need to be evidence which tied Oswald directly to the crime, planted at the crime scene. The operative word here is "planted," so that an unwitting Oswald could be implicated into acting suspiciously (leaving his workplace) but not realizing that he was leaving a crime scene with evidence directly connecting him to the crime. Dallas Police Chief Jesse Curry called out the problem with this evidence specifically in his own book, expressing doubts about the Warren Commission's conclusion—"I'm not sure about it. No one has ever been able to put him (Oswald) in the Texas School Book Depository with a rifle in his hand."[476] Curry also was unconvinced that all the shots had come from the rear of the president or that only one shooter was involved.

Curry's observation captures a critical point. An unwitting Oswald could not be expected to directly implicate himself in the attack on the president; it was necessary to plant evidence which could directly connect him to the shooting. The answer to that would be a rifle legally traceable to Oswald, a rifle that he was known to have purchased, which he had owned for some time and shown to others—to be corroborated in the testimony of others after the fact. Of course, knowing such things about Oswald and his rifle implies that the people that framed him had a "history" with him; they would be people he trusted, had talked with at some length—with whom he likely had associated for some time and even traveled with—people very much like those he had met in New Orleans, and even traveled with to Houston and Dallas.

If Oswald was not going to implicate himself, his rifle would have to do the job. And realistically it would unreasonable to ask him to carry his or any other rifle into the building where he worked without his asking questions which would be difficult to answer. Oswald was not someone to take orders or even directions at face value or without questions.

With that context, the problem in framing him was twofold. First, acquire his rifle, if even temporarily, without raising questions and second, get it into the TSBD and plant it where it would remain hidden. As to acquiring the rifle, several options—all speculative—present themselves. The rifle may have arrived in New Orleans wrapped in a blanket, but the rifle and pistol may have left New Orleans with Oswald, in a car or with others, such as those who appeared with him at McKeown's in Houston and Odio's in Dallas. In traveling to Mexico and afterwards to Dallas, it would have been easy enough to conceal a pistol, but not so much a rifle, especially since he stayed first at the YMCA and later in different apartments. Imagining the rifle being left with the people who would ultimately frame him is not that difficult.

Planting the rifle in the building would be another story entirely—it is worth noting that the rifle was recovered from a very concealed location, hidden under stacked boxes. The Warren Commission presented the scenario of an emotionally charged Oswald shooting the president from a sixth-floor window, running from that window, and taking the time to pause and hide the rifle under boxes at the opposite corner of the sixth floor. Yet Oswald was no fool, and hiding a rifle he had ordered by mail and which was sure to be discovered anywhere in the building would surely seem to be the act of one.

The Warren Commission itself never came close to resolving the question of how the rifle had been taken into the building. The one witness they offered who had seen Oswald with a bag that day was adamant that it was not nearly large enough to carry even a broken-down rifle. That witness was shown the bag reportedly found in the TSBD the evening of the assassination and under polygraph denied it was the bag he had seen with Oswald just that morning (the polygraph interview was never entered into evidence).

In reality, the question of building access proved to be irrelevant. Interviews determined the entire building remained unlocked after TSBD working hours, so that book company employees working in the building had open access. The building had even remained unlocked and unsecured the weekend following the assassination. The rifle could have been planted days before the assassination, hidden in an area where no work was in progress—in just the type of location from which police recovered it. Given that the individuals suspected of framing Oswald had been trained to covertly infiltrate Cuba and assassinate Fidel Castro, they would not have found entering and planting a rifle in the TSBD a serious challenge.

In this scenario, we are left with the real mystery of the Kennedy assassination—not with Oswald as an enigma, and not with an explanation of how he might have been unwittingly manipulated and framed for the shooting, but with the larger conspiracy involved with the murder of the president. That conspiracy, its origins, its motives, and the individuals involved in various aspects of the actual attack in Dallas are explored in *Tipping Point: The conspiracy that murdered President John Kennedy.*

In regards to the larger conspiracy, the following remarks from John Martino may provide some insight. Martino was discussed earlier in this epilogue expressing foreknowledge of the assassination; he was a former Castro prisoner inside Cuba and someone personally acquainted with both anti-Castro activists in Miami and CIA operations officers from the JMWAVE station.

In his final words before his death, to his two closest friends, Martino admitted to having a minor role in the conspiracy, though knowing few details. What he did know was that Oswald was being manipulated by anti-Castro people who represented themselves as being pro-Castro.

Oswald was ignorant of their true identities and rather than helping him get out of the country, their plan was simply to kill him. When that failed, the people they were working with were forced to turn to Jack Ruby to eliminate him.

Our focus in this book has been on an exploration of Oswald's personality and character, demonstrating continuity and consistency in both his beliefs and actions. We extended that to speculation regarding a scenario by which he could have been manipulated and framed in the attack on President Kennedy—by individuals he had come to trust at least to a certain extent.

The larger story of those individuals, of the overall conspiracy and its motives, is another story entirely. It is a story that extends far beyond and above the individuals directly involved with Lee Harvey Oswald. It also extends to Oswald's actions following his departure from his workplace, and his murder within two days by Jack Ruby. As noted above, readers can find those questions and the authors' study of the overall conspiracy in *Tipping Point*.

One final question specifically about Oswald himself does deserve comment. When Desmond Fitzgerald, chief of the CIA's Cuba Project / Special Affairs Staff heard the news of Oswald's death, he reportedly lamented, "Now we'll never know."

But what if Oswald had indeed lived? Would the last six decades of history be completely different? Would Oswald have talked, and all the mysteries have been solved?

The question that is virtually never asked is this: If Oswald had talked, would it have made any difference?

We have outlined a scenario in which Oswald could have been covertly contacted, steered, and manipulated into appearing as a dangerous figure, capable of killing either Castro or JFK (remarks made both to Silvia Odio and much later echoed in an unpublished manuscript by David Phillips).[477] That scenario also included involving him in a suspicious series of activities the week and day of the assassination.

But it is a scenario which left him with no knowledge of that attack itself, or even of the fact that evidence directly connected to him had been planted at the Texas School Book Depository.

If Oswald had talked, what could he have said? Could a living Oswald have convinced authorities after the fact that he was a patsy, set up by unknown parties he could not name, at locations he would have been unclear about? Surely no real names would have been used by those in contact with Oswald. And if they had presented themselves as Castro supporters or even agents, certainly not as anyone connected to the CIA, Oswald's story would have only been reinforcing the idea of a Castro-linked conspiracy in the attack.

In short, even if Oswald had lived and talked, would anyone have believed him? If he had told a story like the scenario we have presented in these last few chapters, he would have had little to support such claims beyond that of the Red Bird airfield incident. In short, Oswald could have opened the door to conspiracy, but the authorities might have simply disbelieved him. Indeed, with the federal government's full-on press to downplay foreign involvement in the assassination, Oswald's talk about pro-Castro Cubans would have been most unwelcome. Oswald, on realizing he was framed and the implications of that, might attempt to declare that these Cubans must have been anti-Castro, not pro-Castro. But again, what proof would he have had for these claims?

Only the CIA would have been able to pursue the possibility that the mystery Cubans were real—and anti-Castro rather than pro-Castro. Of course, in doing that they would have been focusing attention on their own Cuban assets. That appears highly unlikely, given their apparent willingness to conceal or obfuscate anything which might have exposed their operations, people, or projects.

Even if Oswald had lived and was determined to tell all he knew, would that have been enough to open the door to an aggressive investigation of conspiracy? Or would we still have been left with the assassination of President Kennedy as the great mystery of the age?

Endnotes

Foreword

1. "50 Years After Assassination, Kennedy Books Offer New Analysis," Lynn Neary, NPR, November 18, 2013

Chapter 1

2. Dan Hardway, "Thank You, Phil Shenon," Real Hillbilly Views, October 27, 2015. https://realhillbillyviews.blogspot.com/2015/10/
3. Katzenbach Memorandum, Mary Ferrell Foundation. https://www.maryferrell.org/pages/Katzenbach_Memo.html
4. Studies of national emergency responses and an exploration of the practice of "seizing the narrative" are documented in Hancock, *Surprise Attack*, 2015, and include Pearl Harbor, the Kennedy assassination, the King assassination, the Reagan shooting, the attacks on the Pueblo and Liberty Navy ships, as well as the attacks of 9/11 and the American consulate in Benghazi, Libya.
5. Charles Nicholas, "Civil Rights Photos," The Commercial Appeal, Memphis Tennessee, April 5, 1968
6. The Light, San Antonio, Texas, November 23, 1963
7. *San Diego Union Tribune*, San Diego, California, November 23, 1963. https://www.sandiegouniontribune.com/news/local-history/story/2020-11-22/from-the-archives-president-kennedy-assassinated-in-dallas
8. "The Press: The Chain Scripps Forged," *Time Magazine*, Friday, Oct. 19, 1962. https://content.time.com/time/subscriber/article/0,33009,827873,00.html
9. Gaeton Fonzi, *The Last Investigation*, 325-326 also Larry Hancock, *Someone Would Have Talked*, 144-145

10. Jim Hougan, *Secret Agenda: Watergate Deep Throat and the CIA* also Larry Hancock, *Someone Would have Talked*, 2010 edition, 100
11. Larry Hancock, *Someone Would have Talked,* 2010 edition, 144-145
12. Pat Speer, Volume 1: The Kennedy Assassination, Politics, and Propaganda, Chapter 3B. https://www.patspeer.com/chapter3bmenatwork
13. Warren Commission Volume 1, 471. https://www.maryferrell.org/showDoc.html?docId=37#relPageId=482
14. Pat Speer, Volume 2: The Cover-Up and The Cover-up of the Cover-up, Chapter 3C, "The Whitewash; The Last Days of the Warren Commission." https://www.patspeer.com/chapter3cthewhitewash
15. Ibid
16. House Select Committee on Assassinations, Volume 11, 232. https://www.maryferrell.org/showDoc.html?docId=83#relPageId=238
17. Pat Speer, Volume 2: The Cover-Up and The Cover-up of the Cover-up, Chapter 3C, "The Whitewash; The Last Days of the Warren Commission". https://www.patspeer.com/chapter3cthewhitewash
18. U.S. Army Edgewood Arsenal, Technical Report CRDLR 3264, March 1965. https://www.maryferrell.org/showDoc.html?docId=62296
19. Hancock, *Someone Would Have Talked*, 2010 edition, 65-66 also David Wrone, *The Zapruder Film: Reframing JFK's Assassination*, 171-172; Gerald McKnight, *Breach of Trust*, 5 and FBI Memoranda Serial Number 44-1639-2142 and 62-109060-427
20. Pat Speer, Volume 2: The Cover-Up and The Cover-up of the Cover-up, Chapter 5, "The Jigsaw Puzzle". https://www.patspeer.com/chapter5thejigsawpuzzle
21. Church Committee, Book V, The Assassination of President Kennedy, 41-44. https://www.maryferrell.org/showDoc.html?docId=1161#relPageId=48
22. David Phillips' endorsement of the Alvarado story remains especially questionable, given Alvarado's details about a meeting in a public area of a Cuban diplomatic facility, and an open discussion of murder, including the public passing of money. The conversation was purportedly so visible that as simply a visitor to the embassy, Alvarado was able to give detailed physical descriptions of all those involved. He was even able to quote their individual remarks – "I want to kill the man," "You're not man enough, I can do it."

    Alvarado even described the passport, and gave an address for the girl involved in the conversation – as well as the exact amount of cash given to Oswald. That such a conversation would have occurred in a public area is highly questionable; the level of detail provided to support it is virtually beyond belief. As a former case officer and propaganda specialist, Phillips should immediately have raised numerous questions, challenging Alvarado.

Instead, Phillips and the senior Mexico City officers continued to support the story until it was totally disproven by the Mexican government and the FBI – after only 48 hours of investigation. Yet even in the face of the embarrassing deconstruction of Alvarado, Phillips continued to support the story, even repeating it in his autobiography, *The Night Watch.* In the book Phillips elaborated on the story, maintaining Oswald had come back to the United States with a large amount of cash.

23. Peter Dale Scott, *Deep Politics II,* 103, also Mexi CIA documents of November 27 and 29 numbers 174-616 and 260-270. David Phillips reference to Oswald carrying back a payment from the Cubans is from his book *The Night Watch*, 182
24. Senate Select Committee (Church Committee); Findings, "The Hosty entry in Oswald's address book pages" 186-189. https://www.archives.gov/research/jfk/select-committee-report/part-1c.html
25. President's Commission on the Assassination of President Kennedy, Executive Session, 1/22/64. https://www.maryferrell.org/showDoc.html?docId=1327
26. "Agent Tells Fate of Oswald Note," *New York Times*, December 12, 1975. https://www.nytimes.com/1975/12/13/archives/agent-tells-fate-of-oswald-note-says-he-flushed-it-down-drain-on.html
27. Senate Select Committee (Church Committee), "Discussion of Lee Oswald's Alleged FBI Connections / More Recent Allegations", 168-171. https://www.maryferrell.org/showDoc.html?docId=1463#relPageId=171
28. FBI agents approached by the Warren Commission and by Senate and House committees officially denied any operational connection to Lee Harvey Oswald, while admitting that he had volunteered information to the FBI in New Orleans, and had been interviewed multiple times by FBI agents. It should be noted that when District Attorney Garrison attempted to interview agents from New Orleans, both the Special Agent in Charge of the office in 1963 (Regis Kennedy) and the agent handling subversive and security files (Warren de Brueys) maintained that they had either not received subpoenas from Garrison or, in the case of Regis Kennedy, were allowed by the Justice Department to claim "executive privilege" and severely limited their testimony. Jim Garrison, *On the Trail of the Assassins*, 182 and an ARRB electronic document, from the files of Philip G. Golrick, Counsel and Chief Analyst for FBI Records at ARRB,

"non-FBI leads/DOJ leads." https://www.maryferrell.org/showDoc.html?docId=207645#relPageId=11

29. Larry Hancock, *Someone Would Have Talked,* 2010 Edition, 202-203 and 226; also Walter House Select Committee Testimony of March 23, 1978 and FBI Memorandum of October 23, 1975 relating to internal FBI communications pertaining to Walter's allegation.
30. Memorandum, SAIC New Orleans to Director, "Nationality Group Coverage – Cuba," August 27, 1962. https://www.maryferrell.org/showDoc.html?docId=74933#relPageId=2
31. Central Intelligence Agency, Oswald 201 File, Volume 1, Folder 2, 67-72. https://www.maryferrell.org/showDoc.html?docId=95569#relPageId=67
32. Warren Commission testimony of FBI agent John Quigley, Warren Commission Hearings, Volume 4, 436-440. https://www.maryferrell.org/showDoc.html?docId=34#relPageId=444
33. Warren Commission Record, John Quigley Affidavit, Commission Exhibit 825, Dallas, Texas. https://www.maryferrell.org/showDoc.html?docId=233452#relPageId=10
34. Senate Select Committee (Church Committee) Preliminary Report of Investigation into the Assassination of President Kennedy, 100-101. https://www.maryferrell.org/showDoc.html?docId=148889#relPageId=101

Chapter 2

35. Warren Commission Report, Chapter 7: Lee Harvey Oswald: Background and Possible Motives, 423
36. Warren Commission Report, Chapter 7: Lee Harvey Oswald: Background and Possible Motives, WC Report Conclusion, 118 – 125, 156, 157, 162, 165, 168, 174-176, 206, 231. This source will be used as a reference for much of Oswald's school age years.
37. *New York Times*, "Oswald's Wife Says He Developed A New Personality; She Recalls His Irritability After His Return from the Soviet," November 24, 1964. https://www.nytimes.com/1964/11/24/archives/oswalds-wife-says-he-developed-2d-personality-she-recalls-his.html
38. The material for Oswald's school years is derived from the FBI background research developed for the Warren Commission, corroborated by interviews with his family and with teachers and school friends. Other sources are identified in separate citations.
39. Researcher Greg Parker notes that while a later, unofficial diagnosis of Oswald's writing problems refers to dyslexia, the actual symptoms shown by Oswald throughout his life (specifically poor spelling both in handwriting and later in typewritten work) are better matched by

dysgraphia – "Impaired handwriting can interfere with learning to spell words in writing and speed of writing text. Children with dysgraphia may have only impaired handwriting, only impaired spelling (without reading problems), or both impaired handwriting and impaired spelling." https://dyslexiaida.org/understanding-dysgraphia/#:~:text=Impaired%20handwriting%20can%20interfere%20with,impaired%20handwriting%20and%20impaired%20spelling. https://speechify.com/blog/dyslexia-vs-dysgraphia-what-are-the-differences/#:~:text=As%20you%20might%20know%2C%20dyslexia,refers%20to%20writing%20by%20hand.

40. Warren Commission Hearings, Volume 8, 202-213. https://www.maryferrell.org/showDoc.html?docId=36#relPageId=210
41. Warren Commission Report, 698. While in the Soviet Union Oswald joined a local chapter of the Belorussian Society of Hunters and Fishermen, a hunting club sponsored by his factory.
42. Robert J Groden, *The Search for Lee Harvey Oswald: A Comprehensive Photographic Record*, Penguin Group, 1995
43. Antisocial vs. Asocial, https://theswaddle.com/the-difference-between-asocial-and-antisocial/
44. "Inner directed" – describing or relating to an individual who is self-motivated and not easily influenced by the opinions, values, or pressures of other people. Compare to other-directed; tradition-directed. [introduced by U.S. sociologist David Riesman (1909–2002)]
45. Warren Commission Report, 681 – Oswald performed various clerical duties such as distributing mail, delivering messages & answering the telephone. He helped file records & operated ditto, letter opening & sealing machines.
46. Ibid

Chapter 3

47. Jack Swike, *The Missing Chapter: Lee Harvey Oswald in the Far East*, 2008, 52-53
48. Michael Benson, *Who's Who in the JFK Assassination*, 1993, commentary from Allen R. Felde, who was with Oswald from bootcamp and Advanced Infantry Training though Aircraft and Powerplant Training
49. Warren Commission Report, 682-683
50. John Newman, *Oswald and the CIA*, 14
51. United States Air Force Combat Command, Searching the Skies: The Legacy of the United Stated Cold War Defense Program, David F. Winkler

52. John Newman, *Oswald and the CIA*, 33-34
53. Ibid, 29-30.
54. Curtis Peebles, *Dark Eagles: A History of Top Secret U.S. Aircraft Programs*, 39; also William Burrows, *By Any Means Necessary*, 238
55. John Newman, *Oswald and the CIA*, 32-33
56. Curtis Peeples, *Shadow Flights: America's Secret Air War Against the Soviet Union*, 142-43
57. Curtis Peeples, *Dark Eagles: A History of Top Secret U.S. Aircraft Programs*, 38-39
58. National Security Archive, https://nsarchive.gwu.edu/briefing-book/intelligence-nuclear-vault/2022-03-08/cia-u-2-collection-signals-intelligence-1956
59. Curtis Peeples, *Shadow Flights: America's Secret Air War Against the Soviet Union*, 145
60. Curtis Peeples, *Dark Eagles: A History of Top Secret U.S. Aircraft Programs*, 42
61. Ibid, 44-45
62. Warren Commission Report, 685
63. Ibid
64. Jack Swike, *The Missing Chapter: Lee Harvey Oswald in the Far East*, 2008, source PFC Jerry Leon, 98
65. Ibid, 194-195
66. Ibid, 113-114
67. Ibid, 192-195
68. Warren Commission Report, 685
69. Greg Parker, http://www.jfkconversations.com/lee-oswald-russian-language
70. Warren Commission Report, 686-687
71. Ibid
72. Ibid

Chapter 4

73. Ibid, 687
74. George Michael Evica, *A Certain Arrogance*, Xlibris US, 2006
75. Ibid, 84-89
76. John Newman, *Oswald and the CIA*, 92
77. Greg Parker, http://coverthistory.blogspot.com/2005/07/oswald-and-albert-schweitzer-college.html
78. Personal communications with researcher Larry Haapanen, July 2023 related to work by David Lifton
79. Warren Commission Report, 689

80. John Newman, *Oswald and the CIA*, Chapter 1 "Defection in Moscow" and Chapter 2 "Paper Trail in Washington"
81. Ibid, 465-467
82. Ibid, 133
83. Ibid, 3
84. Ibid, 3-8
85. John Newman, *Oswald and the CIA*, 3-14
86. Ernst Titovets, *Oswald: Russian Episode*, 5-6
87. Ibid, 12-13
88. Rick Anderson, *Seattle Weekly News*, "The Worst Internal Scandal in NSA History Was Blamed on Cold War Defectors' Homosexuality / But what if they weren't gay?" July 17, 2007. https://web.archive.org/web/20131227190422/ http://www.seattleweekly.com/home/887442-129/story.html
89. Wayne G. Barker and Rodney E. Coffman, *The Anatomy of Two Traitors: The Defection of Bernon F. Mitchell and William H. Martin*, includes appendices that provide the full text of: "Predeparture Declaration Left in a Safe Deposit Box in the U.S.," "Statement Made at Press Conference in Moscow on September 6, 1960," and "Report by the Committee on Un-American Activities," House of Representatives, 87th Congress, 2nd Session, "Security Practices in the National Security Agency."
90. John Newman, *Oswald and the CIA*, 7-8, 18-19 and 67-70
91. Ernst Titovets, *Oswald: Russian Episode;* Ibid, Chapter 2, "Oswald Rushes Things and Wins," 18-31
92. Ibid, 26-27
93. Michael Cline to Deputy Director for Operations, Soviet Volunteer Allegations Re: Oswald Involvement in Kennedy Assassination. https://www.maryferrell.org/showDoc.html?docId=6761#relPageId=72
94. John Newman, *Oswald and the CIA*, 13-14
95. Ernst Titovets, *Oswald: Russian Episode*, 60-61

Chapter 5

96. John Newman, *Oswald and the CIA*, 147
97. Ernst Titovets, *Oswald: Russian Episode,* Chapter 6, "Oswald in Love," 62-66 and "Sobering Up," 136-138
98. Ernst Titovets, *Oswald: Russian Episode*, Chapter 11, "The Queen of Spades"
99. Ibid, 329
100. Ibid, xxi
101. Warren Commission Report, 700

102. Ibid, Exhibit CE 24, Oswald's Historic Diary, 24. https://www.history-matters.com/archive/jfk/wc/wcvols/wh16/pdf/WH16_CE_24.pdf
103. Diane Holloway with Bob Cheney, *Autobiography of Lee Harvey Oswald: My Life in My Own Words*, 2008, 56
104. John Newman, *Oswald and the CIA*, Chapter 14, "Oswald Returns"
105. House Select Committee on Assassinations, Volume 2. https://history-matters.com/archive/jfk/hsca/reportvols/vol2/pdf/HSCA_Vol2_0913_2_Porter.pdf
106. Warren Commission Report, Appendix 15. https://www.archives.gov/research/jfk/warren-commission-report/appendix-15.html#authorization
107. Warren Commission Report, 710

Chapter 6

108. Warren Commission Exhibit No. 25, Volume 16, 122
109. HSCA interview of Donald Deneslya, September 24, 1978. https://www.archives.gov/files/research/jfk/releases/2018/180-10111-10051.pdf
110. Warren Commission Report, 715
111. Ibid, 716
112. Ibid, 717
113. Ernst Titovets, *Oswald: Russian Episode*, 331-333
114. Warren Commission Report, 716
115. Ibid
116. Ibid
117. Ibid
118. Dallas Police Criminal Investigation Report, February 17, 1964. https://www.maryferrell.org/showDoc.html?docId=217811#relPageId=536
119. George de Mohrenschildt, *I Am a Patsy! I Am a Patsy!* http://22november1963.org.uk/george-de-mohrenschildt-i-am-a-patsy-chapter03
120. CIA file memorandum, George de Mohrenschildt, "Haiti," August 1, 1962. https://www.maryferrell.org/showDoc.html?docId=42244
121. Ibid, http://22november1963.org.uk/george-de-mohrenschildt-i-am-a-patsy-chapter02
122. House Select Committee on Assassinations, Volume 6, 62 https://www.maryferrell.org/showDoc.html?docId=84#relPageId=66
123. Warren Commission testimony of George de Mohrenschildt, Volume 9, 168-169; also, House Select Committee on Assassinations, Volume 12, "Allegations of De Mohrenschildt Intelligence Connections" and "Activities in Haiti," 53-65. https://www.maryferrell.org/showDoc.html?docId=84#relPageId=57
124. Memorandum for Director, Central Intelligence from John Waller,

Inspector General, "George de Mohrenschildt," September 22, 1976. https://www.maryferrell.org/showDoc.html?docId=180399#relPageId=3
125. Central Intelligence Agency, "After Action Report on the Findings of the Working Group." https://www.maryferrell.org/showDoc.html?docId=235948#relPageId=23
126. Ibid
127. Warren Commission Hearings, Volume 9, 166-331. https://www.maryferrell.org/showDoc.html?docId=43#relPageId=174
128. Manuscript appended to Volume 12 of the House Select Committee on Assassinations. https://www.aarclibrary.org/publib/jfk/hsca/reportvols/vol12/pdf/HSCA_Vol12_deMohren.pdf
129. George de Mohrenschildt, *I Am a Patsy! I Am a Patsy!* http://22november1963.org.uk/george-de-mohrenschildt-i-am-a-patsy-chapter15
130. Ibid, http://22november1963.org.uk/george-de-mohrenschildt-i-am-a-patsy-chapter06
131. Ibid, http://22november1963.org.uk/george-de-mohrenschildt-i-am-a-patsy-chapter07

Chapter 7

132. Warren Commission Report, 719
133. Ibid
134. Ibid
135. Ibid, 719-720
136. Ibid, 720
137. Ibid
138. Ibid
139. Robert Charles-Dunne, "Was Oswald a Serial Wife Batterer?," Kennedys & King, February 2017. https://www.kennedysandking.com/john-f-kennedy-articles/was-oswald-a-serial-wife-batterer
140. Warren Commission Report, 720
141. Ibid, 721
142. Ibid
143. Ibid
144. Ibid
145. Ibid, 722
146. Ibid
147. Ibid, 722-723
148. Ibid, 723
149. George de Mohrenschildt, *I Am a Patsy! I Am a Patsy!* http://22

november1963.org.uk/george-de-mohrenschildt-i-am-a-patsy-chapter07

150. Ibid
151. Warren Commission Report, 723
152. Marina Oswald Porter testimony, House Select Committee on Assassinations, Volume 2, 252. https://history-hatters.com/archive/jfk/hsca/reportvols/vol2/pdf/HSCA_Vol2_0913_2_Porter.pdf
153. Ernst Titovets, *Oswald: Russian Episode*, 338
154. Ibid, 339

Chapter 8

155. *New York Times*, "First Reports," December 21, 1963. *The Times* report also includes the information that it was at the Secret Service's advice that Mrs. Oswald reached an agreement with the manager of the Six Flags Inn (James Martin), where she was staying in protective custody, to act as her business manager, and with the concurrence of Robert Oswald, to complete a contract allowing Martin to serve as her business agent.
156. FBI - HSCA Administrative Folder A8, Interviews of Marina Oswald; Secret Service Interview by SA Leon Gopodze with FBI Brown and Hosty present, 11/27/63 https://www.maryferrell.org/showDoc.html?docId=9880
157. For context it has to be noted that Marina Oswald offered a series of remarks and testimony over time and under quite different situations, initially interrogated immediately following the assassination, then interrogated again after a note was discovered implicating Oswald in the Walker shooting (proving that Marina had withheld information in her earliest remarks), and then again in testimony taken at different times by Warren Commission staff who focused and positioned her remarks with their questions. One of the most egregious situational examples of her testimony being managed involved her remarks regarding Lee and a visit by Richard Nixon to Dallas, something not mentioned in any of her interviews, but brought to the attention of the Warren Commission by Robert Oswald, after he and Marina had become quite close in the months following the assassination.

    His remarks to the Commission were strictly anecdotal and third party, but Marina was called to testify about the possibility that Oswald might have threatened Nixon – in the end, her testimony suggested nothing more than Oswald having remarked about wanting to see Nixon at an appearance, with her concern that he might have intended to carry his pistol. Readers can evaluate that story and her response to questioning, her admission as to possible confusion with elements of the story, and with Robert Oswald's involvement, by reference to the testimony itself and how the Warren Commission positioned the interview: Warren Commission Report, "Richard Nixon Incident," 187-189. https://www.maryferrell.org/showDoc.html?docId=946#relPageId=211

158. Tom Gram, "Rethinking Oswald's Mail; P.O. Box 2915 and the Missing Change of Address Order." https://drive.google.com/file/d/1XvkmfIq44G8B-B_RV4L90f5AoXYdRTN4/view
159. Warren Commission Exhibit 1785
160. Warren Commission Hearings, Volume 1, 14
161. Letter from the Fair Play for Cuba Committee to Lee Harvey Oswald, May 29, 1963. https://texashistory.unt.edu/ark:/67531/metapth337534/

Chapter 9

162. Marina Oswald testimony, Warren Commission Hearings, Volume 1, 10
163. Warren Commission Report, 723
164. Warren Commission Hearings and Exhibits, Volume 19, Exhibit 24
165. Warren Commission Hearings and Exhibits: The Collective Life of a Russian Worker, Volume 16, Exhibit 92, 287-336 On Communism and Capitalism, Volume 16, Exhibit 25, 106-122 The Communist Party of the United States, Volume 16, Exhibit 97, 422-430 The Athenian System / Outline and Principles, Volume 16, Exhibit 98, 431-434
166. It has been pointed out that in the Athenian monograph Oswald goes so far as to maintain that, in a more perfect system of government, there should even be some limited regulation of personal firearms; individuals would be free to purchase and own handguns and shotguns with no oversight; however, the police would have the authority to register rifles. The statement speaks for itself; however, it would apply only in the more ideal world he was describing – it is balanced by his obvious interest in rifles and his numerous conversations with Adrian Alba about purchasing them while in New Orleans later that same year.
167. Ernst Titovets, *Oswald: Russian Episode*, 162-167
168. Ibid, 1028
169. John Newman, *Oswald and the CIA*, 275
170. Gayle Nix Jackson, *Pieces of the Puzzle: An Anthology*, 2016 edition, 85-86
171. George De Mohrenschildt, *I Am a Patsy! I Am a Patsy!,* House Select Committee on Assassinations, Volume 12, 198
172. Relevant contextual references include:
    http://22november1963.org.uk/george-de-mohrenschildt-i-am-a-patsy-chapter16

https://www.civilrightsteaching.org/1963
https://news.harvard.edu/gazette/story/2022/01/rescuing-the-civil-rights-movement-and-children-of-birmingham/
https://themilitant.com/1963/2710/MIL2710.pdf

173. Federal Bureau of Investigation/ FBI Oswald Headquarters File, FBI 105-82555 Oswald HQ File, Section 60. https://www.maryferrell.org/showDoc.html?docId=57748#relPageId=24 Jerry Rose, *The Fourth Decade*, Volume 3, Issue 2. https://www.maryferrell.org/showDoc.html?docId=48691#relPageId=44
174. Relevant Contextual references include:
https://www.splcenter.org/fighting-hate/extremist-files/group/national-socialist-movement
https://www.facebook.com/OldImagesOfTheBronx/photos/a.439614706093422/482598881795004/?paipv=0&eav=AfZ81UDiWgBm0B5Z0kL0yYUcSzzIVKe1Fk6_lj3s3UhRUYbg8t1yZr_aHKMXWFfmCQ8&_rdr
https://nypost.com/2017/10/28/he-was-a-rising-nazi-leader-until-a-shocking-secret-did-him-in/
175. FBI Memorandum, Tolson to Belmont, December 3, 1963. https://www.maryferrell.org/showDoc.html?docId=57739#relPageId=136
176. FBI investigative memoranda file related to the Oswald note and Walker shooting, Rosen to Belmont, initial memoranda December 3, 1963 https://www.maryferrell.org/showDoc.html?docId=57739#relPageId=134
177. "The Sixth Floor Museum at Dealey Plaza," November 5, 2019. https://www.facebook.com/SixthFloorMuseum/photos/this-note-which-lee-harvey-oswald-wrote-in-russian-to-his-wife-marina-on-the-nig/10157785315033874/ also Hood College, Gerald McKnight collection, Marina Oswald was interviewed at 11611 Farrar Street, December 5, 1963: http://jfk.hood.edu/Collection/McKnight%20Working%20Folders/Part%204/Marina%20Lying/Marina%20Lying%2008.pdf
178. Warren Commission Report, 183-185. https://www.maryferrell.org/showDoc.html?docId=946#relPageId=207
179. FBI Director Hoover to Attorney General's Office, Memorandum on Lee Harvey Oswald, "Technical Surveillance on Marina Oswald," February 24. 1964 also FBI HSCA ADMIN FOLDER-U10: FBI HSCA ADMINISTRATIVE FOLDER, MARINA OSWALD TECHNICAL SURVEILLANCE, RIF#: 124-10371-10106 and FBI HSCA ADMIN FOLDER-U3: CHRONOLOGIES, RIF#: 124-10371-10029
180. Gayle Nix Jackson, *Pieces of the Puzzle: An Anthology*, 113-114

181. House Select Committee on Assassinations, Volume 2, 234-236. https://history-matters.com/archive/jfk/hsca/reportvols/vol2/pdf/HSCA_Vol2_0913_2_Porter.pdf
182. Gayle Nix Jackson, *Pieces of the Puzzle: An Anthology*, 106-107
183. House Select Committee on Assassinations, Volume 6, "The Backyard Photographs." https://history-matters.com/archive/jfk/hsca/reportvols/vol6/pdf/HSCA_Vol6_4B1_Backyard.pdf
184. "A 3-D STABILITY ANALYSIS OF LEE HARVEY OSWALD IN THE BACKYARD PHOTO," Srivamshi Pittala, Emily Whiting, Hany Farid, Department of Computer Science, Dartmouth College. https://farid.berkeley.edu/downloads/publications/jdfsl15.pdf also Physics. Org, https://phys.org/news/2015-10-backyard-photo-lee-harvey-oswald.html
185. *The Washington Post*, Sept 15, 1978, "More Oswald Photo Evidence Said to be Found." https://www.washingtonpost.com/archive/politics/1978/09/15/more-oswald-photo-evidence-said-to-be-found/39265ee1-14b7-498a-921f-fb3416d07f46/
186. House Select Committee on Assassinations, Volume 6, "History of the Backyard Photographs," 139-140. https://history-matters.com/archive/jfk/hsca/reportvols/vol6/pdf/HSCA_Vol6_4B1_Backyard.pdf
187. Steve Roe, "Oswald's Interest in Mail Order." https://steveroeconsulting.wixsite.com/website/post/oswald-s-interest-in-mail-order
188. Gus Russo, *Live by the Sword*, 116-117, Russo interview with Michael Paine, Aug 19, 1993
189. *The Militant*, April, 1963, Letters to the Editor, 7, News and Views from Dallas. https://themilitant.com/1963/2710/MIL2710.pdf
190. Gus Russo, *Live by the Sword*, 116-117, Interview with Sylvia Weinstein June 12, 1993
191. George De Mohrenschildt, *I Am a Patsy! I Am a Patsy!* http://22november1963.org.uk/george-de-mohrenschildt-i-am-a-patsy-chapter22
192. Edward J. Epstein, *The Assassination Chronicles: Inquest, Counterplot, and Legend* [1992], 557-569
193. James Hosty, *Assignment: Oswald*, 107; the FBI had reached out via the American Embassy in Haiti for a reinterview of de Mohrenschildt; he and his wife were reinterviewed circa December 13, 1963. Mrs. de Mohrenschildt also told the FBI that Marina Oswald had told her during a visit to the Oswalds' apartment that Lee Oswald had purchased a gun. https://www.maryferrell.org/showDoc.html?docId=146078 https://www.maryferrell.org/showDoc.html?docId=96244#relPageId=2
194. Seth Galinsky, *The Militant*, "Fair Play for Cuba Committee built defense for

socialist revolution," September 27, 2021 https://themilitant.com/2021/09/18/fair-play-for-cuba-committee-built-defense-for-socialist-revolution/
195. Ibid

Chapter 10

196. Warren Commission Report, 724
197. Ibid, 725
198. Edward J. Epstein, *The Assassination Chronicles: Inquest, Counterplot, and Legend*, 757, Warren Commission Report, 725
199. Warren Commission Report, 726
200. Ibid, 727
201. Ibid, 726
202. Ibid
203. Ibid
204. Ibid, 727
205. Ibid, 726, also Warren Commission Hearings, Testimony of Adrian Alba, Volume 10, 219-229. https://www.maryferrell.org/showDoc.html?docId=44#relPageId=228
206. Warren Commission Report, 727
207. Ibid, 728
208. Ibid, 727, Warren Commission Exhibit 90. https://www.history-matters.com/archive/jfk/wc/wcvols/wh16/pdf/WH16_CE_90.pdf
209. Warren Commission Report, 727
210. John Newman, *Oswald and the CIA*, Oswald's first letter to the Fair Play for Cuba Committee (apparently of some urgency to Oswald, who was normally quite frugal) was sent via Air Mail. The letter expressed his interest in supporting Cuba and described his having already demonstrated for Cuba in Dallas using a handmade placard. The FPCC responded by sending him 50 copies of the standard FPCC leaflet material. While the FBI did not confirm the incident described by Oswald in the letter, there is anecdotal information from the DPD that one officer may have observed such activity. The individual fled upon seeing the officer approach so exact identification was not possible.
211. FBI oversight by United States Congress House Committee on the Judiciary. Subcommittee on Civil and Constitutional Rights, University of Michigan Library https://books.google.com/books?id=HTsiAQAAMAAJ&pg=PA142&lpg=PA142&dq=what+was+the+fbi+sobir+program&source=bl&ots=YjTyzgUy88&sig=ACfU3U3tb8Zavh8iqK2SWg54O1IKeJkdRA&hl=en&sa=X&ved=2ahUKEwi55JLC54X5AhUOkWoF

HZf9C0sQ6AF6BAgiEAM#v=onepage&q=what%20was%20the%20fbi%20sobir%20program&f=false

212. *New York Times*, "F. B. I. Reported to Have Listed Citizens to Detain During Crisis", August 3, 1975. https://www.nytimes.com/1975/08/03/archives/fbi-reported-to-have-listed-citizens-to-detain-during-crisis-fbi.html
213. Warren Commission Report, 728
214. Federal Bureau of Investigation, July 22, 1964, New Orleans, Louisiana, Interview with Lieutenant Roy Alleman, New Orleans Harbor Patrol. https://www.maryferrell.org/showDoc.html?docId=11765#relPageId=7
215. CIA Oswald 201 file, Harold Alderman FBI statement, New Orleans office, November 26, 1963. https://www.maryferrell.org/showDoc.html?docId=95627#relPageId=31
216. Dallas Municipal Archives, Documents Concerning Lee Harvey Oswald's Undesirable Discharge https://texashistory.unt.edu/ark:/67531/metapth339674/
217. Warren Commission Report, 122
218. Lee Harvey Oswald's "Fair Play for Cuba Committee Signed Card," recovered by the Dallas Police. https://www.rrauction.com/auctions/lot-detail/335499904842064-lee-harvey-oswald-s-fair-play-for-cuba-committee-signed-card
219. CIA memo November 26, 1963; presents information taken from FBI Report on Fair Play for Cuba Committee, Warren C. de Brueys, October 25, 1963. https://www.maryferrell.org/showDoc.html?docId=42895#relPageId=2
220. John Newman, *Oswald and the CIA*, 272-73
221. Tom Gram, "Rethinking Oswald's Mail; P.O. Box 2915 and the Missing Change of Address Orders." https://drive.google.com/file/d/1XvkmfIq44G8B-B_RV4L90f5AoXYdRTN4/view
222. Dallas Municipal Archives, photographs of two ID cards for Alek Hidell, a known alias of Lee Harvey Oswald. The first is from the United States Marine Corps. The other is a "Notice of Classification" card. https://texashistory.unt.edu/ark:/67531/metapth337158/
223. Commission Document 1554 - FBI Letter from Director of 14 Oct 1964 also Warren Commission Report, 571-578. https://www.maryferrell.org/showDoc.html?docId=11949#relPageId=64 https://www.maryferrell.org/showDoc.html?docId=946#relPageId=602
224. Warren Commission Hearings, Volume 10, Testimony of Adrian Alba, 220-229 https://www.maryferrell.org/showDoc.html?docId=44#relPageId=228

225. Ibid
226. Martha Moyers, "Ordering the Rifle," Kennedy Assassination Chronicles, Volume 2, Issue 1 with reference to Kleins order form match discovered by Paul Hoch
227. https://www.maryferrell.org/showDoc.html?docId=4254#relPageId=30
228. FBI Memorandum, SAC New Orleans to Director, Report of SA Warren de Brueys, August 14, 1963. https://www.maryferrell.org/showDoc.html?docId=136965#relPageId=5
229. House Select Committee on Assassinations, Betsy Palmer, Draft – MDC, November 14, 1978. https://www.archives.gov/files/research/jfk/releases/2022/180-10142-10409.pdf
230. FBI Memorandum, De Brueys to Director FBI, "Anti-Fidel Castro Activities," October 3, 1963. https://www.maryferrell.org/showDoc.html?docId=129451
231. Earl Golz, Assassinations Archives, March 7, 1979 https://drive.google.com/file/d/1TtUsMXRnT1Jdb0TLT74lZTpC_kbBITmU/view.
232. Earl Golz interview, March 7, 1979. https://drive.google.com/file/d/1TtUsMXRnT1Jdb0TLT74lZTpC_kbBITmU/view https://www.maryferrell.org/showDoc.html?docId=1691#relPageId=3
233. House Select Committee on Assassinations Segregated Collection, Microfilm Reel 44, Folder D - HTLINGUAL SOFT FILE. https://www.maryferrell.org/showDoc.html?docId=55319#relPageId=67

Chapter 11

234. Harold Weisberg, *Oswald in New Orleans*, 343-348
235. Larry Hancock, *Someone Would Have Talked*, 2010 edition, 40-41
236. WDSU footage on International Trade Mart incident and interview with Lee Oswald. https://www.youtube.com/watch?v=tInqL3g6vJw
237. FBI 62-109060 JFK Headquarters File, Section 15, 67. https://www.maryferrell.org/showDoc.html?docId=62265#relPageId=67
238. Warren Commission Report, 728
239. Church Committee, "Oswald in New Orleans," Paul Wallach to Files on Ronald Smith Interview, December 9, 1975, 40. https://www.maryferrell.org/showDoc.html?docId=1462#relPageId=40
240. FBI memorandum, Warren de Brueys, Report on Lee Harvey Oswald with his background, arrest and affiliation, August 31, 1963. https://www.maryferrell.org/showDoc.html?docId=57383
241. Warren Commission Report, 729
242. Assassinations Records Review Board, Jeremy Gunn "Analysis and Review Working Aid for the JFK Assassination." https://www.maryferrell.org/showDoc.html?docId=207532#relPageId=47

243. House Select Committee on Assassinations, Testimony of Richard Cotter, May 5, 1976, 28. https://www.maryferrell.org/showDoc.html?docId=1414#relPageId=28
244. FBI Headquarters file, Report on Fair Play for Cuba Committee, New Orleans Division, Lee H. Oswald, 15. https://www.maryferrell.org/showDoc.html?docId=9533#relPageId=15
245. Warren Commission Document 1085 - FBI Letter from Director of 11 Jun 1964 with Attached Memoranda and Reports, New Orleans, Louisiana, June 3, 1964. https://www.maryferrell.org/showDoc.html?docId=11481#relPageId=14
246. David Von Pein, "Lee Harvey Oswald on the Radio," Oswald radio appearance recording collection. https://drive.google.com/file/d/1-nD3-311FoqejIWCdBXJvA52PmFSdqBF/view
247. WDSU radio debate featuring Lee Oswald and Carlos Bringuier. https://www.youtube.com/watch?v=umLEVBIcZ0g
248. Jefferson Morley, "Revelation 19.63," *The New Times*, April 12, 2002
249. FBI 105-82555 Oswald HQ File, Section 1, 135. https://www.maryferrell.org/showDoc.html?docId=57690#relPageId=135
250. Jefferson Morley, "Revelation 19.63," *The New Times*, April 12, 2002. https://www.miaminewtimes.com/news/revelation-1963-6353139
251. David Phillips was initially recruited as a contract employee, largely because he owned *The South Pacific Mail*, South America's oldest English language newspaper; the paper gave him a media cover as well as providing a controlled press outlet for the Agency. His rise within the agency was relatively swift; he was assigned to the CIA's Guatemala project as a propaganda specialist, and praised for its success in successfully ousting the elected leader of that nation. More contract work followed; in Cuba he worked under cover, as the operator of an advertising agency. After becoming known to Cuban intelligence, he returned to the United States and was assigned to a new effort against the Castro regime. By 1963 he was in Mexico City, conducting counter intelligence and propaganda activities, and by the fall of 1963 assigned to a new effort against the Castro regime, reporting to Desmond Fitzgerald on his Special Affairs Staff. Phillips became quite involved with the story of Lee Harvey Oswald in Mexico City, officially and in his own books following his retirement. In *The Night Watch,* Phillips describes Oswald absolutely not being on the CIA's radar during his visit to the Cuban Consulate in Mexico City (a claim totally repudiated even in the CIA's own documents); in that book and others he also wrote of Oswald being paid to assassinate President Kennedy and returning to the United States with several thousand dollars

in cash as payment for the murder (a claim refuted and deconstructed in the week following the assassination by an FBI investigation). Phillips would go on to become CIA station chief in Chile, involved with a CIA project which ousted yet another elected president, and ultimately go on to serve as the head of the CIA's Latin American operations under its Western Hemisphere Directorate. Larry Hancock, *Someone Would Have Talked*, 2010 edition, 135-147.

252. Jefferson Morley, "Revelation 19.63," *The New Times*, April 12, 2002
253. Ibid
254. Information Council of the Americas, "Lee Harvey Oswald; Self Portrait in Red." https://www.amazon.com/Oswald-Harvey-Coversation-Carte-Blanche/dp/B001F8AUPQ
255. Jefferson Morley, JFK Facts, "Lee Oswald Self Portrait in Red." https://jfkfacts.org/%E2%96%B6-hear-lee-harvey-oswald-talking-about-cuba-in-august-1963/
256. William Davy, *Let Justice Be Done*, 1999
257. Emilio Americo Rodriguez, CIA Cryptonym AMIRE-1, Mary Ferrell Foundation. https://www.maryferrell.org/php/cryptdb.php?id=AMIRE-1
258. Emilio Rodriquez, Procurement of Domestic Documentation and Security Clearance Approval. https://www.maryferrell.org/showDoc.html?docId=234733 https://www.maryferrell.org/showDoc.html?docId=226615
259. CIA Provisional Operational Approval, Dr. Augustine Guitart. https://www.maryferrell.org/showDoc.html?docId=225781 https://www.maryferrell.org/showDoc.html?docId=197079#relPageId=60
260. Ed Brackett. "JFK files: 15-year lawsuit over mysterious CIA agent drags as final files await release," *USA Today*, March 18, 2019. https://www.usatoday.com/story/news/politics/2018/03/19/jfk-files-15-year-lawsuit-over-mysterious-cia-agent-drags-final-files-await-release/435989002/
261. "Memorandum for the Record: Transcripts of October 1975 Telephone Conversations Between Director Colby, Mrs. Clare Booth Luce and Mr. Justin McCarthy," CIA Executive Registry Files, "Clare Booth Luce Weaves a Fascinating Tale," Betty Beale, *Washington Star*, November 16, 1975. https://www.maryferrell.org/showDoc.html?docId=41853#relPageId=6
262. Bill Simpich, "Fair Play for Cuba and the Cuban Revolution," Counterpunch, July 4, 2009. https://www.counterpunch.org/2009/07/24/fair-play-for-cuba-and-the-cuban-revolution/
263. Mary Ferrell Foundation, CIA Cryptonym AMSANTA. https://www.maryferrell.org/php/cryptdb.php?id=AMSANTA

Chapter 12

264. Warren Commission Hearings, Volume 16, "Oswald's Speech," 441-442. https://www.maryferrell.org/showDoc.html?docId=1133#relPageId=464 also Warren Commission Hearings, Volume 25, FBI interview of John Murret and others at Mobile, https://www.maryferrell.org/showDoc.html?docId=1141#relPageId=954
265. Central Intelligence Agency Memorandum, LBJ papers, Cuban Training of Latin American Subversives, March 27, 1963, RIF #177-10001-10305. https://www.maryferrell.org/showDoc.html?docId=236454
266. Jefferson Morley, *Our Man in Mexico*, 88-92
267. Warren Commission Report, 729-730
268. Ibid, 730, also Commission Exhibits 2478, 2481
269. FBI HQ file, Oswald, Lee H. - Post-Russian Period - Jan 1964 https://www.maryferrell.org/showDoc.html?docId=233297#relPageId=179
270. Warren Commission Report, 730
271. FBI 105-82555 Oswald HQ File, Section 106. https://www.maryferrell.org/showDoc.html?docId=58226#relPageId=101 https://www.maryferrell.org/showDoc.html?docId=10110#relPageId=117
272. Warren Commission Report, 731
273. Ernst Titovets, *Oswald: Russian Experience*, 335
274. Ibid, 338
275. House Select Committee on Assassinations, Lopez Report. https://history-matters.com/archive/jfk/hsca/lopezrpt_2003/html/LopezRpt_0206a.htm
276. FBI Memorandum to Warren Commission staff, J. Lee Rankin, August 4, 1964. https://www.history-matters.com/archive/jfk/wc/wcvols/wh22/pdf/WH22_CE_1412.pdf
277. Memorandum Slawson to Willens, "Oswald's Trip to Mexico; Outline and Recommendations for Further Inquiries," March 25, 1964. https://www.cia.gov/readingroom/docs/CIA-RDP10M00666R000503450002-3.pdf
278. FBI Memorandum to Warren Commission staff, J. Lee Rankin, August 4, 1964, 1111-1114
279. Sylvia Duran signed statement forwarded to Warren Commission (excerpted in HSCA Lopez Report). https://www.archives.gov/files/research/jfk/releases/180-10142-10081.pdf
280. Warren Commission Report, 734
281. Sylvia Duran signed statement forwarded to Warren Commission (excerpted in HSCA Lopez Report). https://history-matters.com/archive/jfk/hsca/lopezrpt_2003/html/LopezRpt_0204a.htm
282. Warren Report, 734

283. Warren Commission Hearings, Volume 16, Commission Exhibit 161, Clothing found at Beckley, also personal communications with Steve Roe, August 2023. https://www.maryferrell.org/showDoc.html?docId=1133#relPageId=544
284. During the HSCA interviews of the Mexico CIA translators, they made no mention of having translated/transcribed the intercept of a call on September 28, one involving both female and male callers.
285. Warren Commission Hearings, Volume 24, Commission Exhibit 2121, Warren Commission Report, 734
286. "Transcripts in Spanish and Some in English of Telephone Conversations, 27 Sept to 1 Oct, 1963," in CIA Russ Holmes Work File, #104-10413-10074. https://www.maryferrell.org/showDoc.html?docId=5742#relPageId=17
287. Ibid
288. Jason Fagone, "The Amazing Story of the Russian Defector Who Changed his Mind," *Washingtonian*, February 18, 2018. https://www.washingtonian.com/2018/02/18/the-amazing-story-of-the-russian-defector-who-changed-his-mind-vitaly-yurchenko/
289. Ernst Titovets, *Oswald Russian Episode*, Chapter 30 "Revealing Tape Recordings," also 343, 410
290. Sylvia Duran signed statement forwarded to Warren Commission (excerpted in HSCA Lopez Report). https://history-matters.com/archive/jfk/hsca/lopezrpt_2003/html/LopezRpt_0204a.htm
291. Jefferson Morley, *Our Man in Mexico*, 237

Chapter 13

292. House Select Committee on Assassinations, Lopez Report, Part IV. https://aarclibrary.org/publib/jfk/hsca/lopezrpt/pdf/LopezRpt_4_Reconstruction.pdf
293. CIA documents in HSCA Segregated Collection, "Pretext call to Soviet Embassy on 20 July 1964" and "Photocopies of all Cables Sent from Mexico City During Surveillance" November 18, 1963. https://www.maryferrell.org/showDoc.html?docId=56792#relPageId=2 https://www.maryferrell.org/showDoc.html?docId=99895#relPageId=78
294. Jefferson Morley, *Our Man in Mexico*; also CIA document RIF #104-10132-10243. https://www.maryferrell.org/showDoc.html?docId=49131
295. Bill Simpich, *State Secret* citing Gus Russo interview of Jeremy Gunn (ARRB staff) in Russo's book, *Brothers in Arms*, September 8, 2003
296. "Mexico City Station History, Excerpts," in CIA Russ Holmes Work File, Anne Goodpasture. https://www.maryferrell.org/showDoc.html?docId=5874

297. Bill Simpich, *State Secret*, Chapter 4: "Mexico City Intrigue – The World of Surveillance." https://www.maryferrell.org/pages/State_Secret_Chapter4.html
298. House Select Committee on Assassinations, Lopez Report, Part IV. https://aarclibrary.org/publib/jfk/hsca/lopezrpt/pdf/LopezRpt_4_Reconstruction.pdf
299. History Matters Archive, Lopez Report, 2003 release. https://history-matters.com/archive/jfk/hsca/lopezrpt_2003/html/LopezRpt_0260a.htm
300. "Transcript: Cuban Embassy, Mexico City, September 28, 1963," in CIA Russ Holmes Work File. https://www.maryferrell.org/showDoc.html?docId=5099#relPageId=3
301. House Select Committee on Assassinations interview of David Atlee Phillips, November 27, 1976, 14. https://www.maryferrell.org/showDoc.html?docId=255
302. Jefferson Morley interview of Andres Goyenechea, "She Took Lee Harvey Oswald's Picture for the CIA," October 29, 2023, also Mary Ferrell Foundation, CIA Cryptonym LIEMPTY-14. https://jfkfacts.substack.com/p/she-took-lee-harvey-oswalds-picture https://www.maryferrell.org/php/cryptdb.php?id=LIEMPTY-14
303. Jefferson Morley, *Our Man in Mexico*, 178
304. House Select Committee on Assassinations interview of David Atlee Phillips, November 27, 1976, 52. https://www.maryferrell.org/showDoc.html?docId=255
305. "Relevant information from Oswald 201 related to David Phillips", in House Select Committee on Assassinations Segregated Collection. https://www.maryferrell.org/showDoc.html?docId=41321#relPageId=4
306. Church Committee staff memorandum to Senators Schweiker and Hart, "References to FBI review of tapes of Oswald's Oct. 1, 1963 Mexico City Conversation," March 5, 1976 also Rex Bradford, "More Mexico City Mysteries," May 2002. https://www.maryferrell.org/showDoc.html?docId=1465#relPageId=3 https://www.history-matters.com/essays/frameup/MoreMexicoMysteries/MoreMexicoMysteries_3.htm
307. Larry Hancock, *Someone Would Have Talked*, Chapter 15, 216-210 also Exhibits 15-19 for *Someone Would Have Talked*, larry-hancock.com. http://www.larry-hancock.com/documents/index.html
308. Mexico City to CIA Director, MEXI 6453, October 8, 1963. https://www.maryferrell.org/showDoc.html?docId=6670
309. CIA Headquarters to State, FBI, Navy, DIR 74673, October 10, 1963. https://www.maryferrell.org/showDoc.html?docId=4223

310. CIA Director to Mexico City, DIR 74830, October 10, 1963. https://www.maryferrell.org/showDoc.html?docId=4224
311. Jefferson Morley, *Our Man in Mexico*, Chapter 15, 196-97
312. Rex Bradford, "More Mexico City Mysteries," History Matters, May 2002. https://history-matters.com/essays/frameup/MoreMexicoMysteries/MoreMexicoMysteries_5.htm
313. "Sylvia Duran's Previous Statements Re LHO's Visit to the Cuban Consul," 30-31. https://www.maryferrell.org/showDoc.html?docId=50428#relPageId=25
314. Bill Simpich, *State Secret*, Chapter 3: "The Cuban Compound in Mexico City Was Ground Zero"
315. Kennedys and King, David Josephs, Research and Essays on Oswald and Mexico City, 2014/2015. https://www.kennedysandking.com/john-f-kennedy-articles/mexico-city-part-1; https://www.kennedysandking.com/john-f-kennedy-articles/mexico-city-part-2-the-trip-down-part-1; https://www.kennedysandking.com/john-f-kennedy-articles/mexico-city-part-3-the-trip-down-part-2
316. Rex Bradford, History Matters, "2003 Release: Oswald, the CIA, and Mexico City" ("Lopez Report"). https://history-matters.com/archive/jfk/hsca/lopezrpt_2003/contents.htm
317. House Select Committee on Assassinations, Lopez Report, 121. https://history-matters.com/archive/jfk/hsca/lopezrpt_2003/html/LopezRpt_0018a.htm
318. House Select Committee on Assassinations, Lopez Report, Part IV. https://history-matters.com/archive/jfk/hsca/lopezrpt_2003/html/LopezRpt_0094a.htm
319. When notified of the American in Mexico City being tentatively identified as Lee Oswald, the Mexico City station had requested contemporary photos; in return CIA Headquarters queried the Navy for photographs of Oswald. However, neither CIA headquarters nor the Navy responded, so Mexico City never received photographs which would have immediately shown the "mystery man" at the Russian Embassy not to have been Oswald. "The Photo of an Unidentified Individual in the Warren Commission Report: A Factual Chronological Survey," memorandum from David Belin, 15, April 1975, in House Select Committee on Assassinations Segregated Collection. https://www.maryferrell.org/showDoc.html?docId=80090#relPageId=23
320. House Select Committee on Assassinations, Lopez Report, 23
321. "Memo: Meeting with Anne Goodpasture," Breckenridge memo to the

record, question 5 on page 3. https://www.maryferrell.org/showDoc.html?docId=24365#relPageId=3
322. ARRB Interview with Anne Goodpasture, 1993, 23. https://www.maryferrell.org/showDoc.html?docId=80090#relPageId=23
323. "Mexico City: A New Analysis," by John Newman, presented at the 1999 November in Dallas conference. https://web.archive.org/web/20060315205154fw_/ http://www.jfklancer.com/backes/newman/newman_1.html
324. FBI memorandum, "Lee H. Oswald/Soviet Activities in Mexico City," November 27, 1963. https://www.maryferrell.org/showDoc.html?docId=8277#relPageId=4
325. CIA Mexico City Station History, 209. https://www.maryferrell.org/showDoc.html?docId=189921#relPageId=209
326. Larry Hancock, *Someone Would Have Talked*, Chapter 15, 216-210 also Exhibits 15-19 for *Someone Would Have Talked*, larry-hancock.com. http://www.larry-hancock.com/documents/index.html

Chapter 14

327. On the afternoon of November 22, 1963, Hoover telephoned Robert Kennedy and related what was known so far about Oswald. Hoover said that Oswald "went to Russia and stayed three years," which is accurate, and then went on to state that Oswald "went to Cuba on several occasions but would not tell us what he went to Cuba for." This statement has never been explained. https://www.maryferrell.org/showDoc.html?docId=62251#relPageId=96
328. This call, the first recorded one between the new President Johnson and Director Hoover, was later erased. See "The Fourteen Minute Gap" on the Mary Ferrell website. https://www.maryferrell.org/pages/The_Fourteen_Minute_Gap.html
329. Ernst Titovets, *Oswald: Russian Experience*, 304-396
330. CIA Historical Review Program, Robert Vandaveer, *Studies in Intelligence*, "Operation Lincoln." https://www.cia.gov/readingroom/docs/doc_0000608379.pdf
331. HSCA Defector evaluation criteria; Oswald investigation
    Date of defection
    Defected with whom
    Rejection of American citizenship
    Length of time for Soviets to grant residence
    Type of residence permit granted
    Circumstances after defection and prior to resettlement
    Propaganda statements made to Soviet press

Relationships with Soviet citizens
Place of residence in Soviet Union
Military training prior to defection
Employment in Soviet Union
Income provided
Financial aid provided
Contact with Soviet officials, especially KGB personnel
Known surveillance
Time period for Soviets to grant exit visa
Time period for United States to grant entrance visa
Time period for spouse or children to obtain exit visa
Time period for spouse or children to obtain entrance visa

332. "The Defector Study," HSCA Staff Report, March, 1979, XI: Webster. https://www.jfk-assassination.net/russ/jfkinfo4/jfk12/defector.htm#WEBSTER
333. During the 1950s Soviet operations were relatively challenging as far as commercial recruiting was concerned, but in other regions the CIA established relationships with senior executives, facilitating the use of their companies' personnel and resources for intelligence collection, and their business infrastructure and assets in covert operations. Commercially valuable information was also shared with the executives. Examples from Latin America included United Fruit, Standard Oil, the American Coffee Company, and even The King Ranch (via connections to David Phillips). Larry Hancock, *Shadow Warfare*, 87-88
334. General CIA Records, Raymond Anderson, *New York Times*, "CIA USED STUDENTS AS SPIES, REDS SAY," *New York Times*, 1987; "3 Deny Pravda's CIA-Tie Charges," *Baltimore Sun*. https://www.cia.gov/readingroom/document/cia-rdp75-00149r000700530016-3 https://www.cia.gov/readingroom/docs/CIA-RDP75-00149R000400300006-2.pdf
335. The Red Bird and Red Sox activities should not be confused with those of Red Cap, which appears to have involved "cultivation" (using a variety of devices including sexual compromise), targeting primarily Soviet and Eastern European diplomats, but possibly administrative and political figures as well. Overt defection was one objective of the activities of Red Cap and its associated LCIMPROVE operations, but compromise in support of CIA political action operations was another.
336. Global Security, Intelligence/Soviet Russia, REDBIRD and REDSOX. https://www.globalsecurity.org/intell/ops/ussr-redsox.htm

337. CIA Cryptonym AMLAW-3, Carlos Lechuga, Mary Ferrell Foundation. https://www.maryferrell.org/php/cryptdb.php?id=AMLAW-3
338. CIA files on Silvia Tirado Bozan de Duran. https://www.archives.gov/files/research/jfk/releases/104-10102-10145.pdf
339. Bill Simpich, *State Secret: Wiretapping in Mexico City, Double Agents, and the Framing of Lee Oswald*, Chapter 3: "The Cuban Compound in Mexico City Was Ground Zero." https://www.maryferrell.org/pages/State_Secret_Chapter3.html
340. "Memo: Political Operations in Cuba - The Proenza Case," CIA Executive Registry Files, July 26, 1978. https://www.maryferrell.org/showDoc.html?docId=162401#relPageId=4
341. Ibid
342. CIA Dispatch, Chief of Station, Mexico City to Chief, SAS, "Operational/TYPIC/CI/Eusebio Azcue Lopez." https://www.maryferrell.org/showDoc.html?docId=224926
343. Peter Dale Scott, "Oswald and the Hunt for Popov's Mole," The Fourth Decade, March, 1996. https://www.maryferrell.org/showDoc.html?docId=48692#relPageId=3
344. Bill Simpich, *State Secret*, Chapter 1, "The Double Dangle"
345. Peter Dale Scott, "Oswald and the Hunt for Popov's Mole," The Fourth Decade, March, 1996
346. John Newman, *Oswald and the CIA*, 24-28
347. Ibid, Chapter 4, "I Am Amazed," 47-59
348. Alan Dale and Malcolm Blunt, *The Devil is in The Details*, 29-33
349. Tom Mangold, *Cold Warrior*, 43
350. Ibid, 42
351. Michael Holtzman, James Jesus Angleton; *The CIA and the Craft of Intelligence*, 139-142, also Chapter 9
352. Charles A Briggs, Memorandum for the Record, to Chief Information Services Staff, Memorandum for Chief of Counter Intelligence, "Destruction of Angleton's Files," February 4, 1976. https://www.maryferrell.org/showDoc.html?docId=16066#relPageId=3
353. Charles A. Briggs Sr., Obituary Notice, *Washington Post*. http://www.legacy.com/obituaries/washingtonpost/obituary.aspx?n=charles-a-briggs&pid=176359949&fhid=17018#sthash.qbuQXzQ5.dpuf
354. "Memorandum for Chief, Information and Privacy Staff, Subject: Weisberg FOIA request on MLK and James Earl Ray," September 21, 1976. https://www.maryferrell.org/showDoc.html?docId=59737#relPageId=2
355. "Memorandum for Chief, Information and Privacy Staff, Subject: Request for E. Howard Hunt's Records While in Domestic Operations

Division," August 30, 1976. https://www.maryferrell.org/showDoc.html?docId=58793#relPageId=2

356. Ibid
357. Memorandum for Chief, Counter Intelligence Staff, Memorandum for the Record Dated 4 February 1976, Mary Ferrell Foundation. https://www.maryferrell.org/showDoc.html?docId=16066#relPageId=3
358. FBI to Director, Central Intelligence Agency, Deputy Director Plans, Report of James Hosty, September 10, 1963. https://www.maryferrell.org/showDoc.html?docId=95569#relPageId=50
359. "Memorandum for the Record, Subject: 1963-64 Miami Station Action to Aid USG Investigation of the Murder of John F. Kennedy," March 22, 1977. https://www.archives.gov/files/research/jfk/releases/2022/104-10103-10024.pdf
360. Warren Commission Report, 735
361. Ibid, 736
362. Ibid, 734
363. Warren Commission Exhibit 1792

Chapter 15

364. Warren Commission Report, 737
365. Warren Commission Hearings, Volume 10, Testimony of Robert S. Stovall, March 30, 1964. https://history-matters.com/archive/jfk/wc/wcvols/wh10/pdf/WH10_Stovall.pdf
366. Warren Commission Report, 737
367. Ibid, 737, Warren Commission Hearings, Testimony of Mary E. Bledsoe, Volume 6, 404
368. Warren Commission Report, 737
369. Ibid, 740
370. Larry Hancock, *Someone Would Have Talked*, 2010 edition, 203; with additional confirmation in personal communications with Dallas researcher Gary Mack, who had verified Oswald's signature on an Adolphus Hotel job application – a lead rejected by the FBI.
371. Dallas Police Department, Dallas City Archives, Memorandum – Lee Harvey Oswald Job Application, October 15, 1963. https://texashistory.unt.edu/ark:/67531/metapth190981/m1/3/
372. CIA "second installment" of "Lee Harvey Oswald: Biography, Appendix A," James Whitten, December 27, 1963. https://www.maryferrell.org/showDoc.html?docId=230696
373. Warren Commission Hearings, Volume 3, 15. https://www.maryferrell.org/showDoc.html?docId=39#relPageId=23

374. Warren Commission Hearings, Volume 1, Testimony of Marina Oswald, 65-66. https://www.history-matters.com/archive/jfk/wc/wcvols/wh1/html/WC_Vol1_0039b.htm

Chapter 16

375. Louis Jacobson Bill McCarthy, "False flags are real but far less real than social media suggests," Poynter, February 9, 2022. https://www.poynter.org/fact-checking/2022/what-is-a-false-flag/
376. Memorandum for the Secretary of Defense, "Justification for Military Intervention in Cuba," prepared for the Chief of Operations, Cuba Project, March 13, 1962. https://nsarchive2.gwu.edu/news/20010430/northwoods.pdf
377. Mae Brussell, "The Last Words of Lee Harvey Oswald," David Wallechinsky and Irving Wallace, *The Peoples Almanac #2*, NY: Bantam Books, 1978, 47-52
378. At the time of his arrest in the Texas Theater, Oswald has been described as stating "This is it" or "Well, It's all over now" – remarks quoted by Patrolman M. N. McDonald who confronted him in the theatre. The officer closest to the two men, Ray Hawkins, did not hear any such remarks from Oswald, nor could other officers confirm them.
379. Television footage of Dallas news broadcasts of Lee Harvey Oswald on the evening of November 22, sourced from Realtime 1960s and CNN: https://www.youtube.com/watch?v=IhmAHlcZHt0; https://www.youtube.com/watch?v=jY8fRTLtgzA
380. Mae Brussell, "The Last Words of Lee Harvey Oswald," David Wallechinsky and Irving Wallace, *The Peoples Almanac #2*, NY: Bantam Books, 1978, 47-52
381. "Memorandum for the Record, Subject: 1963-64 Miami Station Action to Aid USG Investigation of the Murder of John F. Kennedy," March 22, 1977. https://www.maryferrell.org/showDoc.html?docId=223159
382. Larry Hancock, *Someone Would Have Talked*, 2010 edition, Chapter 15 "If I Told You," 209-244
383. FBI 105-82555 Oswald HQ File, Section 214. https://www.maryferrell.org/showDoc.html?docId=59644#relPageId=61

Chapter 17

384. Hancock, *Tipping Point: The Conspiracy that murdered President John Kennedy*, 82-83
385. Memo to Director FBI, "DRE Internal Security, Neutrality Matters," April 23, 1963. https://www.maryferrell.org/showDoc.html?docId=81693#relPageId=11

386. "Anti-Castro Activities and Organizations and LHO in New Orleans," HSCA Segregated Collection, 1979. https://www.maryferrell.org/showDoc.html?docId=196928#relPageId=151
387. HSCA Segregated Collection, Microfilm Reel 17, Folder D - JUAN MANUEL SALVAT ROQUE. https://www.maryferrell.org/showDoc.html?docId=55050#relPageId=35
388. Gaeton Fonzi to G. Robert Blakey, "Interview with Juan Manuel Salvat Roque," February 7, 1978, House Select Committee on Assassinations, 3. https://www.maryferrell.org/showDoc.html?docId=63368#relPageId=3
389. "Memorandum for the Record: Transcripts of October 1975 Telephone Conversations Between Director Colby, Mrs. Clare Booth Luce and Mr. Justin McCarthy," CIA Executive Registry Files, "Clare Booth Luce Weaves a Fascinating Tale," Betty Beale, Washington Star, November 16, 1975. https://www.maryferrell.org/showDoc.html?docId=41853#relPageId=6
390. "DRE Draft," House Select Committee on Assassinations, November 27, 1978, 12. https://www.maryferrell.org/showDoc.html?docId=109635#relPageId=12
391. Warren Commission Report, 730

Chapter 18

392. "CIA DISPATCH: OPERATIONAL/AMSPELL PROGRESS REPORT - JULY 1962." https://www.maryferrell.org/showDoc.html?docId=52396#relPageId=8
393. "PROVISIONAL OPERATIONAL APPROVAL, Subject: Salvat Roque," October 19, 1960, HSCA Segregated Collection. https://www.maryferrell.org/showDoc.html?docId=67691#relPageId=2
394. "CIA CABLE: DRE PROP SEC MANUEL SALVAT REPORTS THAT DRE ACTION (NOT PROP)," November 18, 1960, HSCA Segregated Collection, Microfilm Reel 17: Ruiz - Webster. https://www.maryferrell.org/showDoc.html?docId=67688#relPageId=2
395. "CIA CABLE: MEETING AMBIDDY-1, ALBERTO MULLER, CORBUSTON HELD AFTERNOON, September 3, 1960, HSCA Segregated Collection, Microfilm Reel 17: Ruiz - Webster. https://www.maryferrell.org/showDoc.html?docId=67701#relPageId=2
396. "AMSPELL (DRE) PROGRESS REPORT FOR AUGUST 1969," [sic: 1962] 4, House Select Committee on Assassinations Segregated Collection, Microfilm Reel 26: DRE - JURE. https://www.maryferrell.org/showDoc.html?docId=23849#relPageId=4
397. Ibid, 8. https://www.maryferrell.org/showDoc.html?docId=23849#relPageId=8

398. Ibid, 16. https://www.maryferrell.org/showDoc.html?docId=23849 #relPageId=16
399. List of DRE personnel involved in Havana Harbor Raid and 8th International Youth Festival in Helsinki, Finland, CIA, "CIA Outside Contact Report," House Select Committee on Assassinations. https:// www.maryferrell.org/showDoc.html?docId=147349#relPageId=10
400. Anna Gloria Diaz-Silveira Tamargo was the young woman's true, full name. As with other Latin names, this is often confusing in CIA documents where only partial names are used, sometimes misspelled as well. Some differences can be explained by the use of patronym and matronym variations of Diaz-Silveira. Diaz-Silveira was her father's name; Tamargo her mother's name (matronym). The use of hyphenated names caused some confusion for the FBI as well. FBI documents refer to Diaz-Silveira as just Silveira, dropping the Diaz (or just Diaz, dropping the Silveira). It appears that Anita was simply a nickname for Anna, and in various places she was referred to as Anita Diaz, Anna Diaz, Anna Silveira, and on occasion by the apparent alias of Mirta Dortico. Diaz-Silveira's use of the name Mirta Dortico is not well documented (which is not unusual for an alias) other than in certain photographs, especially those taken early after her arrival in the United States when she was in the company of Frank Sturgis and Rolando Masferrer. References to her may be found in a variety of CIA and FBI documents. A CIA list of all participants in the Eighth World Youth Festival in Helsinki, Finland includes the full names of CIA-sponsored participants including Carlos Hernandez, Juan Manuel Salvat, John Koch, Anna Diaz-Silveira and Francisco Chao Hermida.
401. https://www.maryferrell.org/showDoc.html?docId=83391&relPage Id=3; https://www.maryferrell.org/showDoc; html?docId=57746#relPage Id=28; https://www.maryferrell.org/showDoc.html?docId=145526#relPage Id=19; https://www.maryferrell.org/showDoc.html?docId=10649 #relPageId =27; The FBI referred to her simply as Anna Diaz-Silveira: https:// www.maryferrell.org/showDoc.html?docId=10672#relPageId=650; Federal Bureau of Investigation, FBI 105-82555 Oswald HQ File, Section 215, September 8, 1964. https://www.maryferrell.org/showDoc.html?do cId=59645#relPageId=220
402. "AMSPELL (DRE) PROGRESS REPORT FOR AUGUST 1969," [sic: 1962]. https://www.maryferrell.org/showDoc.html?docId=23849&rel PageId=4
403. "AMSPELL (DRE) PROGRESS REPORT FOR OCTOBER 1962," HSCA Segregated Collection, Microfilm Reel 25: Garrison,

Agrupacion Montecristi - DRE. https://www.maryferrell.org/showDoc.html?docId=23764

404. "AMSPELL (DRE) Status," November 10, 1962. https://www.maryferrell.org/showDoc.html?docId=23765
405. Memo to Director FBI, "Correlation Summary, aka, See References, Assoc, MRR, MIRR, Anti-Castro Organizations," May 13, 1968, 10. https://www.maryferrell.org/showDoc.html?docId=165380#relPageId=10
406. FBI Document, DRE, Internal Security, Neutrality Matters, August, 1962, 11. https://www.maryferrell.org/showDoc.html?docId=81693#relPageId=11
407. CABLE: AMHINT-2 REPORTED AT 1400 HOURS 25 AUG THAT AMSPELL MISSION, August 24, 1962. https://www.maryferrell.org/showDoc.html?docId=52393#relPageId=2
408. Larry Hancock, *In Denial: Secret Wars with Air Strikes and Tanks*, 44
409. FBI Document, DRE, Internal Security, Neutrality Matters, August, 27, 1962. http://www.latinamericanstudies.org/belligerence/Directorio.pdf
410. CIA Report on DRE, December 11, 1978, 10
411. Jefferson Morley, "Revelation 19.63," *The New Times*, April 12, 2002

Chapter 19

412. https://www.maryferrell.org/showDoc.html?docId=129190#relPageId=13
413. https://www.maryferrell.org/showDoc.html?docId=77005#relPageId=219
414. CIA Cuba Project Files, Cuban Counterrevolutionary Handbook. https://www.maryferrell.org/showDoc.html?docId=77005#relPageId=219 https://www.maryferrell.org/showDoc.html?docId=81349#relPageId=6
415. Zarraga was both an FBI informant and a member of JMWAVE's Cuban Intelligence group, the AMOTs. He was AMOT-133. He debriefed Diaz-Garcia on July 30 and in September, 1963. Both would go on missions with Tony Cuesta, Commandos-L and RECE until May 1966 when Cuesta was captured and Diaz-Garcia killed in an infiltration attempt in Cuba. https://www.maryferrell.org/showDoc.html?docId=47897#relPageId=3
416. Memo from SAC, Miami, to Director, FBI, subjects: Shell Oil Refinery Cuba / Conspiracy / Suspects / Plane, Explosives, June 15, 1963. https://www.maryferrell.org/showDoc.html?docId=137119#relPageId=2
417. FBI Special Agent in Charge New Orleans to Director, FBI, "Neutrality Matters," September 27, 1963. https://www.maryferrell.org/showDoc.html?docId=136965#relPageId=5
418. Memo to Director, FBI, subjects: FBI Search Warrant / Bombing Raid

/ Explosives, September 8, 1963, 13. https://www.maryferrell.org/showDoc.html?docId=137079#relPageId=13

Chapter 20

419. Harold Weisberg, *Oswald in New Orleans*, 303-323
420. FBI Airtel, Special Agent in Charge, New Orleans to Director, FBI, re: material seized at LaCombe, Louisiana, September 27, 1963. https://www.maryferrell.org/showDoc.html?docId=136965#relPageId=5
421. Larry Hancock and David Boylan, "The Wheaton Lead: An Exploration", Appendix C: Coming together in Louisiana. https://www.maryferrell.org/pages/Essay_-_The_Wheaton_Lead.html
422. James O'Connor, FBI Subject Report, Miami Florida, March 3, 1964 Memorandum, Weisberg subject files, Hood College. http://jfk.hood.edu/Collection/Weisberg%20Subject%20Index%20Files%20Original/A%20Disk/Agent%20Oswald%20ExSess/Item%20032.pdf
423. Larry Hancock, *Someone Would Have Talked*, 3rd Edition, 62, 79, 195
424. Ibid, 58-59
425. FBI memo from Miami to HQ, Subjects: Carlos Prio Soccaras, Robert Ray McKeown, March 13, 1958, FBI #124-90061-10016. https://www.archives.gov/files/research/jfk/releases/docid-32327291.pdf
426. Executive Session Testimony of Robert McKeown, Gunrunner, House Select Committee on Assassinations, April 12, 1978. https://www.realhistoryarchives.com/collections/assassinations/jfk/mckeown.htm
427. CIA Cryptonym YEAST, Mary Ferrell Foundation. https://www.maryferrell.org/php/cryptdb.php?id=YEAST

Chapter 21

428. Larry Hancock, *Someone Would Have Talked*, 2010 edition, Appendix H: Odio Revisited
429. Larry Hancock, *Tipping Point: The Conspiracy that murdered President John Kennedy*, 235-240
430. House Select Committee on Assassinations, Interview of Silvia Odio. https://www.maryferrell.org/showDoc.html?docId=233230#relPageId=268
431. Warren Commission Document 205 - FBI Report of 23 Dec 1963 re: Oswald. https://www.maryferrell.org/showDoc.html?docId=10672#relPageId=646
432. https://www.maryferrell.org/showDoc.html?docId=137079#relPageId=31

433. https://www.maryferrell.org/showDoc.html?docId=100184#relPageId=28
434. https://www.maryferrell.org/showDoc.html?docId=52163#relPageId=109
435. https://www.maryferrell.org/showDoc.html?docId=137079#relPageId=27
436. https://www.maryferrell.org/php/pseudodb.php?id=TEELS_CARL
437. https://www.maryferrell.org/php/cryptdb.php?id=AMSERF-1
438. https://www.maryferrell.org/showDoc.html?docId=1212#relPageId=66
439. https://www.maryferrell.org/showDoc.html?docId=197037#relPageId=85
440. https://www.maryferrell.org/showDoc.html?docId=13079#relPageId=2
441. https://www.maryferrell.org/showDoc.html?docId=40912#relPageId=2
442. https://www.maryferrell.org/showDoc.html?docId=233230#relPageId=254
443. https://www.maryferrell.org/showDoc.html?docId=52163#relPageId=109
444. Bartes held up an M-2 rifle for "purely psychological reasons" and mentioned that he had purchased this gun with contributions from the CRC members. https://www.maryferrell.org/showDoc.html?docId=74924#relPageId=3
445. https://www.maryferrell.org/showDoc.html?docId=123739#relPageId=10
446. https://www.maryferrell.org/showDoc.html?docId=136961#relPageId=17
447. https://www.maryferrell.org/showDoc.html?docId=136961#relPageId=16
448. Silvia Odio testimony to Warren Commission, July 22, 1964, 16 https://www.maryferrell.org/showDoc.html?docId=233230#relPageId=251

Chapter 22

449. In October the DRE was promoting its intentions to launch a new series of maritime attacks against Cuba – although as noted in a report from JMWAVE, it only had some 15 experienced military personnel available at the time. There was also no obvious source for funds to support such an initiative (or for buying weapons) although DRE leaders had been in touch with Paulino Sierra who was in Chicago. Sierra had managed to secure a level of financial support which he was offering to groups who might become associated with his new political initiative, the JDGE (generally known as the Junta). The Junta itself was largely a paper entity, with a handful of members. Sierra had obtained some funding, both from old-line Cuban conservatives in New York and, according to FBI investigations, other money that had come from individuals out of Las

Vegas – possibly representing former Havana casino figure Jake Lansky. Details on Sierra and the JDGE may be found in *Someone Would Have Talked*, 2010 edition, 264-295.

Although the DRE appears to have had contact with Sierra in both Miami and Chicago (via Juan Francisco Blanco and Homer Echeveria), details from its Chicago efforts in November and December suggest that at best it would have had to bring Sierra himself into any negotiations for weapons, and there is no sign anything of that nature came about in Dallas. Details on those Chicago activities may be found in *Tipping Point*, 242-246.

With regards to the Chicago area, there the DRE did have longstanding contacts with a well-known weapons dealer, the same individual who had supplied dynamite for its abortive late summer aerial mission against Cuba. No such history of contacts existed in the Dallas area and the October 1963 weapons shopping there appears to have been almost random, taking them to an individual suspected of dealing with ultra-right groups such as the Minutemen and already under serious investigation by the ATF.

450. Masen was acquainted with an Army ordinance officer stationed at Fort Hood Texas named George Nonte, who was also a gun enthusiast. Masen had re-barreled weapons for Nonte, and in turn Nonte had exchanged ammunition with Masen. Both men were interested in and worked with ammunition, doing cartridge reloads and other specialty work. At the time the DRE contacted Masen in October, he and Nonte had been exploring setting up a company focused on chemicals for commercial sales to ammunition manufacturers. Nonte was within a year of retirement, and he and Masen teamed with LeRoy Barker (a Dallas chemist) and James Melton (a Dallas gun shop owner) to begin organizing a company to be named Black Hawk Chemicals. See *Someone Would Have Talked*, 171.

451. ATF agent Frank Ellsworth had become interested in Masen due to his reported contacts with Minuteman figures and activities which might have violated the National Firearms Act. There appears to have been additional interest due to Masen's travel to Mexico in 1963 and his meeting with Mexican arms manufacturers. Ellsworth himself carried out a "sting" on Masen, contacting him as a local Irving police officer interested in making money on the side and starting up conversations. Masen himself admitted to Mexican travel and related that in the past he had smuggled weapons into the United States from Mexico. In his initial contact with Masen, Ellsworth purported to have a customer in New Mexico, someone interested in military class weapons including mortars,

anti-tank guns, and of course automatic weapons. After introducing the presumed buyer, another ATF agent named William Fuller, Masen did supply some automatic weapons and also rifle parts in response and eventually was charged, fined and lost his license over the sale. (Dick Russell, interview with Masen, *The Man Who Knew Too Much*, 358-359).

In further conversations, Masen represented that he could indeed get almost anything in the way of ordinance through an Army contact, even placing a telephone call so they could talk to that contact, Captain George Nonte at Fort Hood. That call was especially interesting to Ellsworth, as he knew the Army had been having problems with weapons going unaccounted for at Fort Hood.

Whether or not Nonte might have done some previous sales of weapons would never be discerned. However, when Ellsworth showed up at Fort Hood to question him, Nonte immediately revealed that he had already reported a call from Masen to Army security. In that call, Masen had described a virtual shopping list he had received from a Cuban exile group preparing for a new invasion of Cuba. Investigation determined that the call and the shopping list had indeed come from meetings between Masen and DRE members in Dallas. He had gone into some detail about the claims that it would be a major military action and speculated on the possible value of advance knowledge of such an event. In turn, Nonte had immediately reported the Cuban exile dialogue to Army Intelligence, who had in turn shared it with the FBI. By the time Ellsworth turned up at Fort Hood, Nonte himself had already joined in a sting to cultivate Masen for more information from the Cubans. That continued over several weeks, from mid-October into November, and Nonte eventually met with some of the local DRE members who had talked with Masen. (details in *Someone Would Have Talked*, 3rd Edition, 171-172).

It remains uncertain as to how the DRE leaders from Miami were introduced to Masen; possibly it was through local anti-Communists, or even Minutemen who had attended the October DRE meetings in Dallas. We do know that the initial contact was by Joaquin Martinez de Pinnillos, who had come to Dallas from Miami with Manuel Salvat. Martinez had also brought in local DRE members for the conversations, including George Perrel and Ferman de Goicochia (a fellow student of Sarita Odio at the University of Dallas). Perrel had been a member of Brigade 2506, surviving the landings at the Bay of Pigs, and had only recently moved to Dallas from New York City.

Overall, there is certainly no doubt that Miami-based and local DRE individuals were in contact with Masen and Nonte from late October though much of November, with all parties being of interest to the ATF, the FBI and Army Intelligence.

452. Issues with the recovery, functioning, and provenance of the clip purported to have been found in the TSBD rifle are discussed in extensive detail in Gary Murr's unpublished manuscript *Forgotten*, Part II, Chapter 10.
453. Gary Murr, *Forgotten*, Volume 1, Part V, Chapter 36, 529-559
454. Warren Commission Document 778 - FBI Letterhead Report of 01 Apr 1964 re: Investigation as result of testimony by Mrs. Marina Oswald before the Warren Commission. https://www.maryferrell.org/showDoc.html?docId=11176#relPageId=5
455. The FBI reported that the rifle taken into custody was in a "well oiled" condition; see Warren Commission Exhibit 2974.
456. Ian Griggs, *No Case to Answer*, 173-214
457. FBI agent Vincent Drain exchange with DPD Detective and polygraph operator R. D. Lewis, Weisberg Archives Hood College, also FBI Headquarters file 105-8255 Section 17, page 100. http://jfk.hood.edu/Collection/Meagher%20Sylvia%20Folders/Paper%20Bag/Paper%20Bag%2008.pdf
458. "Chemical and Forensic Analysis of JFK Assassination Bullet Lots; Is a Second Shooter Possible," The Annals of Applied Statistics, Spiegleman, Tobin, James, Sheather, Wexler and Roundhill, 2007. https://arxiv.org/pdf/0712.2150#:~:text=One%20of%20the%20bullets%20analyzed,of%20this%20type%20is%20unique
459. House Select Committee on Assassinations Report, Volume 7, "Was the CE399 bullet found at Parkland Hospital fired from the CE139 Mannlicher-Carcano rifle?" https://www.maryferrell.org/showDoc.html?docId=82#relPageId=378
460. John Hunt, "Breakability: CE-399 and the Diminishing Velocity Theory," History Matters. https://history-matters.com/essays/jfkmed/Breakability/Breakability.htm
461. Gary Aguilar and Josiah Thompson, "The Magical Bullet, Even More Magical Than We Knew," History Matters. https://history-matters.com/essays/frameup/EvenMoreMagical/EvenMoreMagical.htm
462. Interview tape transcript, Col. Bob and Trudy Castorr at their home, January 3, 1968, Weisberg Archives, Hood College
463. Ibid
464. Ibid

Chapter 23

465. A review of FBI post-assassination interviews shows that asking about a Ruby connection was something of a standard question added only to interviews with individuals reporting having seen Oswald before the assassination – including several incidents related to his purported downtown job inquiries. What the purpose of adding that question would be is unclear, but it's obvious that the implication that the individual might be connected to Ruby or the assassination in some way was perceived as intimidating, and served to shut down witness elaborations.
466. Warren Commission Document 205 - FBI Report of 23 Dec 1963 re: Oswald. https://www.maryferrell.org/showDoc.html?docId=10672#relPageId=227
467. Warren Commission Document 87 - Secret Service report of 08 Jan 1964 re: Oswald. https://www.maryferrell.org/showDoc.html?docId=10490#relPageId=779
468. Transport Security International, "The Cuban Hijackings, Their Significance and Impact Sixty Years On," October 19, 2018

Epilogue

469. "Memorandum for the Record, Subject: 1963-64 Miami Station Action to Aid USG Investigation of the Murder of John F. Kennedy," 4-5. https://www.maryferrell.org/showDoc.html?docId=223159#relPageId=5
470. Donald R. Heath, Memorandum for the Inspector General, May 16, 1977. https://www.maryferrell.org/showDoc.html?docId=223158
471. David Corn, *Blonde Ghost*, 1994, 107-108
472. JMWAVE Chief of Station to Chief Special Affairs Staff, "Dispatch 'Maritime After Action Report – Operation TILT," June 6, 1963 https://www.maryferrell.org/showDoc.html?docId=28893; http://www.larry-hancock.com/photos/p-ch01/Tilt1.jpg; and http://www.larry-hancock.com/photos/p-ch01/TILT2.jpg
473. CIA memorandum, "Discussion Operation TILT," June 15, 1963. https://www.maryferrell.org/showDoc.html?docId=28896
474. "John Martino's Confessions," Mary Ferrell Foundation, also Anthony Summers on Martino, "*Conspiracy*," 1980. https://www.maryferrell.org/pages/John_Martinos_Confessions.html
475. Larry Hancock and David Boylan, "The Wheaton Lead," Mary Ferrell Foundation. https://www.maryferrell.org/pages/Essay_-_The_Wheaton_Lead.html

476. Jesse Curry, "Kennedy Assassination Oswald Statement by Dallas Police Chief," University Archives. https://auction.universityarchives.com/auction-lot/kennedy-assassination-oswald-statement-by-dallas_6DD4B1D80A
477. Memo from Richard S. Sampson, Chief Latin America Division to John M. Reeves, Office of Security, Subject: LA Division Comments on Mr. David Phillips' manuscript, 1976. https://www.archives.gov/files/research/jfk/releases/2023/104-10105-10132.pdf

Index